THE LITERATURE OF THE LAW

THE LITERATURE
OF THE LAW

AN ANTHOLOGY
OF GREAT WRITING
IN AND ABOUT THE LAW

SELECTED AND INTRODUCED BY
LOUIS BLOM-COOPER

FOREWORD BY
LORD BIRKETT

PREVIOUSLY PUBLISHED AS
The Law as Literature

THE MACMILLAN COMPANY
NEW YORK

Library of Congress Catalog Card Number: 67-12654

First Printing

THE MACMILLAN COMPANY, NEW YORK

Printed in the United States of America

ACKNOWLEDGMENTS

The editor and publishers gratefully acknowledge permission to reprint copyright material to the following:

The Macmillan Company, New York, for 'Cross-examination of Pigott Before the Parnell Commission' from *The Art of Cross-Examination* by Francis L. Wellman. Copyright 1903, 1904, 1923, 1936 by the Macmillan Company. Copyright 1931, 1932 by Francis Wellman.

S. T. Felstead for 'Notes for the Prosecution of Dr Crippen' from his *Sir Richard Muir: Memoirs of a Public Prosecutor* (Bodley Head).

Patrick Duncan and *Contact* for 'Statement Made in the Regional Court, Cape Town' printed in *Contact* for December 1960.

Mrs Frida Laski and *Atlantic Monthly* for 'My Day in Court' by Harold Laski, first printed in *Atlantic Monthly*, November 1952.

The *Baltimore Sun* and *New York Times* for dispatches by H. L. Mencken on the Scopes Trial.

Kenneth Tynan and *The Observer* for 'Lady Chatterley's Trial' from *The Observer*, November 1960.

James Morris and *The Guardian* for 'The Powers Trial', from *The Guardian*, July 1960.

The Harvard Law Review for 'The Right to Privacy' by Samuel D. Warren and Louis D. Brandeis, 4 *Harvard Law Review*, 193–220, (1890), copyright 1890 by The Harvard Law Review Association; and for *The Path of the Law* by Oliver Wendell Holmes, 10 *Harvard Law Review* 457–478, (1897), copyright 1897 by The Harvard Law Review Association.

The Yale Review and Harcourt Brace Inc. for 'Law and Literature' by Benjamin N. Cardozo.

Professor H. L. A. Hart and *The Listener* for 'Immorality and Treason'.

E. P. Dutton Co. for 'Lord Monboddo and Lord Braxfield' from *Some Old Scots Judges* by W. Forbes Gray.

C. H. S. Fifoot and Stevens & Co. for 'Judge and Jurist, 1837–1901' from *Judge and Jurist in the Reign of Queen Victoria*.

The Clarendon Press for Sir Frank Mackinnon's 'Life of Lord Justice Scrutton' from *Dictionary of National Biography*.

ACKNOWLEDGMENTS

The Incorporated Council of Law Reporting for England and Wales for Younger J. in *Glyn v Weston Film Feature Co.* (1916) 1 Ch. 261; Lord Sumner in *Bowman v Secular Society* (1917) AC 452; Eve J. in *Cummins v Bond* (1927) 1 Ch. 167; Lord Atkin in *Ambard v A.G. for Trinidad and Tobago* (1936) AC 322 and *Liversidge v Anderson* (1942) AC 206; Stable J. in *R v Martin Secker and Warburg* (1954) 1 WLR 1138; Harman L. J. in *Solihull Corporation v Gas Council* (1961) 1 WLR 619 and *Re Shaw deceased* (1959) 1 WLR 729.

Judge David L. Bazelon for his Brandeis Memorial Lecture, 'The Dilemma of Punishment.

Calmann-Levy, publishers of *Evergreen Review*, for 'Reflections on the Guillotine' by Albert Camus and Grove Press Inc., for Richard Howard's translation.

CONTENTS

Foreword Lord Birkett, ix

Editor's Note Louis Blom-Cooper, xiii

1. PROSECUTION AND DEFENCE

2. THE COURTROOM SCENE

3. ON LAW

4. ON LAWYERS

5. FROM THE BENCH

6. CRIME AND PUNISHMENT

FOREWORD

By LORD BIRKETT

Mr Blom-Cooper is a man of law with his roots in the Middle Temple, but he is also a man of letters, as Counsellor Pleydell in *Guy Mannering* wished every lawyer to be. He has kindly invited me to write a short Foreword to this admirable anthology which he has made, and I very gladly do so. Lawyers need no reminding from me that law and literature have been long and closely associated. Words are said to be the raw material of the legal profession, and the assiduous study of words, and the proper use of words have always been part of the lawyer's most desirable accomplishments. Many of our judges have been great masters of the spoken and the written word, and the Law Reports are not only a great treasury of law but they are a great treasury of literature. More than three hundred years ago the judges were called in to advise the House of Lords in a peerage claim when the Earl of Oxford died without issue. The famous speech delivered by Chief Justice Crewe has always been regarded as a superb piece of English prose with its magnificent opening and its majestic conclusion—

'And yet Time hath its revolutions; there must be a period and an end to all temporal things—an end of names, and dignities and whatsoever is terrene, and why not of De Vere? For where is Bohun? Where is Mowbray? Where is Mortimer? Nay, which is more and most of all, Where is Plantagenet? They are entombed in the urns and sepulchres of mortality. And yet let the name and dignity of De Vere stand so long as it pleaseth God'.

Not the least of the services rendered by Mr Blom-Cooper is that he has brought out from the obscurity of the Law Reports some examples of judicial learning clothed in the dress of the finest prose. Many of our advocates, too, have been orators of the first rank. When Erskine made his first speech before Lord Mansfield and won the rapturous praise of Lord Campbell, and when John Somers 'broke the rod of the oppressor' in defence of the Seven Bishops, and won the acclaim of Macaulay, they enriched the annals of law, but at the same time they made a lasting contribution to literature. The two greatest biographies in the language were written by lawyers, Boswell's Life of Johnson, and Lockhart's Life of Scott. The Inns of Court long ago won the famous tribute from Ben Jonson in *Every Man out of his Humour* as the nurseries of humanity and liberty, but they are equally famous for their literature as well as for their law. Selden and Bacon, Clarendon and More are among the great and shining names from the four Inns, and Charles Lamb and Thackeray, together with Dickens, for evermore have their home in the Temple. Mr Blom-Cooper has now selected from this rich domain of law an anthology of legal writing, a bold thing to do, for literature has come to mean for many people something austere and elevated and a little removed from ordinary life. To all such it must come with a slight shock to find in this present anthology the notes made by that formidable prosecutor, Sir Richard Muir, when he opened the case for the Crown against Hawley Harvey Crippen at the Old Bailey on the charge of murdering his wife.

But those nineteen pages of notes, so carefully prepared and so dramatically displayed, tell the most thrilling story in the most fascinating way and are properly described as literature, if literature is writing of great excellence destined to live beyond the immediate hour. The romance and tragedy of Crippen are revealed in Muir's notes with a power and a precision that no lengthy, wordy narrative could ever achieve. Similarly, the cross-examination of Pigott before the Parnell Commission by Sir Charles Russell, as described by the American lawyer, Francis Wellman, owes little to the writing, but almost everything to the overmastering forensic skill of Russell. It is well therefore to remember the nature of an anthology such as this. It was F. L. Lucas of King's College, Cambridge who reminded us in that memorable Introduction to his selections and translations from the Greek Anthology, that all the anthologies of the world date from the collection of poems made by Meleager ninety years before Christ. He likened his collection to a 'garland of diverse flowers'— 'the lilies of Anyte . . . and of Sappho, few but roses'. Mr Blom-Cooper has followed the same tradition and includes in his 'flower-gatherings' contributions of the most diverse, and sometimes of the most curious kind. Harold Laski, describing with some bitterness the day he spent in Court before the Lord Chief Justice; Richard Carlile, now almost forgotten, defending himself at Guildhall in 1819 on a charge of blas-

phemous libel before the Lord Chief Justice of that day; Benjamin
Cardozo writing brilliantly on this very topic of *Law and Literature*
and praising with genuine warmth the English judges for their
'quotable good things, for pregnant aphorisms, for touchstones of
ready application' which together are 'a mine of instruction and a
treasury of joy'; C. H. S. Fifoot's description of the great legal
figures in Victoria's long reign; Gibbon, Dickens, Albert Camus,
Oliver Wendell Holmes, Plato, Gandhi—surely a man might say
with truth 'Here's Richness'. But the section entitled *From the Bench*
reveals most fully the riches of the law as literature, not merely by
what is included but by what is necessarily left out. It is particularly
gratifying to see the judgment of Mr Justice Harman (as he then was)
on the Will of Bernard Shaw taken from the sombre setting of the Law
Reports and presented in this form, for it is a perfect example of the
blending of law and literature, and will hold its place in any company
in any age. But how one misses Lord Bowen, Lord Macnaghten and
Lord Mansfield from the English judges, and Chief Justice John
Marshall and Judge Learned Hand from across the Atlantic. Mr
Justice Eve 'On Spiritual Copyright' is a joy to read, but how the
humour brings the wish for Frank Lockwood and Theo. Mathew. It
is the merit of Mr Blom-Cooper's anthology that his wonderfully-
varied selection creates the desire for more; and I can wish him no
better reward than a clear call for a second volume. In the meantime I
very warmly commend this present volume to lawyers and laymen
alike.

EDITOR'S NOTE

ROBERT GRAVES has claimed that a well-chosen anthology of poetry is a complete dispensary for the more common mental disorders. This anthology of legal writings is not intended as a panacea for mental disorders caused by the law. But it *is* intended as an antidote to one common lay complaint: the view that the law is something abstruse, entirely beyond normal human comprehension. Its purpose is to bridge the gap to some extent between lawyer and layman by providing a selection of writings which, in addition to the insight they provide into the law, stand out as literature—direct, comprehensible and entertaining—in their own right.

Emphasis has been first upon the modern. Thus I have deliberately selected topics which are under active discussion today—the relationship of sin to crime, the limits of the right to publish, the dilemma of criminal responsibility, capital punishment and so on. But none of the items have been selected for their topicality alone.

Any anthology of law as literature must give prominence to the judgments of English judges. The form of the English judgment lends itself naturally to literary treatment (in contrast to the Continent, where legal procedure imposes a set formula on the Court's decision), and a host of English judges have seized their opportunity. The field of selection here is vast and I can only hope that the eight judgments here printed give a fair idea of this rich source of legal literature. Three judges, Lords Bowen, Macnaghten and Sumner are already represented in a literary anthology, the Oxford Book of English Prose. I was therefore tempted to leave all three out but ended by including one.

Many of the judges will be unknown to the wider audience to whom this book is addressed. In the cases of judges who are dead I have appended brief thumbnail portraits. Where necessary I have also provided background information to the particular case concerned. This practice I have adopted too for the other items in the anthology, but only when I felt that some explanation was called for. Where the items seemed self-explanatory, any note from me would I felt have been supererogatory and I therefore refrained from editorial comment.

I cannot sign off this editorial note without a word of thanks. There is no man alive today who has epitomized more the harmony of law and literature than Lord Birkett. His profound knowledge of both worlds is most amply demonstrated in his most gracious foreword.

1

PROSECUTION
AND DEFENCE

'In my youth,' said his father, 'I took to the law'
And argued each case with my wife;
And the muscular strength which it gave to my jaw
Has lasted the rest of my life.'

Lewis Carroll, *Alice's Adventures in Wonderland*

Francis Wellman

Sir Charles Russell's Cross-examination of Pigott before the Parnell Commission

———

Francis Wellman (1854–1942) was an American lawyer who ventured to present professional colleagues and aspiring advocates with a primer on that most difficult of arts—cross-examination. His book, The Art of Cross-examination, *was first published in 1903 and went through four editions.*

The extract from the Parnell Commission of 1888 represents a happy choice of the best in English advocacy. Sir Charles Russell, who became Lord Chief Justice, was called by Lord Coleridge, 'the biggest advocate of the [19th] century'.

Charles Stuart Parnell, an Irish protestant, was the leader of a group of Irish nationalists at Westminster who followed a much more militant programme for the attainment of independence than had previously been experienced. The publication of the facsimile letter in The Times *in which Parnell appeared to condone the murder of one of the victims of the Phoenix Park crime was a political sensation. Opinion varied among politicians as to the letter's authenticity and Parnell denounced it as villainous and bare-faced forgery. Although the Commission did finally establish the complicity of the Parnellites in the spread of agrarian crime in Ireland, Parnell himself was absolved of authorship of the damning letter. This was achieved entirely by the devastating cross-examination of Pigott by Sir Charles Russell.*

PROBABLY ONE of the most dramatic and successful of the more celebrated cross-examinations in the history of the English courts is Sir Charles Russell's cross-examination of Pigott, the chief witness in the investigation growing out of the attack upon Charles S. Parnell and sixty-five Irish members of Parliament, by name, for belonging to a lawless and even murderous organization, whose aim was the overthrow of English rule. . . .

[The method of cross-examination adopted by Sir Charles Russell was unusual.] After adroitly leading Pigott to commit himself irretrievably to certain absolute statements, Russell suddenly confronted him with his own letters in a way that was masterly—and deadly to Pigott. The case is also an admirable illustration of the importance of so using a damaging letter that a dishonest witness cannot escape its effect by ready and ingenious explanations, when given an opportunity, as is often done by an unskilful cross-examiner. . . . The cross-examination of Pigott shows that Sir Charles Russell thoroughly understood this branch of the art, for he read to Pigott only a portion of his damaging letter, and then mercilessly impaled him upon the sharp points of his questions before dragging him forward in a bleeding condition to face other portions of his letter, and repeated the process until Pigott was cut to pieces.

The principal charge against Parnell, and the only one that interests us in the cross-examination of the witness Pigott, was the writing of a letter by Parnell which *The Times* claimed to have obtained and published in facsimile, in which he excused the murderer of Lord Frederick Cavendish, Chief Secretary for Ireland, and of Mr Burke, Under Secretary, in Phoenix Park, Dublin, on 6th May, 1882. One particular sentence in the letter read, 'I cannot refuse to admit that Burke got no more than his deserts.'

The publication of this letter naturally made a great stir in Parliament and in the country at large. Parnell stated in the House of Commons that the letter was a forgery, and later asked for the appointment of a select committee to inquire whether the facsimile letter was a forgery. The Government refused this request, but appointed a special committee, composed of three judges, to investigate all the charges made by *The Times*.

In order to undertake this defence of Parnell, Russell returned to *The Times* the retainer he had enjoyed from them for many previous years. It was known that *The Times* had bought the letter from Mr Houston, the secretary of the Irish Loyal and Patriotic Union, and that Mr Houston had bought it from Pigott. But how did Pigott come by it? That was the question of the hour, and people looked forward to the day when Pigott should go into the box and tell his story, and when Sir Charles Russell should rise to cross-examine him. Pigott's evidence in chief, so far as the letter was concerned, came practically to this: he had been employed by the Irish Loyal and Patriotic Union to hunt up documents which might incriminate Parnell, and he had bought the facsimile letter, with other letters, in Paris from an agent of the Clan-na-Gael, who had no objection to injuring Parnell for a valuable consideration.

Addressing the witness with much courtesy, while a profound silence fell upon the crowded court, Lord Russell began his cross-examination: 'Mr Pigott, would you be good enough, with my Lords' permission, to write some words on that sheet of paper for me? Perhaps you will sit down in order to do so?' A sheet of paper was then handed to the witness. I thought he looked for a moment surprised. This clearly was not the beginning he had expected. He hesitated, seemed confused. Perhaps Russell observed it. At all events he added quickly:

'Would you like to sit down?'

'Oh, no, thanks,' replied Pigott, a little flurried.

THE PRESIDENT: Well, but I think it is better that you should sit down. Here is a table upon which you can write in the ordinary way—the course you always pursue.

RUSSELL: Will you write the word 'livelihood'?

Pigott wrote.

RUSSELL: Just leave a space. Will you write the word 'likelihood'?

Pigott wrote.

RUSSELL: Will you write your own name? Will you write the word 'proselytism', and finally (I think I will not trouble you at present with any more) 'Patrick Egan' and 'P. Egan'?

He uttered these last words with emphasis, as if they imported something of great importance. Then, when Pigott had written, he added carelessly, 'There is one word I had forgotten. Lower down, please, leaving spaces, write the word "hesitancy".' Then, as Pigott was about to write, he added, as if this were the vital point, 'with a small "h".' Pigott wrote and looked relieved.

RUSSELL: Will you kindly give me the sheet?

Pigott took up a bit of blotting paper to lay on the sheet, when Russell, with a sharp ring in his voice, said rapidly, 'Don't blot it, please'. It seemed to me that the sharp ring in Russell's voice startled Pigott. While writing he had looked composed; now again he looked flurried, and nervously handed back the sheet. The Attorney-General looked keenly at it, and then said, with the air of a man who had himself scored, 'My Lords, I suggest that had better be photographed, if your Lordships see no objection.'

RUSSELL (*Turning sharply towards the Attorney-General, and with an angry glance and an Ulster accent, which sometimes broke out when he felt irritated*): Do not interrupt my cross-examination with that request.

Little did the Attorney-General at the moment know that, in the ten minutes or quarter of an hour which it had taken to ask these questions, Russell had gained a decisive advantage. Pigott had in one of his letters to Pat Egan spelt 'hesitancy' thus, 'hesitency'. In one of the incriminatory letters 'hesitancy' was so spelt; and in the sheet now handed back to Russell, Pigott had written 'hesitency', too. In fact it was Pigott's spelling of this word that had put the Irish members on his scent. Pat Egan, seeing the word spelt with an 'e' in one of the incriminatory letters, had written to Parnell, saying in effect, 'Pigott is the forger. In the letter ascribed to you "hesitancy" is spelt "hesitency". That is the way Pigott always spells the word.' These things were not dreamt of in the philosophy of the Attorney-General when he interrupted Russell's cross-examination with the request that the sheet 'had better be photographed'. So closed the first round of the combat.

Russell went on in his former courteous manner, and Pigott, who had now completely recovered confidence, looked once more like a man determined to stand to his guns.

Russell, having disposed of some preliminary points at length (and after he had been perhaps about half an hour on his feet), closed with the witness.

RUSSELL: The first publication of the articles 'Parnellism and Crime' was on the 7th March, 1887?

PIGOTT (*Sturdily*): I do not know.

RUSSELL (*Amiably*): Well, you may assume that is the date.

PIGOTT (*Carelessly*): I suppose so.

RUSSELL: And you were aware of the intended publication of the correspondence, the incriminatory letters?

PIGOTT (*Firmly*): No, I was not at all aware of it.

RUSSELL (*Sharply, and with the Ulster ring in his voice*): What?

PIGOTT (*Boldly*): No, certainly not.

RUSSELL: Were you not aware that there were grave charges to be made against Mr Parnell and the leading members of the Land League?

PIGOTT: I was not aware of it until they actually commenced.

RUSSELL: What?

PIGOTT: I was not aware of it until the publication actually commenced.

RUSSELL: Do you swear that?

PIGOTT: I do.

RUSSELL (*Making a gesture with both hands, and looking towards the bench*): Very good, there is no mistake about that.

Then there was a pause; Russell placed his hands beneath the shelf in front of him, and drew from it some papers—Pigott, the Attorney-General, the judges, everyone in court looking intently at him the while. There was not a breath, not a movement. I think it was the most dramatic scene in the whole cross-examination, abounding as it did in dramatic scenes. Then, handing Pigott a letter, Russell said calmly:

'Is that your letter? Do not trouble to read it; tell me if it is your letter.'

Pigott took the letter, and held it close to his eyes as if reading it.

RUSSELL: Do not trouble to read it.

PIGOTT: Yes, I think it is.

RUSSELL: Have you any doubt of it?

PIGOTT: No.

RUSSELL (*Addressing the judges*): My Lords, it is from Anderton's Hotel, and it is addressed by the witness to Archbishop Walsh. The date, my Lords, is the 4th of March, three days before the first appearance of the first of the articles, 'Parnellism and Crime'.

He then read:

'Private and confidential.'

'My Lord: The importance of the matter about which I write will doubtless excuse this intrusion on your Grace's attention. Briefly, I wish to say that I have been made aware of the details of certain proceedings that are in preparation with the object of destroying the influence of the Parnellite party in Parliament.'

Having read this much Russell turned to Pigott and said:

'What were the certain proceedings that were in preparation?'

PIGOTT: I do not recollect.

RUSSELL: Turn to my Lords and repeat the answer.

PIGOTT: I do not recollect.

RUSSELL: You swear that—writing on the 4th of March, less than two years ago?

PIGOTT: Yes.

RUSSELL: You do not know what that referred to?

PIGOTT: I do not really.

RUSSELL: May I suggest to you?

PIGOTT: Yes, you may.

RUSSELL: Did it refer to the incriminatory letters among other things?

PIGOTT: Oh, at that date? No, the letters had not been obtained, I think, at that date, had they, two years ago?

RUSSELL (*Quietly and courteously*): I do not want to confuse you at all, Mr Pigott.

PIGOTT: Would you mind giving me the date of that letter?

RUSSELL: The 4th of March.

PIGOTT: The 4th of March.

RUSSELL: Is it your impression that the letters had not been obtained at that date?

PIGOTT: Oh, yes, some of the letters had been obtained before that date.

RUSSELL: Then, reminding you that some of the letters had been obtained before that date, did that passage that I have read to you in that letter refer to these letters among other things?

PIGOTT: No, I rather fancy they had reference to the forthcoming articles in *The Times*.

RUSSELL: I thought you told us you did not know anything about the forthcoming articles.

PIGOTT: Yes, I did. I find now I am mistaken—that I must have heard something about them.

RUSSELL: Then try not to make the same mistake again, Mr Pigott. 'Now,' you go on (*continuing to read from Pigott's letter to the archbishop*), 'I cannot enter more fully into details than to state that the proceedings referred to consist in the publication of certain statements purporting to prove the complicity of Mr. Parnell himself, and some of his supporters, with murders and outrages in Ireland, to be followed, in all probability, by the institution of criminal proceedings against these parties by the Government.'

Having finished the reading, Russell laid down the letter and said, turning towards the witness, 'Who told you that?'

PIGOTT: I have no idea.

RUSSELL (*Striking the paper energetically with his fingers*): But that refers, among other things, to the incriminatory letters.

PIGOTT: I do not recollect that it did.

RUSSELL: Do you swear that it did not?

PIGOTT: I will not swear that it did not.

RUSSELL: Do you think it did?

PIGOTT: No, I do not think it did.

RUSSELL: Do you think that these letters, if genuine, would prove or would not prove Parnell's complicity in crime?

PIGOTT: I thought they would be very likely to prove it.

RUSSELL: Now, reminding you of that opinion, I ask you whether you did not intend to refer—not solely, I suggest, but among other things—to the letters as being the matter which would prove complicity or purport to prove complicity?

PIGOTT: Yes, I may have had that in my mind.

RUSSELL: You could have had hardly any doubt that you had?

PIGOTT: I suppose so.

RUSSELL: You suppose you may have had?

PIGOTT: YES.

RUSSELL: There is the letter and the statement (*reading*), 'Your Grace may be assured that I speak with full knowledge, and am in a position to prove, beyond all doubt and question, the truth of what I say.' Was that true?

PIGOTT: It could hardly be true.

RUSSELL: Then did you write that which was false?

PIGOTT: I suppose it was in order to give strength to what I said. I do not think it was warranted by what I knew.

RUSSELL: You added the untrue statement in order to add strength to what you said?

PIGOTT: Yes.

RUSSELL: You believe these letters to be genuine?

PIGOTT: I do.

RUSSELL: And did at this time?

PIGOTT: Yes.

RUSSELL (*Reading*): 'And I will further assure your Grace that I am also able to point out how these designs may be successfully combated and finally defeated.' How, if these documents were genuine documents, and you believed them to be such, how were you able to assure his Grace that you were able to point out how the design might be successfully combated and finally defeated?

PIGOTT: Well, as I say, I had not the letters actually in my mind at that time. So far as I can gather, I do not recollect the letter to Archbishop Walsh at all. My memory is really a blank on the circumstance.

RUSSELL: You told me a moment ago, after great deliberation and consideration, you had both the incriminatory letters and the letter to Archbishop Walsh in your mind.

PIGOTT: I said it was probable I did; but I say the thing has completely faded out of my mind.

RUSSELL (*Resolutely*): I must press you. Assuming the letters to be genuine, what were the means by which you were able to assure his Grace that you could point out how the design might be successfully combated and finally defeated?

PIGOTT (*Helplessly*): I cannot conceive, really.

RUSSELL: Oh, try. You must really try.

PIGOTT (*In manifest confusion and distress*): I cannot.

RUSSELL (*Looking fixedly at the witness*): Try.

PIGOTT: I cannot.

RUSSELL: Try.

PIGOTT: It is no use.

RUSSELL (*Emphatically*): May I take it, then, your answer to my Lords is that you cannot give any explanation?

PIGOTT: I really cannot absolutely.

RUSSELL (*Reading*): 'I assure your Grace that I have no other motive except to respectfully suggest that your Grace would communicate the substance to some one or other of the parties concerned, to whom I could furnish details, exhibit proofs, and suggest how the coming blow may be effectually met.' What do you say to that, Mr Pigott?

PIGOTT: I have nothing to say except that I do not recollect anything about it absolutely.

RUSSELL: What was the coming blow?

PIGOTT: I suppose the coming publication.

RUSSELL: How was it to be effectively met?

PIGOTT: I have not the slightest idea.

RUSSELL: Assuming the letters to be genuine, does it not even now occur to your mind how it could be effectively met?

PIGOTT: No.

Pigott now looked like a man, after the sixth round in a prize fight, who had been knocked down in every round. But Russell showed him no mercy. I shall take another extract.

RUSSELL: Whatever the charges in 'Parnellism and Crime', including the letters, were, did you believe them to be true or not?

PIGOTT: How can I say that when I say I do not know what the charges were? I say I do not recollect that letter to the archbishop at all, or any of the circumstances it refers to.

RUSSELL: First of all you knew this: that you procured and paid for a number of letters?

PIGOTT: Yes.

RUSSELL: Which, if genuine, you have already told me, would gravely implicate the parties from whom these were supposed to come.

PIGOTT: Yes, gravely implicate.

RUSSELL: You would regard that, I suppose, as a serious charge?

PIGOTT: Yes.

RUSSELL: Did you believe that charge to be true or false?

PIGOTT: I believed that charge to be true.

RUSSELL: You believed that to be true?

PIGOTT: I do.

RUSSELL: Now I will read this passage [from Pigott's letter to the archbishop], 'I need hardly add that, did I consider the parties really guilty of the things charged against them, I should not dream of suggesting that your Grace should take part in an effort to shield them; I only wish to impress on your Grace that the evidence is apparently convincing, and would probably be sufficient to secure conviction if submitted to an English jury.' What do you say to that, Mr Pigott?

PIGOTT (*Bewildered*): I say nothing, except that I am sure I could not have had the letters in my mind when I said that, because I do not think the letters conveyed a sufficiently serious charge to cause me to write in that way.

RUSSELL: But you know that was the only part of the charge, so far as you have yet told us, that you had anything to do in getting up?

PIGOTT: Yes, that is what I say; I must have had something else in my mind which I cannot at present recollect—that I must have had other charges.

RUSSELL: What charges?

PIGOTT: I do not know. That is what I cannot tell you.

RUSSELL: Well, let me remind you that that particular part of the charges—the incriminatory letters—were letters that you yourself knew all about.

PIGOTT: Yes, of course.

RUSSELL (*Reading from another letter of* PIGOTT'S *to the archbishop*): 'I was somewhat disappointed in not having a line from your Grace, as I ventured to expect I might have been so far honoured. I can assure your Grace that I have no other motive in writing save to avert, if possible, a great danger to people with whom your Grace is known to be in strong sympathy. At the same time, should your Grace not desire to interfere in the matter, or should you consider that they would refuse me a hearing, I am well content, having acquitted myself of what I conceived to be my duty in the circumstances. I will not further trouble your Grace save to again beg that you will not allow my name to transpire, seeing that to do so would interfere injuriously with my prospects, without any compensating advantage to anyone. I make the request all the more confidently because I have had no part in what is being done to the prejudice of the Parnellite party, though I was enabled to become acquainted with all the details.'

PIGOTT: Yes.

RUSSELL: What do you say to that?

PIGOTT: That it appears to me clearly that I had not the letters in my mind.

RUSSELL: Then if it appears to you clearly that you had not the letters in your mind, what had you in your mind?

PIGOTT: It must have been something far more serious.

RUSSELL: What was it?

PIGOTT: I cannot tell you. I have no idea.

RUSSELL: It must have been something far more serious than the letters?

PIGOTT: Far more serious.

RUSSELL: Can you give my Lords any clue of the most indirect kind to what it was?

PIGOTT: I cannot.

RUSSELL: Or from whom you heard it?

PIGOTT: No.

RUSSELL: Or when you heard it?

PIGOTT: Or when I heard it.

RUSSELL: Or where you heard it?

PIGOTT: Or where I heard it.

RUSSELL: Have you ever mentioned this fearful matter—whatever it is—to anybody?

PIGOTT: No.

RUSSELL: Still locked up, hermetically sealed in your own bosom?

PIGOTT: No, because it has gone away out of my bosom, whatever it
was.

Pigott's cross-examination was finished the following day, and the
second day he disappeared entirely, and later sent back from Paris a
confession of his guilt, admitting his perjury, and giving the details of
how he had forged the alleged Parnell letter by tracing words and
phrases from genuine Parnell letters, placed against the window pane,
and admitting that he had sold the forged letter for £605. After the
confession was read, the Commission 'found' that it was a forgery, and
The Times withdrew the facsimile letter.

A warrant was issued for Pigott's arrest on the charge of perjury, but
when he was tracked by the police to a hotel in Madrid, he asked to be
given time enough to collect his belongings, and, retiring to his room,
blew out his brains.

Sir Richard Muir

Notes for the Prosecution of Dr Crippen

———

The crime of Dr Hawley Harvey Crippen will always rank as one of the curiosities in the murder stories of England. A respectable middle-class medical practitioner with a profound knowledge of anatomy, which proved to be his ultimate undoing, poisoned his wife (known professionally in the variety world as Belle Elmore) and hid her dismembered body under the floorboards of their semi-detached house in the (then) suburb of Camden Town. Crippen tried to cover up his foul deed by pretending that his wife had left him for another man in California where she had fallen ill and died of natural causes. He then openly paraded his mistress, Ethel Le Neve, before his wife's friends until the two of them fled from England aboard the S.S. Montrose. *His capture aboard the ship just off Montreal harbour in 1916 was itself a dramatic event since the message sent from Scotland Yard in London was delivered by telegraph, then a novel mode of communication.*

Crippen and Le Neve were tried separately before the Lord Chief Justice, Lord Alverstone, at the Old Bailey. Crippen was found guilty and subsequently hanged in Pentonville Prison. Le Neve was acquitted of being an accessory after the fact to murder and is thought to be still alive.

Sir Richard (then Mr) Muir was at the time the senior Treasury Counsel, which means the senior Crown prosecutor at the Old Bailey. His eminence as the greatest criminal lawyer of his day was such that in the rare instance of a trial of murder by poisoning the Attorney-General chose not to exercise a well-established precedent of conducting the prosecution himself but left it in the capable hands of Muir. Muir's brilliant grasp of the essentials of the case is reflected in this remarkable document, found among his papers after his death, which concisely sets out the issues and the arguments. It is a model of how any counsel might provide himself with the signposts for conducting a case.

HAWLEY HARVEY CRIPPEN,
M.D. Hospital College,
Cleveland, USA
48 years of age

Agent and Manager for
Munyon's Remedies, Albion House
Advertising Business
Tooth
Eye
Ear remedies

	Cora Crippen
	'Belle Elmore'
1900	Music Hall Singer
1906	of Brooklyn, USA
3 Sep. 1873	About 37 years of age
1892–3	Marries Crippen

as his second wife
Comfortably off,
lived at 39 Hilldrop Crescent,
£50 p.a.

21 Sep. 1905

Well furnished
Latterly kept no servant.
Life together.
On affectionate terms
Kind & attentive husband.
Contrast Crippen's statement
'Ungovernable temper'
'Often threatened to leave me'
'Not co-habited since 1906'
Boasted of attentions from other men
e.g. Bruce Miller.
In Fact Crippen carrying on
an intrigue with his typist
Ethel Le Neve for 3 years.
She had been typist to Crippen
for 8 years.
Money.
Crippen says he provided all
the money for the
home.

If so
　　For four years he had been
supporting a wife for whom
he had no affection.
A lady with expensive
tastes in furs, jewellery
& clothes.
While for three of those
years his affections were
fixed upon another woman,
with whom he 'frequently
stayed at Hotels' but 'was
never away from home at
night.'
The wife during this time was
　　threatening to leave him
saying she was fond of another man
receiving love letters from another man
seeming to think Crippen not good
　　　　enough for her
saying she had a man to go to and
　　　　would end it all.
Not easy to tolerate by a husband if
such a state of things really existed.

FINANCIAL POSITION

31 Jan. 1910

15 March, 1906	Between them had put by £600
24 March, 1909	on deposit at Charing Cross Bank.
Nov. 1909	Crippen ceased to draw £3 weekly
	Became sole agent but it did
	not pay.
15 Dec. 1909	Notice to withdraw deposits by
	(Cora Crippen) Belle Elmore
	on Dec. 15, 1910.
31 Jan. 1910	Connection with Munyon's ceased.
31 Jan. 1910	Crippen had other businesses
	but doubtful if any of
	them a source of income
	then.

Certain that current account with
Charing Cross Bank then overdrawn
£2. 7. 8.
Clearly pressed for money.

MOTIVE

Belle Elmore
                        stood between him
and the closer relations he
wishes to establish with Ethel
Le Neve
Belle Elmore's
                        money (and other
property convertible into money)
would enable him to keep Ethel
Le Neve

                        31 Jan. 1910
             Invitation
4 and 6 p.m.   Twice repeated to Mr and
             Mrs Martinetti to dinner.
8 p.m.   Dinner party.
1 Feb. 1.30 a.m.

             The Martinettis witnesses to
             the affectionate terms on
             which husband and wife
             then were.
             1 Feb. 1910
noon   Crippen called and inquired
                 for Paul.
             How is Belle?
                 A. 'All right.'
             If Crippen saw her that
                 day no one else
                 did.
             Cora Crippen
                        never seen again.

DISAPPEARANCE OF CORA CRIPPEN

Heaps of friends
        England and America
        Some relations there.

37 years of age
>Best of Health and spirits
>Bright, vivacious,
Fond of life
>>dress
>>>jewellery.
>A good correspondent
Never heard of again.
Passed out of the world which
>knew her
>>as completely as if she
>>were dead.
Left behind her
>everything she would
>have left behind her
if she had died on that
day:
>>Money
>>>Jewels
>>>>Furs
>>>>>Clothes
>>>>>>Home
>>>>>>>Husband

Would she return?
Never to Return.
Crippen's certainty.
He very early made up his mind that
it was certain she would not return.
He immediately appropriated her
property:

2 Feb.	Pawned
	Pair of earrings &
	Marquise Ring for £80
9 Feb.	Pawned
	Diamond Brooch and
	6 diamond rings for £115
20 Feb.	Gave to Le Neve
	Brooch 'Sunrise'
	Fox Furs.
12 March	Took Le Neve to live in the house
	39 Hilldrop Crescent.
	The house which had been Belle
	Elmore's home.

But he did not tell Cora Crippen's
    friends
        They had parted for ever
        She would never return.
He started a campaign of lies
    to account for her disappearance.
The Music Hall Ladies' Guild.
    Hon Treasurer
    Cheque Book—Deposit Pass Book
    Meetings Wednesday
If missing inquiries
Anticipated by Crippen

1 or 2 Feb.   Letter to Guild (cheque and deposit books enclosed)
Letter to Miss May, the Secretary.
    'Illness of a near relative
    calls me to America at
    a few hours notice.
    Cannot spare a moment to
    call upon you before I go.'
Those lies told—at her request
    To cover up the scandal
    the best way he could with
    their mutual friends and Guild.
The man who
    went to Ball where mutual
    friends and Guild were.
    With his typist
        wearing his wife's jewels.
    Took the typist to live with
        him at his wife's home.
    Seen about with her
        dressed in wife's furs.
    To account for her
        not coming back.
    Invented letters from relatives in
        California saying Belle was
        ill.
    A letter from Belle saying not to
    worry as she was not so bad.

20 March   A cable—dangerously ill with
double pleuro-pneumonia.

23 March   If anything happens to Belle would go
to France for a week.
(in fact going to Dieppe for Easter
with Le Neve).

24 March   Telegram from Victoria Station
'Belle died yesterday at 6 o'clock.'

25 March   Good Friday.
Death advertisement in 'Era'
'to prevent people asking a lot of questions.'

Easter   Visit to Dieppe with Le Neve.
March 23—in California, USA
Miss Belle Elmore
(Mrs Crippen)

INQUIRIES BY FRIENDS

Mrs Martinetti & Mrs Smythson
asked a lot of questions
& extracted some answers.
She died at Los Angeles, Cal.
Her relations with her
His son saw her die
Son's address given.
Wreath useless because to be
Cremated.
Ashes to be brought over
can have ceremony here.

18 May   He had the Ashes at home.
Wanted to know the name of
the boat she sailed in to
America.
Must have been obvious to
Crippen that his statements
were being doubted.
Mr Nash called on Crippen
Nash had been to America
had tried to find Belle Elmore
or get news of her and
had failed.

30 June   Nash went to Scotland Yard
                         and saw Chief Inspector Dew.

                         INQUIRIES BY POLICE
                 Dew made inquiries and then
8 July   called at 39 Hilldrop Crescent.
10 a.m.   Found Le Neve there
                         went with her to Crippen's
                         business address.
                 Albion House
                 Dew said Mrs Crippen's friends were not
                 satisfied as to the stories Crippen had told
                 about his wife's death.
                 Dew had himself made exhaustive inquiries
                 and he also was not satisfied.
                 Did Crippen desire to offer any
                         explanation.
                 Crippen must have seen it was useless to
                         persist in the story he had told up to
                         then, which had been inquired into and
                 so he said:
                 'I suppose I had better tell the truth.
                 It is untrue what I have told them about
                 her death. So far as I know she is still
                 alive.'
                 He then made a statement which was
                 written down and signed.
                 In it he accounts for his wife's disappearance
                 in quite a new way.

1902   While Crippen had been away from
                         her in America she had
                         formed an attachment for a
                         music-hall artist named
                         Bruce Miller.
                 Since his return she gave way to ungovernable
                         outbursts of temper in which
                         she threatened to leave Crippen
                         and join Bruce Miller.
                 She said that when she left him
                         she would go out of his life
                         altogether and he would never
                         hear from her again.

31 Jan.   Because he did not show Mr Martinetti
1.30 a.m.   to the lavatory she, after the
                guests had gone, had one of those
                outbursts of temper.
         She abused Crippen.
                She said that was the finish of it—
                She would leave him to-morrow and
                he would never hear from her
                again.
                He was to arrange to cover up the
                scandal with their mutual friends
                and the Guild the best way he could.

1 Feb.   Went to business
5 or 6 p.m.   Returned—found she had gone
                Sat down to think how to cover
                up her absence without any scandal
                So wrote to the Guild etc.
                    but
                Realized this would not explain her
                    non-return
                      so
                Told people she was ill and
                    afterwards that she was dead, and
                advertised her death in 'Era'
                to prevent people asking a lot of
                questions.
                Why he told lies.
       Those lies were told at her request
            'to cover up the scandal
            the best way he could
            with their mutual friends
            and the Guild.'

       By the man
                Who went to the Ball of the Music
20 Feb.   Hall Benevolent Fund with his
                typist wearing his wife's brooch
                where mutual friends and members
                of the Guild were certain to be met.

       Who took the typist to live with
12 March   him in what had been his wife's
                home.

Who had been seen about with his
18 May   typist wearing his wife's furs.

What ever reason for telling those
lies
It was not to cover up scandal.
Crippen said his wife left jewellery
behind and took the rest with
her.
He had never pawned anything of hers.
Two reasons for her disappearance:
(1) Because he did not show Mr Martinetti to the

lavatory.

(2) To join Bruce Miller.
(1) Too trivial to require comment.
(2) Untrue in fact.

PREPARATIONS FOR FLIGHT
Envelopes had been deposited with Curnow
in safe.
8 July   'Know nothing about things in safe.
If anything happens to me—
Give it to Le Neve.'

9 July   Crippen was early at office
Sent Long to buy boy's clothes.
Cashed a cheque for £37 through
Miss Curnow.

11.30   Le Neve seen at the office
Crippen seen by Rylance and Long
for last time.

4.15   Posted letter to Long
'Wind up my household affairs.'
Also posted a letter to Rylance
'To escape trouble I shall be obliged
to absent myself for a time.'
Hands over business to Rylance to
continue or not as he pleases.

FLIGHT

9 July   Police circulated a description
         of Mrs Crippen.

11 July   They went to Albion House
             to Hilldrop Crescent
         Crippen was gone
         Le Neve was gone
         Neither of them seen again by police

31 July   until they were found on board a s.s.
         off Quebec.
         Crippen disguised by the shaving
             of his moustache
             passing under a false name
             and
         Le Neve with him on the s.s.
             disguised as a boy.
         What had Crippen to fear
             if Cora Crippen was alive?
         What would he have done
             if he believed she was alive?
         He had nothing to fear but
             he fled
                 he disguised himself
                     he used a false name
         He took Le Neve with him
             disguised as a boy
         He said he would do all he could to get
             in touch with her.
         He would have advertised for her
             but he left the advertisement
             which he had prepared
             behind him.
         Did he believe she was alive.
         From what had Crippen fled?

11 July   The police searched the house at
             39 Hilldrop Crescent.
         They found the advertisement which might
             have been Crippen's salvation
             if Cora Crippen was alive—
             derelict—in one of the rooms.

At Albion House
    a suit of Crippen's clothes and
    Le Neve's hat
    Signs of the flight but nothing
    to account for it
    until

13 July   Human remains were found in the cellar
        of 39 Hilldrop Crescent.
    A hole had been dug in that cellar
        the human remains put into it
        and the brick floor relaid.
    Whose remains were they?

14 July   They were examined in the cellar by Dr Pepper
        and Dr Marshall.
    They and some things found with them
        were removed to a mortuary.
    Since then they have been submitted
        to a critical examination.
    They were
           headless
                limbless
                    boneless
    and practically all indications
    of sex had been removed.
    There remained only
        some of the viscera and some
        pieces of flesh.

Sex
(1) Could not be determined with certainty on
anatomical grounds.
(2) Some Hinde's curlers with long human hair and
some feminine undergarments indicated a woman
On the other hand there were parts of a man's
pyjama jacket and a large handkerchief which
was probably not a woman's.

Identity
(1) The hair was brown and had been bleached.
Belle Elmore's hair was brown and had been
bleached.
That was no doubt true of other women besides her.

(2) The undergarments were such as
   Belle Elmore
   and no doubt such as many
   other women wore.

(3) Flesh:
   A piece of the lower abdominal wall and
   bearings—an old scar was among the
   remains.
   Belle Elmore had had an
   abdominal operation
1892 or 1893   which had left a scar.

(4) Stout:
   The remains were those of a
   rather stout person.
   Belle Elmore was rather stout.

(5) Age:
   The remains were those of an adult
   person of young or middle age.
3 Sep. 1873   Belle Elmore was 37 about.

(6) Time of burial:
   The remains had been buried from 8 to 4
   months giving a wide margin.
   Belle Elmore disappeared 1 Feb. and the
   remains were unearthed on 13 July
                              —$5\frac{1}{2}$ months

(7) Place of burial:
   Belle Elmore was last seen alive in
   that house

   Who put those remains into
                        the ground?

   Opportunity:
   Crippen since 21 Sep. 1905 was
   tenant and with Belle Elmore
   sole occupiers.

Mutilation:

   (1) Done by person having
       some knowledge of and some
       dexterity in the anatomy of
       human beings or other animals.
       Crippen had a medical
       training
       Had practised in
       America
       Attended hospitals in
       England to see operations.

   (2) Would require time and
       security from
       interruption.
       Crippen was alone in
       that house on and after
       the 1 Feb.

Carrying:

       To place such remains as
       those in the hole
       prepared for them
       would require something
       in which to carry them.
       A pyjama jacket would
       serve that purpose.

   (3) Pieces of pyjama jacket were
       found with the remains. It was
       probably a whole jacket
       when put there.

There are grounds for saying that
       that jacket was Crippen's.

The Grounds:

   (1) On 14 July Chief Inspector Dew
       found in a box under a bed in
       39 Hilldrop Crescent 3 pairs of
       pyjama trousers and 2 pyjama
       jackets forming two suits and
       one odd pair of trousers.
       The jackets are marked on a label
           Jones Brothers } on the
              Holloway.   } neck part.

(2) The pieces of pyjama jacket found with
     the human remains correspond in material
     and pattern with the odd pair of
     trousers.
(3) One piece—the neck part—is marked
     on a label

                    Jones Brothers
                            Holloway Road.

     identical.
(4) One piece with a button identical.

Arrest

Chief Inspector Dew
               having received information
boarded the s.s. 'Montrose' in the R. St
Lawrence near Quebec and before she had
arrived there from Antwerp.
Crippen had shaved off his moustache.
He had assumed the name of John Robinson
                            of Detroit, USA.
In the same ship
          occupying the same cabin was
                    Ethel Le Neve
          disguised as a boy—hair short
          wearing the brown suit bought
          by Long on 9 July by Crippen's orders.
Chief Inspector told Crippen he would be arrested
for the murder of his wife and cautioned.
Crippen said nothing in answer.
          Later he said:
                    'I am not sorry; the anxiety
                    has been too much.'
He was searched—two cards were found on him. One
intended apparently for Le Neve had written upon
it: 'I cannot stand the horrors I go through
     every night any longer and as I see nothing
     bright ahead and money has come to an
     end I have made up my mind to jump over-
     board tonight. I know I have spoilt your
     life but I hope some day you can learn to
     forgive me. With last word of love. Your H.'

Chief Inspector McCarthy put handcuffs on Crippen.
Chief Inspector Dew said:
>   'We must put these on
>   because a card found on you
>   you have written that you intend
>   jumping overboard.'

Crippen said:
>   'I won't. I am more than satisfied
>   because the anxiety has been too
>   awful.'

Crippen was searched and while
>   that was being done by Dew
Crippen said:
>   'How is Miss Le Neve?'
Chief Inspector said:
>   'Agitated but I am doing all
>   I can for her.'
Crippen said:
>   'It's only fair to say that she
>   knows nothing about it. I
>   never told her anything.'

Sewn to undervest:
>   4 rings.
>   'Rising Sun' brooch.
>   'Butterfly' brooch (paste).

Voyage to England

20 Aug.   Sailed on s.s. 'Megantic'.
21 Aug.   Warrant read—Crippen said: 'Right'

24 Aug.   Crippen said:
>   'When you took me off the ship I
>   did not see Miss Le Neve.
>   I don't know how things will go;
>   they may go all right or they may
>   go all wrong with me.
>   I may never see her again and I want
>   to ask if you will let me see
>   her—but I won't speak to her.

She has been my only comfort for
the last three years.'
He did see Le Neve in the train between Liverpool
and London.

27 Aug.	Charged at Bow Street Police Station. Said nothing.
21 Sep.	Committed—'Not Guilty—no witness.' Opportunities to give explanation of his flight

31 July.	On arrest.
21 Aug.	Warrant read.
27 Aug.	Charged at Bow St. Police Station.
21 Sept.	On committal.

SUMMARIZED FACTS

Motive on 31 Jan.

Disappearance of Belle Elmore.
Crippen only person who professes
to account for that disappearance.
His first account admittedly false.
His second account followed by immediate
flight.
Human remains found in the
house in which she was
last seen alive.
Pyjama jacket missing from
Crippen's pyjama
suits.
Pieces of the missing jacket
found with the human
remains.
The remains mutilated by
some one having the opportunity
and the anatomical knowledge
Crippen possessed.

Cause of Death

Post Mortem:
      Revealed no cause of death.
The viscera were submitted to
      Dr Willcox
      Senior scientific analyst to Home Office.
He examined them:
    (1) for Mineral and organic poisons and
        found arsenic and Cresol, carbolic and
        Sanitas fluid.
    (2) Made extracts for the purpose of
        detecting alkaloids.
    (3) Tested the extracts for alkaloids
           Stomach
           Intestine
           Kidney   } Found Alkaloid
           Liver
    (4) Tested for different kinds of Alkaloids
        Found one of the vegetable Mydriatic
        Alkaloid and it was either

Deadly Nightshade   (1) Atropine
                      (2) Hyoscyamine
Henbane   or
                    (3) Hyoscine
    (5) Tested to see which of those three it was
           Atropine   } are both
           Hyoscyamine } crystalline.
           Hyoscine does not crystallize but
               forms a gummy residue.
           Bromine test.
           Atropine   } under 'Bromine Test'
           Hyoscyamine } give small brown
                     crystals
               but
           Hyoscine gives small brown spheres.
The result of those tests was that Dr Willcox
found in the viscera a quantity of hyoscine
sufficient to show him that in the whole body
there must have been more than half a grain of
the drug 'Hyoscine Hydrobromide' the form in
which hyoscine is sold and used for medicinal
purposes.

Hyoscine Hydrobromide
    is a powerful
    narcotic poison
    not commonly prescribed,
    used as a sedative
    in cases of mania, delirium,
    delirium tremens or meningitis,
    occasionally also as a hypnotic
    in small doses of insomnia.
$\frac{1}{100}$ to $\frac{5}{200}$ part of a grain is the official dose.
If a large dose were taken
    very quickly
    drowsiness and
    complete unconsciousness
    and paralysis would follow
    and death within a few hours.
$\frac{1}{4}$ to $\frac{1}{2}$ a grain is a fatal dose.

Dr Willcox
    therefore found in this body
    indications that more than a
    fatal dose of this deadly poison
    had in some way been taken.

Moreover.
    He found that the distribution
    of the poison indicated that
        (1) it had been taken by the mouth.
        (2) the person lived an hour or more.
    He found nothing in the viscera to account
    for death
        except hyoscine
    and in his opinion
        the cause of death
    was poisoning by hyoscine.

CAUSE OF DEATH

Remains would not have been
    buried where they were
    unless death caused by
    unlawful criminal means.

Remains would not have been mutilated
    as they were except by the
    person criminally responsible
    for the death—
        desiring to conceal
    evidence of his guilt.
If you are satisfied that the
    persons whose remains were
    found in that cellar
        died of hyoscine poisoning
Who administered the poison?
A drug not commonly known
    to persons without
    medical training
    not commonly used even by
    medical men.

PURCHASE OF HYOSCINE

17–19 Jan. 1910   Crippen bought of Lewis & Burrows Ltd
                5 grs Hyoscine Hydrobrom.
    —500 to 1000 doses
Signed 'Poisons Book'.
He purported to do so on
Munyon's behalf for Homeopathic Preparations
    which was untrue.
He had been a customer there for
about ten months and had never
bought hyoscine before.
What did he want it for?
What did he do with it?
Enormous quantity.
    Lewis & Burrows had none
    in stock.
Never in three years had near
    that quantity in stock.

What has become of Belle Elmore?
Whose remains are those?
If they are Belle Elmore's, what is the
Explanation of their being found in that place
and in that mutilated condition?

Robert H. Jackson

Closing Address in the Nuremburg Trial

MR PRESIDENT AND MEMBERS OF THE TRIBUNAL:

An advocate can be confronted with few more formidable tasks than to select his closing arguments where there is great disparity between his appropriate time and his available material. In eight months— a short time as state trials go—we have introduced evidence which embraces as vast and varied a panorama of events as ever has been compressed within the framework of a litigation. It is impossible in summation to do more than outline with bold strokes the vitals of this trial's mad and melancholy record, which will live as the historical text of the twentieth century's shame and depravity.

It is common to think of our own time as standing at the apex of civilization, from which the deficiencies of preceding ages may patronizingly be viewed in the light of what is assumed to be 'progress'. The reality is that in the long perspective of history the present century will not hold an admirable position, unless its second half is to redeem its first. These two-score years in this twentieth century will be recorded in the book of years as one of the most bloody in all annals. Two World Wars have left a legacy of dead which number more than all the armies engaged in any war that made ancient or medieval history. No half-century ever witnessed slaughter on such a scale, such cruelties and inhumanities, such wholesale deportations of peoples into slavery, such annihilations of minorities. The terror of Torquemada pales before the Nazi inquisition. These deeds are the overshadowing historical facts by which generations to come will remember this decade. If we cannot eliminate the causes and prevent the repetition of these barbaric events, it is not an irresponsible prophecy to say that this twentieth century may yet succeed in bringing the doom of civilization.

Goaded by these facts, we have moved to redress the blight on the record of our era. The defendants complain that our pace is too fast. In drawing the Charter of this Tribunal, we thought we were recording an accomplished advance in International Law. But they say that we have outrun our times, that we have anticipated an advance that should be, but has not yet been made. The Agreement of London, whether it originates or merely records, at all events marks a transition in International Law which roughly corresponds to that in the evolution in local law when men ceased to punish local crime by 'hue and cry', and began to let reason and inquiry govern punishment. The society of nations has emerged from the primitive 'hue and cry', the law of 'catch and kill'. It seeks to apply sanctions to enforce International Law, but to guide their application by evidence, law, and reason instead of outcry. The defendants denounce the law under which their accounting is asked. Their dislike for the law which condemns them is not original. It has been remarked before that

> No man e'er felt the halter draw
> With good opinion of the law.

I shall not labour the law of this case. The position of the United States was explained in my opening statement. My distinguished colleague, the Attorney-General of Great Britain, will reply on behalf of all the Chief Prosecutors to the defendants' legal attack. At this stage of the proceedings, I shall rest upon the law of these crimes as laid down in the Charter. The defendants, who except for the Charter would have no right to be heard at all, now ask that the legal basis of this trial be nullified. This Tribunal, of course, is given no power to set aside or to modify the Agreement between the Four Powers, to which eighteen other nations have adhered. The terms of the Charter are conclusive upon every party to these proceedings.

In interpreting the Charter, however, we should not overlook the unique and emergent character of this body as an International Military Tribunal. It is no part of the constitutional mechanism of internal justice of any of the Signatory nations. Germany has unconditionally surrendered, but no peace treaty has been signed or agreed upon. The Allies are still technically in a state of war with Germany, although the enemy's political and military institutions have collapsed. As a Military Tribunal, it is a continuation of the war effort of the Allied nations. As an International Tribunal, it is not bound by the procedural and substantive refinements of our respective judicial or constitutional systems, nor will its rulings introduce precedents into any country's internal civil system of justice. As an International Military Tribunal, it rises above the provincial and transient and seeks guidance not only from

International Law but also from the basic principles of jurisprudence which are assumptions of civilization and which long have found embodiment in the codes of all nations.

Of one thing we may be sure. The future will never have to ask, with misgiving: 'What could the Nazis have said in their favour?' History will know that whatever could be said, they were allowed to say. They have been given the kind of a trial which they, in the days of their pomp and power, never gave to any man.

But fairness is not weakness. The extraordinary fairness of these hearings is an attribute of our strength. The prosecution's case, at its close, seemed inherently unassailable because it rested so heavily on German documents of unquestioned authenticity. But it was the weeks upon weeks of pecking at this case by one after another of the defendants that has demonstrated its true strength. The fact is that the testimony of the defendants has removed any doubts of guilt which, because of the extraordinary nature and magnitude of these crimes, may have existed before they spoke. They have helped write their own judgment of condemnation.

But justice in this case has nothing to do with some of the arguments put forth by the defendants or their counsel. We have not previously and we need not now discuss the merits of all their obscure and tortuous philosophy. We are not trying them for possession of obnoxious ideas. It is their right, if they choose, to renounce the Hebraic heritage in the civilization of which Germany was once a part. Nor is it our affair that they repudiated the Hellenic influence as well. The intellectual bankruptcy and moral perversion of the Nazi regime might have been no concern of International Law had it not been utilized to goose-step the *Herrenvolk* across international frontiers. It is not their thoughts, it is their overt acts which we charge to be crimes. Their creed and teachings are important only as evidence of motive, purpose, knowledge and intent.

We charge unlawful aggression but we are not trying the motives, hopes, or frustrations which may have led Germany to resort to aggressive war as an instrument of policy. The law, unlike politics, does not concern itself with the good or evil in the *status quo*, nor with the merits of grievances against it. It merely requires that the *status quo* be not attacked by violent means and that policies be not advanced by war. We may admit that overlapping ethnological and cultural groups, economic barriers, and conflicting national ambitions created in the

1930s, as they will continue to create, grave problems for Germany as well as for the other peoples of Europe. We may admit too that the world had failed to provide political or legal remedies which would be honourable and acceptable alternatives to war. We do not underwrite either the ethics or the wisdom of any country, including my own, in the face of these problems. But we do say that it is now, as it was for some time prior to 1939, illegal and criminal for Germany or any other nation to redress grievances or seek expansion by resort to aggressive war.

Let me emphasize one cardinal point. The United States has no interest which would be advanced by the conviction of any defendant if we have not proved him guilty on at least one of the counts charged against him in the Indictment. Any result that the calm and critical judgment of posterity would pronounce unjust would not be a victory for any of the countries associated in this prosecution. But in summation we now have before us the tested evidences of criminality and have heard the flimsy excuses and paltry evasions of the defendants. The suspended judgment with which we opened this case is no longer appropriate. The time has come for final judgment and if the case I present seems hard and uncompromising, it is because the evidence makes it so.

I perhaps can do no better service than to try to lift this case out of the morass of detail with which the record is full and put before you only the bold outlines of a case that is impressive in its simplicity. True, its thousands of documents and more thousands of pages of testimony deal with an epoch and cover a continent, and touch almost every branch of human endeavour. They illuminate specialties, such as diplomacy, naval development and warfare, land warfare, the genesis of air warfare, the politics of the Nazi rise to power, the finance and economics of totalitarian war, sociology, penology, mass psychology, and mass pathology. I must leave it to experts to comb the evidence and write volumes on their specialties, while I picture in broad strokes the offences whose acceptance as lawful would threaten the continuity of civilization. I must, as Kipling put it, 'splash at a ten-league canvas with brushes of comet's hair'.

The Crimes of the Nazi Regime

The strength of the case against these defendants under the conspiracy count, which it is the duty of the United States to argue, is in its simplicity. It involves but three ultimate inquiries: first, have the acts defined by the Charter as crimes been committed; second, were they committed pursuant to a common plan or conspiracy; third, are these defendants among those who are criminally responsible?

The charge requires examination of a criminal policy, not of a multitude of isolated, unplanned, or disputed crimes. The substantive crimes upon which we rely, either as goals of a common plan or as means for its accomplishment, are admitted. The pillars which uphold the conspiracy charge may be found in five groups of overt acts, whose character and magnitude are important considerations in appraising the proof of conspiracy.

1. *The Seizure of Power and Subjugation of Germany to a Police State*

The Nazi Party seized control of the German state in 1933. 'Seizure of power' is a characterization used by defendants and defence witnesses, and so apt that it has passed into both history and everyday speech.

The Nazi junta in the early days lived in constant fear of overthrow. Göring, in 1934, pointed out that its enemies were legion and said:

Therefore the concentration camps have been created, where we have first confined thousands of Communists and Social Democrat functionaries.

In 1933 Göring forecast the whole programme of purposeful cruelty and oppression when he publicly announced:

Whoever in the future raises a hand against a representative of the National Socialist movement or of the state, must know that he will lose his life in a very short while.

New political crimes were created to this end. It was made a treason, punishable with death, to organize or support a political party other than the Nazi Party. Circulating a false or exaggerated statement, or one which would harm the state or even the Party, was made a crime. Laws were enacted of such ambiguity that they could be used to punish almost any innocent act. It was, for example, made a crime to provoke 'any act contrary to the public welfare'.

The doctrine of punishment by analogy was introduced to enable conviction for acts which no statute forbade. Minister of Justice Gürtner explained that National Socialism considered every violation of the goals of life which the community set up for itself to be a wrong *per se*, and that the act could be punished even though it was not contrary to existing 'formal' law.

The Gestapo and the SD were instrumentalities of an espionage system which penetrated public and private life. Göring controlled a personal wire-tapping unit. All privacy of communication was abolished. Party Blockleiters, appointed over every fifty households, continuously spied on all within their ken. Upon the strength of this spying, individuals were dragged off to 'protective custody' and to concentration camps, without legal proceedings of any kind, and without statement of any reason therefore. The partisan political police were exempted from effective legal responsibility for their acts.

With all administrative offices in Nazi control and with the Reichstag reduced to impotence, the judiciary remained the last obstacle to this reign of terror. But its independence was soon overcome and it was reorganized to dispense a venal justice. Judges were ousted for political or racial reasons and were spied upon and put under pressure to join the Nazi Party. After the Supreme Court had acquitted three of the four men whom the Nazis accused of setting the Reichstag fire, its jurisdiction over treason cases was transferred to a newly established 'People's Court' consisting of two judges and five Party officials. The German film of this 'People's Court' in operation, which we showed in this chamber, revealed its presiding judge pouring partisan abuse upon speechless defendants. Special courts were created to try political crimes, only Party members were appointed judges, and 'Judges Letters' instructed the puppet judges as to the 'general lines' they must follow.

The result was the removal of all peaceable means either to resist or to change the government. Having sneaked through the portals of power, the Nazis slammed the gate in the face of all others who might also aspire to enter. Since the law was what the Nazis said it was, every form of opposition was rooted out, and every dissenting voice throttled. Germany was in the clutch of a police state, which used the fear of the concentration camp as a means to enforce nonresistance. The Party was the state, the state was the Party, and terror by day and death by night were the policy of both.

2. *The Preparation and Waging of Wars of Aggression*

From the moment the Nazis seized power, they set about by feverish but stealthy efforts, in defiance of the Versailles Treaty, to arm for war. In 1933 they found no air force. By 1939 they had 21 squadrons, consisting of 240 echelons or about 2,400 first-line planes, together with trainers and transports. In 1933 they found an army of 3 infantry and 3 cavalry divisions. By 1939 they had raised and equipped an army of 51 divisions, 4 of which were fully motorized and 4 of which were panzer divisions. In 1933 they found a navy of 1 cruiser and 6 light cruisers. By 1939 they had built a navy of 4 battleships, 1 aircraft carrier, 6 cruisers, 22 destroyers, and 54 submarines. They had also built up in that period an armament industry as efficient as that of any country in the world.

These new weapons were put to use, commencing in September 1939, in a series of undeclared wars against nations with which Germany had arbitration and non-aggression treaties, and in violation of repeated assurances. On 1st September, 1939, this rearmed Germany attacked Poland. The following April witnessed the invasion and occupation of Denmark and Norway, and May saw the overrunning of Belgium, the Netherlands, and Luxembourg. Another spring found Yugoslavia and Greece under attack, and in June 1941 came the invasion of Soviet Russia. Then Japan, which Germany had embraced as a partner, struck without warning at Pearl Harbour in December 1941 and four days later Germany declared war on the United States.

We need not trouble ourselves about the many abstract difficulties that can be conjured up about what constitutes aggression in doubtful cases. I shall show you, in discussing the conspiracy, that by any test ever put forward by any responsible authority, by all the canons of plain sense, these were unlawful wars of aggression in breach of treaties and in violation of assurances.

3. *Warfare in Disregard of International Law*

It is unnecessary to labour this point on the facts. Göring asserts that the Rules of Land Warfare were obsolete, that no nation could fight a total war within their limits. He testified that the Nazis would have denounced the Conventions to which Germany was a party, but that General Jodl wanted captured German soldiers to continue to benefit from their observance by the Allies.

It was, however, against the Soviet people and Soviet prisoners that Teutonic fury knew no bounds, in spite of a warning by Admiral Canaris that the treatment was in violation of International Law.

We need not, therefore, for purposes of the conspiracy count, recite the revolting details of starving, beating, murdering, freezing, and mass extermination admittedly used against the eastern soldiery. Also, we may take as established or admitted that the lawless conduct such as shooting British and American airmen, mistreatment of western prisoners of war, forcing French prisoners of war into German war work, and other deliberate violations of the Hague and Geneva Conventions, did occur, and in obedience to highest levels of authority.

4. *Enslavement and Plunder of Populations in Occupied Countries*

The defendant Sauckel, Plenipotentiary General for the Utilization of Labour, is authority for the statement that 'out of five million foreign workers who arrived in Germany, not even 200,000 came voluntarily'. It was officially reported to defendant Rosenberg that in his territory 'recruiting methods were used which probably have their origin in the blackest period of the slave trade'. Sauckel himself reported that male and female agents went hunting for men, got them drunk, and 'shanghaied' them to Germany. These captives were shipped in trains without heat, food, or sanitary facilities. The dead were thrown out at stations, and the newborn were thrown out of the windows of moving trains.

Sauckel ordered that 'all the men must be fed, sheltered, and treated in such a way as to exploit them to the highest possible extent at the lowest conceivable degree of expenditure'. About two million of these were employed directly in the manufacture of armaments and munitions.

The director of the Krupp locomotive factory in Essen complained to the company that Russian forced labourers were so underfed that they were too weakened to do their work, and the Krupp doctor confirmed their pitiable condition. Soviet workers were put in camps under Gestapo guards, who were allowed to punish disobedience by confinement in a concentration camp or by hanging on the spot.

Populations of occupied countries were otherwise exploited and oppressed unmercifully. Terrorism was the order of the day. Civilians were arrested without charges, committed without counsel, executed without hearing. Villages were destroyed, the male inhabitants shot or sent to concentration camps, the women sent to forced labour, and the children scattered abroad. The extent of the slaughter in Poland alone was indicated by Frank, who reported:

If I wanted to have a poster put up for every seven Poles who were shot, the forests of Poland would not suffice for producing the paper for such posters.

Those who will enslave men cannot be expected to refrain from plundering them. Boastful reports show how thoroughly and scientifically the resources of occupied lands were sucked into the German war economy, inflicting shortage, hunger, and inflation upon the inhabitants. Besides this grand plan to aid the German war effort there were the sordid activities of the Rosenberg *Einsatzstab*, which pillaged art treasures for Göring and his fellow bandits. It is hard to say whether the spectacle of Germany's number two leader urging his people to give up every comfort and strain every sinew on essential war work while he rushed around confiscating art by the trainload should be cast as tragedy or comedy. In either case it was a crime.

International Law at all times before and during this war spoke with precision and authority respecting the protection due civilians of an occupied country, and the slave trade and plunder of occupied countries were at all times flagrantly unlawful.

5. Persecution and Extermination of Jews and Christians

The Nazi movement will be of evil memory in history because of its persecution of the Jews, the most far-flung and terrible racial persecution of all time. Although the Nazi Party neither invented nor monopolized anti-Semitism, its leaders from the very beginning embraced it, incited it, and exploited it. They used it as 'the psychological spark that ignites the mob'. After the seizure of power, it became an official state policy. The persecution began in a series of discriminatory laws eliminating the Jews from the civil service, the professions, and economic life. As it became more intense it included segregation of Jews in ghettos and exile. Riots were organized by Party leaders to loot Jewish business places and to burn synagogues. Jewish property was confiscated and a collective fine of a billion marks was imposed upon German Jewry. The programme progressed in fury and irresponsibility to the 'final solution'. This consisted of sending all Jews who were fit to work to concentration camps as slave labourers, and all who were not fit, which included children under twelve and people over fifty, as well as any others judged unfit by an SS doctor, to concentration camps for extermination.

Adolf Eichmann, the sinister figure who had charge of the extermination programme, has estimated that the anti-Jewish activities resulted in the killing of six million Jews. Of these, four million were killed in extermination institutions, and two million were killed by *Einsatzgruppen*, mobile units of the Security Police and SD which pursued Jews in the ghettos and in their homes and slaughtered them by gas wagons, by mass shooting in anti-tank ditches, and by every device which Nazi ingenuity could conceive. So thorough and uncompromising was this programme that the Jews of Europe as a race no longer exist, thus fulfilling the diabolic 'prophecy' of Adolf Hitler at the beginning of the war.

Of course, any such programme must reckon with the opposition of the Christian church. This was recognized from the very beginning. Defendant Bormann wrote all Gauleiters in 1941 that 'National Socialism and Christian concepts are irreconcilable', and that the people must be separated from the churches and the influence of the churches totally removed. Defendant Rosenberg even wrote dreary treatises advocating a new and weird Nazi religion.

The Gestapo appointed 'church specialists' who were instructed that the ultimate aim was 'destruction of the confessional churches'. The record is full of specific instances of the persecution of clergymen, the confiscation of church property, interference with religious publications, disruption of religious education, and suppression of religious organizations.

The chief instrumentality for persecution and extermination was the concentration camp, sired by defendant Göring and nurtured under the over-all authority of defendants Frick and Kaltenbrunner.

The horrors of these iniquitous places have been vividly disclosed by documents and testified to by witnesses. The Tribunal must be satiated with ghastly verbal and pictorial portrayals. From your records it is clear that the concentration camps were the first and worst weapon of oppression used by the National Socialist state, and that they were the primary means utilized for the persecution of the Christian church and the extermination of the Jewish race. This has been admitted to you by some of the defendants from the witness stand. In the words of defendant Frank:

A thousand years will pass and this guilt of Germany will still not be erased.

These, then, were the five great substantive crimes of the Nazi regime. Their commission, which cannot be denied, stands admitted. The defendant Keitel, who is in a position to know the facts, has given the Tribunal what seems to be a fair summation of the case on these facts:

The defendant has declared that he admits the contents of the general Indictment to be proved from the objective and factual point of view (that is to say, not every individual case) and this in consideration of the law of procedure governing this trial. It would be senseless, despite the possibility of refuting several documents or individual facts, to attempt to shake the Indictment as a whole.

I pass now to the inquiry whether these groups of criminal acts were integrated in a common plan or conspiracy.

The Common Plan or Conspiracy

The prosecution submits that these five· categories of premeditated crimes were not separate and independent phenomena but that all were committed pursuant to a common plan or conspiracy. The defence admits that these classes of crimes were committed but denies that they are connected one with another as parts of a single programme.

The central crime in this pattern of crime, the kingpin which holds them all together, is the plot for aggressive war. The chief reason for international cognizance of these crimes lies in this fact. Have we established the plan or conspiracy to make aggressive war?

Certain admitted or clearly proven facts help answer that question. First is the fact that such war of aggression did take place. Second, it is admitted that from the moment the Nazis came to power, every one of them and every one of the defendants worked like beavers to prepare for *some* war. The question therefore comes to this: were they preparing for the war which did occur, or were they preparing for some war which never has happened? It is probably true that in the early days none of them had in mind what month of what year war would begin, the exact dispute which would precipitate it, or whether its first impact would be Austria, Czechoslovakia, or Poland. But I submit that the defendants either knew or are chargeable with knowledge that the war for which they were making ready would be a war of German aggression. This is partly because there was no real expectation that any power or combination of powers would attack Germany. But it is chiefly because the inherent nature of the German plans was such that they were certain sooner or later to meet resistance and that they could then be accomplished only by aggression.

The plans of Adolf Hitler for aggression were just as secret as *Mein Kampf*, of which over six million copies were published in Germany. He not only openly advocated overthrowing the Treaty of Versailles, but made demands which went far beyond a mere rectification of its alleged injustices. He avowed an intention to attack neighbouring states and seize their lands, which he said would have to be won with 'the power of a triumphant sword'. Here, for every German to hearken to, were the 'ancestral voices prophesying war'.

Göring has testified in this courtroom that at his first meeting with Hitler, long before the seizure of power:

I noted that Hitler had a definite view of the impotency of protest and, as a second point, that he was of the opinion that Germany should be freed of the peace of Versailles. . . . We did not say we shall have to have a war and defeat our enemies; this was the aim and the methods had to be adapted to the political situation.

When asked if this goal were to be accomplished by war if necessary, Göring did not deny that eventuality but evaded a direct answer by saying: 'We did not even debate about those things at that time.' He went on to say that the aim to overthrow the Treaty of Versailles was open and notorious and that 'Every German in my opinion was for its modification, and there was no doubt that this was a strong inducement for joining the Party'. Thus, there can be no possible excuse for any person who aided Hitler to get absolute power over the German people, or took a part in his regime, to fail to know the nature of the demands he would make on Germany's neighbours.

Immediately after the seizure of power the Nazis went to work to implement these aggressive intentions by preparing for war. They first enlisted German industrialists in a secret rearmament programme. Twenty days after the seizure of power Schacht was host to Hitler, Göring, and some twenty leading industrialists. Among them were Krupp von Bohlen of the great Krupp armament works and representatives of I. G. Farben and other Ruhr heavy industries. Hitler and Göring explained their programme to the industrialists, who became so enthusiastic that they set about to raise three million Reichsmarks to strengthen and confirm the Nazi Party in power. Two months later Krupp was working to bring a reorganized association of German industry into agreement with the political aims of the Nazi government. Krupp later boasted of the success in keeping the German war industries secretly alive and in readiness despite the disarmament clauses of the Versailles Treaty, and recalled the industrialists' enthusiastic acceptance of 'the great intentions of the Führer in the rearmament period of 1933–9'.

Some two months after Schacht had sponsored this first meeting to gain the support of the industrialists, the Nazis moved to harness industrial labour to their aggressive plans. In April 1933 Hitler ordered Dr Ley 'to take over the trade unions', numbering some six million members. By Party directive Ley seized the unions, their property, and their funds. Union leaders, taken into 'protective custody' by the SS and SA, were put into concentration camps. The free labour unions were then replaced by a Nazi organization known as the German Labour Front, with Dr Ley as its head. It was expanded until it controlled over twenty-three million members. Collective bargaining was eliminated, the voice of labour could no longer be heard as to working conditions, and the labour contract was prescribed by 'trustees of labour' appointed by Hitler. The war purpose of this labour programme was clearly acknowledged by Robert Ley five days after war broke out, when he declared in a speech that:

We National Socialists have monopolized all resources and all our energies during the past seven years so as to be able to be equipped for the supreme effort of battle.

The Nazis also proceeded at once to adapt the government to the needs of war. In April 1935 the Cabinet formed a Defence Council, the working committee of which met frequently thereafter. In the meeting of 23rd May, 1933, at which defendant Keitel presided, the members were instructed that

No document must be lost since otherwise the enemy propaganda would make use of it. Matters communicated orally cannot be proven; they can be denied by us in Geneva.

In January 1934, with defendant Jodl present, the Council planned a mobilization calendar and mobilization order for some 240,000 industrial plants. Again it was agreed that nothing should be in writing so that 'the military purpose may not be traceable'.

On 21st May, 1933, the top secret Reich Defence Law was enacted. Defendant Schacht was appointed Plenipotentiary General for War Economy with the task of secretly preparing all economic forces for war and, in the event of mobilization, of financing the war. Schacht's secret efforts were supplemented in October 1936 by the appointment of defendant Göring as Commissioner of the Four Year Plan, with the duty of putting the entire economy in a state of readiness for war within four years.

A secret programme for the accumulation of the raw materials and foreign credits necessary for extensive rearmament was also set on foot immediately upon seizure of power. In September 1934 the Minister of Economics was already complaining that:

The task of stockpiling is being hampered by the lack of foreign currency; the need for secrecy and camouflage also is a retarding influence.

Foreign currency controls were at once established. Financing was delegated to the wizard Schacht, who conjured up the MEFO bill to serve the dual objectives of tapping the short-term money market for rearmament purposes while concealing the amount of these expenditures.

The spirit of the whole Nazi administration was summed up by

Göring at a meeting of the Council of Ministers, which included Schacht, on 27th May, 1936, when he said,

All measures are to be considered from the standpoint of an assured waging of war.

The General Staff, of course, also had to be enlisted in the war plans. Most of the Generals, attracted by the prospect of rebuilding their armies, became willing accomplices. The hold-over Minister of War von Blomberg and the Chief of Staff General von Fritsch, however, were not cordial to the increasingly belligerent policy of the Hitler regime, and by vicious and obscene plotting they were discredited and removed in January 1938. Thereupon, Hitler assumed for himself Supreme Command of the Armed Forces, and the positions of von Blomberg and von Fritsch were filled by others who became, as Blomberg said of Keitel, 'a willing tool in Hitler's hands for every one of his decisions'. The Generals did not confine their participation to merely military matters. They participated in all major diplomatic and political manoeuvres, such as the Obersalzburg meeting where Hitler, flanked by Keitel and other top Generals, issued his virtual ultimatum to Schuschnigg.

As early as 5th November, 1937, the plan to attack had begun to take definiteness as to time and victim. In a meeting which included defendants Raeder, Göring, and von Neurath, Hitler stated the cynical objective:

The question for Germany is where the greatest possible conquest could be made at the lowest possible cost.

He discussed various plans for the invasion of Austria and Czecho-slovakia, indicating clearly that he was thinking of these territories not as ends in themselves, but as means for further conquest. He pointed out that considerable military and political assistance would be afforded by possession of these lands and discussed the possibility of constitut-ing from them new armies up to a strength of about twelve divisions. The aim he stated boldly and baldly as the acquisition of additional living space in Europe, and recognized that 'the German question can be solved only by way of force'.

Six months later, emboldened by the bloodless Austrian conquest, Hitler, in a secret directive to Keitel, stated his 'unalterable decision to smash Czechoslovakia by military action in the near future'. On the same day, Jodl noted in his diary that the Führer had stated his final decision to destroy Czechoslovakia soon and had initiated military preparations all along the line. By April the plan had been perfected to attack Czechoslovakia 'with lightning-swift action as the result of an "incident".'

All along the line preparations became more definite for a war of expansion, on the assumption that it would result in world-wide conflict. In September 1938 Admiral Carls officially commented on a 'Draft Study of Naval Warfare Against England':

There is full agreement with the main theme of the study.

1. If according to the Führer's decision Germany is to acquire a position as a world power, she needs not only sufficient colonial possessions but also secure naval communications and secure access to the ocean.

2. Both requirements can only be fulfilled in opposition to Anglo-French interests and will limit their position as world powers. It is unlikely that they can be achieved by peaceful means. The decision to make Germany a world power therefore forces upon us the necessity of making the corresponding preparations for war.

3. War against England means at the same time war against the Empire, against France, probably against Russia as well, and a large number of countries overseas; in fact, against one-half to one-third of the whole world.

It can only be justified and have a chance of success if it is prepared economically as well as politically and militarily and waged with the aim of conquering for Germany an outlet to the ocean.

This Tribunal knows what categorical assurances were given to an alarmed world after the *Anschluss*, after Munich, and after the occupation of Bohemia and Moravia, that German ambitions were realized and that Hitler had 'no further territorial demands to make in Europe'. The record of this trial shows that those promises were calculated deceptions and that those high in the bloody brotherhood of Nazidom knew it.

As early as 15th April, 1938, Göring pointed out to Mussolini and Ciano that the possession of those territories would make possible an attack on Poland. Ribbentrop's Ministry wrote on 26th August, 1938, that:

After the liquidation of the Czechoslovakian question, it will be generally assumed that Poland will be next in turn.

Hitler, after the Polish invasion, boasted that it was the Austrian and

Czechoslovakian triumphs by which 'the basis for the action against Poland was laid'. Göring suited the act to the purpose and gave immediate instructions to exploit for the further strengthening of Germany the war potential, first of the Sudetenland, and then of the whole Protectorate.

By May 1939 the Nazi preparations had ripened to the point that Hitler confided to defendants Göring, Raeder, Keitel, and others, his readiness 'to attack Poland at the first suitable opportunity', even though he recognized that 'further successes cannot be attained without the shedding of blood'. The larcenous motives behind this decision he made plain in words that echoed the covetous theme of *Mein Kampf:*

Circumstances must be adapted to aims. This is impossible without invasion of foreign states or attacks upon foreign property. Living space, in proportion to the magnitude of the state, is the basis of all power—further successes cannot be attained without expanding our living space in the east. . . .

While a credulous world slumbered, snugly blanketed with perfidious assurances of peaceful intentions, the Nazis prepared not merely as before for *a* war, but now for *the* war. The defendants Göring, Keitel, Raeder, Frick, and Funk, with others, met as the Reich Defence Council in June 1939. The minutes, authenticated by Göring, are revealing evidence of the way in which each step of Nazi planning dovetailed with every other. These five key defendants, three months before the first Panzer unit had knifed into Poland, were laying plans for 'employment of the *population* in wartime', and had gone so far as to classify industry for priority in labour supply 'after five million servicemen had been called up'. They decided upon measures to avoid 'confusion when mobilization takes place', and declared a purpose 'to gain and maintain the lead in the decisive initial weeks of a war'. They then planned to use in production prisoners of war, criminal prisoners, and concentration camp inmates. They then decided on 'compulsory work for women in wartime'. They had already passed on applications from 1,172,000 specialist workmen for classification as indispensable, and had approved 727,000 of them. They boasted that orders to workers to report for duty 'are ready and tied up in bundles at the labour offices'. And they resolved to increase the industrial manpower supply by bringing into Germany 'hundreds of thousands of workers' from the Protectorate to be 'housed together in hutments'.

It is the minutes of this significant conclave of many key defendants which disclose how the plan to start the war was coupled with the plan to wage the war through the use of illegal sources of labour to maintain production. Hitler, in announcing his plan to attack Poland, had already foreshadowed the slave-labour programme as one of its corollaries when he cryptically pointed out to defendants Göring, Raeder, Keitel, and others that the Polish population 'will be available as a source of labour.' This was the part of the plan made good by Frank, who, as Governor General notified Göring that he would supply 'at least one million male and female agricultural and industrial workers to the Reich', and by Sauckel, whose impressments throughout occupied territory aggregated numbers equal to the total population of some of the smaller nations of Europe.

Here also comes to the surface the link between war labour and concentration camps, a manpower source that was increasingly used and with increasing cruelty. An agreement between Himmler and the Minister of Justice Thierack in 1942 provided for 'the delivery of anti-social elements from the execution of their sentence to the Reichsführer SS to be worked to death'. An SS directive provided that bedridden prisoners be drafted for work to be performed in bed. The Gestapo ordered forty-five thousand Jews arrested to increase the 'recruitment of manpower into the concentration camps'. One hundred thousand Jews were brought from Hungary to augment the camps' manpower. On the initiative of the defendant Dönitz, concentration-camp labour was used in the construction of submarines. Concentration camps were thus geared into war production on the one hand, and into the administration of justice and the political aims of the Nazis on the other.

The use of prisoner-of-war labour as here planned also grew with German needs. At a time when every German soldier was needed at the front and forces were not available at home, Russian prisoners of war were forced to man anti-aircraft guns against Allied planes. Field Marshal Milch reflected the Nazi merriment at this flagrant violation of International Law, saying,

This is an amusing thing, that the Russians must work the guns.

The orders for the treatment of Soviet prisoners of war were so ruthless that Admiral Canaris, pointing out that they would 'result in arbitrary mistreatments and killings', protested to the OKW against them as breaches of International Law. The reply of Keitel was unambiguous:

The objections arise from the military conception of chivalrous warfare! This is the destruction of an ideology! Therefore I approve and back the measures.

The Geneva Convention would have been thrown overboard openly except that Jodl objected because he wanted the benefits of Allied observance of it while it was not being allowed to hamper the Germans in any way.

Other crimes in the conduct of warfare were planned with equal thoroughness as a means of insuring the victory of German arms. In October 1938, almost a year before the start of the war, the large-scale violation of the established rules of warfare was contemplated as a policy, and the Supreme Command circulated a most secret list of devious explanations to be given by the Propaganda Minister in such cases. Even before this time commanders of the armed forces were instructed to employ any means of warfare so long as it facilitated victory. After the war was in progress the orders increased in savagery. A typical Keitel order, demanding use of the 'most brutal means', provided that:

It is the duty of the troops to use all means without restriction, even against women and children, so long as it insures success.

The German naval forces were no more immune from the infection than the land forces. Raeder ordered violations of the accepted rules of warfare wherever necessary to gain strategic successes. Dönitz urged his submarine crews not to rescue survivors of torpedoed enemy ships in order to cripple merchant shipping of the Allied nations by decimating their crews.

Thus, the war crimes against Allied forces and the crimes against humanity committed in occupied territories are incontestably part of the programme of making the war because, in the German calculations, they were indispensable to its hope of success.

Similarly, the whole group of pre-war crimes, including the persecutions within Germany, fall into place around the plan for aggressive war like stones in a finely wrought mosaic. Nowhere is the whole catalogue of crimes of Nazi oppression and terrorism within Germany so well integrated with the crime of war as in that strange mixture of wind and wisdom which makes up the testimony of Hermann Göring. In describing the aims of the Nazi programme before the seizure of power, Göring said:

The first question was to achieve and establish a different political structure for Germany which would enable Germany to obtain against the Dictate [of Versailles], and not only a protest, but an objection of such a nature that it would actually be considered.

With these purposes, Göring admitted that the plan was made to over-throw the Weimar Republic, to seize power, and to carry out the Nazi programme by whatever means were necessary, whether legal or illegal.

From Göring's cross-examination we learn how necessarily the whole programme of crime followed. Because they considered a strong state necessary to get rid of the Versailles Treaty, they adopted the *Führerprinzip*. Having seized power, the Nazis thought it necessary to protect it by abolishing parliamentary government and suppressing all organized opposition from political parties. This was reflected in the philosophy of Göring that the opera was more important than the Reichstag. Even the 'opposition of each individual person was not tolerated unless it was a matter of unimportance'. To insure the suppression of opposition a secret political police was necessary. In order to eliminate incorrigible opponents, it was necessary to establish concentration camps and to resort to the device of protective custody. Protective custody, Göring testified, meant that

People were arrested and taken into protective custody who had committed no crime but who one might expect, if they remained in freedom, would do all sorts of things to damage the German state.

The same purpose was dominant in the persecution of the Jews. In the beginning, fanaticism and political opportunism played a principal part, for anti-Semitism and its allied scapegoat mythology were a vehicle on which the Nazis rode to power. It was for this reason that the filthy Streicher and the blasphemous Rosenberg were welcomed to a place at Party rallies and made leaders and officials of the state or Party. But the Nazis soon regarded the Jews as foremost amongst the opposition to the police state with which they planned to put forward their plans of military aggression. Fear of their pacifism and their opposition to strident nationalism was given as the reason that the Jews had to be driven from the political and economic life of Germany.

Accordingly, they were transported like cattle to the concentration camps, where they were utilized as a source of forced labour for war purposes.

At a meeting held on 12th November, 1938, two days after the violent anti-Jewish pogroms instigated by Goebbels and carried out by the Party Leadership Corps and the SA, the programme for the elimination of the Jews from the German economy was mapped out by Göring, Funk, Heydrich, Goebbels, and other top Nazis. The measures adopted included confinement of the Jews in ghettos, cutting off their food supply, 'aryanizing' their shops, and restricting their freedom of movement. Here another purpose behind the Jewish persecutions crept in, for it was the wholesale confiscation of their property which helped finance German rearmament. Although Schacht's plan to have foreign money ransom the entire race within Germany was not adopted, the Jews were stripped to the point where Göring was able to advise the Reich Defence Council that the critical situation of the Reich exchequer, due to rearmament, had been relieved 'through the billion Reichsmark fine imposed on Jewry, and through profits accrued to the Reich in the aryanization of Jewish enterprises'.

A glance over the dock will show that, despite quarrels among themselves, each defendant played a part which fitted in with every other, and that all advanced the common plan. It contradicts experience that men of such diverse backgrounds and talents should so forward each other's aims by coincidence.

The large and varied role of Göring was half militarist and half gangster. He stuck a pudgy finger in every pie. He used his SA musclemen to help bring the gang into power. In order to entrench that power he contrived to have the Reichstag burned, established the Gestapo, and created the concentration camps. He was equally adept at massacring opponents and at framing scandals to get rid of stubborn generals. He built up the Luftwaffe and hurled it at his defenceless neighbours. He was among the foremost in harrying the Jews out of the land. By mobilizing the total economic resources of Germany he made possible the waging of the war which he had taken a large part in planning. He was, next to Hitler, the man who tied the activities of all the defendants together in a common effort.

The parts played by the other defendants, although less comprehensive and less spectacular than that of the Reichsmarshal, were nevertheless integral and necessary contributions to the joint undertaking, without any one of which the success of the common enterprise would have been in jeopardy. There are many specific deeds of which these men have been proven guilty. No purpose would be served—nor indeed is time available—to review all the crimes which the evidence has charged up to their names. Nevertheless, in viewing the conspiracy as a whole and as an operating mechanism it may be well to recall briefly the outstanding services which each of the men in the dock rendered to the common cause.

The zealot HESS, before succumbing to wanderlust, was the engineer tending the Party machinery, passing orders and propaganda down to the Leadership Corps, supervising every aspect of Party activities, and maintaining the organization as a loyal and ready instrument of power. When apprehensions abroad threatened the success of the Nazi scheme for conquest, it was the duplicitous RIBBENTROP, the salesman of deception, who was detailed to pour wine on the troubled waters of suspicion by preaching the gospel of limited and peaceful intentions. KEITEL, weak and willing too, delivered the armed forces, the instrument of aggression, over to the Party and directed them in executing its felonious designs.

KALTENBRUNNER, the grand inquisitor, took up the bloody mantle of Heydrich to stifle opposition and terrorize compliance, and buttressed the power of National Socialism on a foundation of guiltless corpses. It was ROSENBERG, the intellectual high priest of the 'master race', who provided the doctrine of hatred which gave the impetus for the annihilation of Jewry, and who put his infidel theories into practice against the eastern occupied territories. His woolly philosophy also added boredom to the long list of Nazi atrocities. The fanatical FRANK, who solidified Nazi control by establishing the new order of authority without law, so that the will of the Party was the only test of legality, proceeded to export his lawlessness to Poland, which he governed with the lash of Caesar and whose population he reduced to sorrowing remnants. FRICK, the ruthless organizer, helped the Party to seize power, supervised the police agencies to insure that it stayed in power, and chained the economy of Bohemia and Moravia to the German war machine.

STREICHER, the venomous vulgarian, manufactured and distributed obscene racial libels which incited the populace to accept and assist the progressively savage operations of 'race purification'. As Minister of Economics FUNK accelerated the pace of rearmament, and as

Reichsbank President banked for the SS the gold teeth fillings of concentration camp victims—probably the most ghoulish collateral in banking history. It was SCHACHT, the façade of starched respectability, who in the early days provided the window-dressing, the bait for the hesitant, and whose wizardry later made it possible for Hitler to finance the colossal rearmament programme, and to do it secretly.

DÖNITZ, Hitler's legatee of defeat, promoted the success of the Nazi aggressions by instructing his pack of submarine killers to conduct warfare at sea with the illegal ferocity of the jungle. RAEDER, the political admiral, stealthily built up the German navy in defiance of the Versailles Treaty, and then put it to use in a series of aggressions which he had taken a large part in planning. VON SCHIRACH, poisoner of a generation, initiated the German youth in Nazi doctrine, trained them in legions for service in the SS and Wehrmacht, and delivered them up to the Party as fanatic, unquestioning executors of its will.

SAUCKEL, the greatest and cruellest slaver since the Pharaohs of Egypt, produced desperately needed manpower by driving foreign peoples into the land of bondage on a scale unknown even in the ancient days of tyranny in the kingdom of the Nile. JODL, betrayer of the traditions of his profession, led the Wehrmacht in violating its own code of military honour in order to carry out the barbarous aims of Nazi policy. VON PAPEN, pious agent of an infidel regime, held the stirrup while Hitler vaulted into the saddle, lubricated the Austrian annexation, and devoted his diplomatic cunning to the service of Nazi objectives abroad.

SEYSS-INQUART, spearhead of the Austrian fifth column, took over the government of his own country only to make a present of it to Hitler, and then, moving north, brought terror and oppression to the Netherlands and pillaged its economy for the benefit of the German juggernaut. VON NEURATH, the old-school diplomat, who cast the pearls of his experience before Nazis, guided Nazi diplomacy in the early years, soothed the fears of prospective victims, and as Reich Protector of Bohemia and Moravia, strengthened the German position for the coming attack on Poland. SPEER, as Minister of Armaments and War Production, joined in planning and executing the programme to dragoon prisoners of war and foreign workers into German war industries, which waxed in output while the labourers waned in starvation. FRITZSCHE, radio propaganda chief, by manipulation of the truth goaded German public opinion into frenzied support of the regime and anaesthetized the independent judgment of the population so that they did without question their masters' bidding. And BOR- MANN, who has not accepted our invitation to this reunion, sat at the throttle of the vast and powerful engine of the Party, guiding it in the ruthless execution of Nazi policies, from the scourging of the Christian church to the lynching of captive Allied airmen.

The activities of all these defendants, despite their varied back-grounds and talents, were joined with the efforts of other conspirators not now in the dock, who played still other essential roles. They blend together into one consistent and militant pattern animated by a com-mon objective to reshape the map of Europe by force of arms. Some of these defendants were ardent members of the Nazi movement from its birth. Others, less fanatical, joined the common enterprise later, after successes had made participation attractive by the promise of rewards. This group of latter-day converts remedied a crucial defect in the ranks of the original true belivers, for as Dr Seimers has pointed out in his summation:

There were no specialists among the National Socialists for the particular tasks. Most of the National Socialist collaborators did not previously follow a trade requiring technical education.

It was the fatal weakness of the early Nazi band that it lacked technical competence. It could not from among its own ranks make up a goverrment capable of carrying out all the projects necessary to realize its aims. Therein lies the special crime and betrayal of men like Schacht and von Neurath, Speer and von Papen, Raeder and Dönitz, Keitel and Jodl. It is doubtful whether the Nazi master plan could have suc-ceeded without their specialized intelligence which they so willingly put at its command. They did so with knowledge of its announced aims and methods, and continued their services after practice had con-firmed the direction in which they were tending. Their superiority to the average run of Nazi mediocrity is not their excuse. It is their condemnation.

The dominant fact which stands out from all the thousands of pages of the record of this trial is that the central crime of the whole group of Nazi crimes—the attack on the peace of the world—was clearly and deliberately planned. The beginning of these wars of aggression was not an unprepared and spontaneous springing to arms by a population excited by some current indignation. A week before the invasion of Poland Hitler told his military commanders:

I shall give a propagandist cause for starting war—never mind whether it be plausible or not. The victor shall not be asked later on whether we told the truth or not. In starting and making a war, not the right is what matters, but victory.

The propagandist incident was duly provided by dressing concentration camp inmates in Polish uniforms, in order to create the appearance of a Polish attack on a German frontier radio station. The plan to occupy Belgium, Holland, and Luxembourg first appeared as early as August 1938 in connection with the plan for attack on Czechoslovakia. The intention to attack became a programme in May 1939, when Hitler told his commanders that:

The Dutch and Belgian air bases must be occupied by armed forces. Declarations of neutrality must be ignored.

Thus, the follow-up wars were planned before the first was launched. These were the most carefully plotted wars in all history. Scarcely a step in their terrifying succession and progress failed to move according to the master blueprint or the subsidiary schedules and time-tables until long after the crimes of aggression were consummated.

Nor were the war crimes and the crimes against humanity unplanned, isolated, or spontaneous offences. Aside from our undeniable evidence of their plotting, it is sufficient to ask whether six million people could be separated from the population of several nations on the basis of their blood and birth, could be destroyed and their bodies disposed of, except that the operation fitted into the general scheme of government. Could the enslavement of five millions of labourers, their impressment into service, their transportation to Germany, their allocation to work where they would be most useful, their maintenance —if slow starvation can be called maintenance—and their guarding have been accomplished if it did not fit into the common plan? Could hundreds of concentration camps located throughout Germany, built to accommodate hundreds of thousands of victims, and each requiring labour and materials for construction, manpower to operate and supervise, and close gearing into the economy—could such efforts have been expended under German autocracy if they had not suited the plan? Has the Teutonic passion for organization become famous for its toleration of nonconforming activity? Each part of the plan fitted into every other. The slave-labour programme meshed with the needs of industry and agriculture, and these in turn synchronized with the military machine. The elaborate propaganda apparatus geared with the programme to dominate the people and incite them to a war their sons would have to fight. The armament industries were fed by the concentration camps. The concentration camps were fed by the Gestapo. The Gestapo was fed by the spy system of the Nazi Party. Nothing was permitted under the Nazi iron rule that was not in accordance with the programme. Everything of consequence that took place in this regimented society was but a manifestation of a premeditated and unfolding purpose to secure the Nazi state a place in the sun by casting all others into darkness.

Common Defences Against the Charge of Common Responsibility

The defendants meet this overwhelming case, some by admitting a limited responsibility, some by putting the blame on others, and some by taking the position, in effect, that while there have been enormous crimes there are no criminals. Time will not permit me to examine each individual and peculiar defence, but there are certain lines of defence common to so many cases that they deserve some consideration.

Counsel for many of the defendants seek to dismiss the conspiracy or common-planning charge on the ground that the pattern of the Nazi plan does not fit the concept of conspiracy applicable in German law to the plotting of a highway robbery or a burglary. Their concept of conspiracy is in the terms of a stealthy meeting in the dead of night, in a secluded hideout, in which a group of felons plot every detail of a specific crime. The Charter forestalls resort to such parochial and narrow concepts of conspiracy taken from local law by using the additional and nontechnical term, 'common plan'. Omitting entirely the alternative term of 'conspiracy', the Charter reads that 'leaders, organizers, instigators, and accomplices participating in the formulation or execution of a common plan to commit' any of the described crimes 'are responsible for all acts performed by any persons in execution of such plan'.

The Charter concept of a common plan really represents the conspiracy principle in an international context. A common plan or conspiracy to seize the machinery of a state, to commit crimes against the peace of the world, to blot a race out of existence, to enslave millions, and to subjugate and loot whole nations cannot be thought of in the same terms as the plotting of petty crimes, although the same underlying principles are applicable. Little gangsters may plan which will carry a pistol and which a stiletto, who will approach a victim from the front and who from behind, and where they will waylay him. But in planning a war the pistol becomes a Wehrmacht, the stiletto a Luftwaffe. Where to strike is not a choice of dark alleys, but a matter of world geography.

The operation involves the manipulation of public opinion, the law of the state, the police power, industry, and finance. The baits and bluffs must be translated into a nation's foreign policy. Likewise, the degree of stealth which points to a guilty purpose in a conspiracy will depend upon its object. The clandestine preparations of a state against international society, although camouflaged to those abroad, might be quite open and notorious among its own people. But stealth is not an essential ingredient of such planning. Parts of the common plan may be proclaimed from the housetops, as anti-Semitism was, and parts of it kept undercover, as rearmament for a long time was. It is a matter of strategy how much of the preparation shall be made public, as was Göring's announcement in 1935 of the creation of an air force, and how much shall be kept covert, as in the case of the Nazis' use of shovels to teach 'labour' corps the manual of arms. The forms of this grand type of conspiracy are amorphous, the means are opportunistic, and neither can divert the law from getting at the substance of things.

The defendants contend, however, that there could be no conspiracy involving aggressive war because: (1) none of the Nazis wanted war; (2) rearmament was only intended to provide the strength to make Germany's voice heard in the family of nations; and (3) the wars were not in fact aggressive wars but were defensive against a 'Bolshevik menace'.

When we analyse the argument that the Nazis did not want war it comes down, in substance, to this: 'The record looks bad indeed—objectively—but when you consider the state of my mind—subjectively I hated war. I knew the horrors of war. I wanted peace.' I am not so sure of this. I am even less willing to accept Göring's description of the General Staff as pacifist. However, it will not injure our case to admit that as an abstract proposition none of these defendants liked war. But they wanted things which they knew they could not get without war. They wanted their neighbours' lands and goods. Their philosophy seems to be that if the neighbours would not acquiesce, then they are the aggressors and are to blame for the war. The fact is, however, that war never became terrible to the Nazis until it came home to them, until it exposed their deceptive assurances to the German people that German cities, like the ruined one in which we meet, would be invulnerable. From then on war was terrible.

But again the defendants claim: 'To be sure we were building guns. But not to shoot. They were only to give us weight in negotiating.' At its best this argument amounts to a contention that the military forces were intended for blackmail, not for battle. The threat of military invasion which forced the Austrian *Anschluss*, the threats which preceded Munich, and Göring's threat to bomb the beautiful city of Prague if the President of Czechoslovakia did not consent to the Protectorate, are examples of what the defendants have in mind when they talk of arming to back negotiation.

But from the very nature of German demands, the day was bound to come when some country would refuse to buy its peace, would refuse to pay Danegeld—

> For the end of that game is oppression and shame,
> And the nation that plays it is lost.

Did these defendants then intend to withdraw German demands, or was Germany to enforce them and manipulate propaganda so as to place the blame for the war on the nation so unreasonable as to resist? Events have answered that question, and documents such as Admiral Carls's memorandum, quoted earlier, leave no doubt that the events occurred as anticipated.

But some of the defendants argue that the wars were not aggressive and were only intended to protect Germany against some eventual danger from the 'menace of Communism', which was something of an obsession with many Nazis.

At the outset this argument of self-defence falls because it completely ignores this damning combination of facts clearly established in the record: first, the enormous and rapid German preparations for war; second, the repeatedly avowed intentions of the German leaders to attack, which I have previously cited; and third, the fact that a series of wars occurred in which German forces struck the first blows, without warning, across the borders of other nations.

Even if it could be shown—which it cannot be—that the Russian war was really defensive, such is demonstrably not the case with those wars which preceded it.

It may also be pointed out that even those who would have you believe that Germany was menaced by Communism also compete with each other in describing their opposition to the disastrous Russian venture. Is it reasonable that they would have opposed that war if it were undertaken in good-faith self-defence?

The frivolous character of the self-defence theory on the facts it is sought to compensate, as advocates often do, by resort to a theory of law. Dr Jahrreiss, in his scholarly argument for the defence, rightly points out that no treaty provision and no principle of law denied Germany, as a sovereign nation, the right of self-defence. He follows with the assertion, for which there is authority in classic International Law, that:

. . . every state is alone judge of whether in a given case it is waging a war of self-defence.

It is not necessary to examine the validity of an abstract principle which does not apply to the facts of our case. I do not doubt that if a nation arrived at a judgment that it must resort to war in self-defence, because of conditions affording reasonable grounds for such an honest judgment, any tribunal would accord it great and perhaps conclusive weight, even if later events proved that judgment mistaken.

But the facts in this case call for no such deference to honest judgment because no such judgment was even pretended, much less honestly made.

In all the documents which disclose the planning and rationalization of these attacks, not one sentence has been or can be cited to show a good-faith fear of attack. It may be that statesmen of other nations lacked the courage forthrightly and fully to disarm. Perhaps they suspected the secret rearmament of Germany. But if they hesitated to abandon arms, they did not hesitate to neglect them. Germany well knew that her former enemies had allowed their armaments to fall into decay, so little did they contemplate another war. Germany faced a Europe that not only was unwilling to attack, but was too weak and pacifist even adequately to defend, and went to the very verge of dishonour, if not beyond, to buy its peace. The minutes we have shown you of the Nazis' secret conclaves identify no potential attacker. They bristle with the spirit of aggression and not of defence. They contemplate always territorial expansion, not the maintenance of territorial integrity.

Minister of War von Blomberg, in his 1937 directive prescribing general principles for the preparation for war of the armed forces, has given the lie to these feeble claims of self-defence. He stated at that time:

The general political situation justifies the supposition that Germany need not consider an attack on any side. Grounds for this are, in addition to the lack of desire for war in almost all nations, particularly the Western Powers, the deficiencies in the preparedness for war in a number of states and of Russia in particular.

Nevertheless, he recommended

... a continuous preparedness for war in order to (a) counter-attack at any time, and (b) to enable the military exploitation of politically favourable opportunities should they occur.

If these defendants may now cynically plead self-defence, although no good-faith need of self-defence was asserted or contemplated by any responsible leader at the time, it reduces nonaggression treaties to a legal absurdity. They become only additional instruments of deception in the hands of the aggressor, and traps for well-meaning nations. If there be in nonaggression pacts an implied condition that each nation may make a *bona fide* judgment as to the necessity for self-defence against imminent, threatened attack, they certainly cannot be invoked to shelter those who never made any such judgment at all.

In opening this case I ventured to predict that there would be no serious denial that the crimes charged were committed, and that the issue would concern the responsibility of particular defendants. The defendants have fulfilled that prophecy. Generally, they do not deny that these things happened, but it is contended that they 'just happened', and that they were not the result of a common plan or conspiracy.

One of the chief reasons the defendants say there was no conspiracy is the argument that conspiracy was impossible with a dictator. The argument runs that they all had to obey Hitler's orders, which had the force of law in the German state, and hence obedience cannot be made the basis of a criminal charge. In this way it is explained that while there have been wholesale killings, there have been no murderers.

This argument is an effort to evade Article 8 of the Charter, which provides that the order of the government or of a superior shall not free a defendant from responsibility but can only be considered in mitigation. This provision of the Charter corresponds with the justice and with the realities of the situation, as indicated in defendant Speer's description of what he considered to be the common responsibility of the leaders of the German nation:

. . . with reference to utterly decisive matters, there is total responsibility. There must be total responsibility insofar as a person is one of the leaders, because who else could assume responsibility for the development of events, if not the immediate associates who work with and around the head of the state?

And again he told the Tribunal:

. . . it is impossible after the catastrophe to evade this total responsibility. If the war had been won, the leaders would also have assumed total responsibility.

Like much of the defence counsel's abstract arguments, the contention that the absolute power of Hitler precluded a conspiracy crumbles in face of the facts of record. The *Führerprinzip* of absolutism was itself a part of the common plan, as Göring has pointed out. The defendants may have become slaves of a dictator, but he was *their* dictator. To make him such was, as Göring has testified, the object of the Nazi movement from the beginning. Every Nazi took this oath:

I pledge eternal allegiance to Adolf Hitler. I pledge unconditional obedience to him and the Führers appointed by him.

Moreover, they forced everybody else in their power to take it. This oath was illegal under German law, which made it criminal to become a member of an organization in which obedience to 'unknown superiors or unconditional obedience to known superiors is pledged'. These men destroyed free government in Germany and now plead to be excused from responsibility because they became slaves. They are in the position of the fictional boy who murdered his father and mother and then pleaded for leniency because he was an orphan.

What these men have overlooked is that Adolf Hitler's acts are their acts. It was these men among millions of others, and it was these men leading millions of others, who built up Adolf Hitler and vested in his psychopathic personality not only innumerable lesser decisions but the supreme issue of war or peace. They intoxicated him with power and adulation. They fed his hates and aroused his fears. They put a loaded gun in his eager hands. It was left to Hitler to pull the trigger, and when he did they all at that time approved. His guilt stands admitted, by some defendants reluctantly, by some vindictively. But his guilt is the guilt of the whole dock, and of every man in it.

But it is urged that these defendants could not be in agreement on a common plan or in a conspiracy because they were fighting among themselves or belonged to different factions or cliques. Of course, it is not necessary that men should agree on everything in order to agree on enough things to make them liable for a criminal conspiracy. Unquestionably there were conspiracies within the conspiracy, and intrigues and rivalries and battles for power. Schacht and Göring disagreed, but over which of them should control the economy, not over whether the economy should be regimented for war. Göring claims to have departed from the plan because through Dahlerus he conducted some negotiations with men of influence in England just before the Polish war. But it is perfectly clear that this was not an effort to prevent aggression against Poland, but to make that aggression successful and safe by obtaining English neutrality. Rosenberg and Göring may have had some differences as to how stolen art should be distributed but they had none about how it should be stolen. Jodl and Goebbels may have disagreed about whether to denounce the Geneva Convention, but they never disagreed about violating it. And so it goes through the whole long and sordid story. Nowhere do we find an instance where any one of the defendants stood up against the rest and said: 'This thing is wrong and I will not go along with it.' Wherever they differed, their differences were as to method or disputes over jurisdiction, but always within the framework of the common plan.

Some of the defendants also contend that in any event there was no conspiracy to commit war crimes or crimes against humanity because cabinet members never met with the military to plan these acts. But these crimes were only the inevitable and incidental results of the plan to commit the aggression for *Lebensraum* purposes. Hitler stated, at a conference with his commanders, that:

The main objective in Poland is the destruction of the enemy and not the reaching of a certain geographical line.

Frank picked up the tune and suggested that when their usefulness was exhausted,

. . . then, for all I care, mincemeat can be made of the Poles and Ukranians and all the others who run around here—it does not matter what happens. .

Reichskommissar Koch in the Ukraine echoed the refrain:

I will draw the very last out of this country. I did not come to spread bliss. . . .

This was *Lebensraum* on its seamy side. Could men of their practical intelligence expect to get neighbouring lands free from the claims of their tenants without committing crimes against humanity?

The last stand of each defendant is that even if there was a conspiracy, he was not in it. It is therefore important in examining their attempts at avoidance of responsibility to know, first of all, just what it is that a conspiracy charge comprehends and punishes.

In conspiracy we do not punish one man for another man's crime. We seek to punish each for his own crime of joining a common criminal plan in which others also participated. The measure of the criminality of the plan and therefore of the guilt of each participant is, of course, the sum total of crimes committed by all in executing the plan. But the gist of the offence is participation in the formulation or execution of the plan. These are rules which every society has found necessary in order to reach men, like these defendants, who never get blood on their own hands but who lay plans that result in the shedding of blood. All over Germany today, in every zone of occupation, little men who carried out these criminal policies under orders are being convicted and punished. It would present a vast and unforgivable caricature of justice if the men who planned these policies and directed these little men should escape all penalty.

These men in this dock, on the face of the record, were not strangers to this programme of crime, nor was their connection with it remote or obscure. We find them in the very heart of it. The positions they held show that we have chosen defendants of self-evident responsibility. They are the very top surviving authorities in their respective fields and in the Nazi state. No one lives who, at least until the very last moments of the war, outranked Göring in position, power, and influence. No soldier stood above Keitel and Jodl, and no sailor above Raeder and Dönitz. Who can be responsible for the duplicitous diplomacy if not the Foreign Ministers, von Neurath and Ribbentrop, and the diplomatic handy man, von Papen? Who should be answerable for the oppressive administration of occupied countries if Gauleiters, Protectors, Governors, and Commissars such as Frank, Seyss-Inquart, Frick, von Schirach, von Neurath, and Rosenberg are not? Where shall we look for those who mobilized the economy for total war if we overlook Schacht and Speer, and Funk? Who was the master of the great slaving enterprise if it was not Sauckel? Where shall we find the hand that ran the concentration camps if it is not the hand of Kaltenbrunner? And who whipped up the hates and fears of the public, and manipulated the Party organizations to incite these crimes, if not Hess, von Schirach, Fritzsche, Bormann, and the unspeakable Julius Streicher? The list of defendants is made up of men who played indispensable and reciprocal parts in this tragedy. The photographs and the films show them again and again together on important occasions. The documents show them agreed on policies and on methods, and all working aggressively for the expansion of Germany by force of arms.

Each of these men made a real contribution to the Nazi plan. Every man had a key part. Deprive the Nazi regime of the functions performed by a Schacht, a Sauckel, a von Papen, or a Göring, and you have a different regime. Look down the rows of fallen men and picture them as the photographic and documentary evidence shows them to have been in their days of power. Is there one whose work did not substantially advance the conspiracy along its bloody path towards its bloody goal? Can we assume that the great effort of these men's lives was directed towards ends they never suspected?

To escape the implications of their positions and the inference of guilt from their activities, the defendants are almost unanimous in one defence. The refrain is heard time and again: these men were without authority, without knowledge, without influence, indeed without importance. Funk summed up the general self-abasement of the dock in his plaintive lament that,

I always, so to speak, came up to the door. But I was not permitted to enter.

In the testimony of each defendant, at some point there was reached the familiar blank wall: nobody knew anything about what was going on. Time after time we have heard the chorus from the dock:

I only heard about these things here for the first time.

These men saw no evil, spoke none, and none was uttered in their presence. This claim might sound very plausible if made by one defendant. But when we put all their stories together, the impression which emerges of the Third Reich, which was to last a thousand years, is ludicrous. If we combine only the stories from the front bench, this is the ridiculous composite picture of Hitler's government that emerges. It was composed of:

A number two man who knew nothing of the excesses of the Gestapo which he created, and never suspected the Jewish extermination programme although he was the signer of over a score of decrees which instituted the persecutions of that race;

A number three man who was merely an innocent middleman transmitting Hitler's orders without even reading them, like a postman or delivery boy;

A Foreign Minister who knew little of foreign affairs and nothing of foreign policy;

A Field Marshal who issued orders to the armed forces but had no idea of the results they would have in practice;

A security chief who was of the impression that the policing functions of his Gestapo and SD were somewhat on the order of directing traffic;

A Party philosopher who was interested in historical research, and had no idea of the violence which his philosophy was inciting in the twentieth century;

A Governor General of Poland who reigned but did not rule;

A Gauleiter of Franconia whose occupation was to pour forth filthy writings about the Jews, but who had no idea that anybody would read them;

A Minister of the Interior who knew not even what went on in the interior of his own office, much less the interior of his own department, and nothing at all about the interior of Germany;

A Reichsbank President who was totally ignorant of what went in and out of the vaults of his bank;

And a Plenipotentiary for the War Economy who secretly marshalled the entire economy for armament, but had no idea it had anything to do with war.

This may seem like a fantastic exaggeration, but this is what you would actually be obliged to conclude if you were to acquit these defendants.

They do protest too much. They deny knowing what was common knowledge. They deny knowing plans and programmes that were as public as *Mein Kampf* and the Party Programme. They deny even knowing the contents of documents they received and acted upon.

Nearly all the defendants take two or more conflicting positions. Let us illustrate the inconsistencies of their positions by the record of one defendant—one who, if pressed, would himself concede that he is the most intelligent, honourable, and innocent man in the dock. That is Schacht. And this is the effect of his own testimony—but let us not forget that I recite it not against him alone, but because most of its self-contradictions are found in the testimony of several defendants:

Schacht did not openly join the Nazi movement until it had won, nor openly desert it until it had lost. He admits that he never gave it public opposition, but asserts that he never gave it private loyalty. When we demand of him why he did not stop the criminal course of the regime in which he was a minister, he says he had not a bit of influence. When we ask why he remained a member of the criminal regime, he tells us that by sticking on he expected to moderate its programme. Like a Brahmin among untouchables, he could not bear to mingle with the Nazis socially, but never could he afford to separate from them politically. Of all the Nazi aggressions by which he now claims to have been shocked, there is not one that he did not support before the world with the weight of his name and prestige. Having armed Hitler to blackmail a continent, his answer now is to blame England and France for yielding.

Schacht always fought for his position in a regime he now affects to despise. He sometimes disagreed with his Nazi confederates about what was expedient in reaching their goal, but he never dissented from the goal itself. When he did break with them in the twilight of the regime, it was over tactics, not principles. From then on he never ceased to urge others to risk their positions and their necks to forward his plots, but never on any occasion did he hazard either of his own. He now boasts that he personally would have shot Hitler if he had had the opportunity, but the German newsreel shows that even after the fall of France, when he faced the living Hitler, he stepped out of line to grasp the hand he now claims to loathe and hung upon the words of the man he now says he thought unworthy of belief. Schacht says he steadily 'sabotaged' the Hitler government. Yet, the most relentless secret service in the world never detected him doing the regime any harm until long after he knew the war to be lost and the Nazis doomed. Schacht, who dealt in hedges all his life, always kept himself in a position to claim that he was in either camp. The plea for him is as specious on analysis as it is persuasive on first sight. Schacht represents the most dangerous and reprehensible type of opportunism—that of the man of influential position who is ready to join a movement that he knows to be wrong because he thinks it is winning.

These defendants, unable to deny that they were the men in the very top ranks of power, and unable to deny that the crimes I have outlined actually happened, know that their own denials are incredible unless they can suggest someone who is guilty.

The defendants have been unanimous, when pressed, in shifting the blame on other men, sometimes on one and sometimes on another. But the names they have repeatedly picked are Hitler, Himmler, Heydrich, Goebbels, and Bormann. All of these are dead or missing. No matter how hard we have pressed the defendants on the stand, they have never pointed the finger at a living man as guilty. It is a temptation to ponder the wondrous workings of a fate which has left only the guilty dead and only the innocent alive. It is almost too remarkable.

The chief villain on whom blame is placed—some of the defendants vie with each other in producing appropriate epithets—is Hitler. He is the man at whom nearly every defendant has pointed an accusing finger.

I shall not dissent from this consensus, nor do I deny that all these dead or missing men shared the guilt. In crimes so reprehensible that degrees of guilt have lost their significance they may have played the most evil parts. But their guilt cannot exculpate the defendants. Hitler did not carry all responsibility to the grave with him. All the guilt is not wrapped in Himmler's shroud. It was these dead whom these living chose to be their partners in this great conspiratorial brotherhood, and the crimes that they did together they must pay for one by one.

It may well be said that Hitler's final crime was against the land that he had ruled. He was a mad Messiah who started the war without cause and prolonged it without reason. If he could not rule he cared not what happened to Germany. As Fritzsche has told us from the stand, Hitler tried to use the defeat of Germany for the self-destruction of the German people. He continued the fight when he knew it could not be won, and continuance meant only ruin. Speer, in this courtroom, has described it as follows:

The sacrifices which were made on both sides after January 1945 were without sense. The dead of this period will be the accusers of the man responsible for the continuation of that fight, Adolf Hitler, just as much as the destroyed cities, destroyed in that last phase, who had lost tremendous cultural values and tremendous numbers of dwellings. . . . The German people remained faithful to Adolf Hitler until the end. He has betrayed them knowingly. He has tried to throw it into the abyss. . . .

Hitler ordered everyone else to fight to the last and then retreated into death by his own hand. But he left life as he lived it, a deceiver; he left the official report that he had died in battle. This was the man whom these defendants exalted to a Führer. It was they who conspired to get him absolute authority over all of Germany. And in the end he and the system they created for him brought the ruin of them all. As stated by Speer on cross-examination:

. . . the tremendous danger, however, contained in this totalitarian system only became abundantly clear at the moment when we were approaching the end. It was then that one could see what the meaning of the principle was, namely, that every order should be carried out without any criticism. Everything . . . you have seen in the way of orders which were carried out without any consideration, did after all turn out to be mistakes. . . . This system— let me put it like this—to the end of the system it has become clear what tremendous dangers are contained in any such system, as such, quite apart from Hitler's principle. The combination of Hitler and this system, then, brought about this tremendous catastrophe to this world.

But let me for a moment turn devil's advocate. I admit that Hitler was the chief villain. But for the defendants to put all blame on him is neither manly nor true. We know that even the head of a state has the same limits to his senses and to the hours of his day as do lesser men. He must rely on others to be his eyes and ears as to most that goes on in a great empire. Other legs must run his errands; other hands must execute his plans. On whom did Hitler rely for such things more than upon these men in the dock? Who led him to believe he had an invincible air armada if not Göring? Who kept disagreeable facts from him? Did not Göring forbid Field Marshal Milch to warn Hitler that in his opinion Germany was not equal to the war upon Russia? Did not Göring, according to Speer, relieve General Gallant of his air force command for speaking of the weaknesses and bungling of the air force? Who led Hitler, utterly untravelled himself, to believe in the indecision and timidity of democratic peoples if not Ribbentrop, von Neurath, and von Papen? Who fed his illusion of German invincibility if not Keitel, Jodl, Raeder and Dönitz? Who kept his hatred of the Jew inflamed more than Streicher and Rosenberg? Who would Hitler say deceived him about conditions in concentration camps if not Kaltenbrunner, even as he would deceive us? These men had access to Hitler, and often could control the information that reached him and on which he must base his policy and his orders. They were the Praetorian Guard, and while they were under Caesar's orders, Caesar was always in their hands.

If these dead men could take the witness stand and answer what has been said against them, we might have a less distorted picture of the parts played by these defendants. Imagine the stir that would occur in the dock if it should behold Adolf Hitler advancing to the witness box, or Himmler with an armful of dossiers, or Goebbels, or Bormann with the reports of his Party spies, or the murdered Röhm or Canaris. The ghoulish defence that the world is entitled to retribution only from the cadavers, is an argument worthy of the crimes at which it is directed.

We have presented to this Tribunal an affirmative case based on incriminating documents which are sufficient, if unexplained, to require a finding of guilt on Count One against each defendant. In the final analysis, the only question is whether the defendants' own testimony is to be credited as against the documents and other evidence of their guilt. What, then, is their testimony worth?

The fact is that the Nazi habit of economizing in the use of truth pulls the foundations out from under their own defences. Lying has always been a highly approved Nazi technique. Hitler, in *Mein Kampf*, advocated mendacity as a policy. Von Ribbentrop admits the use of the 'diplomatic lie'. Keitel advised that the facts of rearmament be kept secret so that they could be denied at Geneva. Raeder deceived about rebuilding the German navy in violation of Versailles. Göring urged Ribbentrop to tell a 'legal lie' to the British Foreign Office about the *Anschluss*, and in so doing only marshalled him the way he was going. Göring gave his word of honour to the Czechs and proceeded to break it. Even Speer proposed to deceive the French into revealing the specially trained among their prisoners.

Nor is the lie direct the only means of falsehood. They all speak with a Nazi doubletalk with which to deceive the unwary. In the Nazi dictionary of sardonic euphemisms 'final solution' of the Jewish problem was a phrase which meant extermination; 'special treatment' of prisoners of war meant killing; 'protective custody' meant concentration camp; 'duty labour' meant slave labour; and an order to 'take a firm attitude' or 'take positive measures' meant to act with unrestrained savagery. Before we accept their word at what seems to be its face, we must always look for hidden meanings. Göring assured us, on his oath, that the Reich Defence Council never met 'as such'. When we produced the stenographic minutes of a meeting at which he presided and did most of the talking, he reminded us of the 'as such' and explained this was not a meeting of the Council 'as such' because other persons were present. Göring denies 'threatening' Czechoslovakia— he only told President Hácha that he would 'hate to bomb the beautiful city of Prague'.

Besides outright false statements and doubletalk, there are also other circumventions of truth in the nature of fantastic explanations and absurb professions. Streicher has solemnly maintained that his only thought with respect to the Jews was to resettle them on the island of Madagascar. His reason for destroying synagogues, he blandly said, was only because they were architecturally offensive. Rosenberg was stated by his counsel to have always had in mind a 'chivalrous solution' to the Jewish problem. When it was necessary to remove Schuschnigg after the *Anschluss*, Ribbentrop would have had us believe that the Austrian Chancellor was resting at a 'villa'. It was left to cross-examination to reveal that the 'villa' was Buchenwald Concentration Camp. The record is full of other examples of dissimulations and evasions. Even Schacht showed that he, too, had adopted the Nazi attitude that truth is any story which succeeds. Confronted on cross-examination with a long record of broken vows and false words, he declared in justification:

I think you can score many more successes when you want to lead someone if you don't tell them the truth than if you tell them the truth.

This was the philosophy of the National Socialists. When for years they have deceived the world, and masked falsehood with plausibilities, can anyone be surprised that they continue the habits of a lifetime in this dock? Credibility is one of the main issues of this trial. Only those who have failed to learn the bitter lessons of the last decade can doubt that men who have always played on the unsuspecting credulity of generous opponents would not hesitate to do the same now.

It is against such a background that these defendants now ask this Tribunal to say that they are not guilty of planning, executing, or conspiring to commit this long list of crimes and wrongs. They stand before the record of this trial as bloodstained Gloucester stood by the body of his slain King. He begged of the widow, as they beg of you: 'Say I slew them not.' And the Queen replied, 'Then say they were not slain. But dead they are. . . .' If you were to say of these men that they are not guilty, it would be as true to say there has been no war, there are no slain, there has been no crime.

Richard Carlile

An Account of his 'Mock-trial' for Blasphemy

Of those who fought in the nineteenth century for the right of free speech and the right to publish, Richard Carlile is a figure of immense importance whose deeds are now almost forgotten. In his publisher's shop at 55 Fleet Street he printed and published both Thomas Paine's Theological Works and Palmer's Principles of Nature.

In 1819 he faced his first trial—Carlile preferred to call this and all his other appearances in the criminal courts 'mock-trials'—for blasphemous libel before Lord Chief Justice Abbott and a special jury at the Guildhall, London. His passionate defence of the right to publish anti-Christian literature was undying. His first trial resulted in a fine of £1,500, imprisonment for three years and the providing of a surety for his good behaviour for the rest of his life. Undaunted, he and his wife continued to publish. Indeed Mary Carlile was herself convicted of publishing a correct account of the judicial proceedings in which Richard was convicted; to publish an account of a trial which contained matter of a scandalous, blasphemous or indecent nature was at that time unlawful and punishable with imprisonment.

In Dorchester prison where Carlile and his family were incarcerated together with his printer who was also convicted, the presses continued to work and his publications were disseminated by his friends at great personal risk. Although he passionately believed in his right to publish matter which was clearly blasphemous Carlile appears not to have been an agnostic or atheist himself. In his later years, the only time when he was not intermittently in prison, he became a fervent religionist and denounced the works of Paine which he had fought so hard to publish.

The following piece is taken from the published transcript of the first day of his trial in October 1819.

MR CARLILE rose, and spoke to the following effect:

I rise in my own defence, and I stand before you with a deep impression of the importance of the question now under your consideration; that question is of no less importance, than, whether the doctrines or creeds of any man or sect of persons shall be deemed infallible and screened from investigation, or whether we shall in this country, where toleration and the liberty of the press are so much boasted of, be placed under the continual fear of being harassed with prosecution and ruinous expense, similar to this under which I am now struggling, for a fair, candid, honest, calm, and argumentative inquiry into the origin of the religious establishments of this and other countries. It is a question of the first magnitude; it is a question that requires the most open and extensive research and examination, it is a question that requires open and unrestrained discussion; it is a question that, on your part, requires the most mature deliberation. I feel an imperative necessity in examining it in all its bearings; and the justification of defending not only my intentions as a publisher of the *Age of Reason*, but the intentions of its author also, presuming that we were actuated by similar motives; which motives, Gentlemen of the Jury, I shall make appear to you were good, and not wicked and blasphemous as the Information falsely sets forth; I have, therefore, Gentlemen of the Jury, to entreat your patience to a full investigation of the real merits of this publication, and that you will not think the time (however long) mis-spent, when the eyes of the whole world are anxiously turned towards you, with a hope that you will not hesitate to give a verdict according to your consciences and the evidence adduced before you.

Gentlemen of the Jury, I have said the eyes of the whole country are turned towards you; it is a question in which all feel interested, for amongst the immense number of communications I have received from various parts of the country, some with congratulations and some for condolence, on the subject of the prosecutions, I have found many avowing their belief in the Christian doctrines and the validity of the books called the Old and New Testament, and yet deprecating the prosecution of any person for inquiring into them. I am satisfied that all the reasonable and unprejudiced part of the community will sympathize with me, and hail with pleasure the verdict of Not Guilty. But they who would call for a verdict of Guilty are persons of like dispositions to those who formerly kindled the flames in Smithfield and have sanctioned all the massacre and torture that have been predominant since the origin of Christianity; I have no hesitation in saying, that where the disposition has been intolerant, depraved, and oppressive, Christianity has had no restraint on it, but has been a cloak for its vices.

Before I go further into the argument, I will make some few observations on what has fallen from Mr Attorney-General.

The Learned Gentleman has opened his speech with the usual cant, yes, cant I may call it, which all Attorneys-General and prosecutors have used for many years, about the liberty of the press and the importance of free discussion. But I do not think he has evinced much of the spirit of either in the observations he has just addressed to you. He calls upon you to stop both in their progress, and his whole charge amounts to no more than has often been made before, and made in very nearly the same terms. His whole speech is no more than a parody on the speeches of former Attorneys-General. He talks of the liberty and the licentiousness of the Press, but how has he attempted to define it? There is no novelty in the arguments he has used, nor no difficulty in refuting them. He states, Gentlemen, that the eyes of the country are upon you, and I say so too, and I hope to make it appear to you that I am not the person described by that Learned Gentleman. He has said that the Christian religion proceeds from God, that the Christian religion teaches mildness and forbearance; then why does he bring me here? Because his ideas differ from mine as regards the Deity—that Deity who does not need the Attorney-General to protect him. The Learned Gentleman says, there is a law applicable to this case, but he went no further than asserting it. And if there really be a law applicable to the case, I am sure he will have no hesitation to admit that the Thirty-nine Articles are part and parcel of the law. Now, the first of these articles, entitled 'Of Faith in the Holy Trinity', sets out, that:

'There is but one living and true God, everlasting, without body, parts or passions; of infinite power, wisdom, and goodness; the Maker, and Preserver of all things both visible and invisible. And in unity of this Godhead there be three Persons, of one substance, power, and eternity; the Father, the Son, and the Holy Ghost.'

The doctrine of the Trinity cannot therefore be denied by the Attorney-General—or if it be denied, he does not admit the divinity of what is called Christianity. The Learned Gentleman has quoted, with others, the case of Eaton, which was the last case of the kind, with the exception of Mr Hone's case, where the charge was the same, although the charged was different; but subsequent to that case an Act of Parliament was passed for the especial relief of those who impugned the doctrine of the Trinity. Now, how will he be able to reconcile this? The first of the Thirty-nine Articles says one thing, and the Act of Parliament says another—they contradict each other, in point of fact, and yet such are the things represented by the Learned Gentleman as part and parcel of the law of the land. I hold in my hand, Gentlemen, the Act of the 53d of the King, which I shall read to you, an Act expressly passed for the relief of the Unitarians and all other persons who disbelieve the doctrine of the Trinity:

An Act to relieve persons who impugn the doctrine of the Holy Trinity from certain penalties. 21st July, 1813.

'Whereas, in the nineteenth year of his present Majesty an act was passed, intituled an act for the further relief of Protestant Dissenting ministers and schoolmasters; and it is expedient to enact as hereinafter provided; Be it therefore enacted by the King's most excellent majesty, by and with the advice and consent of the Lords spiritual and temporal, and Commons, in this present Parliament assembled, and by the authority of the same, That so much of an act passed in the first year of the right of King William and Queen Mary, intituled an act for exempting his Majesty's Protestant subjects dissenting from the Church of England, from the penalties of certain laws, as provides that that act or anything therein contained should not extend or be construed to extend to give any ease, benefit, or advantage to persons denying the Trinity as therein mentioned, be and the same is hereby repealed.

'II. And it be further enacted, That the provisions of another act passed in the ninth and tenth years of the reign of King William intituled an act for the more efficient suppressing blasphemy and profaneness, so far as the same relate to persons denying as therein mentioned, respecting the Holy Trinity, be and the same are hereby repealed.

'III. And whereas it is expedient to repeal an act, passed in the Parliament of Scotland in the first Parliament of King Charles the Second, intituled an act against the crime of blasphemy; and another act, passed in the Parliament of Scotland in the first Parliament of King William, intituled act against blasphemy; which acts respectively ordain the punishment of death; be it therefore enacted, That the said acts and each of them shall be, and the same are and is hereby repealed.'

Now, Gentlemen, I have no hesitation in asserting, that this act is a repeal of all former acts upon the subject of holding doctrines differing from those of the Trinity; it is, in short, a repeal of the first article of those thirty-nine, which are held to be divine by the great majority of those who call themselves Christians, and without a belief in which they cannot be considered what they profess themselves to be. The latter act, I imagine, ought to have the first operation; and where two acts are made upon one subject, such as the 9th and 10th of William and Mary, and the 53d of the King, but the latter repealing the former, I should take the latest as the existing law upon the subject. And if that be the case, which cannot be denied, Deism is also a part and parcel of the law of the land. For myself, I believe the Deity to be single and without any appendages. As such I worship and revere him, and cannot imagine why the open avowal of my belief should call for the interference of this or any other court. The Act before me tolerates the impugning of the Trinity—it relieves those who so impugn it, from all the penalties enforced or contained in all former Acts upon the subject, and therefore most decidedly admits Deism, and should, to deal out justice, protect its professors from all punishment. I know of no law, or of any court of law that can properly take cognizance of a charge of blasphemy, which consisting in speaking ill or irreverently of the Deity, is a matter between the person offending and the Deity offended. It is for him alone to deal as he thinks proper with a blasphemer. But this Act which I have read, allows persons to disbelieve the Trinity, and so far to blaspheme or impugn that doctrine, on which Christianity rests for its support. It is difficult, however, to define the meaning of the word blasphemy.

The Attorney-General says, the information against me is founded on the common law; but I think resort should never be had to the common law in preference to the statute law, and under the statute I have cited to you, I felt myself justified in publishing the *Age of Reason* by Mr Paine. I am aware there is a statute called the 9th and 10th of William and Mary, entitled 'An Act for the more effectual suppressing of blasphemy and profaneness'.

*   *   *

Carlisle read the Act

But, Gentlemen, you must perceive that the act of 53d of the King goes to repeal the Act of William and Mary, as far as it relates to persons denying or impugning the Holy Trinity. As to the charge of blasphemy, there are parts of the Act of William and Mary, under which I might be prosecuted; and I believe it is the only statute which we have as applicable to a charge of that nature. There is, as I have said, an unrepealed part of the old Act, under which I might be prosecuted, namely, that which incapacitates persons denying 'the Holy Scripture of the Old and New Testament to be of Divine authority', from holding any office or employment, civil, ecclesiastical, or military. But the present information is not founded upon this Statute, and, Gentlemen, I will tell you the reason, because in case of conviction, the punishment would not be equal to what the Learned Gentleman's disposition aims at. He says he has grounded the information on the common law, in preference to that of the statute law, but I do not know what the common law is. The lawyers say, the decisions of judges are the common law, that it resides in their breasts; but I am not satisfied the law should rest upon the dictum of the Judge. All laws should be plain and simple, in order to be easily understood—that we might know what to do and what to avoid. It should be reduced to a written code, in order that the people might know what they had to expect. But this is not the case in the present instance. There is, in fact, no law by which I can be now properly brought before you; there is no Court of Justice competent to try a question of honest difference of opinion on religious matters. I challenge the Attorney-General to produce any such law if he can. I know he cannot, but he relies on the Court to make out that case, which he is not capable of doing himself. He says it would be waste of time, it would be quite idle for him, to defend the doctrines of Christianity; but if he could do so, I do not think it would be such an idle waste of time, as the Learned Gentleman has thought proper to say it would be. If he does not defend it, you will know why he does not; but that is a matter which I do not at this moment mean to press on your attention. If he goes on to state in the usual way, in the way always adopted by all Attorneys-General, when bringing a charge of blasphemy against any individual, that you are bound by your oaths to return a verdict of guilty. Then why do any more than swear you? For it would spare a considerable time, if you pronounced your verdict immediately upon entering that box. He says you are pledged by your oaths, and under the sanction of your holy religion you cannot do otherwise than find me guilty; but this I deny. You are merely sworn to try the question at issue between me and the Attorney-General. You are sworn to ascertain if I had any malicious intention in publishing the works of Paine; and if I had not such intention, I am entitled to a verdict of acquittal. I published the works of Paine for a good and useful purpose, and I trust I shall show you, Gentlemen, there is nothing in them of an immoral tendency.

The Attorney-General frequently repeated that there were laws, under which I might be prosecuted for the alleged crime of blasphemy, but he contented himself with repeating it merely, and never attempting to state definitely what the law was. But there is a law! Yes, no doubt, but with the repetition of 'there is such a law', the Learned Gentleman seemed satisfied. Yet after all this repetition, I hope, Gentlemen of the Jury, I have already satisfied you, that there is no such law.

Prior to the Act of 1813, there was a statute in existence on this subject, but it has since been repealed, which is of itself an admission that the former law was unjust. Blasphemy cannot be defined; for what one man may consider blasphemy, another may look upon in a contrary light. The first case cited by the Attorney-General was that of *Taylor*, who, he said, used blasphemous expressions of so horrid a nature that he could not read them to the Jury. They were not worse, however, he observed, than those contained in the *Age of Reason*. But, notwithstanding all this statement, he read copious extracts from the work. What the expressions were he could not tell; but it appeared that Sir Matthew Hale would not let the man justify them. Now, it is worthy of observation, that Sir Matthew Hale sat on the Bench, and condemned two women to be burned at the stake for witchcraft. And if he had such an opinion with respect to witchcraft, he might also be fallible on the subject of blasphemy. Sir Matthew Hale might have been a very moral man, and yet believe in witchcraft or other equally ridiculous absurdities. The Attorney-General says it is an offence to say religion is a cheat, but he made no observation on their varieties, where Jews called Christianity a cheat; where Christians called the religion of the Jews a cheat, the Bramins called that of the Mohammedans a cheat, the Mohammedans that of the Bramins a cheat, and so on *ad infinitum*. All religions call those that differ from them cheats, or as often as one obtained the ascendancy it never failed to crush and revile the others. The Attorney-General next quoted the case of Woollston. At the time of that prosecution there was a very prevalent tendency towards free-thinking. Woollston, when apprehended for publishing his book, insisted there was no Judge or Jury capable of trying him, on account of his opinion. He was a man of most extensive erudition and research, well acquainted with the Hebrew and other languages, and insisted on it, that from the ignorance of the Judge and Jury in those languages, they were not competent to try him. I know the objection was overruled, and he was convicted, and sent to the King's Bench Prison. But what was the consequence? So conscious was he of the rectitude of his conduct, that he sold his book in the Prison, and was assisted and supported by many persons called devout and learned divines. The Attorney-General likewise quoted the case of Williams, who originally published the first and second parts of the *Age of Reason*. But he was a man who did not venture to defend himself. He left his defence in the hands of Mr Kyd, who came into Court determined to defend himself; but being a barrister, he suffered himself to be put down and silenced by Lord Kenyon. He wished to justify Paine's expressions by reading part of the Bible, but Lord Kenyon prevented him.

*　　　*　　　*

The Attorney-General has said, in the course of his observations, that this publication would have no effect on the morals of learned and intelligent men, but that it is calculated to corrupt the principles of the lower classes of society. And I would ask the Learned Gentleman, whether, in the present state of the country, any of the lower orders could lay down their half-guinea for the book? Three thousand copies have been sold since December last, and let the Attorney-General show a single instance, if he can, in which the work has been productive of an evil tendency. It was circulated amongst that class of society which was capable of spending half-a-guinea and I do not believe a solitary instance could be adduced of its having corrupted the mind of any person. The Learned Gentleman said, he was disgusted with the work, and that the duty of reading it was a most painful one. But however painful it might be, the question was brought into court by his predecessor in office, and he has himself thought fit to lay it before the Jury. The Learned Gentleman has made an appeal to the feelings of the Jury, whom he sought to influence by a reference to their duties as fathers of families. He did not, however, refer to the book itself, in which there is not an immoral sentence. In the work it is said that the Bible contains 'obscene stories, voluptuous debaucheries, cruel and torturous executions, and unrelenting vindictiveness'. If this is not the case, the assertions must fall to the ground—but if it can be justified, then that which the Jury will avoid placing in the hands of their children, is the work which contains those voluptuous stories. The Attorney-General said, he felt it to be his duty to investigate this question thoroughly. He has not, however, done so. But I will go through the book, paragraph by paragraph, and show that there is not a single immoral expression in it. Gentlemen, the Attorney-General's speech is full of repetitions. He said more than once that the Jury were bound to find me guilty, upon their oaths! Of course, if he were right, all inquiry and investigation are unnecessary and the Jury, by the oath they have taken—and merely, for having taken such oath—are bound to bring in a verdict of guilty. Gentlemen, the Attorney-General read the matter in the third and fourth counts of the information, without making any observation whatever upon them; sometimes, indeed, he made gestures, and at other times he favoured you with smiles, but he said nothing in the way of refutation. Gentlemen, the Attorney-General said that he could not read the observations on the New Testament, contained in this book, without the utmost pain. He first, indeed, said he could not bring himself to read them at all, but this you must see was mere declamation and sophistry; he did read those observations. Gentlemen, the Attorney-General has next attacked Mr Paine's opinion of the miraculous conception, but we all know that the Unitarians treat this part of the story with the same contempt, and that they have actually published a New Testament, omitting that part of it as a falsehood. He calls the work a coarse attack on the religious profession of the country. For myself, I do not know what religious profession he means—I know not what particular profession he is of now, but if I have been rightly informed, he was educated an Unitarian; his whole family, his father, his brothers, and nearest relations, have been, and still are Unitarians—are of that very body, for whose protection the Act of Parliament I have cited has been passed; but whether the Learned Gentleman changed his religion since he has been promoted to his profession, it is not for me to say, but I have been told that he was one of those who held up his hand for the passing of this statute law. Gentlemen, the Attorney-General says he hoped for my reformation, as well as the author of this work; he said that in his calmer moments Mr Paine, and the Defendant himself must have felt the truths of the Christian religion. Gentlemen, for myself I am free to declare that I have strong doubts of the truth of that religion, and as for Mr Paine, who has gone to his account, he expressed himself on this subject in terms sufficiently strong not to have his sentiments mistaken. The Attorney-General declared that this prosecution was not instituted for the purposes of persecution; but, Gentlemen, I hope to make it clear to you, that it is for persecuting purposes the prosecution is instituted; for the purpose of persecution on a mere difference of opinion. Gentlemen, the Attorney-General has told you that Christianity did not stand in need of the assistance of the secular arm. And, if Christianity does not stand in need of his interference, is it not gross presumption in him to come into this Court to protect it! If he believes it to be of divine origin, is it not extremely presumptuous in him to defend it! This conduct, Gentlemen, furnishes strong proof that the present Attorney-General, like many of the law-officers of the Crown before him, feels it necessary to hold up the terrors of prosecution against free inquiry on this most important of all subjects. Gentlemen, the Attorney-General has stated to you, that it is an offence against the common law of the land to revile Christianity. Gentlemen, what is Christianity? The articles of the Christian church expressly state, that the Christian God is composed of three persons; Father, Son, and Holy Ghost; the doctrine of the Trinity is the first, the most essential, and the most indispensible doctrine of Christians; yet those who do not believe in that doctrine, those who have openly disavowed it, those who have, in the words of the Attorney-General, reviled this religion have not only not been punished, but are protected by the statute law of the land. Gentlemen, the Attorney-General has told you, that my trial has been delayed, and he has put the causes of this delay on my shoulders; but he is not justifiable in doing so. Why was not this trial brought on after the Easter sittings? It might have been brought on then with as little inconvenience as now; it is true, that other causes were fixed for trial before it, but it is equally true that it is now put out of order, and takes precedence of one hundred previous causes; it might have been brought before you, Gentlemen, at all events, in the beginning of last June. But the Attorney-General has said, that I took advantage of the forms of law, and that I traversed. I did, Gentlemen, traverse for one short term, by which the hearing of the case was postponed from January to April, but the Crown has ever since lain by. Gentlemen of the Jury, the Attorney-General has confidently called for your verdict of guilty, because he says, it is manifest I have offended God. If this were the mere charge against me—if he could only hope to snatch a verdict of guilty, by saying to impartial men that in the publication of this work I have offended my God, I should have nothing to fear—I could not doubt of the protecting verdict of honest men. How can he prove—why should he say, that in this act I have offended my God? Why should he thus presumptuously come between me and my Creator? He cannot, in this instance, make guilt apparent—for here guilt exists in the mind alone, and that mind tells me that I have not given offence to God, by giving publicity to what I consider a moral and a useful work, by extending the field of fair inquiry, into which every man might enter. Gentlemen, the Attorney-General again told you, that by the obligation of your oath, you were bound to find me guilty. What is this but to shut up the avenues of justice, and to confound my defence? This, Gentlemen, is not candid. He also said that he did not mean to excite prejudice against me; but what was his address but an endeavour, from beginning to end, to stir latent prejudices, which must necessarily, if excited, militate against my defence? Gentlemen, I shall, I trust, be able to show you, that there is not one immoral expression in the entire of this publication, unless they are quotations from that book which it labours to refute. Here, Gentlemen, are twelve copies of the publication, which, if it be your wish, I shall send up to your box. You will read it with candour, and I have not a doubt, that when every word it contains is freely and fairly considered, ample justice will be done.

Gentlemen, the book which I now hold in my hand, and which forms the subject of this prosecution, is entitled *The Theological Works of Thomas Paine.* I have already stated my motives for publishing it, which were of the best and purest description, namely to promote morality and free discussion on every subject. In a short preface to the work, I have stated my reasons for its publication, and I shall read it, in order that they may not be mistaken.

'In presenting to the public the Theological Works of THOMAS PAINE, against which so senseless a clamour has hitherto been raised, the Publisher is actuated by but one simple motive, namely, an inquiry after truth. The very numerous inquiries for the *Age of Reason* since the reappearance of the Political Works, have been to the publisher an irresistible inducement to bring forth the present edition. From the applications that have been made to him, he is completely convinced, that the minds of his fellow citizens are fully and adequately prepared to discuss the merits and demerits of the system of religion which forms so prominent a feature in the establishments of the country. He fully anticipates the senseless and unmeaning charges of "impiety" and "blasphemy" that will be exhibited against him by the ignorant and the interested; by the bigot and the hypocrite; to these, however, he is perfectly indifferent, satisfied as he is that this object is to arrive at the truth, and to promote the interests of fair and honest discussion.

'The publisher flatters himself that the present collection will be published from time to time, so as to defeat the hopes and wishes of those whose object it has been to suppress them. He confidently anticipates, that when free discussion on all subjects, whether political or theological, literary or scientific, shall be tolerated, that then, and then only, will the human mind, by progressive improvement, arrive at that state, which may be deservedly termed the Age of Reason.'

Gentlemen, my only reason for publishing the works of Mr Paine has been an anxious and sincere desire to promote the cause of truth and free discussion. I am convinced in my own mind, that they are calculated to improve morality by promoting inquiry; that they tend to exalt our notions of the Deity; and lead us to a belief of his excellence and love for man. These were my motives for republishing his works, and these are motives which produce a satisfaction within me, that no prosecution, that no persecution, will be able to destroy. I consider the publication as essential to the interest and welfare of the country, and having acted under that impression, I stand acquitted of all the malicious intention imputed to me by my persecutors. Gentlemen, I now proceed to call your attention to the work, which, is divided into Three Parts, and is called *The Age of Reason, Part the First being an Investigation of True and Fabulous Theology, by Thomas Paine.* It commences thus:

'It has been my intention, for several years past to publish my thoughts upon religion; I am well aware of the difficulties that attend the subject, and from that consideration, had reserved it to a more advanced period of life. I intended it to be the last offering I should make to my fellow citizens of all nations, and that at a time when the purity of the motive that induced me to it, could not admit of a question, even by those who might disapprove the work.'

Gentlemen, Mr Paine was nearly 60 years of age when he wrote the paragraph I have just read to you. He was then in France, it was at the period of the French revolution, when he could not be sure of his existence for a single day; and when, having written under such circumstances, he must certainly be entitled to the praise of sincerity, and of a thorough conviction of the rectitude of his intentions.

*   *   *

Carlile proceeded to quote at length from Paine's theological works

This, Gentlemen, finishes the first part of the *Age of Reason*, and I now ask you, or rather I leave you to judge for yourselves, whether there is to be found in it a single sentence hostile to the cause of justice, or morality, or tending to discourage the mind of man? No Gentlemen, it does not, but on the contrary it contains a finer system of ethics, and is more calculated to improve and exact the human faculties, than any thing which can be congregated, or formed from that Book which it so ably investigates. Two extracts only have been made from all that I have just read, and inserted in the Indictment which my persecutors have so zealously put together for the purpose of overwhelming me—and these two passages I have already noticed. I shall now, Gentlemen, proceed to read the *Second Part of Paine's Age of Reason, being the continuation of an investigation of True and Fabulous Theology.*

*   *   *

While Mr Carlile was reading this paragraph, the Chief Justice ordered candles to be brought into the Court. While the candles were preparing, he addressed the Chief Justice as follows:

My Lord, I wish your Lordship would relieve me by adjourning the Court until tomorrow morning, for I feel exhausted, and find I cannot proceed much further.

CHIEF JUSTICE: I cannot yet adjourn the Court; but you can retire for a few minutes, and take some refreshment.

Mr Carlile then withdrew with a few friends. Candles were introduced at half past five; the law-officers of the Crown appeared in close conversation, and after an absence of about five minutes, Mr Carlile returned, and was about to proceed, when

The Chief Justice observed that one of the Jury was absent from the box, although within hearing, and that the Defendant had better wait until he was in his place. On the return of this Juryman, he proceeded . . .

*   *   *

I have now gone through the whole of the three books which are brought into the information, and you must be convinced, Gentlemen, that there is not an immoral expression in them, save where it be a quotation. I think I have shown you that the author has evinced an enlarged and liberal mind. The opinions and sentiments of Mr Paine on the subject under discussion are my opinions and sentiments. This work contains a body of truth to which I subscribe. The author has certainly spoken disrespectfully of certain passages in the Old and New Testament, but it should be considered that he believed nothing of the character given them, and his own apology is that, he cannot pay complaisance to error and falsehood. An apology quite sufficient to satisfy any reasonable mind.

I now feel exhausted, and beg your Lordship to adjourn the Court till to-morrow.

CHIEF JUSTICE: Have you much more to offer the Jury in defence?

MR CARLILE: If my bodily strength permits I have enough to last till Saturday night.

CHIEF JUSTICE: As I would not willingly curtail your defence, if you request me, I shall now adjourn till tomorrow.

MR CARLILE: I request it, my Lord.

The Chief Justice, addressing the Jury, said that he was not desirous of imposing upon them any restraints. They would of course take care not to hold communications with any persons on the subject of the trial. The Jury signified their acquiescence; and the Chief Justice addressed himself to Mr Carlile, saying, perhaps you would leave your books and notes with the Officer of the Court.

MR CARLILE: I thank you, my Lord, I had rather not.

On leaving the Court the Defendant, accompanied by Mr Hunt, Mr Sherwin, and Mr Fry, was received with warm applause by the people gathered about the Hall.

Plato

Socrates' Address to the Jurors after being found Guilty of Impiety and Corrupting the Youth*

THERE ARE many reasons why I am not grieved, O men of Athens, at the vote of condemnation. I expected it, and am only surprised that the votes are so nearly equal; for I had thought that the majority against me would have been far larger; but now, had thirty votes gone over to the other side, I should have been acquitted. And I may say, I think, that I have escaped Meletus. I may say more; for without the assistance of Anytus and Lycon, any one may see that he would not have had a fifth part of the votes, as the law requires, in which case he would have incurred a fine of a thousand drachmae.

And so he proposes death as the penalty. And what shall I propose on my part, O men of Athens? Clearly that which is my due. And what is my due? What returns shall be made to a man who has never had the wit to be idle during his whole life; but has been careless of what the many care for—wealth, and family interests, and military offices, and speaking in the assembly, and magistracies, and plots, and parties. Reflecting that I was really too honest a man to be a politician and live, I did not go where I could do no good to you or to myself; but where I could do the greatest good privately to every one of you, thither I went, and sought to persuade every man among you that he must look to himself, and seek virtue and wisdom before he looks to his private interests, and look to the State before he looks to the interests of the State; and that this should be the order which he observes in all his actions. What shall be done to such an one? Doubtless some good thing, O men of Athens, if he has his reward; and the good should be of a kind suitable to him. What would be a reward suitable to a poor man who is your benefactor, and who desires leisure that he may instruct you? There can be no reward so fitting as maintenance in the Prytaneum, O men of Athens, a reward which he deserves far more than the citizen who has won the prize at Olympia in the horse or chariot race, whether the chariots were drawn by two horses or by

* From the *Apology*

many. For I am in want, and he has enough; and he only gives you the appearance of happiness, and I give you the reality. And if I am to estimate the penalty fairly, I should say that maintenance in the Prytaneum is the just return.

Perhaps you think that I am braving you in what I am saying now, as in what I said before about the tears and prayers. But this is not so. I speak rather because I am convinced that I never intentionally wronged any one, although I cannot convince you—the time has been too short; if there were a law at Athens, as there is in other cities, that a capital cause should not be decided in one day, then I believe that I should have convinced you. But I cannot in a moment refute great slanders; and, as I am convinced that I never wronged another, I will assuredly not wrong myself. I will not say to myself that I deserve any evil, or propose any penalty. Why should I? Because I am afraid of the penalty of death which Meletus proposes? When I do not know whether death is a good or an evil, why should I propose a penalty which would certainly be an evil? Shall I say imprisonment? And why should I live in prison, and be the slave of the magistrate of the year—of the Eleven? Or shall the penalty be a fine, and imprisonment until the fine is paid? There is the same objection. I should have to lie in prison, for money I have none, and cannot pay. And if I say exile (and this may possibly be the penalty which you will affix), I must indeed be blinded by the love of life, if I am so irrational as to expect that when you, who are my own citizens, cannot endure my discourses and words, and have found them so grievous and odious that you will have no more of them, others are likely to endure me. No, indeed, men of Athens, that is not very likely. And what a life should I lead, at my age, wandering from city to city, ever changing my place of exile, and always being driven out! For I am quite sure that wherever I go, that, as here, the young men will flock to me; and if I drive them away, their elders will drive me out at their request; and if I let them come, their fathers and friends will drive me out for their sakes.

Some one will say: Yes, Socrates, but cannot you hold your tongue, and then you may go into a foreign city, and no one will interfere with you? Now, I have great difficulty in making you understand my answer to this. For if I tell you that to do as you say would be a disobedience to the God, and therefore that I cannot hold my tongue, you will not believe that I am serious; and if I say again that daily to discourse about virtue, and of those other things about which you hear me examining myself and others, is the greatest good of man, and that the unexamined life is not worth living, you are still less likely to believe me. Yet I say what is true, although a thing of which it is hard for me to persuade you. Also, I have never been accustomed to think that I deserve to suffer any harm. Had I money I might have estimated the offence at what I was able to pay, and not have been much the worse. But I have none, and therefore I must ask you to proportion the fine to my means. Well, perhaps I could afford a mina, and therefore I propose that penalty: Plato, Crito, Critobulus, and Apollodorus, my friends here, bid me say thirty minae, and they will be the sureties. Let thirty minae be the penalty; for which sum they will be ample security to you.

Socrates is condemned to death

Not much time will be gained, O Athenians, in return for the evil name which you will get from the detractors of the city, who will say that you killed Socrates, a wise man; for they will call me wise, even although I am not wise, when they want to reproach you. If you had waited a little while, your desire would have been fulfilled in the course of nature. For I am far advanced in years, as you may perceive, and not far from death. I am speaking now not to all of you, but only to those who have condemned me to death. And I have another thing to say to them: You think that I was convicted because I had no words of the sort which would have procured my acquittal—I mean, if I had thought fit to leave nothing undone or unsaid. Not so; the deficiency which led to my conviction was not of words—certainly not. But I had not the boldness or impudence or inclination to address you as you would have liked me to do, weeping and wailing and lamenting, and saying and doing many things which you have been accustomed to hear from others, and which, as I maintain, are unworthy of me. I thought at the time that I ought not to do anything common or mean when in danger: nor do I now repent of the style of my defence; I would rather die having spoken after my manner, than speak in your manner and live. For neither in war nor yet at law ought I or any man use every way of escaping death. Often in battle there can be no doubt that if a man will throw away his arms, and fall on his knees before his pursuers, he may escape death; and in other dangers there are other ways of escaping death, if a man is willing to say and do anything. The difficulty, my friends, is not to avoid death, but to avoid unrighteousness; for that runs faster than death. I am old and move slowly, and the slower runner has overtaken me, and my accusers are keen and quick, and the faster runner, who is unrighteousness, has overtaken them. And now I depart hence condemned by you to suffer the penalty of death—they too go their ways condemned by the truth to suffer the penalty of villainy and wrong; and I must abide by my award—let them abide by theirs. I suppose that these things may be regarded as fated—and I think that they are well.

And now, O men who have condemned me, I would fain prophesy to you; for I am about to die, and in the hour of death men are gifted with prophetic power. And I prophesy to you who are my murderers, that immediately after my departure punishment far heavier than you have inflicted on me will surely await you. Me you have killed because you wanted to escape the accuser, and not to give an account of your lives. But that will not be as you suppose: far otherwise. For I say that there will be more accusers of you than there are now; accusers whom hitherto I have restrained: and as they are younger they will be more inconsiderate with you, and you will be more offended at them. If you think that by killing men you can prevent some one from censuring your evil lives, you are mistaken; that is not a way of escape which is either possible or honourable; the easiest and the noblest way is not to be disabling others, but to be improving yourselves. This is the prophecy which I utter before my departure to the judges who have condemned me.

Friends, who would have acquitted me, I would like also to talk with you about the thing which has come to pass, while the magistrates are busy, and before I go to the place at which I must die. Stay then a little, for we may as well talk with one another while there is time. You are my friends, and I should like to show you the meaning of this event which has happened to me. O my judges—for you I may truly call judges—I should like to tell you of a wonderful circumstance. Hitherto the divine faculty of which the internal oracle is the source has constantly been in the habit of opposing me even about trifles, if I was going to make a slip or error in any matter; and now as you see there has come upon me that which may be thought, and is generally believed to be, the last and worst evil. But the oracle made no sign of opposition, either when I was leaving my house in the morning, or when I was on my way to the court, or while I was speaking, at anything which I was going to say; and yet I have often been stopped in the middle of a speech, but now in nothing I either said or did touching the matter in hand has the oracle opposed me. What do I take to be the explanation of this silence? I will tell you. It is an intimation that what has happened to me is a good, and that those of us who think that death is an evil are in error. For the customary sign would surely have opposed me had I been going to evil and not to good.

Let us reflect in another way, and we shall see that there is great reason to hope that death is a good; for one of two things—either death is a state of nothingness and utter unconsciousness, or, as men say, there is a change and migration of the soul from this world to another. Now, if you suppose that there is no consciousness, but a sleep like the sleep of him who is undisturbed even by dreams, death will be an unspeakable gain. For if a person were to select the night in which his sleep was undisturbed even by dreams, and were to compare with this the other days and nights of his life, and then were to tell us how many days and nights he had passed in the course of his life better and more pleasantly than this one, I think that any man, I will not say a private man, but even the great king will not find many such days or nights, when compared with the others. Now, if death be of such a nature, I say that to die is gain; for eternity is then only a single night. But if death is the journey to another place, and there, as men say, all the dead abide, what good, O my friends and judges, can be greater than this? If, indeed, when the pilgrim arrives in the world below, he is delivered from the professors of justice in this world, and finds the true judges who are said to give judgment there, Minos and Rhadamanthus and Aeacus and Triptolemus, and other sons of God who were righteous in their own life, that pilgrimage will be worth making. What would not a man give if he might converse with Orpheus and Musaeus and Hesiod and Homer? Nay, if this be true, let me die again and again. I myself, too, shall have a wonderful interest in there meeting and conversing with Palamedes, and Ajax the son of Telamon, and any other ancient hero who has suffered death through an unjust judgment; and there will be no small pleasure, as I think, in comparing my own sufferings with theirs. Above all, I shall then be able to continue my search into true and false knowledge; as in this world, so also in the next; and I shall find out who is wise, and who pretends to be wise, and is not. What would not a man give, O judges, to be able to examine the leader of the great Trojan expedition; or Odysseus or Sisyphus, or numberless others, men and women too! What infinite delight would there be in conversing with them and asking them questions! In another world they do not put a man to death for asking questions: assuredly not. For besides being happier than we are, they will be immortal, if what is said is true.

Wherefore, O judges, be of good cheer about death, and know of a certainty, that no evil can happen to a good man, either in life or after death. He and his are not neglected by the gods; nor has my own approaching end happened by mere chance. But I see clearly that the time had arrived when it was better for me to die and be released from trouble; wherefore the oracle gave no sign. For which reason, also, I am not angry with my condemners, or with my accusers; they have done me no harm, although they did not mean to do me any good; and for this I may gently blame them.

Still, I have a favour to ask of them. When my sons are grown up, I would ask you, O my friends, to punish them; and I would have you trouble them, as I have troubled you, if they seem to care about riches, or anything, more than about virtue; or if they pretend to be something when they are really nothing—then reprove them, as I have reproved you, for not caring about that for which they ought to care, and thinking that they are something when they are really nothing. And if you do this, both I and my sons will have received justice at your hands.

The hour of departure has arrived, and we go our ways—I to die, and you to live. Which is better God only knows.

Gandhi

A Plea for the Severest Penalty upon his Conviction for Sedition

———

Mohandas Karamchand Gandhi (1869–1948) was the architect and first exponent of civil disobedience or non-violence against the State. He learnt the technique which he called Satyagraha *while he was in South Africa. He had come to the Union in 1893 to appear in a law case on behalf of some fellow Indians. (He had been called to the English Bar and was therefore entitled to practise law in any British colony.) A few days after his arrival in Durban he experienced the humiliation of racial discrimination when he was summarily extruded from a first-class train compartment. Gandhi stayed on in South Africa devoting himself more and more to testing his theories of non-violence in that increasingly race-conscious society. He gave up law practice altogether in 1900 but stayed until the First World War.*

'The term Satyagraha *was coined by me in South Africa,' said Gandhi, 'to express the force that the Indians there used for full eight years, and it was coined in order to distinguish it from the movement then going on in the United Kingdom and South Africa under the name of passive resistance. Its root meaning is "holding on to truth", hence truth-force. I have also called it love-force or soul-force. In the application of* Satyagraha, *I discovered in the earliest stages that pursuit of truth did not admit of violence being inflicted on one's opponent, but that he must be weaned from error by patience and sympathy. For what appears to be truth to the one may appear to be error to the other. And patience means self-suffering. So the doctrine came to mean vindication of truth, not by the infliction of suffering on the opponent but on one's self.'*

Gandhi returned to India having forced many changes on the Smuts administration in the Union. He now set himself to do for the Indians what he had done for their brethren in South Africa. His policy of Satyagraha, *backed by large scale strikes, had a paralysing effect throughout British India. With ever-increasing self-confidence in his policy of non-violence, he took over the leadership of the Indian National Congress in 1920.*

Thereafter he was in constant conflict with the authorities, particularly as a result of the speeches which he made up and down the vast hinterland of India. Finally, in 1922 he was arrested and charged with sedition for three articles he had written in his magazine, Young India. *At the conclusion of the trial and before sentence was passed Gandhi was asked whether he wished to make any statement. Gandhi first set out extempore what his policy of non-violence involved and then almost patronizingly—in Gandhi's mouth it sounded utterly sincere and humbling—told the judge that if he was an upholder of the law he must pass the severest sentence on an implacable opponent of the British. Gandhi elaborated this theme in a prepared statement which he then read.*

The judge, obviously impressed by this saintly little man who could move the Indian crowds to undying devotion, was himself not unaffected by this simple plea. He sentenced Gandhi to six years' imprisonment, not by any means an inordinate sentence. Gandhi thereby became the first nationalist leader in modern times to suffer imprisonment at the hands of the British before becoming his country's first prime minister on attaining ultimate independence.

BEFORE I read this statement, I would like to state that I entirely endorse the learned Advocate-General's remarks in connection with my humble self. I think that he was entirely fair to me in all the statements that he has made, because it is very true and I have no desire whatsoever to conceal from this court the fact that to preach disaffection toward the existing system of government has become almost a passion with me; and the learned Advocate-General is also entirely in the right when he says that my preaching of disaffection did not commence with my connection with *Young India*, but that it commenced much earlier; and in the statement that I am about to read, it will be my painful duty to admit before this court that it commenced much earlier than the period stated by the Advocate-General. It is the most painful duty with me, but I have to discharge that duty knowing the responsibility that rests upon my shoulders, and I wish to endorse all the blame that the learned Advocate-General has thrown on my shoulders, in connection with the Bombay occurrences, Madras occurrences, and the Chauri Chaura occurrences. Thinking over these deeply and sleeping over them night after night, it is impossible for me to dissociate myself from the diabolical crimes of Chauri Chaura or the mad outrages of Bombay. He is quite right when he says that as a man of responsibility, a man having received a fair share of education, having had a fair share of experience of this world, I should have known the consequences of every one of my acts. I know that I was playing with fire. I ran the risk, and if I was set free, I would still do the same. I have felt it this morning that I would have failed in my duty, if I did not say what I said here just now.

I wanted to avoid violence, I want to avoid violence. Non-violence is the first article of my faith. It is also the last article of my creed. But I had to make my choice. I had either to submit to a system which I considered had done an irreparable harm to my country, or incur the risk of the mad fury of my people bursting forth, when they understood the truth from my lips. I know that my people have sometimes gone mad. I am deeply sorry for it and I am therefore here to submit not to a light penalty but to the highest penalty. I do not ask for mercy. I do not plead any extenuating act. I am here, therefore, to invite and cheerfully submit to the highest penalty that can be inflicted upon me for what in law is a deliberate crime and what appears to me to be the highest duty of a citizen. The only course open to you, the judge, is, as I am just going to say in my statement, either to resign your post or inflict on me the severest penalty, if you believe that the system and law you are assisting to administer are good for the people. I do not expect that kind of conversion, but by the time I have finished with my statement, you will perhaps have a glimpse of what is raging within my breast to run this maddest risk which a sane man can run.

[The following statement was then read.]

I owe it perhaps to the Indian public and to the public in England, to placate which this prosecution is mainly taken up, that I should explain why from a staunch loyalist and co-operator I have become an uncompromising disaffectionist and non-co-operator. To the court too I should say why I plead guilty to the charge of promoting disaffection toward the government established by law in India.

My public life began in 1893 in South Africa in troubled weather. My first contact with British authority in that country was not of a happy character. I discovered that as a man and as an Indian I had no rights. More correctly, I discovered that I had no rights as a man because I was an Indian.

But I was not baffled. I thought that this treatment of Indians was an excrescence upon a system that was intrinsically and mainly good. I gave the government my voluntary and hearty co-operation, criticising it freely where I felt it was faulty but never wishing its destruction.

Consequently, when the existence of the Empire was threatened in 1899 by the Boer challenge, I offered my services to it, raised a volunteer ambulance corps, and served at several actions that took place for the relief of Ladysmith. Similarly in 1906, at the time of the Zulu revolt, I raised a stretcher-bearer party and served till the end of the 'rebellion'. On both these occasions I received medals and was even mentioned in dispatches. For my work in South Africa I was given by Lord Hardinge a Kaiser-i-Hind Gold Medal. When the war broke out in 1914 between England and Germany, I raised a volunteer ambulance corps in London consisting of the then resident Indians in London, chiefly students. Its work was acknowledged by the authorities to be valuable. Lastly, in India, when a special appeal was made at the War Conference in Delhi in 1918 by Lord Chelmsford for recruits, I struggled at the cost of my health to raise a corps in Kheda, and the response was being made when the hostilities ceased and orders were received that no more recruits were wanted. In all these efforts at service I was actuated by the belief that it was possible by such services to gain a status of full equality in the Empire for my countrymen.

The first shock came in the shape of the Rowlatt Act, a law designed to rob the people of all real freedom. I felt called upon to lead an intensive agitation against it. Then followed the Punjab horrors beginning with the massacre at Jallianwala Bagh and culminating in crawling orders, public floggings, and other indescribable humiliations. I discovered too that the plighted word of the Prime Minister to the Mussulmans of India regarding the integrity of Turkey and the holy places of Islam was not likely to be fulfilled. But in spite of the forebodings and the grave warnings of friends, at the Amritsar Congress in 1919, I fought for co-operation and working with the Montagu-Chelmsford reforms, hoping that the Prime Minister would redeem his promise to the Indian Mussulmans, that the Punjab wound would be healed, and that the reforms, inadequate and unsatisfactory though they were, marked a new era of hope in the life of India.

But all that hope was shattered. The Khilafat promise was not to be redeemed. The Punjab crime was whitewashed and most culprits went not only unpunished but remained in service and in some cases continued to draw pensions from the Indian revenue, and in some cases were even rewarded. I saw too that not only did the reforms not mark

a change of heart, but they were only a method of further draining
India of her wealth and of prolonging her servitude.

I came reluctantly to the conclusion that the British connection had
made India more helpless than she ever was before, politically and
economically. A disarmed India has no power of resistance against any
aggressor if she wanted to engage in an armed conflict with him. So
much is this the case that some of our best men consider that India
must take generations before she can achieve Dominion status. She
has become so poor that she has little power of resisting famines.
Before the British advent, India spun and wove in her millions of
cottages just the supplement she needed for adding to her meagre
agricultural resources. This cottage industry, so vital for India's
existence, has been ruined by incredibly heartless and inhuman processes as described by English witnesses. Little do town dwellers
know how the semi-starved masses of India are slowly sinking to
lifelessness. Little do they know that their miserable comfort represents
the brokerage they get for the work they do for the foreign exploiter,
that the profits and the brokerage are sucked from the masses. Little
do they realize that the government established by law in British
India is carried on for this exploitation of the masses. No sophistry, no
jugglery in figures can explain away the evidence that the skeletons in
many villages present to the naked eye. I have no doubt whatsoever
that both England and the town dwellers of India will have to answer,
if there is a God above, for this crime against humanity which is
perhaps unequalled in history. The law itself in this country has been
used to serve the foreign exploiter. My unbiased examination of the
Punjab Martial Law cases has led me to believe that at least ninety-five
per cent of convictions were wholly bad. My experience of political
cases in India leads me to the conclusion that in nine out of every ten
the condemned men were totally innocent. Their crime consisted in
the love of their country. In ninety-nine cases out of a hundred justice
has been denied to Indians as against Europeans in the courts of India.
This is not an exaggerated picture. It is the experience of almost every
Indian who has had anything to do with such cases. In my opinion,
the administration of the law is thus prostituted consciously or un-
consciously for the benefit of the exploiter.

The greatest misfortune is that Englishmen and their Indian
associates in the administration of the country do not know that they
are engaged in the crime I have attempted to describe. I am satisfied

that many Englishmen and Indian officials honestly believe that they are administering one of the best systems devised in the world and that India is making steady though slow progress. They do not know that a subtle but effective system of terrorism and an organized display of force on the one hand, and the deprivation of all powers of retaliation or self-defence on the other, have emasculated the people and induced in them the habit of simulation. This awful habit has added to the ignorance and the self-deception of the administrators. Section 124(a), under which I am happily charged, is perhaps the prince among the political sections of the Indian Penal Code designed to suppress the liberty of the citizen. Affection cannot be manufactured or regulated by law. If one has an affection for a person or system, one should be free to give the fullest expression to his disaffection, so long as he does not contemplate, promote, or incite to violence. But the section under which Mr Banker [a colleague in non-violence] and I are charged is one under which mere promotion of disaffection is a crime. I have studied some of the cases tried under it, and I know that some of the most loved of India's patriots have been convicted under it. I consider it a privilege, therefore, to be charged under that section. I have endeavoured to give in their briefest outline the reasons for my disaffection. I have no personal ill-will against any single administrator, much less can I have any disaffection toward the King's person. But I hold it to be a virtue to be disaffected toward a government which in its totality has done more harm to India than any previous system. India is less manly under the British rule than she ever was before. Holding such a belief, I consider it to be a sin to have affection for the system. And it has been a precious privilege for me to be able to write what I have in the various articles, tendered in evidence against me.

In fact, I believe that I have rendered a service to India and England by showing in non-co-operation the way out of the unnatural state in which both are living. In my humble opinion, non-co-operation with evil is as much a duty as is co-operation with good. But in the past, non-co-operation has been deliberately expressed in violence to the evildoer. I am endeavouring to show to my countrymen that violent non-co-operation only multiplies evil and that as evil can only be sustained by violence, withdrawal of support of evil requires complete abstention from violence. Non-violence implies voluntary submission to the penalty for non-co-operation with evil. I am here, therefore, to invite and submit cheerfully to the highest penalty that can be inflicted upon me for what in law is a deliberate crime and what appears to me to be the highest duty of a citizen. The only course open to you, the judge, is either to resign your post, and thus dissociate yourself from evil if you feel that the law you are called upon to administer is an evil and that in reality I am innocent, or to inflict on me the severest penalty if you believe that the system and the law you are assisting to administer are good for the people of this country and that my activity is therefore injurious to the public weal.

Patrick Duncan

A Statement in Answer to the Charge of Seditious Libel, made in the Regional Court, Cape Town, November 1960

The great South African writer Olive Schreiner wrote some years ago with prophetic insight that 'it is ordered by the laws of human life that a nemesis should follow the subjection and use, purely for the purposes of their own, of any race by another which lives among them. . . . The continual association with creatures who are not free will ultimately take from us our strength and our own freedom and men will see in our faces the reflection of that on which we are always treading and looking down. If we raise the dark man we shall rise with him; if we kick him under our feet, he will hold us fast by them.'

Patrick Duncan, the son of a former Governor-General of the Union of South Africa, is one of a handful of white South Africans who have strenuously continued to preach the words of Olive Schreiner during the years of increasing repression since 1948 of the non-white citizens of the Union under the yoke of apartheid. During the emergency of 1960 Duncan, as editor of Contact, *the only undiluted radical journal in the Union, continued to publish information about what was going on in defiance of the emergency regulations. He was repeatedly hauled before the courts for 'issuing subversive statements'. While he refused to plead to the charge he was intermittently put in gaol.*

On 17th November, 1960, the second day of the hearing of charges against the proprietors of Contact *before the magistrate at the Regional Court, Cape Town, Patrick Duncan addressed the magistrate. This address was later reprinted in full in an issue of* Contact *after the charges against Duncan had been dropped.*

I WAS astonished when the summons in this case was served on me, for I had thought that the government would have hesitated, from a sense of shame, to revive the painful memories of what it did to the people of South Africa in March and April of this year.

The prosecution has alleged that eight articles, published on 2nd and 16th April this year in *Contact*, were 'subversive statements', and that I have broken the law by having distributed them. These articles describe, and comment on, certain acts done by the government. These acts include large-scale murder by the police, and two treacherous breaches of faith.

Other articles in the issues which are before the court include reports of barbaric floggings of innocent people by the Cape Town police. These criminal acts, perpetrated by and in the name of the government, achieved world notoriety, and shocked the conscience of the whole human race.

Now that the clamour of world publicity has somewhat abated I should have thought that a government of guilty men, such as is the South African government, would have left these horrors alone, to be forgotten. I thought that these guilty men at least had shame. I now see that I was mistaken.

These words that I have used of the government are hard. I have not used them lightly. I have pondered long the question of whether to use them or not. I have decided to use them, and I am prepared to prove that my use of them is justified.

The charge against me is that I infringed the emergency regulations by having distributed subversive statements, it being alleged that the eight articles mentioned in the indictment are subversive statements, within the meaning of those regulations.

I do not wish to waste the time of the court. I did distribute the articles in question. *I am solely and wholly responsible for what they say.* With this heavy charge hanging over me I should like the court to know precisely why I did distribute them, well knowing that material of this kind might be held to conflict with government policy and regulations.

The principal reason for my decision to go ahead and publish them in these circumstances was that I deny that the emergency regulations ever were or are law in the true sense of the word, or that they were or are in any way binding on the conscience.

I maintain that the regulations are lacking in two essential ingredients of true law, and that they are not, therefore, true law.

The missing ingredients are, firstly, the legitimacy of parliament, and, secondly, the morality of the law.

I contend that only just laws made by a legitimate government are true laws, and I am going to show this court why these regulations are fatally defective.

Some people who have been charged under these regulations have contended that all the institutions of government, and therefore all the laws passed since Union, have no legitimacy because the non-Whites had no part in establishing the state.

A case could, I believe, be made in support of their contention. There are, after all, many rules in life that want the full force of law. Children playing in their sand-pits make rules; bandits make and can often enforce rules; usurper kings and governments purport to make rules. But only governments which are, and which are believed to be, legitimate can make laws in the fullest sense of that word, laws which are binding on the people that are governed.

It is obvious that not all who exercise power can bind the consciences of the ruled. During the Nazi occupation of Europe, Hitler's gauleiters made rules, and often succeeded in enforcing obedience to them, because they had a victorious army behind them. These rules did not, however, have the character of law. A case could be made in support of the contention that the government in South Africa is as illegitimate as that of Hitler's occupying armies. It is, however, not necessary for me to enter too deeply into this question, nor to pursue this line of argument, for I rest my case on the simple statement that these regulations are fatally defective by reason of their injustice.

The civilizations of Greece and of Rome, the traditions of Christianity, both Catholic and Reformed, on which our whole culture is based, proclaim unanimously that an unjust law is no true law and cannot bind the conscience of the subject, and that the subject has no duty to obey such a law.

This question is of such tremendous importance that I have spent some time in looking up authoritative statements which will help the court to reach a decision on the subject.

One of the earliest statements of this truth is contained in Sophocles' tragedy *Antigone*. In this play Creon, a king, makes a proclamation that no one may bury the corpse of Polynices, a warrior who died attacking the city-state of Thebes. But, according to Greek religion, an absolute duty lay on the family of a dead man to see that his body got burial rites, as without them he might be prejudiced in the next world. Antigone, a sister of the dead man, deliberately disobeys the king's law, so that she may obey the divine law.

The dilemma is brilliantly portrayed by Sophocles. The king says: 'Whomsoever the city-state may appoint, that man must be obeyed, in little things and in great, in things just and unjust' (lines 666–667). But Antigone says: 'I did not believe that your (i.e. the king's) proclamations were of such force that a mortal could override the unwritten and unfailing laws of heaven' (lines 452–455). The play ends in a triumphant statement that Antigone was right in her opposition to the laws of man.

Over the two-and-a-half-thousand years since the *Antigone* was written the great thinkers of the world have consistently supported the view of Sophocles. Aristotle, in *Rhetoric* (1, 15, para. 6) quotes the above passage from Sophocles in support of the view that equity takes precedence over the written law.

And the same view was held by Cicero. In *De Republica III*, 22, he says:

'. . . True law is right reason in agreement with nature; it is of universal application, unchanging and everlasting; it summons to duty by its commands, and averts from wrongdoing by its prohibitions. And it does not lay its commands or prohibitions upon good men in vain, though neither have any effect on the wicked. It is a sin to try to alter this law, nor is it allowable to attempt to repeal any part of it, and it is impossible to abolish it entirely. We cannot be freed from its obligations by senate or people, and we need not look outside ourselves for an expounder or interpreter of it.'

This measuring of human laws by eternal standards of justice is basic to the Christian idea of law, and is found clearly stated in St Thomas Aquinas' *Summa Theologica*:

'A tyrannical law, through not being according to reason, is not a law, absolutely speaking, but rather a perversion of law' (Prima Secundae Q. 92, Art. 1). Again: 'Human law has the nature of law in so far as it partakes of right reason; and it is clear that, in this respect, it is derived from the eternal law. But in so far as it deviates from reason, it is called an unjust law, and has the nature, not of law, but of violence' (Prima Secundae Q. 93, Art. 3). Again: 'As Augustine says, that which is not just is no law at all: wherefore the force of law depends on the extent of its justice' (Prima Secundae Q. 95, Art. 2).

And, lastly, Aquinas says: 'Laws framed by man are either just or unjust. If they be just, they have the power of binding in conscience, from the eternal law whence they are derived, according to Prov. viii, 15: "By Me kings reign, and law-givers decree just things." Now laws are said to be just, both from the end, when, to wit, they are ordained to the common good—and from their author, that is to say, when the law that is made does not exceed the power of the law-giver—and from their form, when, to wit, burdens are laid on the subjects according to an equality of proportion and with a view to the common good. For, since one man is a part of the community, each man in all that he is and has, belongs to the community; just as a part, in all that it is, belongs to the whole; wherefore nature inflicts a loss on the part, in order to save the whole; so that on this account, such laws as these, which impose proportionate burdens, are just and binding in conscience, and are legal laws.

'On the other hand, laws may be unjust in two ways: first, by being contrary to human good, through being opposed to the things mentioned above—either in respect of the end, as when an authority imposes on his subjects burdensome laws, conducive, not to the common good, but rather to his own cupidity or vainglory—or in respect of the author, as when a man makes a law that goes beyond the power committed to him—or in respect of the form, as when burdens are imposed unequally on the community, although with a view to the common good. The like are acts of violence rather than laws; because, as Augustine says (*De Lib. Arb.* i., 5): "a law that is not just, seems to be no law at all". Wherefore such laws do not bind in conscience.'

Another Christian legal philosopher, Lucas de Penna (Ullmann's commentary in *The Medieval Idea of Law*, London, 1946, p. 54), says:

'The ruler cannot claim the validity of, and demand obedience to, his command when it contradicts the counsels in the holy scriptures ... Furthermore, any command of the ruler which contradicts the divine idea of natural justice or the dictates of natural reason fails to constitute law.'

This tradition is comprehensively Christian, and is not limited to Roman Catholic thought. Thus, Theodore Beza, the Calvinist statesman, in his *Rights of Rulers over their Subjects* (H.A.U.M. edition, p. 25), says that princes must be obeyed, but that

'such obedience must be made subject to the following condition, namely that they command nothing impious, nothing unjust ... Unjust behests, however, I call those by which the performance of that, which every man in accordance with his calling ... is in charity bound to render to his neighbour, is either prevented or forbidden.'

Nor is this tradition merely theological. Grotius, one of the fathers of our South African system of law, clearly recognizes that a statute is not law if it clashes with morality. In his *Jurisprudence of Holland* (I, ii, 6) occur the following passages:

'Law (which is also sometimes called Right because it determines what is right) is a product of reason ordaining for the common good what is honourable.' And, again, 'that which is forbidden by the law of nature (which Grotius elsewhere defines more or less as morality) may not be enjoined by positive law (which he defines as what we would call statute law), nor that which is enjoined by the first forbidden by the second.' And Grotius also says: 'for men must obey not from fear alone, but also for conscience' sake.'

Again, John Locke, on whose thought was erected the whole philosophy and practice of the American constitution, in his *Second Treatise of Civil Government* (Hafner Classics, 1947, pp. 188–194), says:

'The legislative or supreme authority cannot assume to itself a power to rule by arbitrary decrees, but is bound to dispense justice . . .

'These are the bounds which the trust that is put in them by the society and the law of God and nature have set to the legislative power of every commonwealth, in all forms of government: First: they are to govern by promulgated established laws, not to be varied in particular cases, but to have one rule for rich and poor, for the favourite at court and the countryman at plough. Secondly, these laws also ought to be designed for no other end ultimately but the good of the people. Thirdly, they must not raise taxes on the property of the people without the consent of the people.'

The foremost thinkers of the western European Christian tradition, and the fathers of South African law, are therefore at one in proclaiming that an unjust law is no true law.

These regulations, this piece of paper in front of the court, were doubly unjust. For not only were they unjust in themselves: they were the culmination of many years of unjust legislation.

An indication that they were immoral and unjust in themselves is that the notorious 'death regulation' (Proclamation No. 97, *Union Gazette Extraordinary* of 2nd April, 1960) was issued under their authority. This regulation contained the following words:

'MAINTENANCE OF ORDER

'3. (1) Whenever any magistrate or any commissioned or non-commissioned officer in the Forces is of opinion that the presence or conduct of any person or persons at any place endangers or may endanger the public safety or the maintenance of public order or exposes or may expose life or property to danger, he may in a loud voice order such person or persons to stop or to proceed to any place indicated in the order or to desist from such conduct, and shall thereupon warn such person or persons that force will be used if the order is not obeyed forthwith.

'(2) If any such order is not obeyed forthwith, the magistrate or commissioned or non-commissioned officer may apply or authorize the application of force (including force resulting in death) in order to remove or prevent the suspected danger.'

The import of this regulation was seen in the streets of Cape Town on 4th April, when the South African police force was turned by order of the government into a tribal impi. Armed with sticks and sjamboks they combed the streets of Cape Town, hunting for Africans. They chased any person they believed to be a 'kaffir', and perpetrated hundreds, perhaps thousands, of brutal and unprovoked assaults on these persons.

On 7th April a friend of mine was sitting quietly in his own house in Nyanga. He heard someone knocking at his door, so he went to open it. He saw police and soldiers outside. One was armed with a sort of club. He attacked my friend and broke the bones of his left forearm and his right thumb with this club.

As St Thomas Aquinas said, 'unjust laws have "the nature of violence".'

I will not weary the court with further details. It is sufficient to say that at that time the police force acted illegally, immorally, and inhumanely. All this was done under the authority of the emergency regulations, and I therefore stigmatize them as immoral and unjust in themselves.

I accuse them with injustice, also in this respect, in that they were the culmination and logical consequence of a mass of other unjust apartheid legislation.

It is a first rule of the law of reason and nature, a first requirement of justice, that no human being shall be unjustly deprived of his life. Yet, from the point of view of non-Whites, much of the apartheid legislation is anti-life. That is to say, they are laws, not designed for the common good, not made, in Christ's words, 'that they might have life, and that they might have it more abundantly', but that the non-Whites' claim to life be denied.

Apartheid legislation was condemned by anticipation in the pages of both Locke and St Thomas Aquinas. Locke, as quoted above, said that for a decree to be a law, and for it not to be merely arbitrary, there must be 'one rule for rich and poor, for the favourite at court and the countryman at plough'. If he had lived in modern South Africa he would no doubt have added the words 'and one law for Black and White'.

St Thomas Aquinas cuts even nearer the bone when he says that a law is unjust 'when burdens are imposed unequally on the community'.

Some apartheid laws impose such unequal burdens on the community that I have stigmatized them as 'anti-life' because they appear hostile to the non-Whites.

How else can one explain the cruel cancellation of the African school-feeding scheme, while White children continue to be fed by the State? How else can one explain the mean attempt to abridge and constrict, by administrative action, the pension scheme for non-Whites which this government inherited from its predecessors? How else can one explain the present intention of this government to institute family allowances—for Whites only?

Some laws then, actually seek to deny life to non-Whites. Others, while not exhibiting hostility to this extent, yet shamelessly deny justice. I instance:

(1) The Natives Prohibition of Interdicts Act, which subverts the courts by preventing Africans from going to court to defend their rights in certain matters.

(2) The Separate Amenities Act, which empowers the authorities to make separate *but unequal* facilities for Whites and non-Whites.

(3) The sacrilegious 'church clause' of the Native Laws Amendment Act, which forbids Africans to go to church in certain circumstances.

(4) The greedy Group Areas Act, designed (despite the pious and lying promises made by Minister Dönges when he introduced it in parliament) to give the Whites a monopoly of nearly all the desirable areas and suburbs, and, in particular, to strangle the business of many South Africans of Indian origin. This subversive act, by destroying the validity of title deeds, has undermined the respect for and value of property on which our whole economic system is based, and which is indispensable to real liberty.

(5) The unholy Urban Areas Act which, through its so-called influx control, breaks up families, encourages the running wild of children, and reserves family happiness 'for Europeans only'.

(6) The grasping Land Act of 1913, under which some eighty-five per cent of the surface of our common fatherland is closed to ownership to some sixty-six per cent of our fellow-citizens—the Africans.

(7) The feudal pass law, codified under the deceitfully-named Abolition of Passes Act, which chains many of our fellow-citizens to one job or one farm, and which prevents millions from selling their labour where it is most needed.

(8) The greedy job-reservation law which seeks to reserve to the White minority in perpetuity all the good jobs.

(9) The regressive Bantu Authorities Act, which seeks to turn the clock back to a tribal past, instead of helping the people into the modern world as equals.

(10) The repressive Bantu Education Act, which seeks to condition African children to serfdom.

The making of these hostile and unjust regulations is consistent only with a state of mind in the legislator of deep and inveterate enmity borne towards the majority of the people of South Africa.

They are not law. Law, as we have seen, to be true law must nurture life, must promote the common good, must be imposed equally on the community.

It may, however, be argued that however violent, unjust, or anti-life these regulations were, they were necessary for the preserving of law and order.

I admit immediately that this is superficially the most plausible argument against me. I am confident, however, that what I have said remains valid despite this allegation. For one has to consider what law, what order, is being preserved at such cost. It is clear from everything that I have said that the law to be preserved is the law of greedy race supremacy, and the order to be preserved is the order of apartheid.

I would remind this court that Himmler and Hitler did little that was not legal. Like this government, they took the trouble to pass regulations to give the appearance of legality to their dark deeds. Before their genocidal attack on the Jewish communities of Europe they passed the Nuremburg race laws.

Mere order, mere law, I say, are not ends in themselves. They must be related to life, to morality, and to justice.

It might also be argued that it was my patriotic duty to obey, at a time of difficulty and danger to the State, the State's regulations, and that it was my duty to do nothing that could draw on my country the opprobrium of the world.

I say that the opposite was my duty. I am unquestioningly loyal to South Africa, to the fifteen millions of people of all races who are my fellow citizens, and to the lovely land which is ours. I have therefore a duty to protect my people and my country against any group which is hostile to the majority of our people, even though by a series of historic swindles, such a group has been able temporarily to arrogate to itself the name of government.

The anger of the world is not against South Africa. The anger of the world is against this greedy oligarchy that battens on the people that it hates. So far from trying to diminish the world's anger, I believe that it was my patriotic duty to do all in my power to increase it.

I also believe that it was my patriotic duty to speak up for another reason. The injustices done in March and April purported to have been done in the name of all South Africans. For the whole of South Africa to have kept silence then would have been for the whole country to stand arraigned before the highest tribunal of the human race, the Security Council of the United Nations, as steeped in a uniform guilt. I spoke up because I wished to protect the majority of my fifteen million fellow-citizens from the righteous detestation of the whole human race.

It was also, as I see it, my duty to speak the truth then, for no other newspaper in the country felt free to do so. These regulations had dealt an intentional blow against the press of South Africa, whose freedom was thereby curtailed, and curtailed more completely than at any time since the governorship of Lord Charles Somerset. I knew that if only one newspaper were to continue to publish the truth and to comment without fear, other newspapers might follow suit. I acted in the interests of the freedom of the press, which is the most precious freedom left to us in South Africa, though even this freedom has been whittled away and is now finally menaced by a new Bill.

To summarize: I decided to ignore these regulations because they were not worthy of the name of law, because to do so was patriotic and in the interests of our country.

In this trial I am not the accused, though I appear in the dock. On the contrary I am the accuser. I accuse the emergency regulations, and the unjust laws which they arose out of and which they were intended to protect, and those men who perpetrated them, for they have destroyed peace, and outraged justice in our country.

I desire now to turn to consider, briefly, and one by one, the articles which, the Crown alleges, were subversive statements.

The first article which the Crown does not like is one entitled 'Massacre at Sharpeville' which appeared on 2nd April.

I firstly defend the use of the word 'massacre'. A reading of the text of the article, the only eye-witness account by a journalist of the killing, will show that the word was fully justified. The author, Mr Humphrey Tyler, Assistant Editor of *Drum*, described how police, armed with sten guns, fired into an unaggressive fleeing crowd. As is known in every country in the world, some seventy people were shot dead. The Oxford English Dictionary defines 'massacre' as 'a general slaughter', and even today, now that passions have somewhat cooled, I can think of no more suitable word to have used as a headline.

Why then did I run the article? Because it was written by a journalist of repute, because it concerned a historical event which touched us all, because I was given exclusive South African rights to use it, and above all because I felt it to be my duty to publicize to South Africans of all races the things that the South African police are capable of doing.

I turn now to the second article which has earned the Crown's displeasure, 'Pass Campaign Success at Langa and Nyanga'. I am not sure whether the Crown dislikes my use of the word 'success' as showing sympathy. I should like to state here that *Contact* stood, and stands, in complete support of the Pan-African campaign in Langa. That campaign, after all, was totally non-violent, and totally lacking in racialistic attacks on the White minority. What do these White rulers want? Would they rather have a Black Hitler inciting violent race war against them? No doubt they imagine that there is a third possibility, that the African people of this country are going to say 'Ja, baas' for ever, are going to accept apartheid cheerfully and obediently for ever. Let me undeceive them. That possibility does not exist. The alternatives before South Africa are liberation with violence and liberation without violence. As a South African patriot and as a democrat I chose and I choose the way of non-violence wherever it is possible.

The third article for which I have to answer is 'Fortune Favours the Brave'. This was an editorial giving praise to the Pan-Africanist leadership for their qualities of courage, which, as I felt, had enabled their campaign to succeed where no other campaigns had succeeded.

This courage was of a self-sacrificing nature. The leaders were, as they said, prepared to die, but not to kill, for freedom. There can hardly be anything nobler than such courage. I praised it then, and still praise it. I commented as I did hoping that my praise would inspire other South Africans, and perhaps future campaign leaders, with something of · the greatness shown by Mangaliso Robert Sobukwe and his lieutenants.

The fourth article with which I am charged is 'United Nations Must Intervene'. I would prefer to deal with this article later, as in my view it is the most important editorial ever published in *Contact*, and its logical place in this survey is after certain other articles.

The next article which the Crown dislikes is 'The Kgosana Speech' published on 16th April. Why did I publish it? Because it was a historic speech. A young man, scarcely out of his teens, leaps into prominence, leads the two townships of Langa and Nyanga in their pass campaign, and shakes the house of apartheid to the foundations. He launches his campaign with a speech, of which the precious text comes into my hands. The daily press has carried nothing of this speech. The speech includes instructions from the leader of the Pan-Africanist Congress, Mr Sobukwe, which, if obeyed, will strengthen the campaign. The speech contains memorable and important passages which I should like to quote:

'We are not fighting Dr Verwoerd simply because he is Dr Verwoerd; we are not fighting against the Nationalist Party or the United Party. We are not fighting against Europeans or Indians or Chinese. In short we are fighting against nobody. Our energies and forces are directed against a set-up, against a conception and a myth. This myth—others call it racial superiority, others call it herrenvolkism, others White leadership with justice, or White supremacy. We are fighting against the Calvinistic doctrine that a certain nation was specially chosen by God to lead, guide and protect other nations.

'We are not a horde of stupid, barbaric things which will fight against a White man simply because he is White. No sensible person can do that.'

* * *

'I wish here to quote the final instructions of the President of the Pan-Africanist Congress, Mr Mangaliso Robert Sobukwe:

"To All Regions and Branches of P.A.C.:

"Sons and Daughters of the Soil, Remember Africa!

"Very soon, now, we shall be launching. The step we are taking is historical, pregnant with untold possibilities. We must, therefore, appreciate our role. We must appreciate our responsibility. The African people have entrusted their whole future to us. And we have sworn that we are leading them, not to death, but to life abundant.

"My instructions, therefore, are that our people must be taught NOW and CONTINUOUSLY, THAT IN THIS CAMPAIGN we are going to observe ABSOLUTE NON-VIOLENCE.

"There are those in our own ranks who will be speaking irresponsibly of bloodshed and violence. They must be firmly told what our stand is.

"Results of violence: Let us consider, for a moment, what violence will achieve. I say quite POSITIVELY, without fear of contradiction, that the only people who will benefit from violence are the government and the police. Immediately violence breaks out we will be taken up with it and give vent to our pent-up emotions and feel that by throwing a stone at a Saracen or burning a particular building we are small revolutionaries engaged in revolutionary warfare. But after a few days, when we have buried our dead, and made moving grave-side speeches and our emotions have settled again, the police will round up a few people and the rest will go back to the Passes, having forgotten what our goal had been initially.

"What we are not going to do:

"We are not going to burn or damage any part of the Pass Book in any manner. We are not going to fight or attempt to fight, insult or attempt to insult, provoke or attempt to provoke the police in their lawful duties. We are not going to throw stones at the police or do anything that is going to obstruct the police. Any person who does all these things shall be dealt with by the police of course and we, as an organization, shall further deal with him. Nobody is carrying money, knives or any dangerous weapon with himself tomorrow." '

Admittedly the passages I have quoted are accompanied by other passages which are militant calls to action. Those it is not necessary to quote here. All I would say is that nothing in the whole speech incites hatred against any group, White or non-White, and that nothing in the speech falls below the highest levels of modern political thought.

If it is a crime to try to help such a man speaking on such a platform, then I eagerly plead guilty to that crime.

White South Africa does not yet know how lucky it is. Instead of a Black Hitler, or a terrorist movement, people like Mr Kgosana and the P.A.C. have been thrown up by the oppressed people of our country. One day the Whites of our land may well thank almighty God for their undeserved luck.

Reading through *Contact* of 16th April, I note that the article 'The Monday Beatings' has not been included in the indictment. This despite the fact that it contains a photograph of a police officer chasing a man at Langa and trying to beat him with a stick, [and despite the fact that much of the text of the article was taken from embargoed foreign press reports, the publication of which was forbidden in all the rest of the South African press. The article also contains my own eye-witness account of a vicious and unprovoked assault by uniformed police on African pedestrians. I am surprised that this article was missed by the Crown as it combed the two guilty issues for subversion. Is it possible that the Crown is ashamed of the behaviour of members of the police force? I hope so.]*

I pass now to two editorials which the Crown has alleged are subversive. The first describes how, on 25th March, the following pledge was given by the Cape Town police chief to the Cape Town Pan-Africanist leadership: 'Until things return to normal I will see to it that in this area no one is asked to carry passes again.' And, on the evening of the same day, the suspension of the pass laws was made country-wide by General Rademeyer, the then commissioner.

It also described how, some ten days later, long before things had returned to normal (for it was only the first week of the five months' emergency), Minister Erasmus announced that the police would again ask for passes.

The second editorial told the story of the more important betrayal. I quote the first part of it:

In 1838, Dingane lured Piet Retief and his party into a trap. The Boers put down their arms, and were then dealt with, and murdered, by the Zulus. This was treachery.

One hundred and twenty years later, Mr Philip Kgosana, a young South African, aged twenty, negotiated from a position of strength with the Union authorities. He, too, was induced to put down his weapon, the presence of a peaceful and orderly crowd of thirty thousand Africans. In good faith he asked them to go home, for he had been promised an interview with the Minister, Mr Erasmus.

When he had disarmed, after he had willingly put away his only defence, when he came for the promised interview, he was seized and gaoled.

Mr Erasmus had only two honourable courses before him. Either he might decide that the police officers who had given the pledge to Mr Kgosana had acted beyond their authority. In this case nothing less than a public reprimand could make known the Government's displeasure and refusal to accept responsibility for the promise. Or he might decide to honour the pledge made in his name by an honourable official, and to give Mr Kgosana the interview.

* Mr Duncan was told by the Magistrate that this was not relevant to his argument.

In the event Mr Erasmus did neither. To the best of our knowledge the interview has never taken place.

In our view Mr Erasmus is as guilty of treachery as was Dingane.

Here were two clear cases of betrayal. I called them so. If it is a crime to plead the cause of good faith, to criticize governments that break solemn promises, then I am happy to be guilty of such a crime.

The last article which, it is alleged, is a subversive statement, is the column 'Sam Sly' in the same issue. I have searched the column, trying to see what the Crown finds to be subversive. I have reached the conclusion that the subversive bit is a passage describing how an Archbishop, various television personalities, and some Africans had a pleasant drink together in the Mount Nelson Hotel.

In a country afflicted with apartheid, a country in which very few White persons enjoy being near Africans unless they are making money out of them, I now understand that to have printed this passage was seriously subversive. To bring this review to a close, I would turn the attention of the court to the article 'United Nations Must Intervene' published on 2nd April. I published this article when it became clear that the government had lost control of the situation, and that it would be compelled to proclaim a state of emergency. I realized that what had happened in Cape Town and elsewhere was merely a foretaste of future demonstrations, and that if the government lost control for so small a cause, chaos would be likely as a result of future bigger and better-organized demonstrations.

As a patriotic South African I was, and still am, disturbed by the prospect of apartheid-induced chaos in my country. I realized that there is only one force in the world able to intervene to keep chaos at bay, the United Nations. As a democrat I realized that it was possible to hope that if the United Nations were to intervene they would introduce free elections on the basis of the Universal Declaration of Human Rights, that is to say, on a basis of adult suffrage.

United Nations intervention would thus be likely to rid our country of the crushing weight of apartheid, to bring our people democratic freedom, and to guarantee the security of the White and other minorities. It was to bring so glorious a day nearer that I wrote the editorial.

To summarize: I decided to publish all the articles in the heat of the crisis of April. Looking back from this somewhat calmer period I would omit nothing, add nothing, and change nothing. I leave it to a future South Africa to justify or to condemn what I did.

2

THE COURTROOM SCENE

Injustice is relatively easy to bear; what stings is justice.

H. L. Mencken

I must say that, as a litigant, I should dread a lawsuit beyond almost anything else short of sickness and death.

Judge Learned Hand

Harold Laski

My Day in Court

On 16th June 1945, Professor Harold Laski, then Chairman of the Labour Party, went to Newark in Nottinghamshire to speak on behalf of the local candidate in the General Election. During questions, a member of the audience, Mr Wentworth Day, asked a question, an account of which was given in the Newark Advertiser a few days later. The account of the meeting said, 'Mr Day asked the Professor why he had openly advocated "revolution by violence" in speaking at Bishops Stortford and Bournemouth during the war. . . . Professor Laski replied that . . . if Labour did not obtain what it needed by general consent, "we shall have to use violence even if it means revolution." When people felt it was the moment for great experiment, for innovation, because when war is over people so easily forget—especially those who had the power in their hands —that was the time for experiment. Great changes were so urgent in this country, and if they were not made by consent they would be made by violence, and judging by the temper his questioner had displayed he would be perfectly naturally one of the objects of violence when it came.' Many other newspapers repeated the article.

Laski's version of his heckler's intervention and the reply he gave was that after the great upheaval of war the people of a country were conditioned to change. If change was not forthcoming the workers felt it was an intolerable burden. In that way a society drifted into violence. But since Britain had the power to achieve change by consent, we were not committed as other nations to achieving evolution by violence.

Laski was bound to start libel proceedings against the various newspapers, since his recorded remarks, if they went unchallenged, were reckoned to do incalculable harm to the Labour cause. Once he was committed by the issue of a writ, his pride and reputation were at stake so that the action could not decently be discontinued.

The case inevitably attracted wide publicity. Laski himself was a popular figure among his students at the London School of Economics, and his position in the Labour Party commanded respect. The trial was held in the Lord Chief Justice's Court before Lord Goddard and a City of London Special Jury. Mr. G. O. (now Mr Justice) Slade, Q.C., an *expert in libel law appeared for Laski, and Sir Patrick Hastings, the leading advocate of his day, appeared for the* Daily Express, *the paper chosen to fight the test action.*

It was the duel between Laski and Hastings that may have determined the action. Hastings, at his most subtle and incisive, made Laski look helpless and evasive. His first question was devastating [Hastings always made a point of selecting his first question carefully]. He asked: 'Mr Laski, do you believe that the use of violence to achieve your political ends is practically inevitable?' Laski could not supply an answer, yes or no. Even the 'no' had to be qualified, but Laski's insistence to qualify it at length gave the jury an immediate bad impression and allowed Hastings—perhaps unfairly—to cut him short with an additional question. 'Is the answer "No!"' ' to which Laski, cut off in full flight of oratorical explanation, could say only 'The answer is "no"'.

The jury, after retiring for forty minutes, found that the report in the Newark Advertiser *was a fair and accurate report of a public meeting. They spared Laski the humiliation of having to hear a possibly adverse verdict from the jury on the question whether his speeches and writings throughout his life advocated and incited his fellow countrymen to violence and revolution.*

IF HOPE is a stimulant beyond any other, nothing is quite so decisive as failure. You may be beaten in a game and enjoy, nevertheless, the pleasure of combat. You may be 'plucked' in an examination and yet know that it is a temporary setback you will overcome in a month. You may even be routed in a skirmish and rest confident in the knowledge that it is only part of a larger campaign. But when you are beaten in the Courts of Law there is a kind of dumb finality about it which I can only compare with the ultimate emphasis of death.

Every element in a civil trial goes to deepen this sense of finality. In the proceedings themselves you are almost bound to feel like a marionette. The speeches on both sides seem remote from the events you knew; they are like blood in a test tube compared with blood in a living person. You know, of course, that it is about you the lawyers are talking, but all that they say seems to have lost its colour, its vividness, its sense of life, and to be reduced to a shadowlike skeleton which will never be clothed once more in flesh and blood. You only seem a human being when you are in the witness box and counsel on the other side is speaking about you and cross-examining you.

As you listen to this speech and watch the mask-like faces in the jury box, you wonder if it is about yourself that he is talking. You remember the ardour of the incident, the enthusiasm of your effort—the devotion that sent you on a journey of hours for those seventy or eighty minutes of propaganda. Are you really that figure of evil, was your intent always so evil, did you always seem to those political opponents whom you sought to convince an enemy so bitter and so maleficent? Did the pages you wrote over so many years, in so eager an effort to persuade, to find a common mind in which your fellow citizens could share, really read to them all the while like the effort of an Iago pouring some subtle poison into the ears of your opponents? Did that crowd really think you a Catiline, weaving the web of some vile conspiracy, when you thought that what you were urging was the magnanimity that gives birth to conciliation?

The *persona* which the leader of your opponents makes with so much artifice from the complex alchemy of your character is well calculated to leave you certainly disturbed, and possibly almost stunned—but you must listen to it all with passive restraint. It is your enemies' hour, and they must enjoy it to the full. It is for the pleasure of this barrage that they have unmasked their batteries, probed all your motives, dissected with all the hostility they could muster ends and ideas that you do not even recognize as your own.

And you are then handed over to that same counsel whose life has so largely been passed in pricking men until they bleed. He performs his war dance about you like a dervish intoxicated by the sheer ecstasy of his skill in his own performance, ardent in his knowledge that, if you trip for one second, his knife is at your throat. He makes a pattern from bits and pieces picked with care from a pattern of life you have been steadily weaving for a quarter of a century to prove either that you never meant what you intended, or that you lacked every element of skill to give the world the sense of your intent. He moves between the lines of sarcasm and insult. It is an effort to tear off, piece by piece, the skin which he declares no more than a mask behind which any man of understanding could have grasped the foulness of your purpose. He treats you, not as a human being, but as a surgeon might treat some specimen he is demonstrating to students in a dissecting room.

And, all the time, there sits above you the brooding and impassive judge, to whom this operation is no more than another day in an endless routine of similar days; while facing you are the seven impassive

men and women to whom it is a kind of play in which they are half
actors, half spectators. You know that no small part of your fate is in
their hands; and not the least barbarous pain in this grim process is
your tortured doubt of whether they have grasped even a small part
of your effort to draw some thread of clarity through the vast web of
organized confusion your executioner has sought to thrust upon them.
You dare not answer too fully lest they be wearied; and you dare not
answer too briefly lest they should misunderstand. And at every
moment the fear shoots across your mind that every nuance of this
embittered argument is, in fact, a passage in a play they have never
seen before and judged quite worthless even before they were chosen—
mostly against their will—to witness its staging.

For some time you cease to be the principal villain, and move,
though always in the sight of the audience, to the wings of the stage.
Then you must watch the effort of your enemies to break in pieces the
confidence of the witnesses who have come to support your fate.
Mostly, they are simple folk, honest, straightforward, unsubtle.
Mostly, they have never been in the High Court before, let alone
appeared there as witnesses. Counsel for the defendant is mainly concerned to throw them off their balance, to confuse them, to shrug them
with a lift of his shoulders into people about whom he and the jury
share a common and private contempt.

When the witnesses on both sides have been done with, you have to
sit once more with Buddha-like impassivity while the counsel for your
opponent sums up for his client. Here, at least, he is simple and direct;
he knows precisely the effect he desires to produce on the jury. He
assures them that he will make the complex material that has been put
before them so simple that their minds can be at ease and confident. He
paints your character in a few incisive sentences. You begin to see the
outlines of an evil enemy of the realm, clever enough to dress up his
long-cherished stratagems in garments skilfully designed to conceal
their nefarious purpose. You are in substance like a figure in one of
those Elizabethan dramas which Machiavelli influenced; noble men
have worked with you, innocent of the ugly ends for which you proposed to use their alliance. You hear attributed to yourself principles
you have never held. You find yourself driven by motives you have
never known yourself to possess. You become, indeed, the supreme and
ardent enemy of the very cause you have sought to serve. But now, he
concludes triumphantly, we have torn the mask off the villain; he can

no longer disguise himself as an honourable servant of a great movement; he stands revealed before you as one who has striven all his life to undermine the foundations of social peace.

To yourself, listening to what seems the demented passion of a rhetoric devoid of any content save its appeal to the emotions of men and women ready to see in any proponent of social change the grim outline of a Marat or a Robespierre, your own counsel's final speech comes as a great relief. If you know his argument by heart, at least it is a profound psychological comfort to hear it marshalled with orderly effectiveness, and to see the vital points of substance given their due emphasis. You feel that the ease with which he pricks the rhetorical bubbles your opponent's counsel has so lustily blown cannot fail to impress itself upon any men and women with open minds. As he drives home a pattern of events in the shape in which it has become part of your own consciousness, you convince yourself, or almost, that the imperturbable figure on the Bench, trained to weigh evidence, skilled in the separation of fact from fiction, careful to eliminate from his own mind and, if he can, from the minds of the jury, all impact that prejudice may have sought to make—that now, at long last, truth will emerge unscathed from all effort to twist and contort it into shapes you do not recognize.

The judge seems a kindly old man, with a winning smile that lights up his eyes. He speaks with unemphatic quietness, so that, sometimes, you have even to bend forward to catch what he says to the jury in an easy, almost conversational tone. When he tells them of some point the defence has made, or, with a half-amused smile, describes to them the nature of a political campaign, or urges them to realize the passionate care the Bench has taken to safeguard the Englishman's right to the fullest freedom of discussion, you almost feel that you are back in some pleasant lecture room of an Oxford college where an elderly don is retailing the details of some ancient trial decided long ago.

Then, suddenly, his transition to another part of the evidence makes you wonder when he is going to stress that point in the first part which told so strongly in your favour; how he is going to comment on the curious methods of this witness, the subtle way in which your opponent's counsel tore endless passages from their context to paint his picture of your ugly purposes. He will not, surely, forget your counsel's comment on this suggestive point; he cannot have failed to notice that vital combination of circumstances so carefully omitted from the speech in which your opponent's counsel sought to prevent the jury from seeing the gap it revealed in his case. You cannot believe that he will studiously refrain from noting that the charges made against all you have ever said or written these twenty years not only have never been made before, but, were they true, ought obviously to have resulted in your appearance in the dock at Old Bailey. At some time, you are confident, he will bid the jury take notice of the massive testimony your own witnesses have given without an effort at serious contradiction. At least, so you think in growing uneasiness, he will remember that in your five-hour duel with opposing counsel, you stood your ground, answered with straightforward clarity, did not fall into the traps he laid that you might grow angry or confused or irritated, and so be led into the situation where he is so notoriously able to have a witness at his mercy.

And then, with a sudden gasp, you realize that he is not going to put your case at all. He makes his point; he is careful always to emphasize to the attentive jury that it is for them, and them only, to choose whether they will accept the points he makes. But they are always your opponent's points, and you note, almost within the first half-hour of his summing up, that he is conveying, not without some subtlety, what Mr Justice Holmes meant when he said that judicial decisions depend upon the 'inarticulate major premises' of the man on the Bench. And you understand at that stage that the case is lost.

The judge not only hates the opinions you hold, but will explain to the jury that they are dangerous opinions. And since, at your opponent's instance, the jury is a 'special' jury, you know how unlikely it is that they will have an atom of concern for anyone with dangerous opinions. What, you swiftly see, is the real issue at stake is not what was said at some place on a definite occasion, but the fact that you hold unpopular opinions which both judge and jury are convinced it is bad to hold and worse by far to express.

That is the moment when you cease to be an actor in the legal drama, and become one more among the packed spectators in the Court. You know the result of your case. Everything that follows is as regular and automatic as winding up a clock. What had enshrouded you in its air of legal majesty is now like a play upon the stage of which you had read the end before ever you had entered the theatre. The actors continue their parts, for the play must be officially closed. But you are already planning what you will say by way of thanks and consolation to your solicitors and counsel, who had worked so hard and been, to your mind, both fair and effective. You are wondering whether there is a back way out of the Court, that you may avoid the relentless stare of the crowds at the door, the inexorable click of the cameramen from the different papers thrust into your face, the comments on the result you are likely to hear if you go home by bus or tube. You pray that some car may be at hand in which you may be hidden from that restless anxiety of the stream of journalists who, with notebooks ready poised, sweep down upon you, like vultures upon a corpse, to seize your private thoughts for a public avid for any sensation even if it take but three lines to express.

There is no safety for you until you sit at your own fireside. There, at least, without the stare of a thousand eyes, you can meditate upon the shades of meaning in the historic phrase 'the equal protection of the laws'. At least you have been given the fulfilment of the Englishman's right to seek his remedy for injustice and have his day in Court.

H. L. Mencken
The Scopes Trial

─────

H. L. Mencken (1880–1956), who came of German-American stock, was a profound commentator on the American scene. He was for years connected with that great journal The Baltimore Sun, *whose columns were enlivened by his pungent, esoteric vocabulary, a feature of all his writings.*

In 1925 Mencken was sent to cover the Scopes trial in Tennessee. His despatches on that famous trial to The Baltimore Sun *and* The New York Times *form the basis of the rewritten version here printed.*

The trial arose out of a statute passed by the Tennessee legislature which stated: 'Be it enacted—that it shall be unlawful for any teacher in any of the universities, normals, and all other public schools in the state which are supported in whole or in part by the public school funds of the state, to teach the theory that denies the story of the divine creation of man as taught in the Bible, and to teach instead that man has descended from a lower order of animals.'

A few strong-minded liberals in the small town of Dayton, Tennessee decided to put the law to a test and persuaded a young teacher of biology, John Thomas Scopes, to allow himself to be caught red-handed in the act of teaching Evolution to his pupils.

William Jennings Bryan, a famous orator, and inveterate Bible thumper, thrice-defeated candidate for the Presidency of the United States and former Secretary of State, volunteered to prosecute. Clarence Darrow, an agnostic liberal and notable criminal lawyer (he had only recently saved the lives of Leopold and Loeb) accepted the plea of the Civil Liberties Union to defend the young High School teacher.

Americans flocked from the surrounding mountains to the courtroom, eager to learn about the 'monkey talk' and to defend their religious ways against any invading notions of life. The town of Dayton was agog both at the issue and at the giant antagonists. Into this maelstrom of fundamentalists and evangelists versus liberal free-thinking evolutionists came Mencken the mercurial reporter. His free-flowing pen which had blasted the stuffy spiritual, moral and cultural institutions of the United States was now turned on the fascinating spectacle being enacted in this small town in Tennessee.

DEEP IN 'THE COCA-COLA BELT'

The Sun, Baltimore, 13th July, 1925

DAYTON, TENNESSEE, 13th July. There is a Unitarian clergyman here from New York, trying desperately to horn into the trial and execution of the infidel Scopes. He will fail. If Darrow ventured to put him on the stand the whole audience, led by the jury, would leap out of the courthouse windows and take to the hills. Darrow himself, indeed, is as much as they can bear. The whisper that he is an atheist has been stilled by the bucolic make-up and by the public report that he has the gift of prophecy and can reconcile Genesis and evolution. Even so, there is ample space about him when he navigates the streets. The other day a newspaperwoman was warned by her landlady to keep out of the courtroom when he was on his legs. All the local sorcerers predict that a bolt from heaven will fetch him in the end. The night he arrived there was a violent storm, the town water turned brown, and horned cattle in the lowlands were afloat for hours. A woman back in the mountains gave birth to a child with hair four inches long, curiously bobbed in scallops.

The Book of Revelation has all the authority, in these theological uplands, of military orders in time of war. The people turn to it for light upon all their problems, spiritual and secular. If a text were found in it denouncing the anti-evolution law, then the anti-evolution law would become infamous overnight. But so far the exegetes who roar and snuffle in the town have found no such text. Instead they have found only blazing ratifications and reinforcements of Genesis. Darwin is the devil with seven tails and nine horns. Scopes, though he is disguised by flannel pantaloons and a Beta Theta Pi haircut, is the harlot of Babylon. Darrow is Beelzebub in person, and Malone is the Crown Prince Friedrich Wilhelm.

I have hitherto hinted an Episcopalian down here in the Coca-Cola belt is regarded as an atheist. It sounds like one of the lies that journalists tell, but it is really an understatement of the facts. Even a Methodist, by Rhea County standards, is one a bit debauched by pride of intellect. It is the four Methodists on the jury who are expected to hold out for giving Scopes Christian burial after he is hanged. They all made it plain, when they were examined, that they were freethinking and independent men, and not to be run amuck by the superstitions of the lowly. One actually confessed that he seldom read the Bible, though he hastened to add that he was familiar with its principles. The fellow had on a boiled shirt and a polka-dot necktie. He sits somewhat apart. When Darrow withers to a cinder under the celestial blowpipe, this dubious Wesleyan, too, will lose a few hairs.

Even the Baptists no longer brew a medicine that is strong enough for the mountaineers. The sacrament of baptism by total immersion is over too quickly for them, and what follows offers nothing that they can get their teeth into. What they have is a continuous experience of the divine power, an endless series of evidence that the true believer is a marked man, ever under the eye of God. It is not enough to go to a revival once a year or twice a year; there must be a revival every night. And it is not enough to accept the truth as a mere statement of indisputable and awful fact; it must be embraced ecstatically and orgiastically, to the accompaniment of loud shouts, dreadful heavings and gurglings, and dancing with arms and legs.

This craving is satisfied brilliantly by the gaudy practices of the Holy Rollers, and so the mountaineers are gradually gravitating toward the Holy Roller communion, or, as they prefer to call it, the Church of God. Gradually, perhaps is not the word. They are actually going in by whole villages and townships. At the last count of noses there were 20,000 Holy Rollers in these hills. The next census, I have no doubt, will show many more. The cities of the lowlands, of course, still resist, and so do most of the county towns, including even Dayton, but once one steps off the state roads the howl of holiness is heard in the woods, and the yokels carry on an almost continuous orgy.

A foreigner in store clothes going out from Dayton must approach the sacred grove somewhat discreetly. It is not that the Holy Rollers, discovering him, would harm him; it is simply that they would shut down their boiling of the devil and flee into the forests. We left Dayton an hour after nightfall and parked our car in a wood a mile or so beyond the little hill village of Morgantown. Far off in a glade a flickering light was visible and out of the silence came a faint rumble of exhortation. We could scarcely distinguish the figure of the preacher; it was like looking down the tube of a dark field microscope. We got out of the car and sneaked along the edge of a mountain cornfield.

Presently we were near enough to see what was going on. From the great limb of a mighty oak hung a couple of crude torches of the sort that car inspectors thrust under Pullman cars when a train pulls in at night. In their light was a preacher, and for a while we could see no one else. He was an immensely tall and thin mountaineer in blue jeans, his collarless shirt open at the neck and his hair a tousled mop. As he preached he paced up and down under the smoking flambeaux and at each turn he thrust his arms into the air and yelled, 'Glory to God!' We crept nearer in the shadow of the cornfield and began to hear more of his discourse. He was preaching on the day of judgment. The high kings of the earth, he roared, would all fall down and die; only the sanctified would stand up to receive the Lord God of Hosts. One of these kings he mentioned by name—the king of what he called Greece-y. The King of Greece-y, he said, was doomed to hell.

We went forward a few more yards and began to see the audience. It was seated on benches ranged round the preacher in a circle. Behind him sat a row of elders, men and women. In front were the younger folk. We kept on cautiously, and individuals rose out of the ghostly gloom. A young mother sat suckling her baby, rocking as the preacher paced up and down. Two scared little girls hugged each other, their pigtails down their backs. An immensely huge mountain woman in a gingham dress cut in one piece, rolled on her heels at every 'Glory to God'. On one side, but half visible, was what appeared to be a bed. We found out afterwards that two babies were asleep upon it.

The preacher stopped at last and there arose out of the darkness a woman with her hair pulled back into a little tight knot. She began so quietly that we couldn't hear what she said, but soon her voice rose resonantly and we could follow her. She was denouncing the reading of books. Some wandering book agent, it appeared, had come to her cabin and tried to sell her a specimen of his wares. She refused to touch it. Why, indeed, read a book? If what was in it was true, then everything in it was already in the Bible. If it was false, then reading it would imperil the soul. Her syllogism complete, she sat down.

There followed a hymn, led by a somewhat fat brother wearing silver-rimmed country spectacles. It droned on for a half a dozen stanzas, and then the first speaker resumed the floor. He argued that the gift of tongues was real and that education was a snare. Once his children could read the Bible, he said, they had enough. Beyond lay only infidelity and damnation. Sin stalked the cities. Dayton itself was a Sodom. Even Morgantown had begun to forget God. He sat down, and the female aurochs in gingham got up.

She began quietly, but was soon leaping and roaring, and it was hard to follow her. Under cover of the turmoil we sneaked a bit closer. A couple of other discourses followed, and there were two or three hymns. Suddenly a change of mood began to make itself felt. The last hymn ran longer than the others and dropped gradually into a monotonous, unintelligible chant. The leader beat time with his book. The faithful broke out with exultations. When the singing ended there was a brief palaver that we could not hear and two of the men moved a bench into the circle of light directly under the flambeaux. Then a half-grown girl emerged from the darkness and threw herself upon it. We noticed with astonishment that she had bobbed hair. 'This sister,' said the leader, 'has asked for prayers.' We moved a bit closer. We could now see faces plainly and hear every word.

What followed quickly reached such heights of barbaric grotesquerie that it was hard to believe it real. At a signal all the faithful crowded up to the bench and began to pray—not in unison, but each for himself. At another they all fell on their knees, their arms over the penitent. The leader knelt, facing us, his head alternately thrown back dramatically or buried in his hands. Words spouted from his lips like bullets from a machine-gun—appeals to God to pull the penitent back out of hell, defiances of the powers and principalities of the air, a vast impassioned jargon of apocalyptic text. Suddenly he rose to his feet, threw back his head, and began to speak in tongues—blub-blub-blub, gurgle-gurgle-gurgle. His voice rose to a higher register. The climax was a shrill, inarticulate squawk, like that of a man throttled. He fell headlong across the pyramid of supplicants.

A comic scene? Somehow, no. The poor half-wits were too horribly in earnest. It was like peeping through a knothole at the writhings of a people in pain. From the squirming and jabbering mass a young woman gradually detached herself—a woman not uncomely, with a pathetic homemade cap on her head. Her head jerked back, the veins of her neck swelled, and her fists went to her throat as if she were fighting for breath. She bent backward until she was like a half of a hoop. Then she suddenly snapped forward. We caught a flash of the whites of her eyes. Presently her whole body began to be convulsed—great convulsions that began at the shoulders and ended at the hips. She would leap to her feet, thrust her arms in air, and then hurl herself upon the heap. Her praying flattened out into a mere delirious caterwauling, like that of a tomcat on a petting party.

I describe the thing as a strict behaviourist. The lady's subjective sen-

sations I leave to infidel pathologists. Whatever they were they were
obviously contagious, for soon another damsel joined her, and then another and then a fourth. The last one had an extraordinarily bad attack.
She began with mild enough jerks of the head, but in a moment she
was bounding all over the place, exactly like a chicken with its head
cut off. Every time her head came up a stream of yells and barking
would issue out of it. Once she collided with a dark, undersized
brother, hitherto silent and stolid. Contact with her set him off as if he
had been kicked by a mule. He leaped into the air, threw back his head,
and began to gargle as if with a mouthful of BB shot. Then he loos-
ened one tremendous stentorian sentence in the tongues and collapsed.

By this time the performers were quite oblivious to the profane universe. We left our hiding and came up to the little circle of light. We
slipped into the vacant seats on one of the rickety benches. The heap of
mourners were directly before us. They bounced into us as they
cavorted. The smell that they radiated, sweating there in that obscene
heap, half suffocated us. Not all of them, of course, did the thing in
the grand manner. Some merely moaned and rolled their eyes. The
female ox in gingham flung her great hulk on the ground and jabbered
an unintelligible prayer. One of the men, in the intervals between fits,
put on his spectacles and read his Bible.

Beside me on the bench sat the young mother and her baby. She
suckled it through the whole orgy, obviously fascinated by what was
going on, but never venturing to take any hand in it. On the bed just
outside the light two other babies slept peacefully. In the shadows,
suddenly appearing and as suddenly going away, were vague figures,
whether of believers or of scoffers I do not know. They seemed to
come and go in couples. Now and then a couple at the ringside would
step back and then vanish into the black night. After a while some
came back. There was whispering outside the circle of vision. A couple
of Fords lurched up in the wood road, cutting holes in the darkness
with their lights. Once someone out of sight loosed a bray of laughter.
All this went on for an hour or so. The original penitent, by this time,
was buried three deep beneath the heap. One caught a glimpse, now
and then, of her yellow bobbed hair, but then she would vanish again.
How she breathed down there I don't know; it was hard enough ten
feet away, with a strong five-cent cigar to help. When the praying
brothers would rise up for a bout with the tongues their faces were
streaming with perspiration. The fat harridan in gingham sweated like

a longshoreman. Her hair got loose and fell down over her face. She fanned herself with her skirt. A powerful mortal she was, equal in her day to obstetrics and a week's washing on the same morning, but this was worse than a week's washing. Finally, she fell in a heap, breathing in great, convulsive gasps.

We tired of it after a while and groped our way back to our automobile. When we got to Dayton, after eleven o'clock—an immensely late hour for these parts—the whole town was still gathered on the courthouse lawn, hanging upon the disputes of theologians. The Bible champion of the world had a crowd. The Seventh Day Adventist missionaries had a crowd. A volunteer from faraway Portland, Oregon, made up exactly like Andy Gump, had another and larger crowd. Dayton was enjoying itself. All the usual rules were suspended and the curfew bell was locked up. The prophet Bryan, exhausted by his day's work for Revelations, was snoring in his bed up the road, but enough volunteers were still on watch to keep the battlements manned.

Such is human existence among the fundamentalists, where children are brought up on Genesis and sin is unknown. If I have made the tale too long, then blame the spirit of garrulity that is in the local air. Even newspaper reporters, down here, get some echo of the call. Divine inspiration is as common as the hookworm. I have done my best to show you what the great heritage of mankind comes to in regions where the Bible is the beginning and end of wisdom, and the mountebank Bryan, parading the streets in his seersucker coat, is pointed out to sucklings as the greatest man since Abraham.

MONKEY BUSINESS IN TENNESSEE

The New York Times, July 21st, 1925

At last it has happened. After days of ineffective argument and legal quibbling, with speeches that merely skirted the edges of the matter which everyone wanted discussed in this Scopes anti-evolution trial, William Jennings Bryan, fundamentalist, and Clarence Darrow, agnostic and pleader of unpopular causes, locked horns today under the most remarkable circumstances ever known to American court procedure.

It was on the courthouse lawn, where Judge Raulston had moved so that more persons could hear, with the Tennessee crowds whooping for their angry champion, who shook his fist in the quizzical, satiric face of Mr Darrow, that Mr Bryan was put on the stand by the defence to prove that the Bible need not be taken literally.

With an aeroplane whizzing overhead, Mr Darrow asked Mr Bryan about Jonah and the whale, Joshua and the sun, where Cain got his wife, the Flood, and the Tower of Babel, until the youthful Attorney-General Stewart, desperately trying to bring the performance within legal bounds, asked, 'What is the meaning of all this harangue?'

'To show up fundamentalism,' shouted Mr Darrow, lifting his voice in one of the few moments of anger he showed, 'to prevent bigots and ignoramuses from controlling the educational system of the United States.'

Mr Bryan sprang to his feet, his face purple, and shook his fist in the lowering, gnarled face of Mr Darrow, while he cried:

'To protect the word of God from the greatest atheist and agnostic in the United States.'

A roar of applause broke from the crowd under the trees and Mr Darrow, looking down at them, called out sarcastically:

'Why don't you folks cheer?'

At the end of a day so crowded with unexpected happenings all Dayton tonight is holding its head, overcome by the drama of the unprecedented trial.

Mr Darrow was cited in contempt as soon as court opened this morning for his defiance of the judge on Friday, and ordered to show cause why he should not be punished.

In the afternoon he apologized to Judge Raulston, who in a talk that was almost a prayer, his voice shaken with emotion, brought Mr. Darrow to the 'mourner's bench', forgave him, and told him to go back home and learn in his heart the words of the man who said, 'Come unto Me and receive eternal life.'

All morning the crowds packed into the courtroom to hear what everybody assumed would be the final argument of the case, until in the afternoon the building was jammed. Judge Raulston did not wish to shut anybody out, and in order that all might hear he moved to a platform built against the wall of the courthouse, under the maple trees, where a week ago Mr Bryan delivered a sermon. On the benches in front nearly everyone could get a seat, and hundreds stood, forming themselves into opposing modernist and fundamentalist cheering sections, although liberals present were in a small minority.

It was a striking scene. Judge Raulston sat at a little table in the centre, with the state attorneys at his left and the defence at his right, while about them were a few newspapermen and fortunate persons who managed to squeeze by the guard. In front was a sea of upturned faces, waiting for what they presumed would be an ordinary argument, faces which became eager when Mr Darrow announced that he would call Mr Bryan as a witness for the defence.

And then for nearly two hours, while those below broke into laughter or applause or cried out encouragement to Mr Bryan, Mr Darrow goaded his opponent. In a blue shirt and suspenders he leaned against the edge of his table, Bible in hand, and asked Mr Bryan if he really believed that the serpent had always crawled on its belly because it tempted Eve, and if he believed that Eve was made from Adam's rib.

Mr Bryan started off as sweetly as a cooing dove. He wanted to confound this agnostic Darrow, he told the court; he wanted to testify to his faith in the revealed word of God and show that scientists did not know what they were talking about.

He overruled the objection of Attorney-General 'Tom' Stewart, who saw his lawsuit vanishing in the battle smoke of debate, but as Mr Darrow prodded him with all the power of his logical mind, the admissions wrung from Mr Bryan roused him to anger, and in a burst of fury he denounced Mr Darrow as having only the purpose of casting slurs on the Bible.

'I have merely the purpose of showing up your fool ideas that no intelligent Christian believes in,' shouted Mr Darrow, stung to anger, and the judge, in the midst of confusion as both antagonists rose to their feet and shook their fists at each other, adjourned the court.

Mr Darrow drew from Bryan that he knew little of comparative religion, very little of geology, nothing of physiology, and hardly anything that would interest a man seeking light on the vast questions of evolution and religion on which he has written for years. He took refuge again and again in his faith in the written word of the Bible. If what science he had learned did not agree with that he did not believe it and did not want to know.

'I have all the information I need to live by and die by,' he declared vehemently.

But his insistence upon the literal acceptance of the Bible was weakened somewhat, for he admitted when questioned about Joshua making the sun stand still that it was one of those things that 'anybody can put his own construction upon', and explained that although there was no doubt that the earth moved around the sun the Bible was 'inspired by the Almighty, and He may have used language that could be understood at that time'.

The problem of what was meant by 'days' in the Genesis account of creation was also one on which Mr Bryan said things pleasing to Mr Darrow, for he admitted that 'days' probably meant 'periods', and that creation might have lasted for millions of years.

All those under the trees were completely absorbed in the conflict between the two men, each representing a point of view as to religion so diametrically opposed. It was as if all the voices of these two great divisions of religious thought, rationalism and faith, were debating in the persons of Mr Darrow and Mr Bryan. It was a burning vital issue to those people of Rhea County who were present, and to the little group of liberals who clustered in front.

Jonah and the whale should be taken literally, said Mr Bryan, for he believed 'in a God who can make a whale and can make a man, and make both do what He pleases.'

'You don't know whether it was the ordinary mine-run of fish, or made for that purpose?' asked Mr Darrow with quiet sarcasm.

'You may guess,' replied Mr Bryan, calmly, fanning himself with a palm-leaf fan, 'an evolutionist guess.'

'You are not prepared to say whether that fish was made especially to swallow a man or not?'

'The Bible doesn't say, so I'm not prepared to say,' replied Mr Bryan, and that was his attitude on nearly every question raised. It was a miracle, and one miracle was just as easy to believe as another, said Mr Bryan.

'A miracle is a thing performed beyond what man performs,' he said. 'When you get beyond what man can do, you get within the realm of miracles, and it is just as easy to believe in the miracle of Jonah as any other miracle in the Bible.'

The attorneys for the state were chuckling over the way Mr Bryan was acquitting himself by this time, but they did not look so pleased as the afternoon wore on.

Joshua and the sun was another miracle that Mr Darrow wanted to know about. How did it happen that the sun stood still, when the earth moves around the sun?

It was the language of the day, Mr Bryan said, and if anything stopped it must have been the earth.

'Now, Mr Bryan, have you ever pondered what would have happened to the earth if it had stood still?'

'No,' replied Mr Bryan. 'The God I believe in could have taken care of that, Mr Darrow.'

'Don't you know it would have been converted into a molten mass of matter?'

'You testify to that when you get on the stand,' retorted Mr Bryan. 'I will give you a chance,' he said, for he had announced that he would call all the defence counsel if they called him, much to the delight of everyone present.

Then they got on to the flood, and attempted to fix the date of it by the Bible, and against the opposition of Mr Stewart, Mr Bryan told the court to let Mr Darrow have all the latitude he wanted.

'I am going to have some latitude when he gets through,' he said grimly.

'You can have latitude and longitude,' said Mr Darrow.

'These gentlemen have not had much chance,' said Mr Bryan, rising to his feet from the witness chair. 'They did not come here to try this case. They came here to try revealed religion. I am here to defend it, and they can ask me any questions they please.'

The applause from the yard brought a snort of disgust from Mr Darrow, and in reproach for what Mr Bryan called his insults, he raised his fist and shouted at him:

'You insult every man of science and learning in the world because he does not believe in your fool religion.'

Judge Raulston calmed them both, and Mr Stewart again stepped forward to protest.

'I have a public duty to perform under my oath,' said the earnest young attorney-general, who, with his case, had been crowded into the background. 'I ask the court to stop it.'

'How long ago was the flood, Mr Bryan?' asked Mr Darrow, and the debate was on again. They figured it up with the help of Bishop Usher's chronology, as being 2348 B.C. Mr Bryan thought the fish might have lived, but everything else was destroyed.

'Don't you know there are any number of civilizations that are traced back to more than five thousand years?' asked Darrow.

'I know we have people who trace things back according to the number of ciphers they have,' replied Bryan; 'but I am not satisfied they are accurate. I am satisfied by no evidence that I have found, that would justify me in accepting the opinions of these men against what I believe to be the inspired word of God.'

There was a civilization before the flood, said Mr Bryan, but when he was asked if he knew a scientific man in the world who believed that all the animals and all the races now inhabiting the world had come here since the flood, he took refuge in saying that he was more interested in what Christians were doing now than in what happened in the past.

'You have never had any interest in the age of the various races and people and civilizations and animals that exist upon the earth today, is that right?' asked Mr Darrow.

'I have never felt a great deal of interest in the effort that has been made to dispute the Bible by the speculation of men, or the investigations of men,' replied Mr Bryan.

The mild manner in which the 'evangelical leader of the prosecution', as Mr Malone has called him, seated himself in his chair, was vanishing rapidly. His face flushed under Mr Darrow's searching words, and he writhed in an effort to keep himself from making heated replies. His eyes glared at his lounging opponent, who stood opposite him, glowering under his bulging brow, speculatively tapping his arm with his spectacles. No greater contrast in men could be imagined. The traps of logic fell from Mr Darrow's lips as innocently as the words of a child, and so long as Mr Bryan could parry them he smiled back, but when one stumped him he took refuge in his faith and either refused to answer directly or said in effect:

'The Bible states it; it must be so.'

'Have you ever investigated to find out how long man has been on the earth?' asked Darrow.

'I have never found it necessary,' said Mr Bryan.

Mr Bryan's complete lack of interest in many of the things closely connected with such religious questions as he has been supporting for many years was strikingly shown again and again by Mr Darrow. He had never made a study of the ancient civilizations of China, or Egypt, he did not know that they couldn't go back beyond the time of creation as given in the Bible.

Mr Bryan was of the opinion that he had heard of records of archaeologists which describe the flood, but he did not know that there were many old religions with traditions of the flood. The origins of religion had not interested him much, either.

'The Christian religion has satisfied me,' he said, 'and I have never felt it necessary to look up some competitive religions.'

The word 'competitive' interested Mr Darrow, and Bryan finally qualified it by saying he meant 'religious unbelievers' in the Christian religion. The religions of Confucius and Buddha he did not regard as competitive, because he thought them inferior, and he insisted on telling Mr Darrow what he thought of both. He did not know, however, how old the religions of Confucius, Buddha, or Zoroaster were.

'I think it much more important to know the differences between them than to know their age.'

Mr Darrow asked him if he knew how many men were on earth at various times, and when told he was the first man Mr Bryan had ever met who was interested in it, he asked:

'Mr Bryan, am I the first man you ever heard of who has been interested in the age of human societies and primitive man?'

He asked Mr Bryan if he did not know there were thousands of books in the libraries on the subjects he had been asking about, and Mr Bryan said he did not, but would take his word for it. He said he hadn't read much on primitive man, and when Mr Darrow asked him if he had ever in his life tried to find out about the civilizations of the earth, how long they had existed, he replied:

'No, sir, I have been so well satisfied with the Christian religion that I have spent no time trying to find arguments against it.'

'You don't care how old the earth is, how old man is, and how long the animals have been here?'

'I am not so much interested in that,' said Mr Bryan.

And then he drew from Mr Bryan the admission that he had never studied anything on the subject he had written about.

'You have never made an investigation to find out?' he was asked.

'No, sir, I have never,' Mr Bryan answered.

Mr Bryan said that Buddhism was a religion of agnosticism, because he had seen in Rangoon that the Buddhists were to send a delegation to the agnostics' congress to be held in Rome.

After more colloquy about the Tower of Babel and some more objections from Mr Stewart, General Ben McKenzie said the defence would no more file Colonel Bryan's testimony as part of the record for the Appellate Court than they would file a rattlesnake.

Mr Darrow, Dudley Field Malone, and Arthur Garfield Hays burst out as one man:

'We will file it, we will file it.'

'File it from Dan to Beersheba,' Mr Bryan said in his deep rumble.

Kenneth Tynan

Lady Chatterley's Trial

For an introduction to the following see under Mr Justice Stable's summing-up in R. v. Secker & Warburg (page 344).

My sex is me as my mind is me, and nobody will make
me feel shame about it.—D. H. LAWRENCE

NOW THAT the case is over, and Lady Chatterley's adventures are speeding two-hundred-thousand-fold to every outpost of literacy in the country, it seems suddenly unthinkable that the jury could have brought in any other verdict. But it was desperately thinkable right up to three o'clock on Thursday afternoon, as anyone knows who sat through the six days of the trial, and sweated out the dragging hours of the jury's retirement; more than most people, Gerald Gardiner knew it, and looked the reverse of optimistic as he prowled up and down like a wounded lion, waiting for those twelve inscrutable citizens to come to their conclusion.

How we had all stared at them, seizing on each smile, each sniffle, each sign of inattentiveness as evidence of sympathy or hostility to Lawrence's cause! The lean, middle-aged man at the right-hand end of the back row seemed prematurely grey: did this betoken sensitivity or hyper-sensitivity? And the quietly eccentric behaviour of the woman upstage right left many of us baffled; she was given to strange, secret smiles, and would take notes at inexplicable moments; a quick, intense burst of scribbling, for instance, followed the information that one of the witnesses had been educated at Tonbridge School.

In front of her sat a younger woman, sedate and pretty, perhaps a teacher; some of us pictured her as the Henry Fonda character whose gentle persistence would finally win over her colleagues, as in 'Twelve Angry Men'.

But against this hope, and against the waves of pro-Lawrence partisanship that flooded the court from the public gallery, stood the unanimous opinion of the professional crime reporters that acquittal was impossible: 'They'll never swallow those words,' as one of them put it, with a kind of cynical smugness that seems, even in memory, peculiarly detestable.

Nor, as we waited, could we forget the summing-up of a judge who, throughout the trial, had displayed no uncontrollable impatience to get the book into the shops. A slight old gentleman with a mild, dry voice, resembling beneath the scarlet weight of his robes some relict of feudal Japan, Mr Justice Byrne could not be accused of having loaded the dice in favour of the defence.

One remembered the tone, discreetly incredulous, of his interjections; as when he had asked Richard Hoggart to repeat the phrase 'virtuous, if not puritanical,' and had written it down with eyebrows eloquently raised; or when he had put to another witness the question: 'Is there really anything else in this book except adultery?' And his summing-up with its reminder to the jury (it was almost a sigh) that the world today seemed to be full of academic experts, struck the same note of weary bewilderment that must have been heard from the bench when first the psychologists and psychiatrists strode into the courts to confuse plain men with their theories.

Here were professors, critics, editors and poets, standing up in the box to deliver lectures on the nature of literature, clouding the air with their semantic evasions, expressing opinions instead of stating facts, and thus dissolving the fabric of concrete truth on which the world of law was founded when it first began. No sooner had one witness dubbed Lawrence a puritan than another would claim him for Catholicism, only to see someone else haul him back, minutes later, into the Protestant camp. Nothing was simple any more; at the Old Bailey, where matters of indecency and obscene behaviour had traditionally been settled by policemen and doctors, respectable men and women were talking about sex as if it were something holy.

It must have seemed to Mr Justice Byrne that chaos was come again; no wonder he felt the need to recall the jury to sanity, to tell them that their views counted for more than those of the experts, to remind them that this was a Christian country, and to ask them rhetorically whether they perceived 'any spark of affection' between Lady Chatterley and her lover. He urged them not to get lost 'in the higher realms of literature,' but to think of factory girls, reading the book in their lunch-hour—a social group for whom he, like the prosecuting counsel, showed a tender, recurrent regard.

This protectiveness overflowed into his exposition of the new obscenity laws. The jury had first to decide whether or not the work tended 'to deprave and corrupt'; if they concluded that it did, they must go on to consider whether its publication could be justified as being 'for the public good' on the grounds of its literary and other merits. It was hereabouts, perhaps, that the vision of those corruptible factory girls, those hitherto innocent lunch hours, passed once more across the judge's mind, prompting him to impress on the jury that, while the expert testimony should be given due weight, the essence of the Act was contained in four words: 'for the public good'. He detached the phrase from its context, dwelling on it with affectionate iteration, so that one almost forgot that this emphasis, if heavily enough applied, would tilt the new Act towards meaningless fantasy; for a few mad moments, it seemed as if the only point at issue were whether it would be 'for the public good' to publish books that tended 'to deprave and corrupt'.

These and other passages from the summing-up haunted us as we waited; we recalled, for example, the judge's failure to mention, in his survey of the defence witnesses, a name that had echoed thrillingly down the corridors of the Old Bailey on the trial's third morning— Edward Morgan Forster, who had bowed most courteously to the bench before declaring, in prose of the greatest fastidiousness, that certainly Lawrence belonged in the puritan tradition, where his antecedents were Bunyan and Blake.

We also remembered the persistence with which both judge and prosecutor had hammered it home that Lady Chatterley was an immoral woman, that she had had sexual relations before marriage, that she had committed adultery under her husband's roof; as if these charges somehow disqualified her from participation in serious literature. Indeed, there were long periods of the trial during which an outsider might well have assumed that a divorce case was being heard; and it often seemed that the Crown was labouring under the same misapprehension, intensified by spasms of uncertainty as to whether the defendant was Constance Chatterley or Frieda von Richthofen. Over much that we heard hung the ancient fallacy that a book whose characters behave 'immorally' is therefore an immoral book; and the further fallacy that an immoral book is by definition an obscene book.

These confusions were inadvertently compounded by some of the defence witnesses, who went rather far in their eulogies of the book's ethical value; and by others who, while confining themselves to its literary merit, seemed unaware that the stress nowadays laid on the moral content of literature is something imperfectly understood by the average legal mind, to which morality means only Victorian morality. It is significant of the modern critical climate that not once in the trial was the word 'aesthetics' mentioned.

We consoled ourselves, as we kept our vigil outside the jury-room, by concentrating on the good, encouraging episodes, and banishing the bad ones. Apart from Mr Forster, we singled out Helen Gardner, bright-eyed and downright, who briskly explained that since the act of sex was not shameful, neither was the word that described it; and Rebecca West, surely a potent name, although the lady's manner, at once firm and rambling, did not always make for perspicuous communication.

We had Walter Allen and Raymond Williams, both splendidly unflappable; Stephen Potter, impressive in the unaccustomed role of Lawrence scholar; and Cecil Day Lewis, as dapper in mind as in bearing. We had the Bishop of Woolwich and the Headmaster of Alleyn's; from the latter pair of witnesses alone, must it not have seemed to the official custodians of our morals that the whole world was ganging up on them?

And there was always, indomitably, Gerald Gardiner, that rock among silks and monument to unassertive sanity, whose final address had left no weakness in the Crown's case unprobed, from its implicit snobbism in the matter of factory girls to its total lack of supporting testimony. Mr Gardiner had coined phrases, too; there was, he said, 'a high breathlessness about beauty that cancels lust'; and he had managed to restate, without boring us, the novel's twin theme—the danger that industrialization would destroy human relationships and the consequent need to affirm the supremacy of instinct over intellect.

Yet had he, perhaps, presented his case with too little passion? For in all our ears there still rang the voice of Mervyn Griffith-Jones, counsel for the prosecution, high-cheek-boned and poker-backed, a veteran of Eton, Trinity Hall (Cambridge), the Coldstream Guards and many previous obscenity cases; a voice passionate only in disdain, but barbed with a rabid belief in convention and discipline; a slow, scaly voice, listening to which one almost felt that if Penguin Books were acquitted, the prostitutes would dance in the streets, as they did after Oscar Wilde's conviction.

On Lawrence as a literary artist, the voice (for so I think of Mr Griffith-Jones, since from where I sat only his head was visible)—the voice had done some dedicated homework. 'Is that expert, artistic writing?' it would ask, having cited a passage in which a phrase was several times repeated. The mind's eye saw a man holding up one brick after another and demanding: 'Is that expert, artistic architecture?' The voice marked Lawrence as if he were an examination paper, and its interrogations had much in common with *vivas*.

It exhaled class-consciousness as effortlessly as air. Would the jury wish their servants to read Lawrence's novel? And was it natural for the lady of a great house to 'run off and copulate with her husband's game-keeper'? The voice took on a positively vengeful rasp when cross-examining people who distinguished between sex as Lawrence saw it and sex as a trivial diversion. Wasn't it true that by 'tenderness' the book actually meant tenderness towards the genital organs? (One wondered how else the voice would want them treated.) And could anyone deny that in the 'bouts' of love-making the emphasis was on the 'pleasure and satisfaction' involved? Leisurely and deadly, the voice hounded Connie Chatterley, a traitress to her class in that she not only enjoyed sex, but enjoyed it with a quasi-peasant. *A propos* of a passage in which she removes her night-dress before making love, the voice inquired why this 'strip-tease' was necessary; one assumed, charitably, that the question had been carelessly phrased. Throughout the trial, one longed for a witness who might challenge Mr Griffith-Jones in Lionel Trilling's words:

I see no reason in morality (or in aesthetic theory) why literature should not have as one of its intentions the arousing of thoughts of lust. It is one of the effects, perhaps one of the functions, of literature to arouse desire, and I can discover no ground for saying that sexual pleasure should not be among the objects of desire which literature presents to us, along with heroism, virtue, peace, death, food, wisdom, God, etc.

But nobody made that answer; and we, anxious in the corridors, had all but persuaded ourselves that no jury could withstand the impact of Mr Griffith-Jones (whom Roland Culver should play in the movie), when the verdict was returned and Lawrence exonerated.

Looking back, I think I can isolate the crucial incident, the exchange wherein the case was psychologically won. It occurred on the third morning during the testimony of Richard Hoggart, who had called

Lawrence's novel 'puritanical'. Mr Hoggart is a short, dark young Midland teacher of immense scholarship and fierce integrity. From the witness box he uttered a word that we had formerly heard only on the lips of Mr Griffith-Jones; he pointed out how Lawrence had striven to cleanse it of its furtive, contemptuous and expletive connotations, and to use it 'in the most simple, neutral way: one fucks'. There was no reaction of shock anywhere in the court, so calmly was the word pronounced, and so literally employed.

'Does it gain anything,' asked Mr Gardiner, 'by being printed "f——"?' 'Yes,' said Mr Hoggart, 'it gains a dirty suggestiveness.'

Rising in cross-examination, Mr Griffith-Jones wanted to know what Mr Hoggart meant by 'puritanical', receiving an answer to the effect that a puritan was a man who felt a profound sense of responsibility to his own conscience. Counsel then read out a series of excerpts from the novel. It must have been by chance that he chose the most impressive passages, the most solemnly ecstatic, the ones about 'the primeval roots of true beauty' and 'the sons of men and the daughters of women'; but slowly, as he recited them, one realized that he genuinely thought them impure and revolting. With every defiling inflection he alienated some part of his audience, seemingly unaware that what he had intended for our scorn was moving us in a way he had never foreseen; yet still he continued, bland and derisive, utterly unconscious of his increasing loneliness. Having finished, he triumphantly asked the witness whether a puritan would feel such 'reverence for a man's balls'. 'Indeed, yes,' said Mr Hoggart, almost with compassion.

I remembered his earlier reply to the suggestion that Lady Chatterley's affair with Mellors was due solely to her husband's impotence. '*It is not*,' he said: and in those words we heard, for the first time in the trial, the stubborn, uncompromising voice of the radical English moralist. Its volume and assurance grew as the cross-examination proceeded; and before long both jury and audience knew that the real battle had at last been joined—between all that Hoggart stood for, and all that Griffith-Jones stood for; between Lawrence's England and Sir Clifford Chatterley's England; between contact and separation; between freedom and control; between love and death.

James Morris

The Powers Trial

James Morris, who is a special correspondent of The Guardian, *was sent by that newspaper in August 1960 to report on the trial of Captain Francis Powers before the military division of the U.S.S.R. Supreme Court in Moscow. Despatches from Morris were sent throughout the three-day hearing but his final summary came from West Berlin where he was able to send his despatch without the close attention of the Soviet censors. (Since the trial censoring of despatches of foreign correspondents has been considerably relaxed.)*

Powers was the pilot of the ill-fated U-2 which had been on an intelligence reconnaissance flight over the Soviet Union at the direction of the American Central Intelligence Agency. When he was brought down on Soviet soil—how he was forced to land, as Morris explains, remains as great an enigma as the character of Powers himself—a major international incident was sparked off. Recriminations from both sides of the cold war were exchanged and the international climate was frosty for many months. Such was the propaganda value of this Russian capture that the Paris summit conference in the autumn was brusquely called off by Mr Khrushchev to the embarrassment of President Eisenhower.

In the midst of this highly-charged political atmosphere the Russians held—or staged, whichever view you take of the proceedings—the trial of Powers on charges of spying. If the hearing in court seemed to be conducted with impeccable fairness there were always the 100 days before the trial when Powers was held incommunicado. It is here that, under the Soviet code, an accused is at a disadvantage. Great emphasis is placed in the Soviet system on the pre-trial procedure in which investigation of the crime is carried out by members of the procuracy, in this case the military procuracy. At this early stage the accused is deprived of the benefit of any legal representation and advice.

It seemed unnecessary for the Soviet authorities to do any 'brainwashing' since the facts spoke for themselves. But as James Morris explains, there was some inexplicable evidence about the altitude of Powers' aircraft which threw some light on the hitting power of the Soviet defences. All this and more are tantalizingly related in the despatch of the first modern Soviet trial to arouse world-wide interest since the Vickers trial in the thirties.

Berlin, 21st August.

SO THE Powers trial has ended, the House of the Trade Unions in Moscow has relaxed into weekend torpor, the international press is sight-seeing in the Kremlin, strolling down to Samarkand, or running away to Berlin, where it can escape the Russian censors and think things over undisturbed.

It was in some ways a cut-and-dried affair, preceded by a complete confession, conducted with scrupulous and unyielding formality, ending with a gesture of magnanimity. But it was also a conundrum, and every moment of our three days in Court was tinged with the old mystery of Russia, which often etches the details in uncanny clarity but leaves the whole cloudy, fogged and inexplicable.

Queerest of all was the behaviour of Powers himself, whose personality remains, to me anyway, an impenetrable enigma. It may be, as many Americans think, that he is no more than an aeroplane driver —simple, half-educated, non-political, deliberately chosen for his lumpish lack of curiosity, genuinely kept in ignorance of the wider implications of his mission and the nature of his equipment. It may be that, since he really understood very little about the deeper secrecies of his job, he had been instructed by the Central Intelligence Agency to tell the Russians all he knew; or it may be that he was scared, as the rest of us would be, and told all anyway, without permission or persuasion.

In Court, though, at least after the first couple of hours, he did not seem to me quite such a simpleton. Sometimes his answers were keenly penetrating. Sometimes he used words of unexpected subtlety. He countered, almost with aplomb, successive efforts by Rudenko, the prosecutor, to put words into his mouth, and throughout the trial he bore himself with an odd air of composure, usually dignified and sometimes moving. He did not, to be sure, seem a clever, cultivated, or very percipient man, but he seemed something more than a vacant, hill-billy technician.

Was he, then, brainwashed, to induce in him this strange combination of submission and apparent independence? If he was, then it was done with extraordinary subtlety, or with drugs of unsuspected perplexity. His own family thought his manner normal, when they met him after the trial—though, to be sure, a platoon of armed guards stood around the table, just to make sure. Any visitor to Moscow knows how bewildering and insidious is the effect of insistent Communist propaganda—just a repetition of Marxist jargon, over and over again, is enough to make you doubt your convictions and even take a second look at your sanity. Perhaps it was simply his 100 days in a Soviet prison, exposed unremittingly to these influences, without the comfort of a single friendly face or homely face, that induced in Powers this almost trance-like, but never sepulchral, condition.

All the same, the Russians must have been sure of their man before they placed him before the world on Wednesday. Just one impassioned intervention, just one wild Byronic speech, and the whole structure of their spectacle would have collapsed, leaving Powers an all-American hero and the rest of us in tears in the gallery.

How could they be certain? Well, their psychologist may have decided that he was simply incapable of such heroics. Or they may have pointed out to him that misbehaviour in the dock was in itself a punishable offence, while 'co-operation with the Court' was a legal ground for remission. They would certainly have suggested that tractable behaviour, coupled with sincere repentance and everything he knew, would assure him a lenient sentence. They may, though, have offered him some specific quid pro quo: say this defendant Powers, and we will promise you that. It could not be simply the provision of technical information—no assurances were needed, I feel sure, to extract that from him—but it might have been some particular deception that he was required to uphold in Court to prove a Soviet point.

If this is so, then the key to the riddle may be the question of the U-2's altitude. The Russians claim, you will recall, that the aircraft was shot down by a rocket at 68,000 ft.—a claim that rudely upset American notions of Soviet anti-aircraft abilities. The Americans, on the other hand, have maintained from the start that the aircraft was already losing height before Powers baled out—that his loss was due, not in the first instance to Soviet rocketry, but to some mechanical failure. It may well have been hit by a rocket, so the Americans say, but not at 68,000 ft.

Could it be that Powers, in return for a light sentence, was induced to suppress in Court the real causes of his ignominy? Certainly, the details of the aircraft's destruction were distinctly fuzzy. Just why Powers could not use his ejection seat is still unclear to me, and it was interesting to learn that he did not bale out from his aircraft until it had fallen several thousand feet. This was, so we were assured, because he failed to unfasten his oxygen tubes, but it might have been because men who bale out at 68,000 ft. do not, I am told, very often survive. Time and again the prosecutor and the Bench returned to the question of height, each time emphasizing more firmly the potentials of the Russian rocket batteries: and it is obviously no coincidence that the launching of their spectacular new sputnik was announced at the very moment when the Court was considering its sentence. Powers himself, all the same, could never be induced to say, in so many words, that his aircraft had been hit by a rocket at that altitude. He was certainly 'struck down by something' but he had no idea what it was—a green flash was all he saw. Could this stubbornness have represented, I wondered as I watched him, an oblique hint that on this particular matter the evidence was not to be believed? Could the truth be that the Russians still cannot destroy aircraft at this height and that they are therefore particularly anxious to demonstrate that they can?

Certainly, I have no doubt the public trial was simply the exposed and floodlit pinnacle of a much larger iceberg and to claim that it demonstrates some genuine change in the principles of Soviet law seems to be nonsensical. There is really no hard evidence to show that it was either a fair trial or an unfair trial. We can only go by the pricking of our thumbs, and my own tell me that it was not really a trial at all, but simply a parade; in other words, that the sentence was predetermined.

Of course, the public proceedings were fairly conducted. They could hardly be otherwise, after so many preliminary fanfares about the purity of the reformed Soviet code. Rights of all kinds were flaunted in high-falutin' theory; the right to be defended, the right to cross-examine witnesses, the right to introduce evidence. But it was not in any way a test of Soviet justice. Powers had pleaded guilty and his confession had been published weeks before. Indeed, the State Department had pleaded guilty for him months and months ago. Defence counsel could only, in the nature of things, offer a plea in mitigation; and (provided only Powers behaved himself) the Russians could lose nothing by honouring all the forms of fair procedure.

Even on the public level, though, the case was shot through with political irrelevancies. Powers was charged with a criminal offence and it made not an iota of difference to his position whether, for example, Turkey was an accomplice of the United States, or Dr Adenauer had old-fashioned lackeys. There was nothing impromptu about the trial, except for one or two interventions by Powers himself. The witnesses were obviously carefully rehearsed, and I did not once see Mikhail Grinev, the defence counsel, exchanging a word with his client. It did not feel to me in the least like a weighing of evidence and if the sentence was not decreed by authorities higher than those three hulking generals on the bench, then I will eat my furlined hat.

The form of the law, as I see it, means almost nothing; all that matters is the principle and whether lofty principles were honoured in this case, we can really have, as Powers would say in his bland drawl, no idea.

Anyway, there we are; we are left, as they say, with the memory, plus a nasty taste in the mouth. The trial felt to me thoroughly artificial. The sentence, I suspect, may well degenerate into something less futile than prison or labour camp. The cloak-and-dagger figures that flitted through the evidence, with their poison pins and their black cloths, sounded at once childish and unwholesome. Powers, though never despicable, never looked the stuff of martyrs. The Powers family looked tragically out of their depth. Through the whole proceedings there stalked the beastly images of war, power, fear and propaganda, acting impartially for accusers and accused.

I hated every minute of it. It was horrible. It was our brave new world in microcosm, and it stank.

3

ON LAW

The life of the law has not been logic; it has been experience.

Mr Justice Holmes, *The Common Law*

James Boswell

From *The Life of Johnson*

I ASKED him whether, as a moralist, he did not think that the practice of the law, in some degree, hurt the nice feeling of honesty. JOHNSON. 'Why no, Sir, if you act properly. You are not to deceive your clients with false representations of your opinion: you are not to tell lies to a Judge.' BOSWELL. 'But what do you think of supporting a cause which you know to be bad?' JOHNSON. 'Sir, you do not know it to be good or bad till the Judge determines it. I have said that you are to state facts fairly; so that your thinking, or what you call knowing, a cause to be bad, must be from reasoning, must be from your supposing your arguments to be weak and inconclusive. But, Sir, that is not enough. An argument which does not convince yourself, may convince the Judge to whom you urge it: and if it does convince him, why, then, Sir, you are wrong, and he is right. It is his business to judge; and you are not to be confident in your own opinion that a cause is bad, but to say all you can for your client, and then hear the Judge's opinion.' BOSWELL. 'But, Sir, does not affecting a warmth when you have no warmth, and appearing to be clearly of one opinion when you are in reality of another opinion, does not such dissimulation impair one's honesty? Is there not some danger that a lawyer may put on the same mask in common life, in the intercourse with his friends?' JOHNSON. 'Why no, Sir. Everybody knows you are paid for affecting warmth for your client; and it is, therefore, properly no dissimulation: the moment you come from the bar you resume your usual behaviour. Sir, a man will no more carry the artifice of the bar into the common intercourse of society, than a man who is paid for tumbling upon his hands will continue to tumble upon his hands when he should walk on his feet.'

* * *

SIR A. 'I think, Sir, almost all great lawyers, such at least as have written upon law, have known only law, and nothing else.' JOHNSON. 'Why no, Sir; Judge Hale was a great lawyer, and wrote upon law; and yet he knew a great many other things, and has written upon other things. Selden too.' SIR A. 'Very true, Sir; and Lord Bacon. But was not Lord Coke a mere lawyer?' JOHNSON. 'Why, I am afraid he was; but he would have taken it very ill if you had told him so. He would have prosecuted you for scandal.' BOSWELL. 'Lord Mansfield is not a mere lawyer.' JOHNSON. 'No, Sir. I never was in Lord Mansfield's company; but Lord Mansfield was distinguished at the University. Lord Mansfield, when he first came to town, "drank champagne with the wits," as Prior says. He was the friend of Pope.' SIR A. 'Barristers, I believe, are not so abusive now as they were formerly. I fancy they had less law long ago, and so were obliged to take to abuse, to fill up the time. Now they have such a number of precedents, they have no occasion for abuse.' JOHNSON. 'Nay, Sir, they had more law long ago than they have now. As to precedents, to be sure they will increase in course of time; but the more precedents there are, the less occasion is there for law; that is to say, the less occasion is there for investigating principles.'

*　　*　　*

SIR JOSHUA REYNOLDS. 'I do not perceive why the profession of a player should be despised; for the great and ultimate end of all the employments of mankind is to produce amusement. Garrick produces more amusement than anybody.' BOSWELL. 'You say, Dr Johnson, that Garrick exhibits himself for a shilling. In this respect he is only on a footing with a lawyer who exhibits himself for his fee, and even will maintain any nonsense or absurdity if the case requires it. Garrick refuses a play or a part which he does not like; a lawyer never refuses.' JOHNSON. 'Why, Sir, what does this prove? Only that a lawyer is worse. Boswell is now like Jack in *The Tale of a Tub*, who, when he is puzzled by an argument, hangs himself. He thinks I shall cut him down, but I'll let him hang.' (Laughing vociferously.) SIR JOSHUA REYNOLDS. 'Mr Boswell thinks that the profession of a lawyer being unquestionably honourable, if he can show the profession of a player to be more honourable, he proves his argument.'

*　　*　　*

I introduced the subject of toleration. JOHNSON. 'Every society has a right to preserve public peace and order, and therefore has a good right to prohibit the propagation of opinions which have a dangerous tendency. To say the *magistrate* has this right, is using an inadequate word: it is the *society* for which the magistrate is agent. He may be morally or theologically wrong in restraining the propagation of opinions which he thinks dangerous, but he is politically right.' MAYO. 'I am of opinion, Sir, that every man is entitled to liberty of conscience in religion; and that the magistrate cannot restrain that right.' JOHNSON. 'Sir, I agree with you. Every man has a right to liberty of conscience, and with that the magistrate cannot interfere. People confound liberty of thinking with liberty of talking; nay, with liberty of preaching. Every man has a physical right to think as he pleases; for it cannot be discovered how he thinks. He has not a moral right, for he ought to inform himself, and think justly. But, Sir, no member of a society has a right to *teach* any doctrine contrary to what the society holds to be true. The magistrate, I say, may be wrong in what he thinks: but while he thinks himself right, he may and ought to enforce what he thinks.' MAYO. 'Then, Sir, we are to remain always in error, and truth never can prevail; and the magistrate was right in persecuting the first Christians.' JOHNSON. 'Sir, the only method by which religious truth can be established is by martyrdom. The magistrate has a right to enforce what he thinks; and he who is conscious of the truth has a right to suffer. I am afraid there is no other way of ascertaining the truth, but by persecution on the one hand and enduring it on the other.' GOLDSMITH. 'But how is a man to act, Sir? Though firmly convinced of the truth of his doctrine, may he not think it wrong to expose himself to persecution? Has he a right to do so? Is it not, as it were, committing voluntary suicide?' JOHNSON. 'Sir, as to voluntary suicide, as you call it, there are twenty thousand men in an army who will go without scruple to be shot at, and mount a breach for fivepence a day.' GOLDSMITH. 'But have they a moral right to do this?' JOHNSON. 'Nay, Sir, if you will not take the universal opinion of mankind, I have nothing to say. If mankind cannot defend their own way of thinking, I cannot defend it. Sir, if a man is in doubt whether it would be better for him to expose himself to martyrdom or not, he should not do it. He must be convinced that he has a delegation from heaven.' GOLDSMITH. 'I would consider whether there is the greater chance of good or evil upon the whole. If I see a man who had fallen into a well, I would wish to help him out; but if there is a greater probability that he shall pull me in, than that I shall pull him out, I would not attempt it. So were I to go to Turkey, I might wish to convert the Grand Signor to the Christian faith; but when I considered that I should probably be put to death without effectuating my purpose in any degree, I should keep myself quiet.' JOHNSON. 'Sir, you must consider that we have perfect and imperfect obligations. Perfect obligations, which are generally not to do something, are clear and positive; as, "thou shalt not kill." But charity, for instance, is not definable by limits. It is a duty to give to the poor; but no man can say how much another should give to the poor, or when a man has given too little to save his soul. In the same manner it is a duty to instruct the ignorant, and of consequence to convert infidels to Christianity; but no man in the common course of things is obliged to carry this to such a degree as to incur the danger of martyrdom, as no man is obliged to strip himself to the shirt in order to give charity. I have said, that a man must be persuaded that he has a particular delegation from heaven.' GOLDSMITH. 'How is this to be known? Our first reformers, who were burnt for not believing bread and wine to be CHRIST'—JOHNSON (interrupting him). 'Sir, they were not burnt for not believing bread and wine to be CHRIST, but for insulting those who did believe it. And, Sir, when the first reformers began, they did not intend to be martyred: as many of them ran away as could.' BOSWELL. 'But, Sir, there was your countryman, Elwal, who you told me challenged King George with his black-guards, and his red-guards.' JOHNSON. 'My countryman, Elwal, Sir, should have been put in the stocks; a proper pulpit for him; and he'd have had a numerous audience. A man who preaches in the stocks will always have hearers enough.' BOSWELL. 'But Elwal thought himself in the right.' JOHNSON. 'We are not providing for mad people; there are places for them in the neighbourhood' (meaning Moorfields). MAYO. 'But, Sir, is it not very hard that I should not be allowed to teach my children what I really believe to be the truth?' JOHNSON. 'Why, Sir, you might contrive to teach your children *extra scandalum;* but, Sir, the magistrate, if he knows it, has a right to restrain you. Suppose you teach your children to be thieves?' MAYO. 'This is making a joke of the subject.' JOHNSON. 'Nay, Sir, take it thus: —that you teach them the community of goods; for which there are as many plausible arguments as for most erroneous doctrines. You teach them that all things at first were in common, and that no man had a right to any thing but as he laid his hands upon it; and that this still is, or ought to be, the rule amongst mankind. Here, Sir, you sap a great principle in society— property. And don't you think the magistrate would have a right to prevent you? Or, suppose you should teach your children the notion of the Adamites, and they should run naked into the streets, would not the magistrate have a right to flog 'em into their doublets?' MAYO. 'I think the magistrate has no right to interfere till there is some overt act.' BOSWELL. 'So, Sir, though he sees an enemy to the state charging a blunderbuss, he is not to interfere till it is fired off?' MAYO. 'He must be sure of its direction against the state.' JOHNSON. 'The magistrate is to judge of that.—He has no right to restrain your thinking, because the evil centres in yourself. If a man were sitting at this table, and chopping off his fingers, the magistrate, as guardian of the community, has no authority to restrain him, however he might do it from kindness as a parent. Though, indeed, upon more consideration, I think he may; as it is probable, that he who is chopping off his own fingers, may soon proceed to chop off those of other people. If I think it right to steal Mr Dilly's plate, I am a bad man; but he can say nothing to me. If I make an open declaration that I think so, he will keep me out of his house. If I put forth my hand, I shall be sent to Newgate. This is the gradation of thinking, preaching, and acting: if a man thinks erroneously, he may keep his thoughts to himself, and nobody will trouble him; if he preaches erroneous doctrine, society may expel him; if he acts in consequence of it, the law takes place, and he is hanged.' MAYO. 'But, Sir, ought not Christians to have liberty of conscience?' JOHNSON. 'I have already told you so, Sir. You are coming back to where you were.' BOSWELL. 'Dr Mayo is always taking a return post-chaise, and going the stage over again. He has it at half price.' JOHNSON. 'Dr Mayo, like other champions for unlimited toleration, has got a set of words. Sir, it is no matter, politically, whether the magistrate be right or wrong. Suppose a club were to be formed, to drink confusion to King George the Third, and a happy restoration to Charles the Third, this would be very bad with respect to the State; but every member of that club must either conform to its rules, or be turned out of it. Old Baxter, I remember, maintains, that the magistrate should "tolerate all things that are tolerable". This is no good definition of toleration upon any principle; but it shows that he thought some things were not tolerable.' TOPLADY. 'Sir, you have untwisted this difficult subject with great dexterity.'

*　　　*　　　*

We got into an argument whether the Judges who went to India might with propriety engage in trade. Johnson warmly maintained that they might. 'For why,' (he urged) 'should not Judges get riches, as well as those who deserve them less?' I said, they should have sufficient salaries, and have nothing to take off their attention from the affairs of the public. JOHNSON. 'No Judge, Sir, can give his whole attention to his office; and it is very proper that he should employ what time he has to himself, to his own advantage, in the most profitable manner.' 'Then, Sir,' (said Davies, who enlivened the dispute by making it somewhat dramatic) 'he may become an insurer; and when he is going to the bench, he may be stopped—"Your Lordship cannot go yet: here is a bunch of invoices: several ships are about to sail".' JOHNSON. 'Sir, you may as well say a Judge should not have a house; for they may come and tell him, "Your Lordship's house is on fire"; and so, instead of minding the business of his Court, he is to be occupied in getting the engine with the greatest speed. There is no end of this. Every Judge who has land, trades to a certain extent in corn or in cattle; and in the land itself, undoubtedly. His steward acts for him, and so do clerks for a great merchant. A Judge may be a farmer; but he is not to geld his own pigs. A Judge may play a little at cards for his amusement; but he is not to play at marbles, or at chuck-farthing in the Piazza. No, Sir; there is no profession to which a man gives a very great proportion of his time. It is wonderful when a calculation is made, how little the mind is actually employed in the discharge of any profession. No man would be a Judge, upon the condition of being totally a Judge. The best employed lawyer has his mind at work but for a small proportion of his time: a great deal of his occupation is merely mechanical. I once wrote for a magazine: I made a calculation, that if I should write but a page a day, at the same rate, I should, in ten years, write nine volumes in folio, of an ordinary size and print.' BOSWELL. 'Such as Carte's *History?*' JOHNSON. 'Yes, Sir. When a man writes from his own mind, he writes very rapidly.* The greatest part of a writer's time is spent in reading, in order to write: a man will turn over half a library to make one book.'

I argued warmly against the Judges trading, and mentioned Hale as an instance of a perfect Judge, who devoted himself entirely to his office. JOHNSON. 'Hale, Sir, attended to other things besides law: he left a great estate.' BOSWELL. 'That was, because what he got, accumulated without any exertion and anxiety on his part.'

* Johnson certainly did, who had a mind stored with knowledge, and teeming with imagery: but the observation is not applicable to writers in general.

While the dispute went on, Moody once tried to say something upon our side. Tom Davies clapped him on the back, to encourage him. Beauclerk, to whom I mentioned this circumstance, said, that 'he could not conceive a more humiliating situation than to be clapped on the back by Tom Davies.'

*　　*　　*

After supper I accompanied him to his apartment, and at my request he dictated to me an argument in favour of the Negro who was then claiming his liberty, in an action in the Court of Session in Scotland. He had always been zealous against slavery in every form, in which I, with all deference, thought that he discovered 'a zeal without knowledge'. Upon one occasion, when in company with some very grave men at Oxford, his toast was, 'Here's to the next insurrection of the Negroes in the West Indies.' His violent prejudice against our West Indian and American settlers appeared whenever there was an opportunity. Towards the conclusion of his *Taxation no Tyranny*, he says, 'How is it that we hear the loudest *yelps* for liberty among the drivers of Negroes?' and in his conversation with Mr Wilkes, he asked, 'Where did Beckford and Trecothick learn English?' That Trecothick could both speak and write good English is well known. I myself was favoured with his correspondence concerning the brave Corsicans. And that Beckford could speak it with a spirit of honest resolution even to his Majesty, as his 'faithful Lord-Mayor of London,' is commemorated by the noble monument erected to him in Guildhall.

The argument dictated by Dr Johnson was as follows:

'It must be agreed that in most ages many countries have had part of their inhabitants in a state of slavery; yet it may be doubted whether slavery can ever be supposed the natural condition of man. It is impossible not to conceive that men in the original state were equal; and very difficult to imagine how one would be subjected to another but by violent compulsion. An individual may, indeed, forfeit his liberty by a crime; but he cannot by that crime forfeit the liberty of his children. What is true of a criminal seems true likewise of a captive. A man may accept life from a conquering enemy on condition of perpetual servitude; but it is very doubtful whether he can entail that servitude on his descendants; for no man can stipulate without commission for another. The condition which he himself accepts, his son or grandson perhaps would have rejected. If we should admit, what perhaps may with more reason be denied, that there are certain relations between man and man which may make slavery necessary and just, yet it can never be proved that he who is now suing for his freedom ever stood in any of those relations. He is certainly subject by no law, but that of violence, to his present master; who pretends no claim to his obedience, but that he bought him from a merchant of slaves, whose right to sell him never was examined. It is said that, according to the constitutions of Jamaica, he was legally enslaved; these constitutions are merely positive; and apparently injurious to the rights of mankind, because whoever is exposed to sale is condemned to slavery without appeal; by whatever fraud or violence he might have been originally brought into the merchant's power. In our own time Princes have been sold, by wretches to whose care they were entrusted, that they might have an European education; but when once they were brought to a market in the plantations, little would avail either their dignity or their wrongs. The laws of Jamaica afford a Negro no redress. His colour is considered as a sufficient testimony against him. It is to be lamented that moral right should ever give way to political convenience. But if temptations of interest are sometimes too strong for human virtue, let us at least retain a virtue where there is no temptation to quit it. In the present case there is apparent right on one side, and no convenience on the other. Inhabitants of this island can neither gain riches nor power by taking away the liberty of any part of the human species. The sum of the argument is this: No man is by nature the property of another: The defendant is, therefore, by nature free: The rights of nature must be some way forfeited before they can be justly taken away: That the defendant has by any act forfeited the rights of nature we require to be proved; and if no proof of such forfeiture can be given, we doubt not but the justice of the court will declare him free.'

I record Dr Johnson's argument fairly upon this particular case; where, perhaps, he was in the right. But I beg leave to enter my most solemn protest against his general doctrine with respect to the *Slave Trade*. For I will resolutely say—that his unfavourable notion of it was owing to prejudice, and imperfect or false information. The wild and dangerous attempt which has for some time been persisted in to obtain an act of our Legislature, to abolish so very important and necessary a branch of commercial interest, must have been crushed at once, had not the insignificance of the zealots who vainly took the lead in it, made the vast body of Planters, Merchants, and others, whose immense properties are involved in that trade, reasonably enough suppose that there could be no danger. The encouragement which the attempt has received excites my wonder and indignation: and though some men of superior abilities have supported it; whether from a love of temporary popularity, when prosperous; or a love of general mischief, when desperate, my opinion is unshaken. To abolish a *status*, which in all ages GOD has sanctioned, and man has continued, would not only be *robbery* to an innumerable class of our fellow-subjects; but it would be extreme cruelty to the African Savages, a portion of whom it saves from massacre, or intolerable bondage in their own country, and introduces into a much happier state of life; especially now when their passage to the West-Indies and their treatment there is humanely regulated. To abolish that trade would be to

—shut the gates of mercy on mankind.

Whatever may have passed elsewhere concerning it, The HOUSE OF LORDS is wise and independent:

Intaminatis fulget honoribus;
Nec sumit aut ponit secures
Arbitrio popularis aurae.

I have read, conversed, and thought much upon the subject, and would recommend to all who are capable of conviction, an excellent Tract by my learned and ingenious friend John Ranby, Esq., entitled *Doubts on the Abolition of the Slave Trade.* To Mr. Ranby's *Doubts* I will apply Lord Chancellor Hardwicke's expression in praise of a Scotch Law Book, called *Dirleton's Doubts;* his *Doubts* (said his Lordship), are better than most people's *Certainties.*

When I said now to Johnson, that I was afraid I kept him too late up. 'No, Sir,' (said he) 'I don't care though I sit all night with you.' This was an animated speech from a man in his sixty-ninth year.

Had I been as attentive not to displease him as I ought to have been, I know not but this vigil might have been fulfilled; but I unluckily entered upon the controversy concerning the right of Great Britain to tax America, and attempted to argue in favour of our fellow-subjects on the other side of the Atlantic. I insisted that America might be very well governed, and made to yield sufficient revenue by the means of *influence*, as exemplified in Ireland, while the people might be pleased with the imagination of their participating of the British constitution, by having a body of representatives, without whose consent money could not be exacted from them. Johnson could not bear my thus opposing his avowed opinion, which he had exerted himself with an extreme degree of heat to enforce; and the violent agitation into which he was thrown, while answering, or rather reprimanding me, alarmed me so, that I heartily repented of my having unthinkingly introduced the subject. I myself, however, grew warm, and the change was great, from the calm state of philosophical discussion in which he had a little before been pleasingly employed.

Samuel D. Warren
and Louis D. Brandeis
The Right to Privacy

━━━━━━━━

Seventy years ago two graduates of the Harvard Law School wrote in the law review of that famous institution an article arguing that the Common Law of England—and hence the United States—gave the individual subject a right of action for any invasion of his privacy which was not justified on the ground of public interest. The two authors were to become respectively a professor of law and a justice of the Supreme Court of the United States.

The prying activities of the press and the intrusion by press representatives in to the homes and lives of the ordinary citizen leading to the wide dissemination of offensive matter has, in Britain, gone on unabated and unchecked by the agency of the law. A Bill was presented in the House of Lords on 13th March, 1961 and was given a second reading by 74 votes to 21. The Bill proclaims that a right of action shall be given to anybody whose personal affairs or conduct are related by any form of mass media without the owner's consent. The publisher of such matter would have a defence to such action if either he genuinely did not intend the offending material to refer to the individual concerned; or the occasion of the publication was privileged; or, most important, the individual and the matter published about him were the subject of reasonable public interest.

The law of defamation is impliedly ineffective to provide the ordinary citizen with a remedy against the purveyors of harmful news of a wholly private character. The enforcement of a right to privacy differs from the action for defamation in that it is not necessary for the statement to bring the person into hatred, ridicule or contempt. There may be instances where publication falls short of injuring a person in any one of those ways and yet be quite harmful. If a person's self-esteem is wounded or an affront to his personal dignity is made there is no question of defamation, although juries are not slow to convert what is merely capable of bearing a defamatory meaning into a defamatory statement whenever there is some offensive invasion of personal privacy.

But a real distinction which cannot be nullified by any perverse finding of a jury is that in defamation the defence of truth deprives the individual of any remedy. It is a cardinal principle of our law that everyone should be free to tell the truth, however unpalatable that truth may be. If anyone is to be penalized for stating the truth there must be some compelling reason why such a rule is to be imposed by law. Is it enough for the law to say that the truth may be told only if the subject matter is of reasonable public interest? And is it right that the courts should be the arbiters of what is 'reasonable public interest'?

'It could be done only on principles of private justice, moral fitness and public convenience, which, when applied to a new subject, make common law without a precedent; much more when received and approved by usage.' Mr Justice Willes in *Miller v. Taylor.*

THAT THE individual shall have full protection in person and in property is a principle as old as the common law; but it has been found necessary from time to time to define anew the exact nature and extent of such protection. Political, social, and economic changes entail the recognition of new rights, and the common law, in its eternal youth, grows to meet the demands of society. Thus, in very early times, the law gave a remedy only for physical interference with life and property, for trespasses *vi et armis*. Then the 'right to life' served only to protect the subject from battery in its various forms; liberty meant freedom from actual restraint; and the right to property secured to the individual his lands and his cattle. Later, there came a recognition of man's spiritual nature, of his feelings and intellect. Gradually the scope of these legal rights broadened; and now the right to life has come to mean the right to enjoy life—the right to be let alone; the right to liberty secures the exercise of extensive civil privileges; and the term 'property' has grown to comprise every form of possession—intangible, as well as tangible.

Thus, with the recognition of the legal value of sensations, the protection against actual bodily injury was extended to prohibit mere attempts to do such injury; that is, the putting another in fear of such injury. From the action of battery grew that of assault. Much later there came a qualified protection of the individual against offensive noises and odours, against the dust and smoke, and excessive vibration. The law of nuisance was developed. So regard for human emotions soon extended the scope of personal immunity beyond the body of the individual. His reputation, the standing among his fellow-men, was considered, and the law of slander and libel arose. Man's family relations became a part of the legal conception of his life, and the alienation of a wife's affections was held remediable. Occasionally the law halted—as in its refusal to recognize the intrusion by seduction upon the honour of the family. But even here the demands of society were met. A mean fiction, the action *per quod servitium amisit*, was resorted to, and by allowing damages for injury to the parents' feelings, an adequate remedy was ordinarily afforded. Similar to the expansion of the right to life was the growth of the legal conception of property. From corporeal property arose the incorporeal rights issuing out of it; and then there opened the wider realm of intangible property, in the products and processes of the mind, as works of literature and art, goodwill, trade secrets, and trademarks.

This development of the law was inevitable. The intense intellectual and emotional life, and the heightening of sensations which came with the advance of civilization, made it clear to men that only a part of the pain, pleasure, and profit of life lay in physical things. Thoughts, emotions, and sensations demanded legal recognition, and the beautiful capacity for growth which characterizes the common law enabled the judges to afford the requisite protection, without the interposition of the legislature.

Recent inventions and business methods call attention to the next step which must be taken for the protection of the person, and for securing to the individual what Judge Cooley calls the right 'to be let alone'. Instantaneous photographs and newspaper enterprise have invaded the sacred precincts of private and domestic life; and numerous mechanical devices threaten to make good the prediction that 'what is whispered in the closet shall be proclaimed from the house-tops'. For years there has been a feeling that the law must afford some remedy for the unauthorized circulation of portraits of private persons; and the evil of the invasion of privacy by the newspapers, long keenly felt, has been but recently discussed by an able writer. The alleged facts of a somewhat notorious case brought before an inferior tribunal in New York a few months ago, directly involved the consideration of the right of circulating portraits; and the question whether our law will recognize and protect the right to privacy in this and in other respects must soon come before our courts for consideration.

Of the desirability—indeed of the necessity—of some such protection, there can, it is believed, be no doubt. The press is overstepping in every direction the obvious bounds of propriety and of decency. Gossip is no longer the resource of the idle and of the vicious, but has become a trade, which is pursued with industry as well as effrontery. To satisfy a prurient taste the details of sexual relations are spread broadcast in the columns of the daily papers. To occupy the indolent, column upon column is filled with idle gossip, which can only be procured by intrusion upon the domestic circle. The intensity and complexity of life, attendant upon advancing civilization, have rendered necessary some retreat from the world, and man, under the refining influence of culture, has become more sensitive to publicity, so that solitude and privacy have become more essential to the individual; but modern enterprise and invention have, through invasions upon his privacy, subjected him to mental pain and distress, far greater than could be inflicted by mere bodily injury. Nor is the harm wrought by such invasions confined to the suffering of those who may be the subjects of journalistic or other enterprise. In this, as in other branches of commerce, the supply creates the demand. Each crop of unseemly gossip, thus harvested, becomes the seed of more, and, in direct proportion to its circulation, results in a lowering of social standards and of morality. Even gossip apparently harmless, when widely and persistently circulated, is potent for evil. It both belittles and perverts. It belittles by inverting the relative importance of things, thus dwarfing the thoughts and aspirations of a people. When personal gossip attains the dignity of print, and crowds the space available for matters of real interest to the community, what wonder that the ignorant and thoughtless mistake its relative importance. Easy of comprehension, appealing to that weak side of human nature which is never wholly cast down by the misfortunes and frailties of our neighbours, no one can be surprised that it usurps the place of interest in brains capable of other things. Triviality destroys at once robustness of thought and delicacy of feeling. No enthusiasm can flourish, no generous impulse can survive under its blighting influence.

It is our purpose to consider whether the existing law affords a principle which can be properly invoked to protect the privacy of the individual; and, if it does, what the nature and extent of such protection is.

Owing to the nature of the instruments by which privacy is invaded, the injury inflicted bears a superficial resemblance to the wrongs dealt with by the law of slander and of libel, while a legal remedy for such injury seems to involve the treatment of mere wounded feelings, as a substantive cause of action. The principle on which the law of defamation rests, covers, however, a radically different class of effects from those for which attention is now asked. It deals only with damage to reputation, with the injury done to the individual in his external relations to the community, by lowering him in the estimation of his fellows. The matter published of him, however widely circulated, and however unsuited to publicity, must, in order to be actionable, have a direct tendency to injure him in his intercourse with others, and even if in writing or in print, must subject him to the hatred, ridicule, or contempt of his fellowmen—the effect of the publication upon his estimate of himself and upon his own feelings not forming an essential element in the cause of action. In short, the wrongs and correlative rights recognized by the law of slander and libel are in their nature material rather than spiritual. That branch of the law simply extends the protection surrounding physical property to certain of the conditions necessary or helpful to worldly prosperity. On the other hand, our law recognized no principle upon which compensation can be granted for mere injury to the feelings. However painful the mental effects upon another of an act, though purely wanton or even malicious, yet if the act itself is otherwise lawful, the suffering inflicted is *damnum absque injuria*. Injury of feelings may indeed be taken account of in ascertaining the amount of damages when attending what is recognized as a legal injury; but our system, unlike the Roman law, does not afford a remedy even for mental suffering which results from mere contumely and insult, from an intentional and unwarranted violation of the 'honour' of another.

It is not however necessary, in order to sustain the view that the common law recognizes and upholds a principle applicable to cases of invasion of privacy, to invoke the analogy, which is but superficial, to injuries sustained, either by an attack upon reputation or by what the civilians called a violation of honour; for the legal doctrines relating to infractions of what is ordinarily termed the common-law right to intellectual and artistic property are, it is believed, but instances and applications of a general right to privacy, which properly understood afford a remedy for the evils under consideration.

The common law secures to each individual the right of determining, ordinarily, to what extent his thoughts, sentiments, and emotions, shall be communicated to others. Under our system of government, he can never be compelled to express them (except when upon the witness-stand); and even if he has chosen to give them expression, he generally retains the power to fix the limits of the publicity which shall be given them. The existence of this right does not depend upon the particular method of expression adopted. It is immaterial whether it be by word or by signs, in painting, by sculpture, or in music. Neither does the existence of the right depend upon the nature or value of the thought or emotion, nor upon the excellence of the means of expression. The same protection is accorded to a casual letter or an entry in a diary and to the most valuable poem or essay, to a botch or daub and to a masterpiece. In every such case the individual is entitled to decide whether that which is his shall be given to the public. No other has the right to publish his productions in any form, without his consent. This right is wholly independent of the material on which, or the means by which, the thought, sentiment or emotion is expressed. It may exist independently of any corporeal being, as in the words spoken, a song sung, a drama acted. Or if expressed on any material, as a poem in writing, the author may have parted with the paper, without forfeiting any proprietary right in the composition itself. The right is lost only when the author himself communicates his production to the public—in other words, publishes it. It is entirely independent of the copyright laws, and their extension into the domain of art. The aim of those statutes is to secure to the author, composer, or artist the entire profits arising from publication; but the common-law protection enables him to control absolutely the act of publication, and in the exercise of his own discretion, to decide whether there shall be any publication at all. The statutory right is of no value, unless there is a publication; the common-law is lost as soon as there is a publication.

What is the nature, the basis, of this right to prevent the publication of manuscripts of works of art? It is stated to be the enforcement of a right of property; and no difficulty arises in accepting this view, so long as we have only to deal with the reproduction of literary and artistic compositions. They certainly possess many of the attributes of ordinary property: they are transferable; they have a value; and publication or reproduction is a use by which that value is realized. But where the value of the production is found not in the right to take the profits arising from publication, but in the peace of mind or the relief afforded by the ability to prevent any publication at all, it is difficult to regard the right as one of property, in the common acceptance of that term. A man records in a letter to his son, or in his diary, that he did not dine with his wife on a certain day. No one into whose hands those papers fall could publish them to the world, even if possession of the documents had been obtained rightfully; and the prohibition would not be confined to the publication of a copy of the letter itself, or of the diary entry; the restraint extends also to a publication of the contents. What is the thing which is protected? Surely, not the intellectual act of recording the fact that the husband did not dine with his wife, but that fact itself. It is not the intellectual product, but the domestic occurrence. A man writes a dozen letters to different people. No person would be permitted to publish a list of the letters written. If the letters or the contents of the diary were protected as literary compositions, the scope of the protection afforded should be the same secured to a published writing under the copyright law. But the copyright law would not prevent an enumeration of the letters, or the publication of some of the facts contained therein. The copyright of a series of paintings or etchings would prevent a reproduction of the paintings as pictures; but it would not prevent a publication of a list or even a description of them. Yet in the famous case of *Prince Albert v. Strange*, the court held that the common-law rule prohibited not merely the reproduction of the etchings which the plaintiff and Queen Victoria had made for their own pleasure, but also 'the publishing (at least by printing or writing), though not by copy or resemblance, a description of them, whether more or less limited or summary, whether in the form of a catalogue or otherwise'. Likewise, an unpublished collection of news possessing no element of a literary nature is protected from piracy.

That this protection cannot rest upon the right to literary or artistic property in any exact sense, appears the more clearly when the subject-matter for which protection is invoked is not even in the form of intellectual property, but has the attributes of ordinary tangible property. Suppose a man has a collection of gems or curiosities which he keeps private: it would hardly be contended that any person could publish a catalogue of them, and yet the articles enumerated are certainly not intellectual property in the legal sense, any more than a collection of stoves or of chairs.

The belief that the idea of property in its narrow sense was the basis of the protection of unpublished manuscripts led an able court to refuse, in several cases, injunctions against the publication of private letters, on the ground that 'letters not possessing the attributes of literary compositions are not property entitled to protection'; and that it was 'evident the plaintiff could not have considered the letters as of any value whatever as literary productions, for a letter cannot be considered of value to the author which he never would consent to have published.' But these decisions have not been followed, and it may now be considered settled that the protection afforded by the common law to the author of any writing is entirely independent of its pecuniary value, its intrinsic merits, or of any intention to publish the same, and, of course, wholly independent of the material, if any, upon which, or the mode in which, the thought or sentiment was expressed.

Although the courts have asserted that they rested their decisions on the narrow grounds of protection to property, yet there are recognitions of a more liberal doctrine. Thus in the case of *Prince Albert v. Strange*, already referred to, the opinions both of the Vice-Chancellor and of the Lord Chancellor, on appeal, show a more or less clearly defined perception of a principle broader than those which were mainly discussed, and on which they both placed their chief reliance. Vice-Chancellor Knight-Bruce referred to publishing of a man that he had 'written to particular persons or on particular subjects' as an instance of possibly injurious disclosures as to private matters, that the courts would in a proper case prevent; yet it is difficult to perceive how, in such a case, any right of property, in the narrow sense, would be drawn in question, or why, if such a publication would be restrained when it threatened to expose the victim not merely to sarcasm, but to ruin, it should not equally be enjoined, if it threatened to embitter his life. To deprive a man of the potential profits to be realized by publishing a catalogue of his gems cannot *per se* be a wrong to him. The possibility of future profits is not a right of property which the law ordinarily recognizes; it must, therefore, be an infraction of other rights which constitutes the wrongful act, and that infraction is equally wrongful, whether its results are to forestall the profits that the individual might himself secure by giving the matter a publicity obnoxious to him, or to gain an advantage at the expense of his mental pain and suffering. If the fiction of property in a narrow sense must be preserved, it is still true that the end accomplished by the gossipmonger is attained by the use of that which is another's, the facts relating to his private life, which he has seen fit to keep private. Lord Cottenham stated that a man 'is entitled to be protected in the exclusive use and enjoyment of that which is exclusively his', and cited with approval the opinion of Lord Eldon, as reported in a manuscript note of the case of *Wyatt v. Wilson*, in 1820, respecting an engraving of George the Third during his illness, to the effect that 'if one of the late King's physicians had kept a diary of what he heard and saw, the court would not, in the King's lifetime, have permitted him to print and publish it'; and Lord Cottenham declared, in respect to the acts of the defendants in the case before him, that 'privacy is the right invaded'. But if privacy is once recognized as a right entitled to legal protection, the interposition of the courts cannot depend on the particular nature of the injuries resulting.

These considerations lead to the conclusion that the protection afforded to thoughts, sentiments, and emotions, expressed through the medium of writing or of the arts, so far as it consists in preventing publication, is merely an instance of the enforcement of the more general right of the individual to be let alone. It is like the right not to be assaulted or beaten, the right not to be imprisoned, the right not to be maliciously prosecuted, the right not to be defamed. In each of these rights, as indeed in all other rights recognized by the law, there inheres the quality of being owned or possessed—and (as that is the distinguishing attribute of property) there may be some propriety in speaking of those rights as property. But, obviously, they bear little resemblance to what is ordinarily comprehended under that term. The principle which protects personal writings and all other personal productions, not against theft and physical appropriation, but against publication in any form, is in reality not the principle of private property but that of an inviolate personality.

If we are correct in this conclusion, the existing law affords a principle which may be invoked to protect the privacy of the individual from invasion either by the too-enterprising press, the photographer, or the possessor of any other modern device for recording or reproducing scenes or sounds. For the protection afforded is not confined by the authorities to those cases where any particular medium or form of expression has been adopted, nor to products of the intellect. The same protection is afforded to emotions and sensations expressed in a musical composition or other works of art as to a literary composition;

and words spoken, a pantomime acted, a sonata performed, is no less entitled to protection than if each had been reduced to writing. The circumstance that a thought or emotion has been recorded in a permanent form renders its identification easier, and hence may be important from the point of view of evidence, but, it has no significance as a matter of substantive right. If, then, the decisions indicate a general right to privacy for thoughts, emotions, and sensations, these should receive the same protection, whether expressed in writing, or in conduct, in conversation, in attitudes, or in facial expression.

It may be urged that a distinction should be taken between the deliberate expression of thoughts and emotions in literary or artistic compositions and the casual and often involuntary expression given to them in the ordinary conduct of life. In other words, it may be contended that the protection afforded is granted to the conscious products of labour, perhaps as an encouragement to effort. This contention, however plausible, has, in fact, little to recommend it. If the amount of labour involved be adopted as the test, we might well find that the effort to conduct one's self properly in business and in domestic relations had been far greater than that involved in painting a picture or writing a book; one would find that it was far easier to express lofty sentiments in a diary than in the conduct of a noble life. If the test of deliberateness of the act be adopted, much casual correspondence which is now accorded full protection would be excluded from the beneficent operation of existing rules. After the decisions denying the distinction attempted to be made between those literary productions which it was intended to publish and those which it was not, all considerations of the amount of labour involved, the degree of deliberation, the value of the product, and the intention of publishing must be abandoned, and no basis is discerned upon which the right to restrain publication and reproduction of such so-called literary and artistic works can be rested, except the privacy, as a part of the more general right to the immunity of the person—the right to one's personality.

It should be stated that, in some instances where protection has been afforded against wrongful publication, the jurisdiction has been asserted, not on the ground of property, or at least not wholly on that ground, but upon the ground of an alleged breach of an implied contract or of a trust or confidence.

Thus, in *Abernethy v. Hutchinson*, 3 L. J. Ch. 209 (1825), where the plaintiff, a distinguished surgeon, sought to restrain the publication in the *Lancet* of unpublished lectures which he had delivered at St Bartholomew's Hospital in London, Lord Eldon doubted whether there could be property in lectures which had not been reduced to writing, but granted the injunction on the ground of breach of confidence, holding 'that when persons were admitted as pupils or otherwise, to hear these lectures, although they were orally delivered, and although the parties might go to the extent, if they were able to do so, of putting down the whole by means of shorthand, yet they could do that only for the purposes of their own information, and could not publish, for profit, that which they had not obtained the right of selling'.

In *Prince Albert v. Strange*, 1 McN. & G. 25 (1849), Lord Cottenham, on appeal, while recognizing a right of property in the etchings which of itself would justify the issuance of the injunction, stated, after discussing the evidence, that he was bound to assume that the possession of the etchings by the defendant had 'its foundation in a breach of trust, confidence or contract', and that upon such ground also the plaintiff's title to the injunction was fully sustained.

In *Tuck v. Priester*, 19 Q.B.D. 639 (1887), the plaintiffs were owners of a picture, and employed the defendant to make a certain number of copies. He did so, and made also a number of other copies for himself, and offered them for sale in England at a lower price. Subsequently, the plaintiffs registered their copyright in the picture, and then brought suit for an injunction and damages. The Lords Justices differed as to the application of the copyright Acts to the case, but held unanimously that independently of those Acts, the plaintiffs were entitled to an injunction and damages for breach of contract.

In *Pollard v. Photographic Co.*, 40 Ch. Div. 345 (1888), a photographer who had taken a lady's photograph under the ordinary circumstances was restrained from exhibiting it, and also from selling copies of it, on the ground that it was a breach of an implied term in the contract, and also that it was a breach of confidence. Mr Justice North interjected in the argument of the plaintiff's counsel the inquiry: 'Do you dispute that if the negative likeness were taken on the sly, the person who took it might exhibit copies?' and counsel for the plaintiff answered: 'In that case there would be no trust or consideration to support a contract.' Later, the defendant's counsel argued that 'a person has no property in his own features; short of doing what is libellous or otherwise illegal, there is no restriction on the photographer's using his negative'. But the court, while expressly finding a breach of contract and of trust sufficient to justify its interposition, still seems to have felt the necessity of resting the decision also upon a right of property, in order to bring it within the line of those cases which were relied upon as precedents.

This process of implying a term in a contract, or of implying a trust (particularly where the contract is written, and where there is no established usage or custom), is nothing more nor less than a judicial declaration that public morality, private justice, and general convenience demand the recognition of such a rule, and that the publication under similar circumstances would be considered an intolerable abuse. So long as these circumstances happen to present a contract upon which such a term can be engrafted by the judicial mind, or to supply relations upon which a trust or confidence can be erected, there may be no objection to working out the desired protection through the doctrines of contract or of trust. But the court can hardly stop there. The narrower doctrine may have satisfied the demands of society at a time when the abuse to be guarded against could rarely have arisen without violating a contract or a special confidence; but now that modern devices afford abundant opportunities for the perpetration of such wrongs without any participation by the injured party, the protection granted by the law must be placed upon a broader foundation. While, for instance, the state of the photographic art was such that one's picture could seldom be taken without his consciously 'sitting' for the purpose, the law of contract or of trust might afford the prudent man sufficient safeguards against the improper circulation of his portrait; but since the latest advances in photographic art have rendered it possible to take pictures surreptitiously, the doctrines of contract and of trust are inadequate to support the required protection, and the law of tort must be resorted to. The right of property in its widest sense, including all possession, including all rights and privileges, and hence embracing the right to an inviolate personality, affords alone that broad basis upon which the protection which the individual demands can be rested.

Thus the courts, in searching for some principle upon which the publication of private letters could be enjoined, naturally came upon the ideas of a breach of confidence, and of an implied contract; but it required little consideration to discern that this doctrine could not afford all the protection required, since it would not support the court in granting a remedy against a stranger; and so the theory of property in the contents of letters was adopted. Indeed, it is difficult to conceive on what theory of the law the casual recipient of a letter, who proceeds to publish it, is guilty of a breach of contract, express or implied, or of any breach of trust, in the ordinary acceptance of that term. Suppose a letter had been addressed to him without his solicitation. He opens it, and reads. Surely, he has not made any contract; he has not accepted any trust. He cannot, by opening and reading the letter, have come under any obligation save what the law declares; and, however expressed, that obligation is simply to observe the legal right of the sender, whatever it may be, and whether it be called his right of property in the contents of the letter, or his right to privacy.

A similar groping for the principle upon which a wrongful publication can be enjoined is found in the law of trade secrets. There, injunctions have generally been granted on the theory of a breach of contract, or of an abuse of confidence. It would, of course, rarely happen that any one would be in the possession of a secret unless confidence had been reposed in him. But can it be supposed that the court would hesitate to grant relief against one who had obtained his knowledge by an ordinary trespass—for instance, by wrongfully looking into a book in which the secret was recorded, or by eavesdropping? Indeed, in *Yovatt v. Winyard*, 1 J. & W. 394 (1820), where an injunction was granted against making any use of or communicating certain recipes for veterinary medicine, it appeared that the defendant, while in the plaintiff's employ, had surreptitiously got access to his book of recipes, and copied them. Lord Eldon 'granted the injunction, upon the ground of there having been a breach of trust and confidence'; but it would seem to be difficult to draw any sound legal distinction between such a case and one where a mere stranger wrongfully obtained access to the book.

We must therefore conclude that the rights, so protected, whatever their exact nature, are not rights arising from contract or from special trust, but are rights as against the world; and as above stated, the principle which has been applied to protect these rights is in reality not the principle of private property, unless that word be used in an extended and unusual sense. The principle which protects personal writings and any other productions of the intellect or of the emotions, is the right to privacy, and the law has no new principle to formulate when it extends this protection to the personal appearance, sayings, acts, and to personal relation, domestic or otherwise.

If the invasion of privacy constitutes a legal *injuria*, the elements for demanding redress exist, since already the value of mental suffering, caused by an act wrongful in itself, is recognized as a basis for compensation.

The right of one who has remained a private individual, to prevent his public portraiture, presents the simplest case for such extension; the right to protect one's self from pen portraiture, from a discussion by the press of one's private affairs, would be a more important and far-reaching one. If casual and unimportant statements in a letter, if handiwork, however inartistic and valueless, if possessions of all sorts are protected not only against reproduction, but against description and enumeration, how much more should the acts and sayings of a man in his social and domestic relations be guarded from ruthless publicity. If you may not reproduce a woman's face photographically without her consent, how much less should be tolerated the reproduction of her face, her form, and her actions, by graphic descriptions coloured to suit a gross and depraved imagination.

The right to privacy, limited as such right must necessarily be, has already found expression in the law of France.

It remains to consider what are the limitations of this right to privacy, and what remedies may be granted for the enforcement of the right. To determine in advance of experience the exact line at which the dignity and convenience of the individual must yield to the demands of the public welfare or of private justice would be a difficult task; but the more general rules are furnished by the legal analogies already developed in the law of slander and libel, and in the law of literary and artistic property.

1. The right to privacy does not prohibit any publication of matter which is of public and general interest.

In determining the scope of this rule, aid would be afforded by the analogy, in the law of slander and libel, of cases which deal with the qualified privilege of comment and criticism on matters of public and general interest. There are of course difficulties in applying such a rule; but they are inherent in the subject-matter, and are certainly no greater than those which exist in many other branches of the law— for instance, in that large class of cases in which the reasonableness or unreasonableness of an act is made the test of liability. The design of the law must be to protect those persons with whose affairs the community has no legitimate concern, from being dragged into an undesirable and undesired publicity; and to protect all persons, whatsoever their position or station, from having matters which they may properly prefer to keep private, made public against their will. It is the unwarranted invasion of individual privacy which is reprehended, and to be, so far as possible, prevented. The distinction, however, noted in the above statement is obvious and fundamental. There are persons who may reasonably claim as a right, protection from the notoriety entailed by being made the victims of journalistic enterprise. There are others who, in varying degrees, have renounced the right to live their lives screened from public observation. Matters which men of the first class may justly contend, concern themselves alone, may in those of the second be the subject of legitimate interest to their fellow-citizens. Peculiarities of manner and person, which in the ordinary individual should be free from comment, may acquire a public importance, if found in a candidate for political office. Some further discrimination is necessary, therefore, than to class facts or deeds as public or private according to a standard to be applied to the fact or deed *per se*. To publish of a modest and retiring individual tha the suffers from an impediment in his speech or that he cannot spell correctly, is an unwarranted, if not an unexampled, infringement of his rights, while to state and comment on the same characteristics found in a would-be congressman could not be regarded as beyond the pale of propriety.

The general object in view is to protect the privacy of private life, and to whatever degree and in whatever connection a man's life has ceased to be private, before the publication under consideration has been made, to that extent the protection is to be withdrawn. Since, then, the propriety of publishing the very same facts may depend wholly upon the person concerning whom they are published, no fixed formula can be used to prohibit obnoxious publication. Any rule of liability adopted must have in it an elasticity which shall take account of the varying circumstances of each case—a necessity which unfortunately renders such a doctrine not only more difficult of application, but also to a certain extent uncertain in its operation and easily rendered abortive. Besides, it is only the more flagrant breaches of decency and propriety that could in practice be reached, and it is not perhaps desirable even to attempt to repress everything which the nicest taste and keenest sense of the respect due to private life would condemn.

In general, then, the matters of which the publication should be repressed may be described as those which concern the private life, habits, acts, and relations of an individual, and have no legitimate connection with his fitness for a public office which he seeks or for which he is suggested, or for any public or quasi-public position which he seeks or for which he is suggested, and have no legitimate relation to or bearing upon any act done by him in a public or quasi-public capacity. The foregoing is not designed as a wholly accurate or exhaustive definition, since that which must ultimately in a vast number of cases become a question of individual judgment and opinion is incapable of such definition; but it is an attempt to indicate broadly the class of matters referred to. Some things all men alike are entitled to keep from popular curiosity, whether in public life or not, while others are only private because the persons concerned have not assumed a position which makes their doing legitimate matters of public investigation.

2. The right to privacy does not prohibit the communication of any matter, though in its nature private, when the publication is made under circumstances which would render it a privileged communication according to the law of slander and libel.

Under this rule, the right to privacy is not invaded by any publication made in a court of justice, in legislative bodies, or the committees of those bodies; in municipal assemblies, or the committees of such assemblies, or practically by any communication made in any other public body, municipal or parochial, or in any body quasi-public, like the large voluntary associations formed for almost every purpose of benevolence, business, or other general interest; and (at least in many jurisdiction) reports of any such proceedings would in some measure be accorded a like privilege. Nor would the rule prohibit any publication made by one in the discharge of some public or private duty, whether legal or moral, or in conduct of one's own affairs, in matters where his own interest is concerned.

3. The law would probably not grant any redress for the invasion of privacy by oral publication in the absence of special damage.

The same reasons exist for distinguishing between oral and written publication of private matters, as is afforded in the law of defamation by the restricted liability for slander as compared with the liability for libel. The injury resulting from such oral communications would ordinarily be so trifling that the law might well, in the interest of free speech, disregard it altogether.

4. The right to privacy ceases upon the publication of the facts by the individual, or with his consent.

This is but another application of the rule which has become familiar in the law of literary and artistic property. The cases there decided establish also what should be deemed a publication—the important principle in this connection being that a private communication or circulation for a restricted purpose is not a publication within the meaning of the law.

5. The truth of the matter published does not afford a defence. Obviously this branch of the law should have no concern with the truth or falsehood of the matters published. It is not for injury to the individual's character that redress or prevention is sought, but for injury to the right of privacy. For the former, the law of slander and libel provides perhaps a sufficient safeguard. The latter implies the right not merely to prevent inaccurate portrayal of private life, but to prevent its being depicted at all.

6. The absence of 'malice' in the publisher does not afford a defence.

Personal ill-will is not an ingredient of the offence, any more than in an ordinary case of trespass to person or to property. Such malice is never necessary to be shown in an action for libel or slander at common law, except in rebuttal of some defence, e.g., that the occasion rendered the communication privileged, or, under the statutes in this State and elsewhere, that the statement complained of was true. The invasion of the privacy that is to be protected is equally complete and equally injurious, whether the motives by which the speaker or writer was actuated are, taken by themselves, culpable or not; just as the damage to character, and to some extent the tendency to provoke a breach of the peace, is equally the result of defamation without regard to the motives leading to its publication. Viewed as a wrong to the individual, this rule is the same pervading the whole law of torts, by which one is held responsible for his intentional acts, even though they are committed with no sinister intent; and viewed as a wrong to society, it is the same principle adopted in a large category of statutory offences.

The remedies for an invasion of the right of privacy are also suggested by those administered in the law of defamation, and in the law of literary and artistic property, namely:

1. An action for tort for damages in all cases. Even in the absence of special damages, substantial compensation could be allowed for injury to feelings as in the action of slander and libel.

2. An injunction, in perhaps a very limited class of cases.

It would doubtless be desirable that the privacy of the individual should receive the added protection of the criminal law, but for this, legislation would be required. Perhaps it would be deemed proper to bring the criminal liability for such publication within narrower limits; but that the community has an interest in preventing such invasions of privacy, sufficiently strong to justify the introduction of such a remedy, cannot be doubted. Still, the protection of society must come mainly through a recognition of the rights of the individual. Each man is responsible for his own acts and omissions only. If he condones what he reprobates, with a weapon at hand equal to his defence, he is responsible for the results. If he resists, public opinion will rally to his support. Has he then such a weapon? It is believed that the common law provides him with one, forged in the slow fire of the centuries, and today fitly tempered to his hand. The common law has always recognized a man's house as his castle, impregnable, often, even to its own officers engaged in the execution of its commands. Shall the courts thus close the front entrance to constituted authority, and open wide the back door to idle or prurient curiosity?

Benjamin N. Cardozo

Law and Literature

*Mr Justice Cardozo (1868–1938), a justice of the Supreme Court of the United States for the last six years of his life, was, after Mr Justice Holmes, the brightest judicial luminary of the American legal scene. Cardozo, who came from Holland of a Sephardi-Jewish family which had originally intended settling in England, displayed the rare combination of immense legal scholarship and a mode of expressing himself both as a judge and jurist with all the qualities of a Lamb or a Hazlitt. Between 1922 and 1928 while he was a member of the Court of Appeals in New York there flowed from his pen three small volumes—*The Nature of the Judicial Process, The Growth of the Law *and* The Paradoxes of Legal Science*—which rank among the most significant works of juristic thought. He wrote with equal distinction when handing down his judicial decisions, many of them in his last years involving important constitutional issues.*

Cardozo had also the humility that goes hand in glove with true greatness. In his essay reprinted below he acclaimed the English judiciary as masters of English prose. In the wielding of the weapons of the epigram and the homely illustration he claimed that the English judges were supreme. Yet it was Cardozo himself, his mentor Holmes, and his colleague Learned Hand (all American judges) who excelled in the art of legal literature within the English-speaking world.

Cardozo's Law and Literature *appeared originally in the* Yale Review *of 1925 and was subsequently included in an issue of the* Harvard Law Review *of 1939 as part of an edition dedicated to the late judge's memory. In it Cardozo confesses to his own secret of success as a great judge. He suggests that a profession of words can only have grandeur if artistry accompanies the written word. If this is the equation of a great judge then Cardozo amply justified the epithet of judge and jurist of pre-eminence.*

I AM told at times by friends that a judicial opinion has no business to be literature. The idol must be ugly, or he may be taken for a common man. The deliverance that is to be accepted without demur or hesitation must have a certain high austerity which frowns at winning graces. I fancy that not a little of this criticism is founded in misconception of the true significance of literature, or, more accurately perhaps, of literary style. To some a clearer insight has been given. There are those who have perceived that the highest measure of condensation, of short and sharp and imperative directness, a directness that speaks the voice of some external and supreme authority, is consistent, none the less, with supreme literary excellence. A dictum of Henri Beyle's, recalled not long ago by Mr Strachey, will point my meaning. The French novelist used to say that 'there was only one example of the perfect style, and that was the Code Napoléon; for there alone everything was subordinated to the exact and complete expression of what was to be said'. The poor man succumbed to its charm to such an extent that he was in the habit of reading a few paragraphs every morning before breakfast. I do not seek to substitute this regimen for the daily exercise in calisthenics. Some of us prefer our literature like our food in less concentrated tablets. I do no more than suggest that the morsel hastily gulped down may have a savour all its own for the discriminating palate.

But I over-emphasize and exaggerate if I seem to paint the picture of any active opposition that is more than sporadic and exceptional to so amiable a weakness as a love of art and letters. A commoner attitude with lawyers is one, not of active opposition, but of amused or cynical indifference. We are merely wasting our time, so many will inform us, if we bother about form when only substance is important. I suppose this might be true if any one could tell us where substance ends and form begins. Philosophers have been trying for some thousands of years to draw the distinction between substance and mere appearance. in the world of matter. I doubt whether they succeed better when they attempt a like distinction in the world of thought. Form is not something added to substance as a mere protuberant adornment. The two are fused into a unity. Not long ago I ran across a paragraph in the letters of Henry James in which he blurts out his impatience of these attempts to divide the indivisible. He is writing to Hugh Walpole, now a novelist of assured position, but then comparatively unknown. 'Don't let any one persuade you—there are plenty of ignorant and ratuous duffers to try to do it—that strenuous selection and comparison are not the very essence of art, and that Form *is* not substance to that degree that there is absolutely no substance without it. Form alone *takes*, and holds and preserves substance, saves it from the welter of helpless verbiage that we swim in as in a sea of tasteless tepid pudding.' This is my own faith. The argument strongly put is not the same as the argument put feebly any more than the 'tasteless tepid pudding' is the same as the pudding served to us in triumph with all the glory of the lambent flame. The strength that is born of form and the feebleness that is born of the lack of form are in truth qualities of the substance. They are the tokens of the thing's identity. They make it what it is.

Up to this point at least, I have little fear of opposition. We shall, most of us, be agreed, I think, not merely that style is not an evil in the Sahara of a judicial opinion, but even that it is a positive good, if only it is the right style. *There* is the disquieting condition which checks the forward movement of triumphal demonstration. What is to be deemed the right style, or the right styles if there are more than one of them? Do the examples of the great masters reveal some uniformity of method for the instruction of the tyro? If uniformity is not discoverable, may there not at least be types or standards? If types or standards do not exist, shall we not find stimulus and interest in the coruscations of genius, however vagrant or irregular? If at times there is neither stimulus nor interest, may there not in lieu of these be the awful warning of example?

I suppose there can be little doubt that in matters of literary style the sovereign virtue for the judge is clearness. Judge Veeder in his interesting and scholarly essay, 'A Century of Judicature', quotes the comment of Brougham upon the opinions of Lord Stowell: 'If ever the praise of being luminous could be bestowed upon human compositions, it was upon his judgments.' How shall his successors in the same or other courts attain that standard or approach it? There is an accuracy that defeats itself by the over-emphasis of details. I often say that one must permit oneself, and that quite advisedly and deliberately, a certain margin of misstatement. Of course, one must take heed that the margin is not exceeded, just as the physician must be cautious in administering the poisonous ingredient which magnified will kill, but in tiny quantities will cure. On the other hand, the sentence may be so overloaded with all its possible qualifications that it will tumble down of its own weight. 'To philosophize,' says Holmes in one of his opinions—I am quoting him from uncertain and perhaps inaccurate recollection—'to philosophize is to generalize, but to generalize is to omit.' The picture cannot be painted if the significant and the insignificant are given equal prominence. One must know how to select. All these generalities are as easy as they are obvious, but, alas! the application is an ordeal to try the souls of men. Write an opinion, and read it a few years later when it is dissected in the briefs of counsel. You will learn for the first time the limitations of the power of speech, or, if not those of speech in general, at all events your own. All sorts of gaps and obstacles and impediments will obtrude themselves before your gaze, as pitilessly manifest as the hazards on a golf course. Sometimes you will know that the fault is truly yours, in which event you can only smite your breast, and pray for deliverance thereafter. Sometimes you will feel that the fault is with counsel who have stupidly misread the obvious, in which event, though you rail against the bar and the imperfect medium of speech, you will be solaced, even in your chagrin, by a sense of injured innocence. Sometimes, though rarely, you will believe that the misreading is less stupid than malicious, in which event you will be wise to keep your feelings to yourself. One marvels sometimes at the ingenuity with which texts the most remote are made to serve the ends of argument or parable. But clearness, though the sovereign quality, is not the only one to be pursued, and even if it were, may be gained through many avenues of approach. The opinion will need persuasive force, or the impressive virtue of sincerity and fire, or the mnemonic power of alliteration and antithesis, or the terseness and tang of the proverb and the maxim. Neglect the help of these allies, and it may never win its way. With traps and obstacles and hazards confronting us on every hand, only blindness or indifference will fail to turn in all humility, for guidance or for warning, to the study of examples.

Classification must be provisional, for forms run into one another. As I search the archives of my memory, I seem to discern six types or methods which divide themselves from one another with measurable distinctness. There is the type magisterial or imperative; the type laconic or sententious; the type conversational or homely; the type refined or artificial, smelling of the lamp, verging at times upon preciosity or euphuism; the type demonstrative or persuasive; and finally the type tonsorial or agglutinative, so called from the shears and the pastepot which are its implements and emblem.

I place first in order, for it is first in dignity and power, the type magisterial or imperative. It eschews ornament. It is meagre in illustration and analogy. If it argues, it does so with the downward rush and overwhelming conviction of the syllogism, seldom with tentative gropings towards the inductive apprehension of a truth imperfectly discerned. We hear the voice of the law speaking by its consecrated ministers with the calmness and assurance that are born of a sense of mastery and power. Thus Marshall seemed to judge, and a hush falls upon us even now as we listen to his words. Those organ tones of his were meant to fill cathedrals or the most exalted of tribunals. The judicial department, he tells us, 'has no will in any case. . . . Judicial power is never exercised for the purpose of giving effect to the will of the judge; always for the purpose of giving effect to the will of the legislature; or in other words, to the will of the law.' The thrill is irresistible. We feel the mystery and the awe of inspired revelation. His greatest judgments are framed upon this plane of exaltation and aloofness. The movement from premise to conclusion is put before the observer as something more impersonal than the working of the individual mind. It is the inevitable progress of an inexorable force. Professor Corwin in an interesting volume, *John Marshall and the Constitution*, shows how even his contemporaries, the bitterest critics of his aggrandizement of federal power, were touched by this illusion. 'All wrong, all wrong,' lamented John Randolph of Roanoke, 'but no man in the United States can tell why or wherein.' I have reread a few of the most famous of his judgments: *Marbury v. Madison; Gibbons v. Ogden; McCulloch v. Maryland*; they are all in the grand style.

Listen to the voice of the magistrate in *Marbury v. Madison*: 'The distinction between a government with limited and unlimited powers is abolished if those limits do not confine the persons on which they are imposed, and if acts prohibited and acts allowed are of equal obligation. It is a proposition too plain to be contested: that the Constitution controls any legislative act repugnant to it; or that the legislature may alter the Constitution by an ordinary act. Between these alternatives there is no middle ground. . . . If two laws conflict with each other, the courts must decide on the operation of each. So if a law be in opposition to the Constitution; if both the law and the Constitution apply to a particular case, so that the court must either decide that case conformably to the law, disregarding the Constitution, or conformably to the Constitution, disregarding the law, the court must determine which of these conflicting rules governs the case. This is of the very essence of judicial duty.' Nothing is here of doubt; nothing of apology; no blurred edges or uncertain lines. 'There is no middle ground.' The choice that is made is 'of the very essence of judicial duty'. The voice has pealed forth. Let the wicked heed it and obey.

One will find this same suggestion of sure and calm conviction in some of the judgments of Lord Mansfield. The slave Somersett captured on the coast of Africa, is sold in bondage in Virginia, and brought to England by his master. The case comes before Mansfield on the return to the writ of habeas corpus: 'The state of slavery is of such a nature that it is incapable of being introduced on any reasons, moral or political, but only positive law, which preserved its force long after the reasons, occasions, and time itself from whence it was created, are erased from memory. It is so odious that nothing can be suffered to support it, but positive law. . . . I care not for the supposed *dicta* of judges, however eminent, if they be contrary to all principle. The *dicta* cited were probably misunderstood, and at all events they are to be disregarded. Villainage, when it did exist in this country, differed in many particulars from West India slavery. The lord never could have thrown his villain, whether *regardant* or *in gross*, into chains, sent him to the West Indies, and sold him there to work in a mine or in a cane field. At any rate villainage has ceased in England, and it cannot be revived. The air of England has long been too pure for a slave, and every man is free who breathes it. Every man who comes into England is entitled to the protection of English law, whatever oppression he may heretofore have suffered, and whatever may be the colour of his skin. "*Quamvis ille niger, quamvis tu candidus esses.*" Let the negro be discharged.'

It is thus men speak when they are conscious of their power. One does not need to justify oneself if one is the mouthpiece of divinity. The style will fit the mood.

I have said that in dignity and power there is no method that can be matched with the method which I have characterized as magisterial or imperative. A changing philosophy of law has tended, none the less, to the use of other methods more conciliatory and modest. The development of law is conceived of, more and more, as a process of adaptation and adjustment. The pronouncements of its ministers are timid and tentative approximations, to be judged through their workings, by some pragmatic test of truth. I find in a dissenting opinion by Mr Justice Brandeis a striking statement of this attitude of mind. Arguing for the restriction of a rule which had proved itself unworkable, he says: 'Such limitations of principles previously announced and such express disapproval of *dicta* are often unnecessary. It is an unavoidable incident of the search by courts of last resort for the true rule. The process of inclusion and exclusion, so often applied in developing a rule, cannot end with its first enunciation. The rule as announced must be deemed tentative. For the many and varying facts to which it will be applied cannot be foreseen. Modification implies growth. It is the life of the law.'

One cannot face the law in this spirit of cautious seeking without showing the changing point of view in a changing style and form. Universals will be handled more charily under the dominance of such a philosophy than in days when the law of nature supplied us with data that were supposed to be eternal and unyielding. Yet there are times even now when the magisterial method is utilized by men who know that they are masters of their calling. It is still utilized in fields where some established principle is to be applied to new facts or where the area of its extension or restriction is fairly obvious or narrow. But alas! even then it is the masters, and no others, who feel sure enough of themselves to omit the intermediate steps and stages, and leap to the conclusion. Most of us are so uncertain of our strength, so beset with doubts and difficulties, that we feel oppressed with the need of justifying every holding by analogies and precedents and an exposure of the reasons. The masters are content to say, 'The elect will understand, there is no need to write for others'. Perhaps there are opinions by Mr Justice Holmes in which this mood can be discerned. The sluggard unable to keep pace with the swiftness of his thought will say that he is hard to follow. If that is so, it is only for the reason that he is walking with a giant's stride. But giants, after all, are not met at every turn, and for most of us, even if we are not pygmies, the gait of ordinary men is the safer manner of advance. We grope and feel our way. What we hand down in our judgments is an hypothesis. It is no longer a divine command.

I pass to other types which run into each other by imperceptible gradations, the laconic or sententious and the conversational or homely. There has been no stage of our legal history in which these methods have been neglected. The Year Books are full of wise saws and homely illustrations, the epigram, the quip, the jest. Perhaps this is but a phase of that use of the maxim or the proverb which is characteristic of legal systems in early stages of development. Dean Pound in a recent paper has traced the growth and function of the maxim with all the resources of his learning. If the maxim has declined in prevalence and importance, now that the truths of the law have become too complex to be forced within a sentence, there has been no abatement of recourse to the laconic or sententious phrase, to drive home and imbed what might otherwise be lost or scattered. Who will resist Lord Nottingham's adjuration: 'Pray let us so resolve cases here, that they may stand with the reason of mankind when they are debated abroad'? Is there any armour proof against a thrust like the dictum of Lord Bowen's: 'The state of a man's mind is as much a fact as the state of his digestion'? Next door to the epigram is the homely illustration which makes its way and sinks deep by its appeal to everyday experience. In the wielding of these weapons, the English judges have been masters. The precept may be doubtful in the beginning. How impossible to fight against it when the judge brings it down to earth and makes it walk the ground, the brother of some dictate of decency or of prudence which we have followed all our lives. Perhaps the kinship is not so close or apparent as it is figured. Who of us will have the hardihood to doubt the reality of the tie when it is so blandly assumed to be obvious to all? The common denominator silences and satisfies. The rule that is rooted in identities or analogies of customary belief and practice is felt and rightly felt to be rooted in reality. We glide into acquiescence when negation seems to question our kinship with the crowd. Something must be set down also to the sense of fellowship awakened when judges talk in ways that seem to make us partners in the deliberate process. 'I entirely agree with my right honourable and learned friend upon the woolsack.' We seem to be let into the mysteries of the conference, the sacrosanct 'arcana', to quote Professor Powell's phrase, to which 'the uninitiated are not admitted'. Given such an atmosphere, with point and pungency thrown into it, the product makes its way into every crack and crevice of our being.

I limit my illustrations, though many are available. Take this by Lord Bramwell: 'It does not follow that if a man dies in a fit in a railway carriage, there is a *prima facie* case for his widow and children, nor that if he has a glass in his pocket and sits on it and hurts himself, there is something which calls for an answer or explanation from the company.' Take this by Lord Blackburn: 'If with intent to lead the plaintiff to act upon it, they put forth a statement which they know may bear two meanings, one of which is false to their knowledge, and thereby the plaintiff, putting that meaning upon it, is misled, I do not think they can escape by saying he ought to have put the other. If they palter with him, in a double sense, it may be that they lie like truth, but I think they lie, and it is a fraud.' One could cite other examples without number. What a cobweb of fine-spun casuistry is dissipated in a breath by the simple statement of Lord Esher in *Ex parte Simonds*, that the court will not suffer its own officer 'to do a shabby thing'. If the word shabby had been left out, and unworthy or dishonourable substituted, I suppose the sense would have been much the same. But what a drop in emotional value would have followed. As it is, we feel the tingle of the hot blood of resentment mounting to our cheeks. For quotable good things, for pregnant aphorisms, for touchstones of ready application, the opinions of the English judges are a mine of instruction and a treasury of joy.

Such qualities on the whole are rarer close at home, yet we have one judge even now who can vie with the best of his English brethren, past as well as present, in the art of packing within a sentence the phosphorescence of a page. If I begin to quote from the opinions of Mr Justice Holmes, I hardly know where I shall end, yet fealty to a master makes me reluctant to hold back. The sheaf will be a tiny one, made up haphazard, the barest sample of the riches which the gleaner may gather where he will. Some hint of the epigrammatic quality of his style may be found in this: 'The Fourteenth Amendment, itself a historical product, did not destroy history for the States and substitute mechanical compartments of law all exactly alike.' In this: 'We are in danger of forgetting that a strong public desire to improve the public condition is not enough to warrant achieving the desire by a shorter cut than the constitutional way of paying for the change.' In this: 'Legal obligations that exist but cannot be enforced are ghosts that are seen in the law but that are elusive to the grasp.' And finally in this, words of solemn dissent, their impressiveness heightened by the knowledge that the cause has been already lost: 'Persecution for the expression of opinions seems to me perfectly logical. If you have no doubt of your premises or your power and want a certain result with all your heart you naturally express your wishes in law and sweep away all opposition. To allow opposition by speech seems to indicate that you think the speech impotent, as when a man says that he has squared the circle, or that you do not care whole-heartedly for the result, or that you doubt either your power or your premises. But when men have realized that time has upset many fighting faiths, they may come to believe even more than they believe the very foundations of their own conduct that the ultimate good desired is better reached by free trade in ideas—that the best test of truth is the power of the thought to get itself accepted·in the competition of the market, and that truth is the only ground upon which their wishes safely can be carried out. That at any rate is the theory of our Constitution. It is an experiment, as all life is an experiment. Every year if not every day we have to wager our salvation upon some prophecy based upon imperfect knowledge. While that experiment is part of our system I think that we should be eternally vigilant against attempts to check the expression of opinions that we loathe and believe to be fraught with death, unless they so imminently threaten immediate interference with the lawful and pressing purposes of the law that an immediate check is required to save the country.'

There is another type or method which I have spoken of as the refined or artificial, smelling a little of the lamp. With its merits it has dangers, for unless well kept in hand, it verges at times upon preciosity and euphuism. Held in due restraint, it lends itself admirably to cases where there is need of delicate precision. I find no better organon where the subject matter of discussion is the construction of a will with all the filigree of tentacles, the shades and nuances of differences, the slender and fragile tracery that must be preserved unmutilated and distinct. Judge Finch of the Court of Appeals of New York was an adept in the writing of opinions which carried with them this suggestion of precision and refinement. Occasionally, it shades into a faint and gentle sarcasm which is sometimes the refuge of the spokesman of a minority expressing his dissent. As an illustration, let me quote from the dissenting opinion in an election controversy which provoked in its day no little warmth of difference. The majority had held that despite the provision of the Constitution making each house of the legislature the judge of the elections, returns, and qualifications of its own members, the courts would refuse affirmative aid to a claimant for such an office if it found him ineligible in its own view of the law. Judge Finch protested against this holding. 'And so,' he said, 'I deny the asserted doctrine of "Invocation"; of a right to do evil that good may come; of excusable judicial usurpation; and if the doctrine has anywhere got its dangerous and destructive hold upon our law, which I do not believe, it should be resolutely shaken off. But let us not deceive ourselves. The excess of jurisdiction is not even excusable, for it has neither occasion nor necessity.' A moment later, he has his fears that he has been betrayed into excessive warmth. His closing words are those of apology and deference: 'If what I have said does not convince the majority of the court, nothing that I can say will do so. I have tried faithfully, and, I hope, with proper respect, for certainly I have not meant to be wanting in that, to point out the mistake which, it seems to me, they are about to make. Theirs, however, must be both the responsibility and its consequences.'

Such a method has its charm and its attraction, though one feels at times the yearning for another more robust and virile. It is here that I pass into the type which I have characterized as demonstrative or persuasive. It is not unlike the magisterial or imperative, yet it differs in a certain amplitude of development, a freer use of the resources of illustration and analogy and history and precedent, in brief, a tone more suggestive of the scientific seeker for the truth and less reminiscent of the priestess on the tripod. One might cite many judges who have used this method with distinction. I think the work of Charles Andrews, for many years a judge and then the Chief Judge of the New York Court of Appeals, is a shining illustration. I can best describe the quality of his opinions in the words of a memorial written upon his death: 'The majesty of his personal appearance,' it was said, 'is reflected in the majesty of his judicial style, the steady and stately march of his opinions from established premises to inevitable conclussions.' Such a method, well pursued, has a sanity and a clarity that make it an admirable medium for the declaration of considered judgments. The form is no mere epidermis. It is the very bone and tissue.

My summary of styles may leave a cheerless impression of the solemn and the ponderous. Flashes of humour are not unknown, yet the form of opinion which aims at humour from beginning to end is a perilous adventure, which can be justified only by success, and even then is likely to find its critics almost as many as its eulogists. The story is told by Bernard Shaw of a man who wished to consult the writings of the great naturalist Buffon, and who startled the clerks in the bookstore by the pompous and solemn query, 'Have you the books of the celebrated Buffoon?' One of the difficulties about the humorous opinion is exposure to the risk of passing from the class of Buffons where we all like to dwell and entering the class of the celebrated Buffoons. The transition at times is distressingly swift, and when once one has entered the new class, it is difficult, if not indeed impossible, to climb over the fences and back into the old. None the less, there are subjects which only the most resolute have been able to discuss without yielding to the temptation of making profert of their sense of humour. A dog or a cat, or a horse if it is the occasion of a horse trade, has been the signal for unexpected outbursts of mirth and occasionally of pathos from judges slowly stirred to emotion by the cinema of life.

Judge Allen's opinion on the 'code duello' among dogs, was on the whole a fine success, but it has been responsible for the writing of some others that were not. There is an opinion by Baron Bramwell which deals with the propensities of pigs. A fence was defective, and the pigs straying did mischief to a trolley car. The decision was that the barrier should have been sufficient to protect the adjoining owner against the incursions, not of all pigs, but of pigs of 'average vigour and obstinacy'. 'Nor do we lay down,' said the learned Baron, 'that there must be a fence so close and strong that no pig could push through it, or so high that no horse or bullock could leap it. One could scarcely tell the limits of such a requirement, for the strength of swine is such that they would break through almost any fence, if there were a sufficient inducement on the other side. But the company are bound to put up such a fence that a pig not of a peculiarly wandering disposition, nor under any excessive temptation, will not get through it.' Perhaps the humour of this ruling was more unwitting than designed. Some may agree with Sir Frederick Pollock that the decision is 'almost a caricature of the general idea of the "reasonable man".' In all this I would not convey the thought that an opinion is the worst for being lightened by a smile. I am merely preaching caution. Other flights and digressions I find yet more doubtful than the humorous. In days not far remote, judges were not unwilling to embellish their deliverances with quotations from the poets. I shall observe towards such a practice the tone of decent civility that is due to those departed.

I have had in mind in this excursus a humour that was conscious and intended. Perhaps I should have classed the opinion that is humorous or playful as an independent type, but I have preferred to treat it incidentally since I am not aware that any judge has employed it consistently or except on rare occasions. Humour also that is unconscious and unintended may be dug out of the reports if we take the trouble to extract it. I once gathered together for my own edification and amusement some gems that I had unearthed from the opinions of one of our local courts in days when it had an appellate branch of its own and handed down opinions which were faithfully reported. Unluckily, I have lost my memorandum, but a few of the items are still vivid in my mind. The question to be determined was the extent of the amendment of a pleading to be permitted upon the trial. The decisive principle was thus expounded: 'The bed that litigants make and lie in up to the trial, should not be then vacated by them. They should continue to lie therein until the jury render their verdict.' I understand that the modern Practice Acts have swept this principle away, and that the suitor, who seems to his adversary to be innocently somnolent, may now jump out of bed at the last moment and prove to be very much awake. This is the new doctrine, but where will you find a more vivid statement of the doctrine of an elder day which decried surprise and haste, and was satisfied that justice herself should have the privilege of a nap? I recall, too, a charge to a jury never reported, but surely fit to be preserved. 'In this case,' said the trial judge, 'I believe that Mr A (the counsel for the plaintiff) knows as much law as Mr B (the counsel for the defendant), and I believe that Mr B knows as much law as Mr A, but I believe that I in my judicial capacity know as much law as both of them together.' Whereupon he forgot to tell the jury anything else, but said they were to consider of their verdict and decide the case in accordance with the rules he had laid down. Well, his charge was sparse, but it enunciated an important truth. Our whole judicial system is built upon some such assumption as the learned judge put forward a trifle crassly and obscurely. This is the great convention, the great fiction, which makes trial in court a fair substitute for trial by battle or by casting lots. The philosopher will find philosophy if he has an eye for it even in a 'crowner's' court.

I must not forget my final type of judicial style, the tonsorial or agglutinative. I will not expatiate upon its horrors. They are known but too well. The dreary succession of quotations closes with a brief paragraph expressing a firm conviction that judgment for plaintiff or for defendant, as the case may be, follows as an inevitable conclusion. The writer having delivered himself of this expression of a perfect faith, commits the product of his hand to the files of the court and the judgment of the ages with all the pride of authorship. I am happy to be able to report that this type is slowly but steadily disappearing. As contrasted with its arid wastes, I prefer the sunny, though rather cramped and narrow, pinnacle of a type once much in vogue: 'We have carefully examined the record and find no error therein; *therefore* the judgment must be affirmed with costs.' How nice a sense of proportion, of the relation between cause and effect, is involved in the use of the illative conjunction 'therefore', with its suggestion that other minds less sensitively attuned might have drawn a different conclusion from the same indisputable premises.

I have touched lightly, almost not at all, upon something more important than mere felicities or turn of phrase. Above and beyond all these are what we may term the architectonics of opinions. The groupings of fact and argument and illustration so as to produce a cumulative and mass effect; these, after all, are the things that count above all others. I should despair, however, of any successful analysis of problems at once so large and so difficult within the limits of this paper. One needs a larger easel if one is to follow such a map. Often clarity is gained by a brief and almost sententious statement at the outset of the problem to be attacked. Then may come a fuller statement of the facts, rigidly pared down, however, in almost every case, to those that are truly essential as opposed to those that are decorative and adventitious. If these are presented with due proportion and selection, our conclusion ought to follow so naturally and inevitably as almost to prove itself. Whether it succeeds in doing this or not is something about which the readers of the opinion are not always in accord. To gain a proper breadth of view, one should consult counsel for the vanquished as well as counsel for the victor.

The thought of the vanquished brings me to the opinion that voices a dissent. The protests and the warnings of minorities overborne in the fight have their interest and significance for the student, not only of law itself, but of the literary forms through which law reaches its expression. Comparatively speaking at least, the dissenter is irresponsible. The spokesman of the court is cautious, timid, fearful of the vivid word, the heightened phrase. He dreams of an unworthy brood of scions, the spawn of careless *dicta*, disowned by the *ratio decidendi*, to which all legitimate offspring must be able to trace their lineage. The result is to cramp and paralyse. One fears to say anything when the peril of misunderstanding puts a warning finger to the lips. Not so, however, the dissenter. He has laid aside the role of the hierophant, which he will be only too glad to resume when the chances of war make him again the spokesman of the majority. For the moment, he is the gladiator making a last stand against the lions. The poor man must be forgiven a freedom of expression, tinged at rare moments with a touch of bitterness, which magnanimity as well as caution would reject for one triumphant.

A French judge, M. Ransson, a member of the Tribunal of the Seine, wrote some twenty years ago an essay on the art of judging, in which he depicts the feelings of a judge of the first instance when a judgment is reversed. I suppose the state of mind of one reversed is akin in quality to the state of mind of one dissenting, though perhaps differing in degree. 'A true magistrate', says M. Ransson, 'guided solely by his duty and his conscience, his learning and his reason, hears philosophically and without bitterness that his judgment has not been sustained; he knows that the higher court is there to this end, and that better informed beyond doubt, it has believed itself bound to modify his decision. Ought we even to condemn him, if having done his best, he maintains in his inmost soul the impression that perhaps and in spite of everything he was right? *Victrix causa deis placuit, sed victa Catoni.*' Cato had a fine soul, but history does not record that he feared to speak his mind, and judges when in the minority are tempted to imitate his candour. We need not be surprised, therefore, to find in dissent a certain looseness of texture and depth of colour rarely found in the *per curiam*. Sometimes, as I have said, there is just a suspicion of acerbity, but this, after all, is rare. More truly characteristic of dissent is a dignity, an elevation, of mood and thought and phrase. Deep conviction and warm feeling are saying their last say with knowledge that the cause is lost. The voice of the majority may be that of force triumphant, content with the plaudits of the hour, and recking little of the morrow. The dissenter speaks to the future, and his voice is pitched to a key that will carry through the years. Read some of the great dissents, the opinion, for example, of Judge Curtis in *Dred Scott v. Sandford*, and feel after the cooling time of the better part of a century the glow and fire of a faith that was content to bide its hour. The prophet and the martyr do not see the hooting throng. Their eyes are fixed on the eternities.

I shall be travelling away from my subject if I leave the writing of opinions and turn to arguments at the bar. A word of digression may be pardoned, however, for the two subjects are allied. One is called upon often to make answer to the question, what sort of argument is most effective in an appellate court? Shall it be long or short, terse or discursive? Shall it assume that the judges know the rudiments of law or shall it attempt in a brief hour to supply the defects in their early training? Shall it state the law or the facts? Shall it take up the authorities and analyse them, or shall it content itself with conclusions and leave analysis for the study? There is, of course, no formula that will fit all situations in appellate courts or elsewhere. If, however, I had to prepare a list of 'Don'ts' for the guidance of the novice, I think I would say that only in the rarest instances is it wise to take up one decision after another for the purpose of dissection. Such autopsies have their value at times, but they are wearisome and gruesome scenes. In my list of Don'ts, I would add, don't state the minutiae of the evidence. The judges won't follow you, and if they followed, would forget. Don't attempt to supplement the defects of early training. Your auditors are hardened sinners, not easily redeemed. Above all, don't be long-winded. I have in mind a lawyer, now lifted to the bench, who argued the appeals for one of the civil subdivisions of the State. His arguments lasted about a quarter of an hour. He told us his point and sat down. The audience in the rear of the court-room might not applaud, but the audience in front did—at least in spirit—and since the latter audience has the votes, it is best to make your play for them. If you faithfully observe these cautions, let not your spirits droop too low when the decision is adverse, even though there be the added gall and wormwood of a failure of the court to crown your brilliant effort with the dignity of an opinion. Many a gallant argument has met the same unworthy fate.

Young men as they approach admission to the bar must sometimes say to themselves that the great problems have been solved, that the great battles of the forum have been fought, that the great opportunities are ended. There are moods in which for a moment I say the same thing to myself. If I do, the calendar of the following day is as likely as not to bring the exposure of the error. It is a false and cramping notion that cases are made great solely or chiefly by reason of something intrinsic in themselves. They are great by what we make of them. *McCulloch v. Maryland*—to chose almost at random—is one of the most famous cases of our history. I wonder, would it not be forgotten, and even perhaps its doctrine overruled, if Marshall had not put upon it the imprint of his genius. 'Not one of his great opinions,' says Professor Corwin, speaking of Marshall's work, 'but might easily have been decided on comparatively narrow grounds in precisely the same way in which he decided it on broad, general principles, but with the probable result that it would never again have been heard of outside the law courts.' So, too, the smaller issues await the transfiguring touch. 'To a genuine accountant,' says Charles Lamb, 'the difference of proceeds is as nothing. The fractional farthing is as dear to his heart as the thousands which stand before it. He is the true actor, who, whether his part be a prince or a peasant, must act it with like authority.' That is the spirit in which judge or advocate is to look upon his task. He is expounding a science, or a body of truth which he seeks to assimilate to a science, but in the process of exposition he is practising an art. The Muses look at him a bit impatiently and wearily at times. He has done a good deal to alienate them, and sometimes they refuse to listen, and are seen to stop their ears. They have a strange capacity, however, for the discernment of strains of harmony and beauty, no matter how diffused and scattered through the ether. So at times when work is finely done, one sees their faces change, and they take the worker by the hand. They know that by the lever of art the subject the most lowly can be lifted to the heights. Small, indeed, is the company dwelling in those upper spaces, but the few are also the elect.

Oliver Wendell Holmes Jr.

The Path of the Law

────────

Oliver Wendell Holmes Jr. (1841–1935), justice of the Supreme Court of the United States, ranks as one of the greatest jurists of the Anglo-Saxon world; his book on the Common Law is a classic. After an outstanding record at Harvard, where he displayed great literary talents, he prepared himself for a career at the Bar in spite of gloomy warnings by his famous father that no lawyer could achieve greatness as a man. In 1902 he was put on to the Supreme Court Bench where his liberal instincts made him as frequent a dissenter as a bold assenter to the Court's decisions.

The essay included here marks the beginning of the American realist theory of law. The essence of this theory is the playing down of abstract rules and a greater emphasis on what the courts actually do. Holmes rejected any idea of law in terms of morality although he did not deny the influence of morality. He maintained that it was just as necessary to look at law through the spectacles of the 'bad man' who cares only for the material consequences of legal administration; the 'bad man' knows nothing nor cares for legal rights and duties in a philosophical sense. Holmes's definition of law was the 'prophecies of what the Courts will do in fact'. This is something of a sociological view of law in which the behaviour patterns of the judges are observed and graphed.

WHEN WE study law we are not studying a mystery but a well-known profession. We are studying what we shall want in order to appear before judges, or to advise people in such a way as to keep them out of court. The reason why it is a profession, why people will pay lawyers to argue for them or to advise them, is that in societies like ours the command of the public force is entrusted to the judges in certain cases, and the whole power of the state will be put forth, if necessary, to carry out their judgments and decrees. People want to know under what circumstances and how far they will run the risk of coming against what is so much stronger than themselves, and hence it becomes a business to find out when this danger is to be feared. The object of our study, then, is prediction, the prediction of the incidence of the public force through the instrumentality of the courts.

The means of the study are a body of reports, of treatises, and of statutes, in this country and in England, extending back for six hundred years, and now increasing annually by hundreds. In these sibylline leaves are gathered the scattered prophecies of the past upon the cases in which the axe will fall. These are what properly have been called the oracles of the law. For the most important and pretty nearly the whole meaning of every new effort of legal thought is to make these prophecies more precise, and to generalize them into a thoroughly connected system. The process is one, from a lawyer's statement of a case, eliminating as it does all the dramatic elements with which his client's story has clothed it, and retaining only the facts of legal import, up to the final analyses and abstract universals of theoretic jurisprudence. The reason why a lawyer does not mention that his client wore a white hat when he made a contract, while Mrs Quickly would be sure to dwell upon it, along with the parcel, gilt goblet and the sea-coal fire, is that he foresees that the public force will act in the same way whatever his client had upon his head. It is to make the prophecies easier to be remembered and to be understood that the teachings of the decisions of the past are put into general propositions and gathered into text-books, or that statutes are passed in a general form. The primary rights and duties with which jurisprudence busies itself again are nothing but prophecies. One of the many evil effects of the confusion between legal and moral ideas, about which I shall have something to say in a moment, is that theory is apt to get the cart before the horse, and to consider the right or the duty as something existing apart from and independent of the consequences of its breach, to which certain sanctions are added afterward. But, as I shall try to show, a legal duty so called is nothing but a prediction that if a man does or omits certain things he will be made to suffer in this or that way by judgment of the court; and so of a legal right.

The number of our predictions when generalized and reduced to a system is not unmanageably large. They present themselves as a finite body of dogma which may be mastered within a reasonable time. It is a great mistake to be frightened by the ever-increasing number of reports. The reports of a given jurisdiction in the course of a generation take up pretty much the whole body of the law, and restate it from the present point of view. We could reconstruct the corpus from them if all that went before were burned. The use of the earlier reports is mainly historical, a use about which I shall have something to say before I have finished.

I wish, if I can, to lay down some first principles for the study of this body of dogma or systematized prediction which we call the law, for men who want to use it as the instrument of their business to enable them to prophesy in their turn, and, as bearing upon the study, I wish to point out an ideal which as yet our law has not attained.

The first thing for a businesslike understanding of the matter is to understand its limits, and therefore I think it desirable at once to point out and dispel a confusion between morality and law, which sometimes rises to the height of conscious theory, and more often and indeed constantly is making trouble in detail without reaching the point of consciousness. You can see very plainly that a bad man has as much reason as a good one for wishing to avoid an encounter with the public force, and therefore you can see the practical importance of the distinction between morality and law. A man who cares nothing for an ethical rule which is believed and practised by his neighbours is likely nevertheless to care a good deal to avoid being made to pay money, and will want to keep out of gaol if he can.

I take it for granted that no hearer of mine will misrepresent what I have to say as the language of cynicism. The law is the witness and external deposit of our moral life. Its history is the history of the moral development of the race. The practice of it, in spite of popular jests, tends to make good citizens and good men. When I emphasize the difference between law and morals I do so with reference to a single end, that of learning and understanding the law. For that purpose you must definitely master its specific marks, and it is for that that I ask you for the moment to imagine yourselves indifferent to other and greater things.

I do not say that there is not a wider point of view from which the distinction between law and morals becomes of secondary or no importance, as all mathematical distinctions vanish in presence of the infinite. But I do say that that distinction is of the first importance for the object which we are here to consider, a right study and mastery of the law as a business with well understood limits, a body of dogma enclosed within definite lines. I have just shown the practical reason for saying so. If you want to know the law and nothing else, you must look at it as a bad man, who cares only for the material consequences which such knowledge enables him to predict, not as a good one, who finds his reasons for conduct, whether inside the law or outside of it, in the vaguer sanctions of conscience. The theoretical importance of the distinction is no less, if you would reason on your subject aright. The law is full of phraseology drawn from morals, and by the mere force of language continually invites us to pass from one domain to the other without perceiving it, as we are sure to do unless we have the boundary constantly before our minds. The law talks about rights, and duties, and malice, and intent, and negligence, and so forth, and nothing is easier, or, I may say, more common in legal reasoning, than to take these words in their moral sense, at some stage of the argument, and so to drop into fallacy. For instance, when we speak of the rights of man in a moral sense, we mean to mark the limits of interference with individual freedom which we think are prescribed by conscience, or by our ideal, however reached. Yet it is certain that many laws have been enforced in the past, and it is likely that some are enforced now, which are condemned by the most enlightened opinion of the time, or which at all events pass the limit of interference as many consciences would draw it. Manifestly, therefore, nothing but confusion of thought can result from assuming that the rights of man in a moral sense are equally rights in the sense of the Constitution and the law. No doubt simple and extreme cases can be put of imaginable laws which the statute-making power would not dare to enact, even in the absence of written constitutional prohibitions, because the community would rise in rebellion and fight, and this gives some plausibility to the proposition that the law, if not a part of morality, is limited by it. But this limit of power is not coextensive with any system of morals. For the most part it falls far within the lines of any such system, and in some cases may extend beyond them, for reasons drawn from the habits of a particular people at a particular time. I once heard the late Professor Agassiz say that a German population would rise if you added two cents to the price of a glass of beer. A statute in such a case would be empty words, not because it was wrong, but because it could not be enforced. No one will deny that wrong statutes can be and are enforced, and we should not all agree as to which were the wrong ones.

The confusion with which I am dealing besets confessedly legal conceptions. Take the fundamental question, What constitutes the law? You will find some text writers telling you that it is something different from what is decided by the courts of Massachusetts, or England, that it is a system of reason, that it is a deduction from principles of ethics or admitted axioms or what not, which may or may not coincide with the decisions. But if we take the view of our friend the bad man we shall find that he does not care two straws for the axioms or deductions, but that he does want to know what the Massachusetts or English courts are likely to do in fact. I am much of this kind. The prophecies of what the courts will do in fact, and nothing more pretentious, are what I mean by the law.

Take again a notion which as popularly understood is the widest conception which the law contains—the notion of legal duty, to which already I have referred. We fill the word with all the content which we draw from morals. But what does it mean to a bad man? Mainly, and in the first place, a prophecy that if he does certain things he will be subjected to disagreeable consequences by way of imprisonment or compulsory payment of money. But from his point of view, what is the difference between being fined and being taxed a certain sum for doing a certain thing? That his point of view is the test of legal principles is shown by the many discussions which have arisen in the courts on the very question whether a given statutory liability is a penalty or a tax. On the answer to this question depends the decision whether conduct is legally wrong or right, and also whether a man is under compulsion or free. Leaving the criminal law on one side, what is the difference between the liability under the Mill Acts or statutes authorizing a taking by eminent domain and the liability for what we call a wrongful conversion of property where restoration is out of the question? In both cases the party taking another man's property has to pay its fair value as assessed by a jury, and no more. What significance is there in calling one taking right and another wrong from the point of view of the law? It does not matter, so far as the given consequence, the compulsory payment, is concerned, whether the act to which it is attached is described in terms of praise or in terms of blame, or whether the law purports to prohibit it or to allow it. If it matters at all, still speaking from the bad man's point of view, it must be because in one case and not in the other some further disadvantages, or at least some further consequences, are attached to the act by the law. The only other disadvantages thus attached to it which I ever have been able to think of are to be found in two somewhat insignificant legal doctrines, both of which might be abolished without much disturbance. One is, that a contract to do a prohibited act is unlawful, and the other, that, if one of two or more joint wrongdoers has to pay all the damages, he cannot recover contribution from his fellows. And that I believe is all. You see how the vague circumference of the notion of duty shrinks and at the same time grows more precise when we wash it with cynical acid and expel everything except the object of our study, the operations of the law.

Nowhere is the confusion between legal and moral ideas more manifest than in the law of contract. Among other things, here again the so-called primary rights and duties are invested with a mystic significance beyond what can be assigned and explained. The duty to keep a contract at common law means a prediction that you must pay damages if you do not keep it, and nothing else. If you commit a tort, you are liable to pay a compensatory sum. If you break a contract, you are liable to pay a compensatory sum unless the promised event comes to pass, and that is all the difference. But such a mode of looking at the matter stinks in the nostrils of those who think it advantageous to get as much ethics into the law as they can. It was good enough for Lord Coke, however, and here, as in many other cases, I am content to abide with him. In Bromage *v.* Genning, a prohibition was sought in the King's Bench against a suit in the marches of Wales for the specific performance of a covenant to grant a lease, and Coke said that it would subvert the intention of the covenantor, since he intends it to be at his election either to lose the damages or to make the lease. Sergeant Harris for the plaintiff confessed that he moved the matter against his conscience, and a prohibition was granted. This goes further than we should go now, but it shows what I venture to say has been the common law point of view from the beginning, although Mr Harriman, in his very able little book upon Contracts has been misled, as I humbly think, to a different conclusion.

I have spoken only of the common law, because there are some cases in which a logical justification can be found for speaking of civil liabilities as imposing duties in an intelligible sense. These are the relatively few in which equity will grant an injunction, and will enforce it by putting the defendant in prison or otherwise punishing ing him unless he complies with the order of the court. But I hardly think it advisable to shape general theory from the exception, and I think it would be better to cease troubling ourselves about primary rights and sanctions altogether, than to describe our prophecies concerning the liabilities, commonly imposed by the law in those inappropriate terms.

I mentioned, as other examples of the use by the law of words drawn from morals, malice, intent, and negligence. It is enough to take malice as it is used in the law of civil liability for wrongs, what we lawyers call the law of torts, to show you that it means something different in law from what it means in morals, and also to show how the difference has been obscured by giving to principles which have little or nothing to do with each other the same name. Three hundred years ago a parson preached a sermon and told a story out of Foxe's *Book of Martyrs* of a man who had assisted at the torture of one of the saints, and afterward died, suffering compensatory inward torment. It happened that Foxe was wrong. The man was alive and chanced to hear the sermons, and thereupon he sued the parson. Chief Justice Wray instructed the jury that the defendant was not liable, because the story was told innocently, without malice. He took malice in the moral sense, as importing a malevolent motive. But nowadays no one doubts that a man may be liable without any malevolent motive at all, for false statements, manifestly calculated to inflict temporal damage. In stating the case in pleading, we still should call the defendant's conduct malicious; but, in my opinion at least, the word means nothing about motives, or even about the defendant's attitude toward the future, but only signifies that the tendency of his conduct under the known circumstances was very plainly to cause the plaintiff temporal harm.

In the law of contract the use of moral phraseology has led to equal confusion, as I have shown in part already, but only in part. Morals deal with the actual internal state of the individual's mind, what he actually intends. From the time of the Romans down to now, this mode of dealing has affected the language of the law as to contract, and the language used has reacted upon the thought. We talk about a contract as a meeting of the minds of the parties, and thence it is inferred in various cases that there is no contract because their minds have not met; that is, because they have intended different things or because one party has not known of the assent of the other. Yet nothing is more certain than that parties may be bound by a contract to things which neither of them intended, and when one does not know of the other's assent. Suppose a contract is executed in due form and in writing to deliver a lecture, mentioning no time. One of the parties thinks that the promise will be construed to them at once, within a week.

The other thinks that it means when he is ready. The court says that it means within a reasonable time. The parties are bound by the contract as it is interpreted by the court, yet neither of them meant what the court declares that they have said. In my opinion no one will understand the true theory of contract or be able even to discuss some fundamental questions intelligently until he has understood that all contracts are formal, that the making of a contract depends not on the agreement of two minds in one intention, but on the agreement of two sets of external signs, not on the parties' having *meant* the same thing but on their having *said* the same thing. Furthermore, as the signs may be addressed to one sense or another—to sight or to hearing—on the nature of the sign will depend the moment when the contract is made. If the sign is tangible, for instance, a letter, the contract is made when the letter of acceptance is delivered. If it is necessary that the minds of the parties meet, there will be no contract until the acceptance can be read—none, for example, if the acceptance be snatched from the hand of the offerer by a third person.

This is not the time to work out a theory in detail, or to answer many obvious doubts and questions which are suggested by these general views. I know of none which are not easy to answer, but what I am trying to do now is only by a series of hints to throw some light on the narrow path of legal doctrine, and upon two pitfalls which, as it seems to me, lie perilously near to it. Of the first of these I have said enough. I hope that my illustrations have shown the danger, both to speculation and to practice, of confounding morality with law, and the trap which legal language lays for us on that side of our way. For my own part, I often doubt whether it would not be a gain if every word of moral significance could be banished from the law altogether, and other words adopted which should convey legal ideas uncoloured by anything outside the law. We should lose the fossil records of a good deal of history and the majesty got from ethical associations, but by ridding ourselves of an unnecessary confusion we should gain very much in the clearness of our thought.

So much for the limits of the law. The next thing which I wish to consider is what are the forces which determine its content and its growth. You may assume, with Hobbes and Bentham and Austin, that all law emanates from the sovereign, even when the first human beings to enunciate it are the judges, or you may think that law is the voice of the Zeitgeist, or what you like. It is all one to my present purpose. Even if every decision required the sanction of an emperor with despotic power and a whimsical turn of mind, we should be interested none the less, still with a view to prediction, in discovering some order, some rational explanation, and some principle of growth for the rules which he laid down. In every system there are such explanations and principles to be found. It is with regard to them that a second fallacy comes in, which I think it important to expose.

The fallacy to which I refer is the notion that the only force at work in the development of the law is logic. In the broadest sense, indeed, that notion would be true. The postulate on which we think about the universe is that there is a fixed quantitative relation between every phenomenon and its antecedents and consequents. If there is such a thing as a phenomenon without these fixed quantitative relations, it is a miracle. It is outside the law of cause and effect, and as such transcends our power of thought, or at least is something to or from which we cannot reason. The condition of our thinking about the universe is that it is capable of being thought about rationally, or, in other words, that every part of it is effect and cause in the same sense in which those parts are with which we are most familiar. So in the broadest sense it is true that the law is a logical development, like everything else. The danger of which I speak is not the admission that the principles governing other phenomena also govern the law, but the notion that a given system, ours, for instance, can be worked out like mathematics from some general axioms of conduct. This is the natural error of the schools, but it is not confined to them. I once heard a very eminent judge say that he never let a decision go until he was absolutely sure that it was right. So judicial dissent often is blamed, as if it meant simply that one side or the other were not doing their sums right, and if they would take more trouble, agreement inevitably would come.

This mode of thinking is entirely natural. The training of lawyers is a training in logic. The processes of analogy, discrimination, and deduction are those in which they are most at home. The language of judicial decision is mainly the language of logic. And the logical method and form flatter that longing for certainty and for repose which is in every human mind. But certainty generally is illusion, and repose is not the destiny of man. Behind the logical form lies a judgment as to the relative worth and importance of competing legislative grounds, often an inarticulate and unconscious judgment, it is true, and yet the very root and nerve of the whole proceeding. You can give any conclusion a logical form. You always can imply a condition in a contract. But why do you imply? It is because of some belief as to the practice of the community or of a class, or because of some opinion as to policy, or, in short, because of some attitude of yours upon a matter not capable of founding exact logical conclusions. Such matters really are battle grounds where the means do not exist for determinations that shall be good for all time, and where the decision can do no more than embody the preference of a given body in a given time and place. We do not realize how large a part of our law is open to reconsideration upon a slight change in the habit of the public mind. No concrete proposition is self-evident, no matter how ready we may be to accept it, not even Mr Herbert Spencer's. Every man has a right to do what he wills, provided he interferes not with a like right on the part of his neighbours.

Why is a false and injurious statement privileged, if it is made honestly in giving information about a servant? It is because it has been thought more important that information should be given freely, than that a man should be protected from what under other circumstances would be an actionable wrong. Why is a man at liberty to set up a business which he knows will ruin his neighbour? It is because the public good is supposed to be best subserved by free competition. Obviously such judgments of relative importance may vary in different times and places. Why does a judge instruct a jury that an employer is not liable to an employee for an injury received in the course of his employment unless he is negligent, and why do the jury generally find for the plaintiff if the case is allowed to go to them? It is because the traditional policy of our law is to confine liability to cases where a prudent man might have foreseen the injury, or at least the danger, while the inclination of a very large part of the community is to make certain classes of persons insure the safety of those with whom they deal. Since the last words were written, I have seen the requirement of such insurance put forth as part of the programme of one of the best known labour organizations. There is a concealed, half-conscious battle on the question of legislative policy, and if any one thinks that it can be settled deductively, or once for all, I only can say that I think he is theoretically wrong, and that I am certain that his conclusion will not be accepted in practice *semper ubique et ab omnibus*.

Indeed, I think that even now our theory upon this matter is open to reconsideration, although I am not prepared to say how I should decide if a reconsideration were proposed. Our law of torts comes from the old days of isolated, ungeneralized wrongs, assaults, slanders, and the like, where the damages might be taken to lie where they fell by legal judgment. But the torts with which our courts are kept busy today are mainly the incidents of certain well-known businesses. They are injuries to person or property by railroads, factories, and the like. The liability for them is estimated, and sooner or later goes into the price paid by the public. The public really pays the damages, and the question of liability, if pressed far enough, is really the question how far it is desirable that the public should insure the safety of those whose work it uses. It might be said that in such cases the chance of a jury finding for the defendant is merely a chance, once in a while rather arbitrarily interrupting the regular course of recovery, most likely in the case of an unusually conspicuous plaintiff, and therefore better done away with. On the other hand, the economic value even of a life to the community can be estimated, and no recovery, it may be said, ought to go beyond that amount. It is conceivable that some day in certain cases we may find ourselves imitating, on a higher plane, the tariff for life and limb which we see in the Leges Barbarorum.

I think that the judges themselves have failed adequately to recognize their duty of weighing considerations of social advantage. The duty is inevitable, and the result of the often proclaimed judicial aversion to deal with such considerations is simply to leave the very ground and foundation of judgments inarticulate, and often unconscious, as I have said. When socialism first began to be talked about, the comfortable classes of the community were a good deal frightened. I suspect that this fear has influenced judicial action both here and in England, yet it is certain that it is not a conscious factor in the decisions to which I refer. I think that something similar has led people who no longer hope to control the legislatures to look to the courts as expounders of the Constitutions, and that in some courts now principles have been discovered outside the bodies of those instruments, which may be generalized into acceptance of the economic doctrines which prevailed about fifty years ago, and a wholesale prohibition of what a tribunal of lawyers does not think about right. I cannot but believe that if the training of lawyers led them habitually to consider more definitely and explicitly the social advantage on which the rule they lay down must be justified, they sometimes would hesitate where now they are confident, and see that really they were taking sides upon debatable and often burning questions.

So much for the fallacy of logical form. Now let us consider the present condition of the law as a subject for study, and the ideal toward which it tends. We still are far from the point of view which I desire to see reached. No one has reached it or can reach it as yet. We are only at the beginning of a philosophical reaction, and of a reconsideration of the worth of doctrines which for the most part still are taken for granted without any deliberate, conscious, and systematic questioning of their grounds. The development of our law has gone on for nearly a thousand years, like the development of a plant, each generation taking the inevitable next step, mind, like matter, simply obeying a law of spontaneous growth. It is perfectly natural and right that it should have been so. Imitation is a necessity of human nature, as has been illustrated by a remarkable French writer, M. Tarde, in an admirable book, *Les Lois de l'Imitation.* Most of the things we do, we do for no better reason than that our fathers have done them or that our neighbours do them, and the same is true of a larger part than we suspect of what we think. The reason is a good one, because our short life gives us no time for a better, but it is not the best. It does not follow, because we all are compelled to take on faith at second hand most of the rules on which we base our action and our thought, that each of us may not try to set some corner of his world in the order of reason, or that all of us collectively should not aspire to carry reason as far as it will go throughout the whole domain. In regard to the law, it is true, no doubt, that an evolutionist will hesitate to affirm universal validity for his social ideals, or for the principles which he thinks should be embodied in legislation. He is content if he can prove them best for here and now. He may be ready to admit that he knows nothing about an absolute best in the cosmos, and even that he knows next to nothing about a permanent best for men. Still it is true that a body of law is more rational and more civilized when every rule it contains is referred articulately and definitely to an end which it subserves, and when the grounds for desiring that end are stated or are ready to be stated in words.

At present, in very many cities, if we want to know why a rule of law has taken its particular shape, and more or less if we want to know why it exists at all, we go to tradition. We follow it into the Year Books, and perhaps beyond them to the customs of the Salian Franks, and somewhere in the past, in the German forests, in the needs of Norman kings, in the assumptions of a dominant class, in the absence of generalized ideas, we find out the practical motive for what now best is justified by the mere fact of its acceptance and that men are accustomed to it. The rational study of law is still to a large extent the study of history. History must be a part of the study, because without it we cannot know the precise scope of rules which it is our business to know. It is a part of the rational study, because it is the first step toward a deliberate reconsideration of the worth of those rules. When you get the dragon out of his cave on to the plain and in the daylight, you can count his teeth and claws, and see just what is his strength. But to get him out is only the first step. The next is either to kill him, or to tame him and make him a useful animal. For the rational study of the law the black-letter man may be the man of the present, but the man of the future is the man of statistics and the master of economics. It is revolting to have no better reason for a rule of law than that so it was laid down in the time of Henry IV. It is still more revolting if the grounds upon which it was laid down have vanished long since, and the rule simply persists from blind imitation of the past. I am thinking of the technical rule as to trespass *ab initio*, as it is called, which I attempted to explain in a recent Massachusetts case.

Let me take an illustration, which can be stated in a few words, to show how the social end which is aimed at by a rule of law is obscured and only partially attained in consequence of the fact that the rule owes its form to a gradual historical development, instead of being reshaped as a whole, with conscious articulate reference to the end in view. We think it desirable to prevent one man's property being misappropriated by another, and so we make larceny a crime. The evil is the same whether the misappropriation is made by a man into whose hands the owner has put the property, or by one who wrongfully takes it away. But primitive law in its weakness did not get much beyond an effort to prevent violence, and very naturally made a wrongful taking, a trespass, part of its definition of the crime. In modern times the judges enlarged the definition a little by holding that, if the wrong-doer gets possession by a trick or device, the crime is committed. This really was giving up the requirement of a trespass, and it would have been more logical, as well as truer to the present object of the law, to abandon the requirement altogether. That, however, would have seemed too bold, and was left to statute. Statutes were passed making embezzlement a crime. But the force of tradition caused the crime of embezzlement to be regarded as so far distinct from larceny that to this day, in some jurisdictions at least, a slip corner is kept open for thieves to contend, if indicted for larceny, that they should have been indicted for embezzlement, and if indicted for embezzlement, that they should have been indicted for larceny, and to escape on that ground.

Far more fundamental questions still await a better answer than that we do as our fathers have done. What have we better than a blind guess to show that the criminal law in its present form does more good than harm? I do not stop to refer to the effect which it has had in degrading prisoners and in plunging them further into crime, or to the question whether fine and imprisonment do not fall more heavily on a criminal's wife and children than on himself. I have in mind more far-reaching questions. Does punishment deter? Do we deal with criminals on proper principles? A modern school of Continental criminalists plumes itself on the formula, first suggested, it is said, by Gall, that we must consider the criminal rather than the crime. The formula does not carry us very far, but the inquiries which have been started look toward an answer of my questions based on science for the first time. If the typical criminal is a degenerate, bound to swindle or to murder by as deep-seated an organic necessity as that which makes the rattlesnake bite, it is idle to talk of deterring him by the classical method of imprisonment. He must be got rid of; he cannot be improved, or frightened out of his structural reaction. If, on the other hand, crime, like normal human conduct, is mainly a matter of imitation, punishment fairly may be expected to help to keep it out of fashion. The study of criminals has been thought by some well-known men of science to sustain the former hypothesis. The statistics of the relative increase of crime in crowded places like large cities, where example has the greatest chance to work, and in less populated parts, where the contagion spreads more slowly, have been used with great force in favour of the latter view. But there is weighty authority for the belief that, however this may be, 'not the nature of the crime, but the dangerousness of the criminal, constitutes the only reasonable legal criterion to guide the inevitable social reaction against the criminal'.

The impediments to rational generalization, which I illustrated from the law of mercy, are shown in the other branches of the law, as well as in that of crime. Take the law of tort or civil liability for damages apart from contract and the like. Is there any general theory of such liability, or are the cases in which it exists simply to be enumerated, and to be explained each on its special ground, as is easy to believe from the fact that the right of action for certain well-known classes of wrongs like trespass or slander has its special history for each class? I think that there is a general theory to be discovered, although resting in tendency rather than established and accepted. I think that the law regards the infliction of temporal damage by a responsible person as actionable, if under the circumstances known to him the danger of his act is manifest according to common experience, or according to his own experience if it is more than common, except in cases where upon special grounds of policy the law refuses to protect the plaintiff or grants a privilege to the defendant. I think that commonly malice, intent, and negligence mean only that the danger was manifest to a greater or less degree, under the circumstances known to the actor, although in some cases of privilege malice may mean an actual malevolent motive, and such a motive may take away a permission knowingly to inflict harm, which otherwise would be granted on this or that ground of dominant public good. But when I stated my view to a very eminent English judge the other day, he said: 'You are discussing what the law ought to be; as the law is, you must show a right. A man is not liable for negligence unless he is subject to a duty.' If our difference was more than a difference in words, or with regard to the proportion between the exceptions and the rule, then, in his opinion, liability for an act cannot be referred to the manifest tendency of the act to cause temporal damage in general as a sufficient explanation, but must be referred to the special nature of the damage, or must be derived from some special circumstances outside of the tendency of the act, for which no generalized explanation exists. I think that such a view is wrong, but it is familiar, and I dare say generally is accepted in England.

Everywhere the basis of principle is tradition, to such an extent that we even are in danger of making the role of history more important than it is. The other day Professor Ames wrote a learned article to show, among other things, that the common law did not recognize the defence of fraud in actions upon specialties, and the moral might seem to be that the personal character of that defence is due to its equitable origin. But if, as I have said, all contracts are formal, the difference is not merely historical, but theoretic, between defects of form which prevent a contract from being made, and mistaken motives which manifestly could not be considered in any system that we should call rational except against one who was privy to those motives. It is not confined to specialties, but is of universal application. I ought to add that I do not suppose that Mr Ames would disagree with what I suggest.

However, if we consider the law of contract, we find it full of history. The distinctions between debt, covenant, and assumpsit are merely historical. The classification of certain obligations to pay money, imposed by the law irrespective of any bargain as quasi contracts, is merely historical. The doctrine of consideration is merely historical. The effect given to a seal is to be explained by history alone. Consideration is a mere form. Is it a useful form? If so, why should it not be required in all contracts? A seal is a mere form, and is vanishing in the scroll and in enactments that a consideration must be given, seal or no seal. Why should any merely historical distinction be allowed to affect the rights and obligations of business men?

Since I wrote this discourse I have come on a very good example of the way in which tradition not only overrides rational policy, but overrides it after first having been misunderstood and having been given a new and broader scope than it had when it had a meaning. It is the settled law of England that a material alteration of a written contract by a party avoids it as against him. The doctrine is contrary to the general tendency of the law. We do not tell a jury that if a man ever has lied in one particular he is to be presumed to lie in all. Even if a man has tried to defraud, it seems no sufficient reason for preventing him from proving the truth. Objections of like nature in general go to the weight, not to the admissibility, of evidence. Moreover, this rule is irrespective of fraud, and is not confined to evidence. It is not merely that you cannot use the writing, but that the contract is at an end. What does this mean? The existence of a written contract depends on the fact that the offerer and offeree have interchanged their written expressions, not on the continued existence of those expressions. But in the case of a bond the primitive notion was different. The contract was inseparable from the parchment. If a stranger destroyed it, or tore off the seal, or altered it, the obligee could not recover, however free from fault, because the defendant's contract, that is, the actual tangible bond which he had sealed, could not be produced in the form in which it bound him. About a hundred years ago Lord Kenyon undertook to use his reason on this tradition, as he sometimes did to the detriment of the law, and, not understanding it, said he could see no reason why what was true of a bond should not be true of other contracts. His decision happened to be right, as it concerned a promissory note, where again the common law regarded the contract as inseparable from the paper on which it was written, but the reasoning was general, and soon was extended to other written contracts, and various absurd and unreal grounds of policy were invented to account for the enlarged rule.

I trust that no one will understand me to be speaking with disrespect of the law, because I criticize it so freely. I venerate the law, and especially our system of law, as one of the vastest products of the human mind. No one knows better than I do the countless number of great intellects that have spent themselves in making some addition or improvement, the greatest of which is trifling when compared with the mighty whole. It has the final title to respect that it exists, that it is not a Hegelian dream, but a part of the lives of men. But one may criticize even what one reveres. Law is the business to which my life is devoted, and I should show less than devotion if I did not do what in me lies to improve it, and, when I perceive what seems to me the ideal of its future, if I hesitated to point it out and to press toward it with all my heart.

Perhaps I have said enough to show the part which the study of history necessarily plays in the intelligent study of the law as it is today. In the teaching of this school* and at Cambridge† it is in no danger of being under-valued. Mr Bigelow here and Mr Ames and Mr Thayer there have made important contributions which will not be forgotten, and in England the recent history of early English law by Sir Frederick Pollock and Mr Maitland has lent the subject an almost deceptive charm. We must beware of the pitfall of antiquarianism, and must remember that for our purposes our only interest in the past is for the light it throws upon the present. I look forward to a time when the part played by history in the explanation of dogma shall be very small, and instead of ingenious research we shall spend our energy on a study of the ends sought to be attained and the reasons for desiring them. As a step toward that ideal it seems to me that every lawyer ought to seek an understanding of economics. The present divorce between the schools of political economy and law seems to me an evidence of how much progress in philosophical study still remains to be made. In the present state of political economy, indeed, we come

* Yale Law School   † i.e. Harvard

again upon history on a larger scale, but there we are called on to consider and weigh the ends of legislation, the means of attaining them, and the cost. We learn that for everything we have to give up something else, and we are taught to set the advantage we gain against the other advantage we lose, and to know what we are doing when we elect.

There is another study which sometimes is undervalued by the practical minded, for which I wish to say a good word, although I think a good deal of pretty poor stuff goes under that name. I mean the study of what is called jurisprudence. Jurisprudence, as I look at it, is simply law in its most generalized part. Every effort to reduce a case to a rule is an effort of jurisprudence, although the name as used in English is confined to the broadest rules and most fundamental conceptions. One mark of a great lawyer is that he sees the application of the broadest rules. There is a story of a Vermont justice of the peace before whom a suit was brought by one farmer against another for breaking a churn. The justice took time to consider, and then said that he had looked through the statutes and could find nothing about churns, and gave judgment for the defendant. The same state of mind is shown in all our common digests and textbooks. Applications of rudimentary rules of contract or tort are tucked away under the head of Railroads or Telegraphs or go to swell treatises on historical subdivisions, such as Shipping or Equity, or are gathered under an arbitrary title which is thought likely to appeal to the practical mind, such as Mercantile Law. If a man goes into law it pays to be a master of it, and to be a master of it means to look straight through all the dramatic incidents and to discern the true basis of prophecy. Therefore, it is well to have an accurate notion of what you mean by law, by a right, by a duty, by malice, intent, and negligence, by ownership, by possession, and so forth. I have in my mind cases in which the highest courts seem to me to have floundered because they had no clear ideas on some of these themes. I have illustrated their importance already. If a further illustration is wished, it may be found by reading the Appendix to Sir James Stephen's *Criminal Law* on the subject of possession, and then turning to Pollock and Wright's enlightened book. Sir James Stephen is not the only writer whose attempts to analyse legal ideas have been confused by striving for a useless quintessence of all systems, instead of an accurate anatomy of one. The trouble with Austin was that he did not know enough English law. But still it is a practical advantage to master Austin, and his predecessors, Hobbes and Bentham, and his worthy successors, Holland and Pollock. Sir Frederick Pollock's recent little book is touched with the felicity which marks all his works, and is wholly free from the perverting influence of Roman models.

The advice of the elders to young men is very apt to be as unreal as a list of the hundred best books. At least in my day I had my share of such counsels, and high among the unrealities I place the recommendation to study the Roman Law. I assume that such advice means more than collecting a few Latin maxims with which to ornament the discourse—the purpose for which Lord Coke recommended Bracton. If that is all that is wanted, the title *De Regulis Juris Antiqui* can be read in an hour. I assume that, if it is well to study the Roman law, it is well to study it as a working system. That means mastering a set of technicalities more difficult and less understood than our own, and studying another course of history by which even more than our own the Roman law must be explained. If any one doubts me, let him read Keller's *Der Romische Civil Process und die Actionen*, a treatise on the praetor's edict, Muirhead's most interesting *Historical Introduction to the Private Law of Rome* and, to give him the best chance possible, Sohm's admirable Institutes. No. The way to gain a liberal view of your subject is not to read something else, but to get to the bottom of the subject itself. The means of doing that are, in the first place, to follow the existing body of dogma into its highest generalizations by the help of jurisprudence; next, to discover from history how it has come to be what it is; and, finally, so far as you can, to consider the ends which the several rules seek to accomplish, the reasons why those ends are desired, what is given up to gain them, and whether they are worth the price.

We have too little theory in the law rather than too much, especially on this final branch of study. When I was speaking of history, I mentioned larceny as an example to show how the law suffered from not having embodied in a clear form a rule which will accomplish its manifest purpose. In that case the trouble was due to the survival of forms coming from a time when a more limited purpose was entertained. Let me now give an example to show the practical importance, for the decision of actual cases, of understanding the reasons of the law, by taking an example from rules which, so far as I know, never have been explained or theorized about in any adequate way. I refer to statutes of limitation and the law of prescription. The end of such rules is obvious, but what is the justification for depriving a man of his rights, a pure evil as far as it goes, in consequence of the lapse of time? Sometimes the loss of evidence is referred to, but that is a secondary matter. Sometimes the desirability of peace, but why is peace more desirable after twenty years than before? It is increasingly likely to come without the aid of legislation. Sometimes it is said that, if a man neglects to enforce his rights, he cannot complain if, after a while, the law follows his example. Now if this is all that can be said about it, you probably will decide a case I am going to put, for the plaintiff; if you take the view which I shall suggest, you possibly will decide it for the defendant. A man is sued for trespass upon land, and justifies under a right of way. He proves that he has used the way openly and adversely for twenty years, but it turns out that the plaintiff had granted a licence to a person whom he reasonably supposed to be the defendant's agent, although not so in fact, and therefore had assumed that the use of the way was permissive, in which case no right would be gained. Has the defendant gained a right or not? If his gaining it stands on the fault and neglect of the landowner in the ordinary sense, as seems commonly to be supposed, there has been no such neglect, and the right of way has not been acquired. But if I were the defendant's counsel, I should suggest that the foundation of the acquisition of rights by lapse of time is to be looked for in the position of the person who gains them, not in that of the loser. Sir Henry Maine has made it fashionable to connect the archaic notion of property with prescription. But the connection is further back than the first recorded history. It is in the nature of man's mind. A thing which you have enjoyed and used as your own for a long time, whether property or an opinion, takes root in your being and cannot be torn away without your resenting the act and trying to defend yourself, however you came by it. The law can ask no better justification than the deepest instincts of man. It is only by way of reply to the suggestion that you are disappointing the former owner, that you refer to his neglect having allowed the gradual dissociation between himself and what he claims, and the gradual association of it with another. If he knows that another is doing acts which on their face show that he is on the way towards establishing such an association, I should argue that in justice to that other he was bound at his peril to find out whether the other was acting under his permission, to see that he was warned, and, if necessary, stopped.

I have been speaking about the study of the law, and I have said next to nothing of what commonly is talked about in that connection —textbooks and the case system, and all the machinery with which a student comes most immediately in contact. Nor shall I say anything about them. Theory is my subject, not practical details. The modes of teaching have been improved since my time, no doubt, but ability and industry will master the raw material with any mode. Theory is the most important part of the dogma of the law, as the architect is the most important man who takes part in the building of a house. The most important improvements of the last twenty-five years are improvements in theory. It is not to be feared as unpractical, for, to the competent, it simply means going to the bottom of the subject. For the incompetent, it sometimes is true, as has been said, that an interest in general ideas means an absence of particular knowledge. I remember in army days reading of a youth who, being examined for the lowest grade and being asked a question about squadron drill, answered that he never had considered the evolutions of less than ten thousand men. But the weak and foolish must be left to their folly. The danger is that the able and practical minded should look with indifference or distrust upon ideas the connection of which with their business is remote. I heard a story, the other day, of a man who had a valet to whom he paid high wages, subject to deduction for faults. One of his deductions was, 'For lack of imagination, five dollars.' The lack is not confined to valets. The object of ambition, power, generally presents itself nowadays in the form of money alone. Money is the most immediate form, and is a proper object of desire. 'The fortune,' said Rachel, 'is the measure of the intelligence.' That is a good text to waken people out of a fool's paradise. But, as Hegel says, 'It is in the end not the appetite, but the opinion, which has to be satisfied.' To an imagination of any scope the most far-reaching form of power is not money, it is the command of ideas. If you want great examples read Mr Leslie Stephen's *English Thought in the Eighteenth Century*, and see how a hundred years after his death the abstract speculations of Descartes had become a practical force controlling the conduct of men. Read the works of the great German jurists, and see how much more the world is governed today by Kant than by Bonaparte. We cannot all be Descartes or Kant, but we all want happiness. And happiness, I am sure from having known many successful men, cannot be won simply by being counsel for great corporations and having an income of fifty thousand dollars.

An intellect great enough to win the prize needs other food beside success. The remoter and more general aspects of the law are those which give it universal interest. It is through them that you not only become a great master in your calling, but connect your subject with the universe and catch an echo of the infinite, a glimpse of its unfathomable process, a hint of the universal law.

Professor H. L. A. Hart

Immorality and Treason

The relationship between crime and sin has been a perennial topic for jurists and philosophers. It was projected on to the wider forum of public debate in 1957 when the Wolfenden report on homosexuality and prostitution made the challenging statement that some sexual behaviour, although, according to some, sinful, was no business of the criminal law; homosexual practices conducted between consenting adults in private were just one such instance.

Whether the mores of society ought to be controlled by the agency of the criminal law was the theme of the Maccabaean lecture in jurisprudence delivered by Lord Justice Devlin in March 1959. It was stoutly rebutted by H. L. A. Hart, Professor of Jurisprudence in the University of Oxford, in the libertarian tradition of Bentham and Mill.

If the moral thinking of society is to be enforced, as Lord Justice Devlin proposes, it means that society will be attempting to punish any deviations from the mores current in society. In this way the criminal law will be underlining heavily the need of individuals to conform; as a result orthodoxy is reinforced. Individualism is thus inhibited to the extent that it is deviationary.

It is equally true that the criminal law must take cognizance of morality. The criminal law and its enforcement relies for much of its efficacy upon the support of public opinion, which in this instance fairly reflects moral feeling. A rule of the criminal law which derives its raison d'être from ideas of deterrence, retribution or reformation alone will quickly receive the disapprobation of society.

This does not mean that laws are inherently bad because they take no account of moral feelings but are directed merely to controlling anti-social conduct and promoting felicific behaviour. But the laws do need to be supported by public approval, which is no more than saying that morals play a part in legislating against human conduct. This is not to say though that morals must actively be enforced through the medium of the criminal law. Morals are a facet of law enforcement but not a motivating factor. 'Morality and criminality,' said Lord Atkin, 'are far from co-extensive.'

THE WOLFENDEN Committee on Homosexual Offences and Prostitution recommended by a majority of 12 to 1 that homosexual behaviour between consenting adults in private should no longer be a criminal offence. One of the Committee's principal grounds for this recommendation was expressed in its report in this way: 'There must remain a realm of private morality and immorality which in brief and crude terms is not the law's business.' I shall call this the liberal point of view: for it is a special application of those wider principles of liberal thought which John Stuart Mill formulated in his essay on Liberty. Mill's most famous words, less cautious perhaps than the Wolfenden Committee's, were:

The only purpose for which power can be rightfully exercised over any member of a civilized community against his will is to prevent harm to others. His own good, either physical or moral, is not a sufficient warrant. He cannot rightfully be compelled to do or forbear . . . because in the opinion of others to do so would be wise or even right.

The liberal point of view has often been attacked, both before and after Mill. I shall discuss here the repudiation of it made by Sir Patrick Devlin, in his recent lecture, which has now been published. This contains an original and interesting argument designed to show that '*prima facie* society has the right to legislate against immorality as such' and that the Wolfenden Committee were mistaken in thinking that there is an area of private immorality which is not the law's business. Sir Patrick's case is a general one, not confined to sexual immorality, and he does not say whether or not he is opposed to the Wolfenden Committee's recommendation on homosexual behaviour. Instead he gives us a hypothetical principle by which to judge this issue. He says: 'If it is the genuine feeling of our society that homosexuality is a vice so abominable that its mere presence is an offence', society has the right to eradicate it by the use of the criminal law.

The publication by Sir Patrick of this lecture is in itself an interesting event. It is many years since a distinguished English lawyer delivered himself of general reasoned views about the relationship of morality to the criminal law. The last to do so with comparable skill and clarity was, I think, the great Victorian judge James Fitzjames Stephen. It is worth observing that Stephen, like Sir Patrick, repudiated the liberal point of view. Indeed his gloomy but impressive book *Liberty, Equality, Fraternity* was a direct reply to Mill's essay *On Liberty*. The most remarkable feature of Sir Patrick's lecture is his view of the nature of morality—the morality which the criminal law may enforce. Most previous thinkers who have repudiated the liberal point of view have done so because they thought that morality consisted either of divine commands or of rational principles of human conduct discoverable by human reason. Since morality for them had this elevated divine or rational status as the law of God or reason, it seemed obvious that the state should enforce it, and that the function of human law should not be merely to provide men with the opportunity for leading a good life, but actually to see that they lead it. Sir Patrick does not rest his repudiation of the liberal point of view on these religious or rationalist conceptions. Indeed much that he writes reads like an abjuration of the notion that reasoning or thinking has much to do with morality. English popular morality has no doubt its historical connection with the Christian religion: 'That,' says Sir Patrick, 'is how it got there'. But it does not owe its present status or social significance to religion any more than to reason.

What, then, is it? According to Sir Patrick it is primarily a matter of feeling. 'Every moral judgment,' he says, 'is a feeling that no right-minded man could act in any other way without admitting that he was doing wrong.' Who then must feel this way if we are to have what Sir Patrick calls a public morality? He tells us that it is 'the man in the street', 'the man in the jury box', or (to use the phrase so familiar to English lawyers) 'the man on the Clapham omnibus.' For the moral judgments of society so far as the law is concerned are to be ascertained by the standards of the reasonable man, and he is not to be confused with the rational man. Indeed, Sir Patrick says 'he is not expected to reason about anything and his judgment may be largely a matter of feeling.'

But what precisely are the relevant feelings, the feelings which may justify use of the criminal law? Here the argument becomes a little complex. Widespread dislike of a practice is not enough. There must, says Sir Patrick, be 'a real feeling of reprobation'. Disgust is not enough either. What is crucial is a combination of intolerance, indignation, and disgust. These three are the forces behind the moral law, without which it is not 'weighty enough to deprive the individual of freedom of choice'. Hence there is, in Sir Patrick's outlook, a crucial difference between the mere adverse moral judgment of society and one which is inspired by feeling raised to the concert pitch of intolerance, indignation, and disgust.

This distinction is novel and also very important. For on it depends the weight to be given to the fact that when morality is enforced individual liberty is necessarily cut down. Though Sir Patrick's abstract formulation of his views on this point is hard to follow, his examples make his position fairly clear. We can see it best in the contrasting things he says about fornication and homosexuality. In regard to fornication, public feeling in most societies is not now of the concert-pitch intensity. We may feel that it is tolerable if confined: only its spread might be gravely injurious. In such cases the question whether individual liberty should be restricted is for Sir Patrick a question of balance between the danger to society in the one scale, and the restriction of the individual in the other. But if, as may be the case with homosexuality, public feeling is up to concert pitch, if it expresses a 'deliberate judgment' that a practice as such is injurious to society, if there is 'a genuine feeling that it is a vice so abominable that its mere presence is an offence', then it is beyond the limits of tolerance, and society may eradicate it. In this case, it seems, no further balancing of the claims of individual liberty is to be done, though as a matter of prudence the legislator should remember that the popular limits of tolerance may shift: the concert-pitch feeling may subside. This may produce a dilemma for the law; for the law may then be left without the full moral backing that it needs, yet it cannot be altered without giving the impression that the moral judgment is being weakened.

If this is what morality is—a compound of indignation, intolerance, and disgust—we may well ask what justification there is for taking it, and turning it as such, into criminal law with all the misery which criminal punishment entails. Here Sir Patrick's answer is very clear and simple. A collection of individuals is not a society; what makes them into a society is among other things a shared or public morality. This is as necessary to its existence as an organized government. So society may use the law to preserve its morality like anything else essential to it. 'The suppression of vice is as much the law's business as the suppression of subversive activities.' The liberal point of view which denies this is guilty of 'an error in jurisprudence': for it is no more possible to define an area of private morality than an area of private subversive activity. There can be no 'theoretical limits' to legislation against immorality just as there are no such limits to the power of the state to legislate against treason and sedition.

Surely all this, ingenious as it is, is misleading. Mill's formulation of the liberal point of view may well be too simple. The grounds for interfering with human liberty are more various than the single criterion of 'harm to others' suggests: cruelty to animals or organizing prostitution for gain do not, as Mill himself saw, fall easily under the description of harm to others. Conversely, even where there is harm to others in the most literal sense, there may well be other principles limiting the extent to which harmful activities should be repressed by law. So there are multiple criteria, not a single criterion, determining when human liberty may be restricted. Perhaps this is what Sir Patrick means by a curious distinction which he often stresses between theoretical and practical limits. But with all its simplicities the liberal point of view is a better guide than Sir Patrick to clear thought on the proper relation of morality to the criminal law: for it stresses what he obscures—namely, the points at which thought is needed before we turn popular morality into criminal law.

No doubt we would all agree that a consensus of moral opinion on certain matters is essential if society is to be worth living in. Laws against murder, theft, and much else would be of little use if they were not supported by a widely diffused conviction that what these laws forbid is also immoral. So much is obvious. But it does not follow that everything to which the moral vetoes of accepted morality attach is of equal importance to society; nor is there the slightest reason for thinking of morality as a seamless web: one which will fall to pieces carrying society with it, unless all its emphatic vetoes are enforced by law. Surely even in the face of the moral feeling that is up to concert pitch—the trio of intolerance, indignation, and disgust—we must pause to think. We must ask a question at two different levels which Sir Patrick never clearly enough identifies or separates. First, we must ask whether a practice which offends moral feeling is harmful, independently of its repercussion on the general moral code. Secondly, what about repercussion on the moral code? Is it really true that failure to translate this item of general morality into criminal law will jeopardize the whole fabric of morality and so of society?

We cannot escape thinking about these two different questions merely by repeating to ourselves the vague nostrum: 'This is part of public morality and public morality must be preserved if society is to exist.' Sometimes Sir Patrick seems to admit this, for he says in words which both Mill and the Wolfenden Report might have used, that there must be the maximum respect for individual liberty consistent with the integrity of society. Yet this, as his contrasting examples of fornication and homosexuality show, turns out to mean only that the immorality which the law may punish must be generally felt to be intolerable. This plainly is no adequate substitute for a reasoned estimate of the damage to the fabric of society likely to ensue if it is not suppressed.

Nothing perhaps shows more clearly the inadequacy of Sir Patrick's approach to this problem than his comparison between the suppression of sexual immorality and the suppression of treason or subversive activity. Private subversive activity is, of course, a contradiction in terms because 'subversion' means over-throwing government, which is a public thing. But it is grotesque, even where moral feeling against homosexuality is up to concert pitch, to think of the homosexual behaviour of two adults in private as in any way like treason or sedition either in intention or effect. We can make it *seem* like treason only if we assume that deviation from a general moral code is bound to affect that code, and to lead not merely to its modification but to its destruction. The analogy could begin to be plausible only if it was clear that offending against this item of morality was likely to jeopardize the whole structure. But we have ample evidence for believing that people will not abandon morality, will not think any better of murder, cruelty and dishonesty, merely because some private sexual practice which they abominate is not punished by the law.

Because this is so the analogy with treason is absurd. Of course 'No man is an island': what one man does in private, if it is known, may affect others in many different ways. Indeed it may be that deviation from general sexual morality by those whose lives, like the lives of many homosexuals, are noble ones and in all other ways exemplary will lead to what Sir Patrick calls the shifting of the limits of tolerance. But if this has any analogy in the sphere of government it is not the overthrow of ordered government, but a peaceful change in its form. So we may listen to the promptings of common sense and of logic, and say that though there could not logically be a sphere of private treason there is a sphere of private morality and immorality.

Sir Patrick's doctrine is also open to a wider, perhaps a deeper, criticism. In his reaction against a rationalist morality and his stress on feeling, he has I think thrown out the baby and kept the bath water; and the bath water may turn out to be very dirty indeed. When Sir Patrick's lecture was first delivered *The Times* greeted it with these words: 'There is a moving and welcome humility in the conception that society should not be asked to give its reason for refusing to tolerate what in its heart it feels intolerable.' This drew from a correspondent in Cambridge the retort: 'I am afraid that we are less humble than we used to be. We once burnt old women because, without giving our reasons, we felt in our hearts that witchcraft was intolerable.'

This retort is a bitter one, yet its bitterness is salutary. We are not, I suppose, likely, in England, to take again to the burning of old women for witchcraft or to punishing people for associating with those of a different race or colour, or to punishing people again for adultery. Yet if these things were viewed with intolerance, indignation, and disgust, as the second of them still is in some countries, it seems that on Sir Patrick's principles no rational criticism could be opposed to the claim that they should be punished by law. We could only pray, in his words, that the limits of tolerance might shift.

It is impossible to see what curious logic has led Sir Patrick to this result. For him a practice is immoral if the thought of it makes the man on the Clapham omnibus sick. So be it. Still, why should we not summon all the resources of our reason, sympathetic understanding, as well as critical intelligence, and insist that before general moral feeling is turned into criminal law it is submitted to scrutiny of a different kind from Sir Patrick's? Surely, the legislator should ask whether the general morality is based on ignorance, superstition, or misunderstanding; whether there is a false conception that those who practise what it condemns are in other ways dangerous or hostile to society; and whether the misery to many parties, the blackmail and the other evil consequences of criminal punishment, especially for sexual offences, are well understood. It is surely extraordinary that among the things which Sir Patrick says are to be considered before we legislate against immorality these appear nowhere; not even as 'practical considerations', let alone 'theoretical limits'. To any theory which, like this one, asserts that the criminal law may be used on the vague ground that the preservation of morality is essential to society and yet omits to stress the need for critical scrutiny, our reply should be: 'Morality, what crimes may be committed in thy name!'

As Mill saw, and de Tocqueville showed in detail long ago in his critical but sympathetic study of democracy, it is fatally easy to confuse the democratic principle that power should be in the hands of the majority with the utterly different claim that the majority, with power in their hands, need respect no limits. Certainly there is a special risk in a democracy that the majority may dictate how all should live. This is the risk we run, and should gladly run; for it is the price of all that is so good in democratic rule. But loyalty to democratic principles does not require us to maximize this risk: yet this is what we shall do if we mount the man in the street on the top of the Clapham omnibus and tell him that if only he feels sick enough about what other people do in private to demand its suppression by law no theoretical criticism can be made of his demand.

4

ON LAWYERS

Mastering the lawless science of our law,
That codeless myriad of precedent,
That wilderness of single instances,
Through which a few, by wit or fortune led,
May beat a pathway out to wealth and fame.

Alfred, Lord Tennyson, *Aylmer's Field*

The function of a trial judge is to be quick, courteous and wrong
That is not to say that the Court of Appeal should be slow,
rude and right; for that would be to usurp the
function of the House of Lords.

Lord Asquith of Bishopsgate

W. Forbes Gray

Lord Monboddo and Lord Braxfield

Lack of communication between lawyers from either side of the Border cannot be explained only by the fact that the two countries have quite separate systems of law. Apart from the mingling of many famous Scottish judges among their English brethren in the House of Lords contact between the professions has always been minimal. No meeting of the legal professions has ever taken place. This is both inexplicable and inexcusable for two nations which have been united politically for over two hundred and fifty years.

English lawyers are thus woefully ignorant of what takes place among the judiciary of Scotland; less so, vice-versa. But Mr Forbes Gray in his book Some Old Scots Judges *in 1914 did a little to repair this omission. From that book are taken biographies of two eighteenth-century judges, Lord Monboddo and Lord Braxfield. While Monboddo displayed the intellectual qualities of a great Scots lawyer, even if when on the bench his eccentricities obscured these qualities, his contemporary, Lord Braxfield, was an illiterate reprobate who did nothing to grace the Scottish bench. Braxfield, who has been compared unfavourably even with the English Jeffreys, was perhaps the quintessence of judicial misconduct. But his gifts as a lawyer at least save him from the full-blown and merited opprobrium reserved for Jeffreys.*

Lord Monboddo (1714–99)

JAMES BURNET, Lord Monboddo, one of the most extraordinary men who ever sat on the judgment seat—'a character rarely to be met with in common life; being fitter for a comedy or novel than anything else' —was born in 1714 of a family more ancient than opulent. His paternal ancestors could be traced back to the days of King Robert the Bruce, and were the owners of the Deeside property of Leys. His father, James Burnet, was the proprietor of a small estate in Kincardineshire, known as Monboddo, in the unpretentious and somewhat dilapidated mansion-house of which the future judge first saw the light. Burnet's lineage on the maternal side was also distinguished, his mother being the only daughter of Sir Arthur Forbes, Bart, of Craigievar.

Of the parents there are few personal details. The father was a strong Jacobite and, along with many other landed gentlemen, got into trouble in connection with the Rebellion of 1715. He was present at the battle of Sheriffmuir, and one incident, recorded by Ramsay of Ochtertyre, shows him in rather an amiable light. An English officer, who had been stunned by a fall from his horse, perceiving, on his recovery, a gentleman on horseback near him, said: 'Sir, I am your prisoner.' 'No,' answered the other (who saw the King's troops approaching), 'I am your prisoner.' 'If that be the case,' said the officer, 'dismount, and I will protect you.' Burnet of Monboddo accordingly walked, while the officer rode his horse, and brought him safely to Stirling Castle.

Burnet received his first schooling from a Robert Milne, designated in the family archives 'Tutor to Monboddo's bairns'. Monboddo, however, does not seem to have rated the tutor's gifts very highly, for in 1722 we find him writing a doleful letter to his spouse from Edinburgh, expressing doubts as to the efficacy of home tuition, and gravely assuring her that 'Jamie will be lost' if she does not send him to a proper school. The advice was taken, and 'Jamie' was despatched forthwith to the parish school of Laurencekirk, where he was taught by Thomas Ruddiman who, in later years, shone as a prince among Latin grammarians and as Keeper of the Advocates' Library, an office in which he was succeeded by no less a person than David Hume. Ruddiman was an apt teacher, a scholar, and, if all reports be true, a gentleman. But, notwithstanding these excellent qualifications, Monboddo had still gloomy forebodings that 'Jamie' was in danger of being 'lost'. The result was that the boy was early recalled from the parish school, and home tuition was given another trial—this time under Dr Francis Skene.

Under his new tutor Burnet made satisfactory progress, and imbibed that love of Greek literature and philosophy which was to become the ruling passion of his life. Skene remained at Monboddo until his appointment to the Chair of Philosophy in King's College, Aberdeen. Thither his pupil followed him. He is even said to have lived under his tutor's roof; but, however that may be, it is certain that, inspired by Skene and Principal Blackwell, the latter one of the most ardent champions of Greek study in Scotland, Burnet became an enthusiastic disciple of Aristotle and Plato, and a contemner of Bacon, Locke, Newton, Hume, and other mere moderns.

Having graduated Master of Arts at Aberdeen University, he removed to Edinburgh, where he began to equip himself for the Scottish Bar. He afterwards went to Holland to learn the maxims of the great Dutch jurists (which then had great weight in the Parliament House), to see the world, and to converse with strangers of figure and fashion. Monboddo, in after years, prided himself not a little upon the fact that he had spent three years studying Civil Law at Groningen, and never lost an opportunity of advocating a similar education for all promising Scottish lawyers.

Returning to Scotland, he happened to arrive in Edinburgh on the day when the notorious Captain Porteous expiated his crime on a dyer's pole in the Grassmarket. When about to retire to rest, Burnet's curiosity was aroused by a tumultuous crowd hurrying along the thoroughfare beneath his window. Instead of going to bed, he made his way to the street, where his scantily clad condition and the nightcap which he wore added a touch of humour to a situation tragic in the extreme. Speedily becoming entangled with the crowd, he soon found himself in the Grassmarket, where he was an involuntary witness of the scene which Scott has painted in indelible colours in his *Heart of Midlothian*. Burnet was so shocked by what he saw that he passed a sleepless night, and next morning seriously meditated leaving Edinburgh as a place unfit for a civilized being to live in. Better counsels prevailed, however, for on learning how Porteous had come by his miserable end, he heroically resolved to hazard his life among the turbulent populace of the Scottish capital.

Burnet became an advocate in 1737 and, with a true sense of the fitness of things, went to reside in Advocates' Close. Here he practised the simple life, partly because briefs were few, and partly because his capacity for convivial enjoyment was limited. One good story has come down to us of those days when Burnet's plight seems to have been that suggested by the cheerless line in Johnson's *London*:

Slow rises worth by poverty dépress'd.

He was junior counsel for the Laird of Stracathro and the tacksman of the Edzell fishings, in an action which they had brought against Mr Scott of Brotherton with reference to the construction of certain 'cruive fishings' near the mouth of the North Esk. The cruives had to be inspected, and Burnet, in doing this, fell into a deep pool. Efforts were made to rescue him, but Scott, the defender, thought this a work of supererogation. 'Let him alone,' he cried, 'the young man wants to go to the bottom of the cause.' Burnet, however, was saved, and did get to the bottom of the cause, though in a different way from what the defender in the case expected.

As a young man, Burnet sedulously attended social entertainments of all kinds, and in fashionable society he speedily rose to honour. There was no more familiar figure at the assemblies in Bell's Wynd, where he generally appeared in a suit of white velvet. Adorned in this garb, which he thought might well have become the person of the Chancellor of France, he would dance a minuet in truly Dutch style, to the delight of the ladies, and to the no small satisfaction of himself. He was unfailing, too, in his devotion to theatricals, though, as will be shown later, his ideas of the drama were decidedly peculiar. When West Digges and the captivating Mrs Ward appeared in the Edinburgh playhouse, Burnet was nightly in attendance, and found scope for his energies in handing the ladies to their seats. He was also fond of hunting and other manly exercises.

The outbreak of the Jacobite rebellion in 1745 brought about a temporary cessation of business in the Court of Session, and Burnet, loathing civil strife, hurried off to London to cement a number of literary and philosophical friendships. In the Metropolis, which, in later life, he visited annually, he mixed in the best society, his company being much sought after by wits, men of letters, and fashionable ladies. Indeed, he knew almost everybody worth knowing, not excepting the King. Among his most intimate London acquaintances were Thomson, the poet of the *Seasons*, in whose house at Richmond he passed many a pleasant hour; David Mallet, that notorious literary adventurer who changed his name 'from Scotch Malloch to English Mallet', and tried to filch from Thomson the honour of having written 'Rule, Britannia'; and Dr John Armstrong—frugal, taciturn, splenetic—who divided his time between a lucrative medical practice and the Muses, cultivating the latter with profit to himself, if not with advantage to the human race.

Burnet was also intimate with a group of law lords, including the great Thurlow, who is remembered by Fox's jest, 'No man was so wise as Thurlow looked', and the greater Mansfield, one of the finest intellects that ever added lustre to the King's Bench. Then there was

Mrs Montagu, 'a faded beauty, a wit, a critic, an author of some fame' who 'might have been admired by the first order of minds, had she not been greedy of more praise than she was entitled to.' It was at Mrs Montagu's that Burnet met Hannah More, whom he exasperated by defending slavery because the Ancients did so, and by maintaining that Home's *Douglas* was the greatest of tragedies. Nor must we forget Mrs Garrick, of whom he saw a good deal in the days of her widowhood. The lady still retained her beauty and charm of manner, so much so that the eccentric judge—now a widower of some years' standing—fell deeply in love with her. Twice the widower offered marriage to the widow, and twice it was politely declined.

Last, but not least, Burnet basked in the sunshine of royal favour. George III became quite interested in the Scottish judge, and frequently welcomed him at the Court of St James. One day Burnet was walking on the terrace at Windsor Castle, when the King, recognizing him, desired him to be called. 'My Lord,' said His Majesty with much affability, 'how did you travel from Scotland?' 'On horseback, please your Majesty.' 'That was too much at your time of life, and in the late bad weather, when even my dragoon officers took chaises; but tell me, does your lordship call a wheel-carriage a *box*?' 'Sire,' replied Monboddo, 'I am afraid I gave it a worse name; for I called it a *close box*.'

Burnet won his legal spurs in the Douglas Cause, which began in 1762. This, by far the most famous of Scottish lawsuits of the eighteenth century, centred in a very small point, regarding which, however, the evidence was extremely conflicting, namely, 'whether Archibald Stewart was or was not the son of Sir John Stewart of Grandtully and Lady Jane Douglas, sister of the Duke of Douglas.' The case created immense interest and excitement, as upon it hung the succession to the extensive estates of the last Duke of Douglas, for which there were several claimants.

'Briefed' on behalf of the Duke of Queensberry, Burnet acquitted himself so well as to make his elevation to the Bench inevitable. His industry and success in collecting evidence amazed his friends and disconcerted his opponents. Thrice did he visit France for this purpose, where his mastery of the language, a legacy of the Groningen days, was of great service. The Paris lawyers employed in the case were not very hopeful of success, and actually drafted a letter to the Duke of Queensberry counselling withdrawal, but Burnet would not hear of his client being so easily vanquished, and the letter was destroyed.

Subsequent events fully justified the line he took. The pleadings lasted no fewer than thirty-one days. Burnet sustaining his part brilliantly all the while. It is true that the Court of Session, by the casting vote of the Lord President, decided against him; but when the case was taken to the House of Lords, where sat Camden and Mansfield, the Douglas side won an easy victory. So ably did Burnet plead his case that the Supreme Court of Appeal, without a vote, reversed the decision of the Scottish judges, who had decided that Archibald Stewart was not the son of Sir John Stewart.

The death in 1767 of Andrew Fletcher, Lord Milton, created a vacancy among the ordinary Lords of Session, and Burnet became his successor, assuming the title of Lord Monboddo. As the Douglas Cause was not yet finally decided, efforts were made to delay the appointment, and not unnaturally, for Burnet's elevation at that moment meant that he would be placed in the invidious position of being called upon to pronounce judgment in a case in which he had played a leading part as an advocate. Burnet, it must be confessed, acted in this matter neither with discrimination nor delicacy, for he allowed the Duke of Queensberry, who was not slow to appreciate the advantage of transforming the man who had pled his cause into being its judge, to go to the King, and secure his appointment. Surely no judge was ever placed in a more embarrassing position than was Monboddo, for on the first occasion on which he appeared in his judicial capacity, the Douglas Cause came up for disposal.

But however inauspicious was the beginning of Monboddo's judicial career, it was fully atoned for. He is credited with having been not only a master of legal principle, but a wise, independent, impartial, and learned judge. Monboddo would probably have subscribed to the dictum of the American orator, 'One man with God is a majority'. Certainly, he often differed from his brethren, and found himself in a minority of one; but it says much for his soundness as a lawyer that his judgments were seldom, if ever, reversed by the House of Lords. Paradoxical Monboddo was in his books and in his talk, but he seems to have kept this dubious accomplishment under rigorous restraint while on the Bench.

Not less creditable is the fact that he was instrumental to some extent in getting rid of the 'law's delay'. One notable improvement instituted by him in a court in which circumlocution had become almost a fetish, was the substitution of what is known, in legal terminology, as 'hearings' for 'pleadings'. Monboddo might have become a judge in the Court of Justiciary, but he declined all overtures, because the duties would have interfered with the pursuit of his Greek studies in the vacation.

The personality of Monboddo is puzzling beyond all belief. He was typically Scottish in his shrewdness, wit, thrift, and 'dourness', but there was also a quixotic element in his nature which unmistakably differentiated him from the normal type of Scotsman. He was not exactly winsome, yet it would be a perversion of truth to say that he had no heart. A staunch if candid friend, an excellent host, a lover of cultivated society, an honest advocate of respectability in high places, and a latitudinarian churchman, Monboddo sat under his own vine and fig tree, none daring to make him afraid.

It cannot be said that he was prepossessing, looking, says Chambers, 'rather like an old stuffed monkey dressed in a judge's clothes, than anything else. His face, however, "sicklied o'er" with the pale cast of thought, bore traces of high intellect.' His manners were brusque; his habits plain, methodical, and frequently odd. He was abstemious, which is saying much, orgies being then in fashion. He was a thoroughgoing champion of sunlight and fresh air, which his contemporaries rigidly economized; and he unfeignedly believed that cleanliness was next to godliness, a doctrine more honoured in the breach than in the observance by his neighbours.

It was his custom, summer and winter, to take a cold bath on rising, usually at a very early hour. When staying at his Kincardineshire seat, he enjoyed this luxury in a structure erected for the purpose at some distance from the mansion, and near a running stream which supplied the water. He took a light dinner about noon, but considerably neutralized his excellent system of hygiene by making his supper the heaviest meal of the day. Before retiring to rest he indulged in an airbath, and then did homage to the Ancients (for whom he considered no sacrifice too great), by applying to his body a lotion composed of rose-water, olive oil, saline, aromatic spirit, and Venetian soap. Besmeared with this formidable concoction, he slept the sleep of the just.

It has been well said that Monboddo earned more fame by his eccentricities than by his acuteness and learning. Unquestionably, he both said and did very odd things—things so odd as to give rise to serious apprehension regarding his sanity. He called forth more ridicule than any other public character of his time. The vagaries of Adam Smith (and they were singular enough) were insignificant compared with the oddities of Monboddo. The queer sayings and doings of this judge were not excrescences, the offspring of affectation; they were part of the man himself. Monboddo could no more do obeisance to tradition and conventionality than he could admit that Shakespeare was a great dramatist, or David Hume an influential philosopher. And this obliquity of conduct and speech, simply because it was innate, has always weighed most in the popular judgment of Monboddo. Whimsical people are often tantalizing, but no one can say they are ever dull.

To chronicle all the stories about this crotchety man would be impossible, and even if it could be done no good purpose would be served, but one or two may be retailed as characteristic. What would be said nowadays of a judge who dispensed justice not from the Bench, but from the well of the court? This Monboddo invariably did. Several reasons have been given for his singular conduct. It is said that when he made his first appearance as a judge, he felt the awkwardness of his situation in connection with the Douglas Cause, and, with doubtful expediency, sought relief from a wounded conscience by delivering his 'opinion' from the well of the court. Cockburn says that some slight had made Monboddo resolve never to sit on the same bench with Lord President Dundas. He, however, adds that by sitting at the clerk's table, Monboddo was enabled to get easily in and out of the court, a more likely reason, for 'whenever there was a pause he was sure to slip off, gown and all, to have a talk in the Outer House'.

But Chambers gives another version. The story goes that his lordship once embroiled himself in an action respecting a horse which he had committed when sick to a farrier, with instructions to give the animal a certain medicine. The farrier, thinking to improve the occasion, administered, along with the medicine, a liberal dose of treacle, no doubt surmising that a horse was as fond of its medicine being made palatable as a child. Unfortunately, the horse died next morning, and the farrier found himself the unhappy victim of a prosecution at the hands of Monboddo, who pleaded his own cause at the Bar. He lost the case, however, and became, Chambers alleges, 'so enraged in consequence at his brethren, that he never afterwards sat with them upon the bench, but underneath, amongst the clerks'.

In Butler's *Hudibras* there is a line which says:

> Great on the bench, great in the saddle.

These words might be fitly applied to Monboddo. He despised a carriage for two reasons. First, because he thought it was degrading to be dragged at the tails of horses instead of being mounted on their backs; and, secondly, because carriages were not in universal use among the Ancients. One wonders what would have been Monboddo's attitude had he lived in this era of motor cars and aeroplanes. The truth is that, apart from his partiality for classical habits, he was very fond of horses. No one delighted more than he in the pleasures of the chase. Mounted on Alburac, his favourite nag, he would scour the country in all weathers. And he was proud of the performance. He told Ramsay of Ochtertyre once that, in a journey from Dalhousie Castle to Monboddo, he had met but one traveller who, to avoid the blast, rode with his face to the tail.

His annual journeys to London were invariably made on horseback. These equestrian performances continued until he was upwards of eighty years of age. On his last journey he took ill, and it was with great difficulty that a friend, who had overtaken him on the road, persuaded him to enter a carriage, which sorely touched his dignity as well as cast a slur upon the Ancients. But he was ill at ease, and, on the following day, he again mounted Alburac, and arrived in Edinburgh without further mishap.

In May 1785, Monboddo was in the court of the King's Bench when a rumour that the building was falling caused a general stampede. The Scottish judge, however, took the matter very coolly, as the following extract from a contemporary newspaper sufficiently testifies: 'In the curious rout of the lawyers' corps, it is singular that the only person who kept his seat was a venerable stranger. Old Lord Monboddo, one of the Scots judges, was in the court of the King's Bench, and being short-sighted and rather dull in his hearing, he sat still during the tumult, and did not move from his place. Afterwards, being questioned why he did not bestir himself to avoid the ruin, he coolly answered "that he thought it was *an annual ceremony* with which, as an alien to our laws, he had nothing to do!" '

When the colonel in *Guy Mannering* informs Mr Pleydell that the usual hour of supper will be anticipated, the latter gaily expresses his delight, and remarks, 'I am of counsel with my old friend Burnet. I love the *cœna*, the supper of the Ancients'. The allusion is to Monboddo's custom of entertaining his friends to what he called 'learned suppers', in imitation of the Ancients. These took place fortnightly at his residence in St John Street. Here of an evening would gather as choice a company of intellectual aristocrats as could be found anywhere, for the colloquial fare was as substantial as the repast. The supper was usually at an early hour, and had all the variety and abundance of the chief meal of the day, Monboddo, in his unquenchable enthusiasm for the Ancients, being intent on reviving as much of the glory of the Attic banquets as was possible in an unattractive house in murky Edinburgh. The table was strewn with roses, for did not Horace love to have it so at his beautiful home among the Sabine hills? Similarly, the master of the feast would garland his flasks of excellent Bordeaux, as Anacreon was wont to do at the court of Polycrates of Samos. And as the sumptuous feast proceeded, Monboddo, who loved to unbend after the labours of the day to a select and admiring company, would discourse upon many things ancient and modern with wit, vivacity, and learning, or would expound some of his eccentric theories regarding the savage state or the diminution of the human race with an ingenuity and eloquence which might have been expended in a better cause.

While Monboddo's conversational powers were exhibited to most advantage at the suppers of the Ancients, his brilliant dialectical skill was in evidence at the meetings of the Select Society. There he met foemen worthy of his steel who by argument, and, occasionally, by sarcasm, sought to demolish his most cherished ideas. But he usually proved more than a match for his antagonists. On one occasion he had an animated encounter with Wedderburn who, in after years, found his way to the Woolsack. The future Lord Chancellor had ventured to say something derogatory to the Ancients which, immediately, brought Monboddo to his feet. 'Mr Preses,' he said, 'the Ancients roasted *above* the fire; the Moderns roast *before* the fire; but methinks this young gentleman would fain roast without any fire at all!'

An ingenious though unsound philosopher, a scholar whose knowledge was extensive rather than profound, a trafficker in paradox, and a man of letters whose judgment ran counter to that of most of his contemporaries, Monboddo had his full share of the trials of the man who is misunderstood. And like most misunderstood men, he made not a few enemies, partly by his intellectual singularity, and partly by a certain acerbity towards those who happened to differ from him. He quarrelled with Hume, whose 'wretched philosophy' he could not abide; he despised his colleague, Kames, and, with perhaps a touch of jealousy, made light of his metaphysics; and he had no love for Dr Johnson because, among other reasons, he had not 'genius enough to comprehend the beauties of Milton,' and held very unorthodox views concerning the Ancients.

Foote said of Monboddo that he was 'an Elzevir edition of Johnson' —a pretty compliment, though some, perplexed as to whether Foote really meant what the phrase usually implies, have asserted that he was only thinking of a pocket edition. Be that as it may, Monboddo and Johnson could forget their feuds, and meet as gentlemen. Boswell, however, was not at all sure on this point, and believing for once that discretion is the better part of valour, he cautiously 'sounded' Monboddo as to whether a visit from Johnson, who was then trudging to the Hebrides, would be acceptable.

It was the vacation, and the judge was as usual living in the guise of a farmer on the ancestral estate. Thither Boswell despatched a letter announcing that Johnson had, with touching magnanimity, expressed a wish to 'go two miles out of his way to see Lord Monboddo'. Boswell's wish was gratified. Lexicographer and judge met, and if they did not fall upon each other's neck nor always return the soft answer which turns away wrath, they, on the whole, spent a pleasant time, and parted better friends than they were when they met.

Boswell gives a fairly full and graphic description of the interview: 'Lord Monboddo received us at his gate most courteously; pointed to the Douglas arms upon his house, and told us that his great-grandmother was of that family. "In such houses (said he) our ancestors lived, who were better men than we." "No, no, my lord (said Dr Johnson). We are as strong as they, and a great deal wiser." This was an assault upon one of Lord Monboddo's capital dogmas, and I was afraid there would have been a violent altercation in the very close, before we got into the house. But his lordship is distinguished not only for "ancient metaphysics" but for ancient *politesse* . . . and he made no reply.'

'His lordship,' Boswell continues, 'was drest in a rustic suit, and wore a little round hat; he told us, we now saw him as Farmer Burnet, and we should have his family dinner, a farmer's dinner. He said: "I should not have forgiven Mr Boswell, had he not brought you here, Dr Johnson." ' The ice once broken, the two men talked genially concerning many topics in which they had a common interest, and soon became conscious that they were not so far apart after all. Both, of course, spoke highly of Homer. 'Johnson: "He had all the learning of his age. The shield of Achilles shows a nation in war, a nation in peace; harvest sport, nay stealing." Monboddo: "Ay, and what we (looking to Boswell) would call a Parliament House scene; a cause pleaded." Johnson: "That is part of the life of a nation at peace. And there are in Homer such characters of heroes, that the united powers of mankind ever since have not produced any but what are to be found there." Monboddo: "Yet no character is described." '

Then the conversation turned to history. 'Monboddo: "The history of manners is the most valuable. I never set a high value on any other history." Johnson: "Nor I; and therefore I esteem biography, as giving us what comes near to ourselves, what we can turn to use." Boswell: "But in the course of general history, we find manners. In wars we see the dispositions of people, their degrees of humanity, and other particulars." Johnson: "Yes: but then you must take all the facts to get this; and it is but a little you get." Monboddo: "And it is that little which makes history valuable." '

Monboddo and Johnson then sharpened their wits on such subjects as the decay of learning, the attainments of bishops, and the momentous problem as to whether a savage or a London shopkeeper had the best existence, the judge characteristically casting his vote for the savage. Johnson subsequently examined his host's son, Arthur, in Latin, an ordeal which the youth seems to have stood fairly well. It remains to be added that Johnson ate a hearty dinner, and that the judge suspected him of gourmandism.

It would have been surprising had Monboddo escaped the unpopularity which ever awaits the man whose tongue is not only sharp but indiscreet. He rushed in where angels fear to tread. His likes and dislikes he expressed with the utmost freedom, regardless of consequences. Candour is a virtue, but if not linked to prudence it may do endless havoc. Monboddo and Kames, between whom there was no love lost, once found themselves at Gordon Castle as guests of Jane, Duchess of Gordon. For this great lady Monboddo had much respect. 'Sir,' he once remarked to a friend, 'her Grace has a brilliancy and radiance about her like the rays round the head of an apostle!'—clumsy but genuine appreciation which ill accorded, however, with the incident about to be mentioned. Discussing his favourite topic—the Ancients —Monboddo remarked to the Duchess that few Moderns could write with elegance. It was suggested that Kames (who was present) was at least one exception to the rule. But Monboddo, with amazing tactlessness, declined to admit the exception. Kames, who thought himself as good as any Ancient, was, of course, highly offended. Happily, the noble hostess, not relishing the prospect of a literary duel in her drawing-room, adroitly relieved a desperate situation by proposing that the protagonists should dance a reel with her.

Monboddo's domestic life was clouded by bereavement. In 1760 he married Miss Farquharson, a relative of Marshal Keith, but the lady died in giving birth to her third child. Then his only son was taken at an early age, and, in 1790, his second daughter, who was the light of his eyes and the pride of his heart, fell a victim to consumption. Her remarkable beauty was the talk of Edinburgh; and she is supposed to have been the person who was elegantly praised in one of the papers of the *Mirror* as rejecting the most flattering offers of marriage in order that she might tend her father in his old age. Burns, who met her on the occasion of his first visit to Edinburgh, surrendered at once to her charms. 'Well,' said his friend Geddes to him when he arrived back in his native Ayrshire, 'and did you admire the young lady?' 'I admired God Almighty more than ever. Miss Burnet is the most heavenly of all His works,' was the unhesitating reply. Writing later to William Chalmers, the bard explained that 'Fair B——is heavenly Miss B., daughter of Lord Monboddo, at whose house I have had the honour to be more than once. There has not been anything nearly like her, in all the combinations of beauty, grace, and goodness, the great Creator has formed, since Milton's Eve on the first day of her existence.'

It would have been strange, indeed, if Burns had not followed up such superlative laudation by singing the praises of Monboddo's fair daughter in verse. Accordingly, there is the well-known allusion to her in the 'Address to Edinburgh':

> Fair Burnet strikes th' adoring eye,
> Heav'n's beauties on my fancy shine;
> I see the Sire of Love on high,
> And own His work indeed divine!

Miss Burnet's death, however, impelled the poet to try something more ambitious, and after several months' 'hammering', he produced the fine elegy of seven stanzas beginning:

> Life ne'er exulted in so rich a prize
> As Burnet, lovely from her native skies;
> Nor envious Death so triumph'd in a blow
> As that which laid th' accomplish'd Burnet low.

Even Clarinda was forced to acknowledge the bewitching beauty of Monboddo's daughter. To 'dear Sylvander', she wrote: 'Miss Burnet sat just behind me. What an angelic girl! I stared at her, having never seen her so near. I remembered you talking of her, etc. What felicity to witness her "softly speak and sweetly smile!" How could you celebrate any other Clarinda! Oh, I would have adored you, as Pope of exquisite taste and refinement, had you loved, sighed, and written upon her for ever!' Whatever foibles Clarinda may have had, certainly jealousy was not one of them.

The death of his beloved daughter was a blow from which Monboddo never recovered. It is said that, after she died, his son-in-law covered her portrait to spare the old man's feelings. 'Quite right—quite right,' said Monboddo, casually looking up from his book. 'Never,' says Ramsay, 'did Lord Monboddo appear in a more advantageous light. . . . He bore his loss like a hero and a Christian, returning to his studies and duties seemingly with increased ardour.' Monboddo survived his daughter for nine years. Shortly before his own death, which occurred at his house in Edinburgh on May 26, 1799, he said to Dr Gregory, his medical adviser and friend: 'I know it is not in the power of Art to cure me: all I wish is euthanasia—a happy death.' And euthanasia he got, for he died in harness.

Monboddo was fortunate in many things—fortunate in possessing a fine intellect, a sound heart, and a good conscience. But his estimable qualities and his undoubted learning were buried beneath as ludicrous a mass of crotchets and idiosyncrasies as ever were credited to a man outside of bedlam. Ridicule was his only portion during his lifetime, and it has not forsaken his memory—so hard is the way of the man who habitually trades in paradox. Of Monboddo's writings something will be said in the next chapter; but here, having regard solely to his personality, there is little to cavil at in the inflated lines which Dr H. W Tytler, author of *Pœdstrophia*, wrote in memory of his friend:

> If wisdom, learning, worth, demand a tear,
> Weep o'er the dust of great Monboddo here;
> A Judge upright, to mercy still inclined;
> A generous friend, a father fond and kind;
> His country's pride, for skill in Grecian lore,
> And all Antiquity's invalued store.

Lord Braxfield (1722–99)

To Lord Braxfield belongs the unenviable reputation of being the most execrated judge in the annals of Scottish jurisprudence. Even Lord Advocate Mackenzie, whose cruelty to the Covenanters earned him the sobriquet of 'Bluidy Mackenzie', was a scholar, a poet, and, some say, a gentleman; but the most ardent apologist for Braxfield is compelled to admit that his good qualities are not easily discoverable.

> Men's evil manners live in brass; their virtues
> We write in water.

The latter part of the Shakespearian dictum hardly applies to the 'Hanging Judge', for the most charitable view of his career leads only to the conclusion that his virtues, if he ever had any, were distinctly elusive. He is popularly regarded as the counterpart of the 'infamous Jeffreys'; but this hardly does him justice. When Cockburn dubbed him 'the Jeffreys of Scotland', he was thinking more of his flagrant conduct in connection with the sedition trials of 1793–4 than of his general character. Braxfield, it must be acknowledged, was a shade better than the English judge. He was a sound and able lawyer, which Jeffreys was not, and he was no sycophant, which Jeffreys was. Nevertheless, no one who has studied in contemporary records the judicial part which he played at a critical period in Scottish affairs, and is familiar with the word-portrait which Cockburn drew from the life, can have any doubt that he came dangerously near being destitute of principle and character. Unscrupulous, tyrannical, coarse, dissipated, illiterate, he was morally almost featureless. He had a hard heart, a tainted mind, a cross-grained, domineering nature, and an uncouth exterior. A noble aspiration or a lofty motive he was incapable of appreciating. Without faith, without hope, without charity, he moved continually in a world of sordid interests and ignoble purposes.

Let it be admitted that Cockburn's ultra-Whiggism did colour to some extent his portrait of Braxfield, but the broad lineaments of the notorious Lord Justice-Clerk are unquestionably there. And what a repulsive portrait it is! 'Strong built and dark, with rough eyebrows, powerful eyes, threatening lips, and a low growling voice, he was like a formidable blacksmith. . . . Illiterate and without any taste for refined enjoyment, strength of understanding, which gave him power without cultivation, only encouraged him to a more contemptuous disdain of all natures less coarse than his own. Despising the growing improvement of manners, he shocked the feelings even of an age which, with more of the formality, had far less of the substance of decorum than our own. Thousands of his sayings have been preserved, and the staple of them is indecency; which he succeeded in making many people enjoy, or at least endure, by hearty laughter, energy of manner, and rough humour.'

The genius of Stevenson has familiarized an immense public with the odiousness of Braxfield's character—a public that Cockburn could not reach. The prototype of Weir of Hermiston was, as everyone knows, no other than the redoubtable judge who sat at the head of the criminal court of Scotland in the closing years of the eighteenth century. 'Mind you,' wrote Stevenson in 1892 from far Vailima, 'I expect *The Justice-Clerk* (afterwards changed to *Weir of Hermiston*) to be my masterpiece. My Braxfield is already a thing of beauty and a joy for ever, and, so far as he has gone, *far* my best character.' Of course, Stevenson, for the purposes of romance, added touches to his portraiture which are not to be found in the original; but as his description was mainly based on Cockburn's account, and from what he could glean from the Raeburn canvas, it is indisputable that the general characteristics of Weir of Hermiston faithfully reflect those of the truculent Braxfield. This judge had a strange fascination for Stevenson, to whom he makes more than one reference in his writings. Readers of *Virginibus Puerisque* will recall his graphic account of the impressions made upon him by the 'Hanging Judge's' portrait when he saw it for the first time at the Raeburn Exhibition in Edinburgh in 1876.

Born in 1722, Robert Macqueen was mainly indebted to himself for his advancement in life, 'being a man of no family and very small estate.' His paternal grandfather was gardener to Charles, Earl of Selkirk, and his son, John Macqueen, the father of the judge, was bred a writer, to qualify him to be a baron-bailie to the Earl. He prospered in business, was sheriff-substitute of the Upper Ward of Lanarkshire, and in due season became the owner of a small property in the county, from which the future judge derived his legal title. His wife also belonged to Lanarkshire, being a daughter of John Hamilton of Gilderscleugh. Robert was the eldest son.

The family being large, and the means to support them small, John Macqueen could not afford to entertain exalted notions respecting the future of his children. Robert got a good, but not an expensive education, the father's intention being that he should succeed him. No stories have come down to us to show what manner of boy young Macqueen was when attending the grammar-school of Lanark, but at Edinburgh University, where he afterwards studied civil law, he seems to have created a favourable impression. At all events, there is the testimony of a class-fellow, Dr Erskine, who affirms that the civil law students 'would have fought for Robbie Macqueen, whose honesty and good nature made him a general favourite'.

Macqueen's ambition at first was to be a Writer to the Signet, and for some time he was an apprentice to an Edinburgh practitioner. When next we hear of him, he is in his father's office in Lanark. Here he came into contact with Dundas, afterwards the second President of that name, whose wife owned the estate of Bonnington. Dundas was struck by Macqueen's shrewdness and legal abilities, and urged him to qualify for the Scottish Bar. The advice was taken, and Macqueen set himself seriously to study for his new vocation. His industry was unflagging, and his enthusiasm great, and in 1744 he found himself wearing the gown of an advocate.

For a number of years he had the ordinary fate of young members of the Bar in having little to do, but gradually agents began to discover his merit, 'which was not inaptly compared to a rough diamond'. When his friend, Dundas, became Lord Advocate, he was made one of his deputies, an office which, if it yielded little money, at least gave a young barrister an opportunity of showing of what stuff he was made. Macqueen had been a careful student of feudal law, and when the litigation arising out of the forfeitures consequent upon the Jacobite rebellion of 1745 came before the Court, he, as one of the counsel for the Crown, was found to be the right man in the right place. His extensive and accurate knowledge, and his clear and forcible exposition of the many complicated points at issue, called forth general admiration.

His good sense and sound law, his candour, his unfailing instinct for what was relevant, made both judges and agents overlook his ungainly presence, his rustic manners, his broad dialect, and his vulgarisms. Macqueen had none of the art of the rhetorician, indeed despised it. He mainly relied upon a vigorous understanding, a thorough mastery of legal principle, and the sheer driving power of a strong virile personality. Many brilliant lawyers there were at the Bar at this time, but ere long he was the rival of the foremost of them. When at the height of his fame he is reputed to have pled from fifteen to twenty causes in a single day. Boswell's lines in the 'Court of Session Garland' is a reminder, too, that he was a proficient draughtsman.

> However, of our cause not being ashamed,
> Unto the whole Lords we straightway reclaimed;
> And our petition was appointed to be seen,
> Because it was drawn by Robbie Macqueen.

Macqueen's success at the Bar, conspicuous though it was, was eclipsed by his success in the tavern. Many outside Parliament House knew him to be a great lawyer, but many more recognized him as a great drinker. He early joined the claret-drinking, card-playing fraternity, and soon rose to be the ideal type of boon companion—coarse, boisterous, dissipated—a man who swore without provocation, 'like an ensign of the last age in his teens', and who, when in high spirits and in congenial company, would exclaim in dubious English, 'What a glorious thing is it to speak nonsense!' As Stevenson says, 'He was a convivial man, a lover of wine, and one who shone peculiarly at tavern meetings.' But though these drinking-bouts were neither infrequent nor slight, they seem hardly to have impaired his powers of work. 'Bacchus,' says Cockburn, 'had never an easy victory over Macqueen.' He is credited with having thriven on a 'stintless regimen of beef, brandy, and claret', being firmly persuaded that a point of law will be more easily studied after drinking a bottle of the favourite beverage than by abstemiousness. It is a novel doctrine, but Macqueen seemed to lend countenance to the idea that it was true.

The character of this man appears to be almost humanly inscrutable. It defies all ordinary standards of comparison. His father is said to have been at much pains to give him a religious upbringing, and he himself, despite his deep potations and his love of strong expletives, took credit for being 'a sincere Christian'. He would have indignantly repudiated any suggestion to the contrary. Of religion, Ramsay of Ochtertyre deliciously remarks, 'he retained all along a due sense, being thoroughly persuaded of its truth, though it did not always produce suitable fruits or make him set a watch on his lips.'

He was illiterate to a degree hardly conceivable in a person occupying his exalted position. He had no interest in literature, or art, or philosophy. With the writings of the Dutch jurists he was tolerably familiar, and for the works of Lord Stair he showed all the reverence he possessed, but it is doubtful whether he ever read a book which did not bear directly upon his professional labours. He fully imbibed the spirit of Prior's lines:

> From ignorance our comfort flows,
> The only wretched are the wise.

The intellectual lustre of the Edinburgh of his day meant nothing to him. He preferred the joviality of the tavern to the learned talk of Monboddo's supper parties. While Kames was struggling hard to get his countrymen to speak and write 'English undefiled', Braxfield was glorying in the vernacular and perpetrating the most outrageous Scotticisms. His humour was broad, but his speech was broader. 'Hae ye ony coonsel, man?' said he to Maurice Margarot, when placed at the bar on a charge of sedition. 'No,' was the laconic reply. 'Dae ye want to hae ony appointit?' continued the judge. 'No,' said Margarot sarcastically, 'I only want an interpreter to make me understand what your lordship says.' When Jeffrey, fresh from Oxford, began his career at the Scottish Bar, his speech gave his lordship much trouble. 'The laddie,' he remarked wittily, 'has clean tint his Scotch and fund nae English.'

After more than thirty years' exacting but eminently successful work as a pleader, Macqueen, in 1776, was raised to the Bench with the title of Lord Braxfield. This post he accepted only after the earnest solicitation of his old friend Dundas, for though it brought him honour, it implied substantial pecuniary loss. Four years later, he succeeded Lord Auchinleck, the father of Johnson's biographer, as a Lord of Justiciary. The appointment was not allowed to pass unnoticed. In the same year there was published an anonymous 'Letter to Robert Macqueen, Lord Braxfield, on his Promotion to be one of the Judges of the High Court.' Cockburn attributes this senseless pamphlet, for such it was, to Boswell. If he was really the author—and it is not difficult to imagine him in that capacity—then the publication may be set down as one of those 'blazing indiscretions' for which the renowned biographer was so famous. Apart from the fact that he was the son of the retiring judge, it was highly presumptuous, if not something worse, to lecture the judges of the criminal court on their partiality, indecorum, and carelessness, as the writer of this pamphlet did in terms neither wise nor moderate. Moreover, it was surely very improper to address the 'Letter' to Braxfield, who as yet had had no opportunities of committing the judicial sins complained of. The only construction that can be put upon the writer's action is that he was taking time by the forelock and warning Braxfield against a course of conduct to which his past record showed him peculiarly liable.

But whatever the explanation of this epistle, we may be sure that it did not hurt the new judge's feelings nor injure his prospects. As at the Bar so on the Bench, his forceful personality carried all before it. In 1788 he became Lord Justice-Clerk, in which capacity his most notorious deeds were done. It is impossible to understand what Braxfield was as a judge unless due allowance is made for his abnormal character—a character devoid of nearly every judicial virtue. He was coarse and jocular when he ought to have been dignified and circumspect; vindictive when he ought to have been dispassionate; cruel when he ought to have been just; boisterous and domineering when he ought to have been serenely calm.

'Judges,' says Bacon, 'ought to be more learned than witty; more reverend than plausible; and more advised than confident.' Braxfield ran counter to all three injunctions. He was a sort of swashbuckler of the Bench. It is true that he once declared (what is usually assumed on the part of a judge), 'I am one of those who are always for giving fair-play to panels'; but this most excellent rule he honoured more in the breach than in the observance. He bullied prisoners, he bullied witnesses, he bullied young advocates if he thought them 'Bar flunkeys' (his term for fops), and, at times, he bullied his colleagues.

'It is impossible,' writes Cockburn, 'to condemn his conduct as a criminal judge too gravely, or too severely. It was a disgrace to the age. A dexterous and practical trier of ordinary cases, he was harsh to prisoners even in his jocularity, and to every counsel whom he chose to dislike. . . . It may be doubted if he was ever so much in his element as when tauntingly repelling the last despairing claim of a wretched culprit, and sending him to Botany Bay or the gallows with an insulting jest; over which he would chuckle the more from observing that correct people were shocked.'

And all the specimens of his lordship's *obiter dicta* that have been chronicled, bear out this amazing indictment by one who was himself a judge. Braxfield was indeed a 'terror of the law'. Lockhart, in his *Life of Scott*, reports him as having said to an eloquent culprit at the bar: 'Ye're a vera clever chiel, man, but ye wad be nane the waur o' a hangin'.' When Muir, the political reformer, was being tried, Braxfield, parting with the last vestige of judicial honour, whispered to the father of Francis Horner (one of the Edinburgh Reviewers), as he entered the jury-box, 'Come awa, Maister Horner, come awa, and help us to hang ane o' thae d—— scoondrels.' At a time when the procedure in criminal cases was more a mystery than it is now, and the line to be taken often seemed doubtful, Braxfield at all events was ready for any emergency. 'Hoot! jist gie me Josie Norrie (a clerk of court well up in forms and precedents) and a gude jury, an' I'll do for the fallow'—a typical example of his lordship's best judicial manner.

In ribaldry and coarseness, Braxfield would have offended the Lord Chesterfield of that day, a man by no means squeamish, if we are to judge by those flagitious letters he wrote to his son. Even the most sacred things were not immune from his ridicule. In one of the sedition trials, the prisoner, Gerrald, ventured to remark that all great men had been reformers, 'even our Saviour Himself'. 'Muckle He made o' that; He was hangit' was the profane reply of the man who prided himself upon being a 'sincere Christian'. On another occasion two young advocates, looking considerably the worse for a protracted orgy, were about to plead before his lordship when they were admonished in the following fashion: 'Gentlemen, ye maun jist pack up yer papers and gang hame, for the tane o' ye's riftin' punch, and the ither's belching claret, and there'll be nae gude got oot o' ye the day.'

And where claret was concerned, Braxfield's opinion was not to be traduced. Being entertained once at Douglas Castle, and observing that port was the only wine produced after dinner, his lordship, with his customary rudeness, asked his host if 'there was nae claret in the castle?' 'I believe there is,' was the reply, 'but my butler tells me it is not good.' 'Let's pree't,' said the senator. The claret having been produced and pronounced excellent, Braxfield, wishing to show that he was not ignorant of ecclesiastical phraseology, proposed that as a *fama clamosa* had gone forth against the wine, the parish minister (who was present) should 'absolve' it. But his lordship had been a little foolhardy. 'I know,' said the clergyman, 'that you are a very good judge in cases of civil and criminal law; but I see you do not understand the laws of the Church. We never absolve till after three appearances.'

In the same year that Braxfield became Lord Justice-Clerk, he was called upon to play the principal judicial part in the trial of the notorious Deacon Brodie, who, for a time, was highly successful in his dual position of town councillor by day and burglar by night. In this, with the single exception of the Douglas Cause, the most famous Scottish trial of the eighteenth century, Braxfield was thoroughly in his element. It was a case well fitted to call forth all his sinister powers, and he made the most of his opportunities. Four other judges sat beside him, but he alone controlled the case.

John Clerk (afterwards Lord Eldin) was counsel for George Smith, one of the Deacon's confederates, and with this young and brilliant advocate Braxfield had several encounters. Clerk, it must be confessed, was rash and pugnacious, and just the type of man to ruffle the not too equable temper of the Lord Justice-Clerk. In the first encounter Clerk did not figure well. In language not very respectful, he charged the Court with admitting improper evidence. He was, of course, reproved, but he persisted in impugning the judgment of the Court, and in asserting that the jury were to judge of the law as well as the facts. 'Sir, I tell you,' exclaimed the infuriated Braxfield, 'that the jury have nothing to do with the law, but to take it *simpliciter* from me.' 'That I deny,' was Clerk's insolent answer. The Court was indignant, but Clerk held his ground, and once more affirmed that the jurors were judges of the whole case. 'You are talking nonsense, sir,' roared Braxfield. 'My lord, you had better not snub me in this way,' was the instant reply, whereupon his lordship merely said, 'Proceed—gang on, sir.' There followed more interruptions, and a tactful counsel would certainly have been more deferential, but Clerk never believed that discretion is the better part of valour. So he went on: 'Gentlemen of the jury, I was just saying to you, when this outbreak on the Bench occurred, that you were the judges of the law and of the facts in this case.' Braxfield: 'We cannot tolerate this, sir. It is an indignity to this High Court—a very gross indignity, deserving of the severest reprobation.' But Clerk would either address the jury in his own way, or not speak at all. Whereupon the Lord Justice-Clerk called upon the counsel for the prisoner, Brodie, to proceed with his address; but the latter shook his head, as if declining to do so. The climax had now been reached. Braxfield was about to charge the jury when Clerk, starting to his feet, and raising a defiant fist to the Bench, shouted, 'Hang my client if you daur, my lord, without hearing me in his defence!' These words produced a great sensation, and the judges immediately retired to hold a consultation. On returning to the court, the Lord Justice-Clerk requested Clerk to resume his speech, which he did without further interruption.

Braxfield's address to the prisoners in passing sentence of death revealed the protean essence of his character. He was surely the last man in the world to reprove the vices of the age, and to point to the consolations of religion, but this he did in the case of Deacon Brodie. Here are his hypocritical words: 'It is much to be lamented that those vices, which are called gentlemanly vices, are so favourably looked upon in the present age. They have been the source of your (Brodie's) ruin; and, whatever may be thought of them, they are such as assuredly lead to ruin. I hope you will improve the short time which you have now to live by reflecting upon your past conduct, and endeavouring to procure, by a sincere repentance, forgiveness for your many crimes. God always listens to those who seek Him with sincerity.' Not bad for a man who could make the Founder of Christianity the subject of a jest!

The most memorable episode in Braxfield's career—the episode which exhibits more clearly than any other his real characteristics, both personal and professional—was the part he played in the trials of Muir, Skirving, Margarot, and others who were charged with sedition in 1793–4. The judicial aspect of the matter, and particularly Braxfield's conduct, was exhaustively investigated by Cockburn in his *Examination of the Trials for Sedition in Scotland* (2 vols, 1888). It would not be difficult to convict Cockburn of bias. He was a staunch Whig, he himself was counsel for three prisoners who were tried for sedition in 1817–19, and he had the good fortune to live in later times when a loftier standard of ethics prevailed on the Bench. These circumstances were almost bound to influence his judgment, and influence it they did. To call the Lord Justice-Clerk 'a coarse and dexterous ruffian' was to betray a spirit which suggested anything but judicial serenity. Such a phrase Cockburn surely ought not to have used. But when every allowance has been made for his Whiggism, it cannot be said that his severe condemnation of Braxfield's methods is unmerited. The harsh, censorious, and avowedly partisan conduct of the Lord Justice-Clerk as revealed by the records of these trials is almost incredible to a person living in the twentieth century.

An attempt has been made to palliate Braxfield's wrongdoing by contending that such a judge as he was needed to curb the lawless spirit of the time. Braxfield may have crushed the lawless spirit; he certainly did not administer justice. Even when the trials were proceeding his judicial conduct was strongly criticised. The attention of Parliament was drawn to the matter, and Lord Advocate Dundas was compelled to inform him that representations had been made against the legality of the sentences on Muir and Palmer. But the Lord Justice-Clerk was utterly unrepentant. He affirmed that the sentences were legal, and gratuitously urged that the royal clemency should not be extended to either prisoner.

Only one influential voice was raised in Braxfield's defence—Lord Mansfield's. Unfortunately, it did not, on this occasion, count for much since Mansfield admitted that he had no personal acquaintance with Braxfield, though he had 'long heard the loud voice of fame that speaks of him as a man of pure and spotless integrity, of great talents, and of a transcendent knowledge of the laws of his country.'

How this man of 'pure and spotless integrity' comported himself in the sedition trials of 1793–4, we shall see presently. Meanwhile, it may be noted that Braxfield was a political partisan of the deepest dye. He was a disciple of Dundas, to whose 'nod every man owed what he got, and looked for what he wished.' And Dundas stood for a Toryism which spelt political degradation, and the triumph of the forces of reaction. Accordingly, Whigs, Radicals, French Revolutionists, and 'siclike enemies o' the King and Constitution' were Braxfield's pet aversion. If he did not exactly hold with Dr Johnson that 'the first Whig was the Devil', he certainly made it his business both on and off the Bench to see that the 'Whig dogs' did not get the best of it. Where politics were concerned, it was impossible to look for justice from Braxfield. 'Bring me prisoners, and I'll find you law' was his attitude during a period of intense political excitement. 'His blamableness in these trials,' says Cockburn, 'far exceeds that of his brethren. They were weak; he was strong. They were frightened; he was not. They followed; he, the head of the Court, led.'

Braxfield's ruling principle in the sedition trials was to obtain a conviction, and having obtained it, to impose a sentence that would strike terror in the hearts of his political adversaries. The ethical sense had become so atrophied that he was prepared to go to any length. Had not Dundas, who trembled lest the Lord Justice-Clerk's zeal for Toryism should carry him too far, counselled moderation, the situation might have been worse. But even as it stands, Braxfield's record is very black. Never, it may be confidently asserted, had the Scottish judiciary sunk so low, never had political passion so blinded judges who ought to have risen superior to all party feeling.

In the trial of Thomas Muir (1793), Braxfield accused the prisoner of trying to overturn 'our present happy Constitution—the happiest, the best, and the most noble Constitution in the world.' Furthermore, he proclaimed the novel doctrine that to promote parliamentary reform was to be guilty of sedition. He also fulminated against the French as 'monsters of human nature.' 'Mr Muir might have known that no attention could be paid (by Parliament) to such a rabble (the advocates of political reform). What right had they to representation? . . . A government in every country should be just like a corporation; and, in this country, it is made of the *landed interest, which alone has a right to be represented.*'

This extraordinary outburst was severely commented upon in Parliament, but so many conflicting interests were at work that the judge was neither censured nor asked to retract. When the jury unanimously found Muir guilty, Braxfield expressed his high approval of the verdict, declared that 'transportation was the proper punishment', and 'only hesitated whether it should be for life or for a term of fourteen years.' In such fashion was justice administered in Scotland in the closing years of the eighteenth century.

An equally violent display of political rancour occurred in connection with the trial of William Skirving (1794), Braxfield more than hinting that he expected the jury to acquit themselves as good partymen. All opposition to the predominant political mood of the hour was sedition. 'I say, gentlemen, that the greatest union in this nation is necessary to support us under a war with a neighbouring nation, consisting of the most profligate monsters that ever disgraced humanity.' This tirade Braxfield wound up as follows: 'It would be very difficult for me to conceive it possible that this man, now at the bar, can be found not guilty.' The jury did not misinterpret his meaning, and poor Skirving received the penalty of political contumacy.

Of all the political prisoners brought before Braxfield, Maurice Margarot gave, perhaps, the most trouble. During his trial (1794) a scene occurred to which it would be difficult to find a parallel in legal history. Margarot was no poltroon. Quite early in the trial he proved himself more than a match for the formidable Braxfield. Learning that the court was being filled with people who had paid the doorkeepers for admission, he demanded that the court should be open to all comers. 'That you have no business with,' was Braxfield's answer. Margarot said no more, but on entering upon his defence, he again threw down the gauntlet. The scene which then took place was so

extraordinary that the passage-at-arms between the prisoner and the
Lord Justice-Clerk may well be reproduced in full.

MARGAROT. Now, my lord, comes a very delicate matter indeed. I
mean to call upon my Lord Justice-Clerk; and I hope that the questions
and the answers will be given in the most solemn manner. I have
received a piece of information which I shall lay before the Court in
the course of my questions. First, my lord, are you on oath?

BRAXFIELD. State your questions, and I will tell you whether I
will answer them or not. If they are proper questions I will answer
them.

MARGAROT. Did you dine at Mr Rochead's at Inverleith in the course
of last week?

BRAXFIELD. And what have you to do with that, sir?

MARGAROT. Did any conversation take place with regard to my
trial?

BRAXFIELD. Go on, sir.

MARGAROT. Did you use these words: 'What should you think of
giving him (Margarot) a hundred lashes together with Botany Bay',
or words to that effect?

BRAXFIELD. Go on. Put your questions if you have any more.

MARGAROT. Did any person—did a lady say to you that the mob
would not allow you to whip me? And, my lord, did you not say that
the mob would be the better for losing a little blood? These are the
questions, my lord, that I wish to put to you at present in the presence
of the Court. Deny them, or acknowledge them.

The consternation which this encounter—surely one of the most
extraordinary that ever took place between a judge of the High Court
and a prisoner—produced, may be more easily imagined than described. Braxfield appealed to his colleagues as to whether he should
answer the questions; but, amazing to relate, all replied that they were
irrelevant, and ought not to be answered. A more despicable piece of
sophistry can hardly be conceived. Braxfield, at all events, knew that
Margarot's questions were not only relevant, but that the story which
gave rise to them was true. In a rash moment he had uttered the sentiments mentioned by Margarot at Mr Rochead's house, and a lady had
indiscreetly repeated them. In point of fact, his lordship never sought
to deny the story. Moreover, at the subsequent trial of Joseph Gerrald,
an offer was made to establish its truth by evidence independent of

Braxfield, but the Court refused to allow the matter to be gone into—
'a proceeding which,' as Cockburn remarks, 'it is difficult to reconcile
with any hypothesis except one.'

Gerrald's trial came on in March 1794, and was conducted with all
the severity and want of fair-play which had been displayed in the
trials of Muir, Skirving, and Margarot. Judging by Braxfield's summing-up, Gerrald's offence seems to have been one of nationality
rather than of sedition. 'Gentlemen,' said his lordship, 'Gerrald has no
relation, nor the least property, in this country, but comes here to
disturb the peace of the country, as a delegate from a society in
England, to raise sedition in this country. I say he appears to me to be
much more criminal than Muir, Palmer, and Skirving, because they
were all natives of this country.' This statement was both irrelevant
and untrue—irrelevant inasmuch as the circumstances of these men
were not before the jury (Palmer had not even been tried before
Braxfield), untrue, because Palmer, at any rate, was an Englishman.

Braxfield's valiant efforts to stem the rising tide of democratic
sentiment gained him many friends who had no reason to be dissatis-
fied with the state of things which existed under the Dundas regime.
But it was otherwise with the great mass of the people. The political
animosity of Braxfield and his colleagues, and the remorseless way in
which they transported men whose chief offence was that they were
'Friends of the People', roused the most unruly passions. For a time
Braxfield was quite as unpopular as Mansfield had been during the
Gordon riots, though for a very different reason. In this very brief
catalogue of virtues, courage occupied a prominent place. There was
nothing clandestine about Braxfield. The man who told the Radicals
to their faces that 'they would a' be muckle the better o' being hangit'
might be lamentably indiscreet, but was certainly no coward. As an
instance of his great nerve, it is recorded that after the sedition trials
were over, which was generally about midnight, he would walk to his
house in George Square, alone and unprotected.

What kind of a domestic life Braxfield led it is impossible to say, but
from what is known of his public character and of his habits, it is
permissible to assume that the family circle would not be the brighter
for his presence. He was twice married. His first wife, by whom he had
two sons and two daughters, was a daughter of Major James Agnew of
the 7th Dragoon Guards, and niece of Sir Andrew Agnew, Bart., of
Lochnaw, Wigtownshire. He married, secondly, Elizabeth, daughter

of Robert Ord, Lord Chief Baron of the Exchequer of Scotland, by whom he had no issue.

When Braxfield paid his addresses to this lady, he did so in a thoroughly business-like fashion. Having satisfied himself as to her suitability, he called upon her, and announced his mission with a brevity and point which all suitors will admire, though few can emulate. 'Lizzy, I am looking out for a wife, and I thought you just the person that would suit me. Let me have your answer, off or on, the morn, and nae mair aboot it.' It is pleasant to add that the lady was quite as business-like. Next day she returned a favourable answer, and the marriage took place with the minimum of delay. Ramsay of Ochtertyre relates an anecdote of this lady upbraiding her husband for niggardliness. The story is to the effect that Lord Hailes and Braxfield were once entering a town where a circuit court was to be held, when Mrs Macqueen remarked upon the shabbiness of their equipage compared with that of Hailes. 'It is a shame,' she said, 'to have horses of different colours.' 'Never mind that, my dear,' said her partner, 'have we not a dog that he wants?'

Braxfield was a near neighbour of the father of Sir Walter Scott, the former residing at 28 and the latter at 25 George Square. Between the two families there appears to have been considerable intimacy; and it is interesting to recall that Scott's thesis on *The Title of the Pandects concerning the Disposal of the Dead Bodies of Criminals*, written in connection with his admission to the Faculty of Advocates, was dedicated to Braxfield—a tribute, no doubt, to the Lord Justice-Clerk's Toryism, which Scott shared to the full.

In his declining years Braxfield, no longer equal to the exacting pleasures of the tavern, became enamoured of the life of a country gentleman. Much of his leisure was passed at his Lanarkshire seat, 'which he loved the more that he had gathered birds' nests there in his boyish years'. As a landed proprietor he did remarkably well. He devoted much time and attention to farming with excellent financial results, he improved and extended Braxfield, and he purchased 'several valuable estates at a time when land was comparatively cheap.'

From his seventieth year onwards, Braxfield suffered much from ill-health, and for more than twelve months prior to his death he was unable to attend the Parliament House. He died at his town residence in 1799, and was buried at Lanark. 'Regardless of the threats and invectives of a misled populace, Braxfield,' wrote a contemporary, 'discharged his duties with a manly firmness of mind, well-tempered intrepidity of conduct, and a wise and faithful application of the law, that must make his memory ever be gratefully remembered by his country.' That so unrighteous a judge should have been graced with so fine an epitaph is one of the travesties of human life. 'He has carried more sound law with him than he has left upon the Bench', observed one of his ablest professional rivals on learning of his death. Posterity will prefer to think of Braxfield the lawyer rather than of Braxfield the judge, or of Braxfield the man.

C. H. S. Fifoot

Judge and Jurist 1837–1901

QUEEN VICTORIA was not born a Victorian; she became one by marriage, widowhood and longevity. Upon the crowded years of her reign no single pattern may be imposed. A few contrasts will mark the gulf between 1837 and 1901. In 1837 Sir Walter Scott was but five years dead, Carlyle published his *French Revolution*, *Pickwick Papers* were appearing in numbers, Disraeli entered the House of Commons for the first time. In 1901 Thomas Hardy had ceased to write novels, Henry James had reached the last stage of refinement, Bernard Shaw had surrendered dramatic criticism to the incomparable Max and was meditating upon *Man and Superman*, Winston Churchill had been a year in Parliament. Today's observer, looking back upon the reign with his own resigned, almost cynical assumption of instability, may see it enveloped in an atmosphere of smug security. The impression is superficial. From 1837 to 1850 England was, or felt itself to be, in constant peril of revolution. These were the years of Corn Law agitation, of the Chartists, of mob disorder, of the reverberations at home of 1848 abroad. They saw the advent of the railway and the company, with their deep impact upon the structure of trade and industry, the first erosion of individual responsibility and the gradual disintegration of provincial life.

If any period invites the reproach of complacency, it is the third quarter of the century. The great exhibition of 1851 symbolized the supremacy of the upper middle class—able, confident, high-minded, broad based upon commercial and agricultural wealth. They and their sons were the fruits of the new public schools inspired by Dr Arnold, who had taught them the importance of being earnest. Their leader was Lord Palmerston, born above them but adopted into their *familia* and, in the cliché of the time, a representative man. His death in October, 1865, still in office and within two days of his eighty-first birthday, was a climacteric. The rivals who sought his place, Gladstone and Disraeli, came from the dominant class, but new men meant new measures. The Reform Act of 1867, if it seemed apt to buttress the structure of society could serve as well to undermine it. Beneath the surface of popular optimism and material prosperity lurked the fear of the future. Thinking men searched their minds and were perturbed at what they found. Anthony Trollope, the mirror of his age and class, portrayed with distaste the transition from the old England of *The Warden* in 1855 to the new England of *Mr Scarborough's Family* in 1882. Froude in 1864 was prophetic. 'We live in times of disintegration, and none can tell what will be after us. What opinions—what convictions—the infant of today will find prevailing on the earth if he and it live out together to the middle of another century, only a bold man would undertake to conjecture.' The testimony of Bagehot, shrewd and detached, is significant. He had been bred to assume the merits of the current 'system of removable inequalities' much as, in a later age, it has become orthodox to assert, rather than to rationalize, the cruder doctrine of equality. It was 'the wholesome competition between class and class and the wholesome migration from class to class' that forged 'the strongest instruments of social improvement'. This assumption he now saw challenged by the advent of democracy—'neither the best nor the highest form which a society can adopt, and one fatal to that development of individual originality by which the past progress of the human race has been achieved and from which alone all future progress is to be anticipated.'

The prophets were justified only too soon. In the last quarter of the century powerful solvents were at work upon English society. The agricultural interests, which had so surprisingly survived and even flourished upon the abolition of the Corn Laws, fell into a decline that proved all but fatal. International competition, inherent in the dogma of Free Trade, at last burst the barriers of insularity, and the produce of the new acres was carried by the new means of transport to flood the domestic markets. In this invasion high and low—landlord, farmer and labourer—were alike engulfed. From the late seventies to the early nineties agricultural was accompanied by trade depression, with its familiar portents—unemployment, strikes, the foundation of the Fabian Society and the rise of the Labour Party. Amid this confusion, political and economic *laissez-faire*, long fashionable if never unquestioned, could not survive unimpaired; and the reaction of anxious Liberals to the new machinery of state control were, according to temperament, tortuous or indignant. Some, like T. H. Green, vindicated the measures of their leaders by insisting that only through order could freedom be realized. Defending the Employers' Liability Act of 1880 against the reproach of authoritarianism, he insisted that contractual licence was 'valuable only as a means to an end—the liberation of the powers of all men equally for contribution to the common good'. Liberty must serve equality. Herbert Spencer, fed on the pure milk of individualism, was not to be comforted by paradox. The servant could too easily become the slave. In 1884 in *The Man versus the State* he vented his anguish at the betrayal of liberal ideas and denounced the 'trend towards regimentation, bureaucracy, socialism and excessive taxation'. Victoria's reign, with its material achievements and its accumulation of wealth, ended, as it had begun, in doubt and misgivings.

Through all these years educated opinion was moulded by a diversity of intellectual interests. The young Victorian inherited the economic theories of Ricardo, modified and disseminated by John Stuart Mill, whose *Principles of Political Economy*, published in 1847, was in 1901 still the one 'set book' on economics in the Oxford History School. By this time, indeed, its premises were widely challenged, nor had they ever lacked critics. Carlyle had rejected them with scorn. Mill's book, he said, was 'well done but not worth doing'. But they helped to form the climate in which were bred most of the judges and jurists of Victoria's reign.

A fresh and stimulating demand upon receptive minds was made by natural science and pre-eminently by the biologist. Opinion was excited in 1844 by the anonymous publication of *Vestiges of the Natural Order of Creation*, attributed *inter alios* to the Prince Consort but in fact written by Robert Chambers of *Chambers's Encyclopaedia*. It popularized 'evolution' and was eagerly embraced and as furiously denounced. The way was prepared for Darwin, whose theory of natural selection met so happily the claims of a competitive society; and in 1869 Bagehot applied biological methods to sociology.

The bias thus imparted to speculative thought seemed to threaten the foundations of religious belief. Newman, as he avowed in his *Apologia* felt instantly the danger to Christian faith, or at least to Christian doctrine, of scientific pretensions; and the appearance in 1860 of the famous *Essays and Reviews* revealed the need felt by the more sensitive leaders of the Anglican Church to trim their lamps to the new revelation. Of the seven contributors Benjamin Jowett, Mark Pattison and Frederick Temple were at once the most distinguished and the most circumspect. Two of their colleagues, more enthusiastic or less discreet, were prosecuted before the Court of Arches for denying the doctrine of eternal punishment. They were convicted, but the conviction was quashed by the Judicial Committee of the Privy Council. The fortunate ambiguity of the Articles enabled the charge of heresy to be eluded. Lord Westbury, who delivered the opinion of the Committee, was said, in a contemporary squib, to have 'dismissed Hell with costs and to have taken away from members of the Church of England their last hope of everlasting damnation'. Outside the ranks of the clergy belief sank only too often into agnosticism. The loss of faith was a catastrophe in itself enough to destroy the picture of a nation engrossed in creature comfort. The best suffered the most. Stable standards of conduct must somewhere be found, and with doubtful hope the religious was replaced by the ethical imperative. George Eliot, while she found it difficult, if not impossible, to accept orthodox Christianity, was not comforted by the prospect of evolution. After reading the *Origin of Species* she wrote: 'To me the Development Theory, and all other explanations of processes by which things came to be, produce a feeble impression compared with the mystery that lies under the processes.' Matthew Arnold, loth to relinquish all conception of a Deity, could describe God only as 'the Eternal not ourselves which makes for righteousness'. Bradley's comment is not unjust. As well term the habit of washing 'the Eternal not ourselves that makes for cleanliness'.

A healthier phenomenon was the emergence from Germany of the 'historical spirit'. Niebuhr, Savigny and above all Ranke may be called the founders of modern history. They proclaimed the need to base all research and all writing upon the study of original sources; and when in 1870 Stubbs published his *Select Charters* he vindicated at once German technique and English scholarship. The influence of Germany was not confined to history. As early as 1792 in Edinburgh a coterie of briefless barristers, among them Walter Scott, formed a German class. The example spread southwards until Coleridge and Carlyle became ardent disciples. English philosophers followed at the heels of Kant and deserted him in the second half of the century only to cultivate the more esoteric rites of Hegel. Theologians, willingly or grudgingly, went again to school. Pusey himself served an apprenticeship with the German divines, though he was proof against the scepticism with which his younger contemporaries were infected.

Dean Stanley defended *Essays and Reviews* by invoking the testimony of the master race. 'The German theologians have lighted the candle which, by God's grace, shall never be put out.'

English law was not insulated from these currents of thought and opinion. Ethical preoccupations coloured the approach to civil and criminal liability. The prevalent political economy demanded, as one of its assumptions, the sanctity of agreements, and it was in the first half of Victoria's reign that the classical formulae of contract were expounded. Expanding trade and industry, with their prolific and costly litigation, drew to the common law and to the commercial bar the eager minds that had previously pursued the mysteries of conveyancing.

The literature of the law reflected the taste for biological investigation. Maine published his *Ancient Law* two years after the *Origin of Species*, and it was the theory of natural selection no less than a sense of the past that provoked his attack on Austin in the final chapters of *The Early History of Institutions*. Holmes thought Darwin the seminal influence of the century. 'No one,' he wrote, 'has done so much to affect our whole way of thinking about the universe.' Maitland saluted Savigny not only as the Romanist and as the historian, but as 'the herald of evolution, the man who substitutes development for manufacture, organism for mechanism, natural laws for Natural Law, the man who is nervously afraid lest a code should impede the beautiful processes of natural growth.'

The ever-increasing interest in historical and especially in mediaeval studies that spread over Victorian scholarship might have been expected to make a peculiar appeal to the English lawyer with his proud consciousness of continuity and his unique records. Yet the response was desultory and belated. Among the practitioners this was, perhaps, not altogether surprising, though there were distinguished exceptions. Serjeant Manning was a mediaevalist and pressed his learning into service both as reporter and as counsel. Mr Justice Willes, here as elsewhere, was pre-eminent. It was he who sent Pollock to the Year Books and set him 'on the path of discovery that modern English law cannot be properly understood without going back to its mediaeval origins and development.' But even in academic circles Maine was at first a lonely missionary. It was not until the last quarter of the nineteenth century that legal history became the subject of serious study. Sir Kenelm Digby was a pioneer when in 1875 he based the first elementary exposition of Real Property upon original sources and applied to the land law the methods so triumphantly exploited by Stubbs in constitutional history. His example was eagerly followed. In 1885 Pike introduced new methods of editing the Year Books. In 1887 the Selden Society was founded; and in 1895 mediaeval scholarship flowered in Pollock and Maitland's *History of English Law before the time of Edward I.*

As Maine's career shows, historical and comparative jurisprudence are near akin. The common lawyers, if they found it less fatiguing to be proud of their past than to know it, had long paid something more than lip service to the advantages of comparative law. Before the reign of Victoria they had frequently sought French analogies, and especially in Pothier and the Code Civile. But here as in other fields France was forced to yield to Germany. Already in the early years of the nineteenth century Austin had leant heavily upon Savigny; and it is curious that, after Austin abandoned his course, German influence took so long to creep into the interstices of English law. The Americans were quicker to change their allegiance. At Harvard historical jurisprudence was taught by a pupil of Savigny from 1848 to 1850; and in the latter year the young American prodigy, William Westmore Story, wrote to Lowell of his remarkable experiences in Berlin. 'Von Savigny, the celebrated jurist, I have seen repeatedly, and I can assure you that of all petrifactions he is the most remarkable. He is as dry as dust. Very courteous and affable and complimentary I found him, but living wholly in a book-world and that book-world a law-book-world. He held up both his hands when he found out that I was an artist, and cried out, "What, an artist and a lawyer! That is impossible." ' In England the infiltration was slow. As late as 1875 Markby complained that eyes were still fixed upon the decadent French and earnestly recommended students to turn to Germany. Markby practised what he preached, but he was now preaching to the converted. The young jurists were eager to imbibe the new culture. Pollock was introduced by Bryce to Savigny as to 'the greatest expounder of legal principles in modern Europe'. Maitland discovered him without assistance and said that it was he who first showed him 'the way in which law should be regarded'. At the close of the century, it is true, voices were heard of deprecation if not of dissent. Pollock and Maitland both came to temper their admiration with criticism. But Savigny was still the master whom to the end both delighted to honour.

Such was the background to the judicial and juristic work of Victoria's reign. But notwithstanding the attraction of scientific and evolutionary studies, despite the 'march of mind' and the 'climate of opinion' and the many facile phrases that serve as substitutes for thought, it remains a vulgar error to suppose that any 'influence' can itself produce books, decide cases and command events. Law, no more than any other human creation, is the automatic result of natural forces or intellectual movements. It is made by men. Whatever the pitfalls, it is less misleading to adopt or adapt Carlyle's creed and approach legal history through biography. English lawyers, of all men, should believe in the power of the great judge. Would the common law have been the same had Bacon and not Coke stood at the parting of the sixteenth and seventeenth centuries, had William Murray not been 'caught young' or had Lord Campbell overlooked Colin Blackburn?

The judicial history of the reign may be surveyed in three periods. From 1837 to 1852 the Bench was dominated by Baron Parke. The son of a Liverpool merchant, he distinguished himself at Trinity College, Cambridge, of which he became a Fellow. He was then for seven years a special pleader and, when at last called to the Bar, had an immediate and striking success. From 1828 to 1834 he was a judge of the King's Bench and from 1834 to 1855 a Baron of the Exchequer, where he made the court his own. In 1856 he was translated, as Lord Wensleydale, to the House of Lords and died, still in office, in 1868. His judgments reveal the diverse and sometimes inconsistent strands interwoven in the professional mind. Lord Mansfield was praised by Dr Johnson for not being 'a mere lawyer': he made law serve life. To Baron Parke law was sometimes the servant and sometimes the master. His early experience tempted him to cherish too tenderly the pleader's craft and to approach a case as if it were an exercise in mathematics for failure in which the hapless litigant must pay. But when he averted his eyes from process he was masterly, quick to penetrate the core of a problem, unerring in the extraction of principle from precedent and endowed with the gift of lucid exposition. The two sides of his personality not unnaturally impressed contemporaries with distaste or delight according to their several tastes. Chief Baron Pollock, for twenty years his colleague, denied him the attributes of greatness. He was only, he insisted, 'a considerable man. His intellectual powers were like the explosive compositions called "fulminating"—very powerful within a limited sphere.' Lord Coleridge, recalling him in later life, allowed his superb qualities but lamented their dissipation upon the 'absurdities of special pleading'. He had heard him 'rejoice at non-suiting a plaintiff in an undefended cause, saying, with a sort of triumphant air, that those who drew loose declarations brought scandal on the law'. But the testimony on the other side is weighty. Mr Justice Willes placed the law 'under greater obligations to him than to any judge within living memory.' Baron Martin, the son-in-law of Chief Baron Pollock and testifying therefore against interest, acclaimed him 'without doubt the ablest and best public servant I was personally acquainted with in the whole course of my life'. Now that the dust has settled on the pages of special pleading and Baron Parke is read for his contributions to the substantive law, the verdict of posterity is emphatically in his favour. He was to Lord Dunedin the 'absolute ideal of a judge'.

The years between the Common Law Procedure Act of 1852 and the Judicature Act of 1875 saw a succession of great judges. Of the many candidates for the First Class the most remarkable figure narrowly to miss the highest honours was Lord Campbell. The son of a Scots minister and destined himself for the ministry, he forsook the manse for London and the law. To pay his way, while he devoted his days to learning, he gave his nights to journalism. As a reporter he was ubiquitous, passing undeterred from Westminster Hall to the more doubtful purlieus of Covent Garden and Drury Lane. He wrote indiscriminately as occasion offered or interest suggested; and his *magnum opus*, the Lives of the Lord Chancellors and of the Chief Justices, though deft and lively, are memorials not of pride but of prejudice. When at length he, too, became successively Chief Justice and Lord Chancellor, he proved, somewhat against expectation, to be an able and resolute judge. Had he reached office earlier in life and had he learned to discipline his tongue, he might have achieved greatness.

To three judges of the golden age, Bramwell, Blackburn and Willes, greatness cannot be denied. Lord Bramwell was the most single-minded of men. Neither by nature nor nurture a scholar, he began his working life as a clerk in his father's bank; and with an instinctive grasp of commercial realities, he yet sought to trace in the business man's contract the reflection, however distorted, of the political economy to whose classical canons he was ever faithful. Not learned in the environs of jurisprudence, he accumulated a prodigious knowledge of the cases but refused to be bullied by precedent into any conclusion that seemed to him contrary to principle or justice. On the Bench he was the embodiment of common sense in law. He wasted no words, suffered no irrelevance and stated his conclusions without refinement and without compromise.

Blackburn was in many ways the antithesis of Bramwell. From Eton and Trinity he went to the Bar, where for twenty years he was but moderately successful. In 1845 he published his Treatise on the Contract of Sale. A learned and original book and an early essay in comparative law, it revealed a cast of mind not always practical and one that must have suggested qualms to those attorneys who preferred to brief counsel whom they could more readily understand. In 1859 his appointment to the Queen's Bench took the profession by surprise. The story is well known, but may be re-told in the words of Lord Campbell who chose him and who had to repel the charge of having turned a duty into a job. 'July 3rd, 1859. I have already got into great disgrace by disposing of my judicial patronage on the principle *detur digniori*. Having occasion for a new judge, I appointed Blackburn, the fittest man in Westminster Hall, although wearing a stuff gown; whereas several Whig Q.C.'s and M.P.'s were considering which of them would be the man, not dreaming that they could all be passed over. They got me well abused in *The Times* and other newspapers, but Lyndhurst has defended me gallantly in the House of Lords.' Blackburn at once justified his choice and was a great power on the Bench for a quarter of a century. He had a brusque manner that concealed some inner doubts. He was not always ruthless to break through authority so as to reach and assert principle and to do justice. There was perhaps enough of the academic in him to pore too anxiously upon all sides of the questions; some at least of his judgments are thus flawed. But, when all deductions are made, he remains one of the great common lawyers of all time.

Bramwell was the son of an English banker and Blackburn a Scot. Willes was Irish. Unlike Blackburn, he won an immediate success at the Bar and, though he, too, never took silk, his gifts were universally acknowledged. He was counsel both for the Treasury and for Lloyd's, and his seniors were accustomed to take notes of his arguments in court. From 1855, when he was made a judge of the Common Pleas, to 1872, when he had a nervous collapse and shot himself, he was supreme. He shared Blackburn's mastery of the reports and his knowledge of foreign jurisprudence, and he added a living interest in the Year Books. While Blackburn was rough in personal relations and too often hesitant on the Bench, Willes—in private life shy, reserved and gauche—was firm and confident in judicial decision. In retrospect his judgments are seen to be masterpieces. All aspects of a case have been reviewed, all arguments weighed and all authorities examined. But the mind has sifted and selected, and the result is the exposition and settlement of a principle so simple and convincing that, once revealed by the master, it seems strange that it had not hitherto been perceived. It is not without cause that Sir Frederick Pollock dedicated his *Law of Torts* to him as to a judge 'wise and valiant'.

The years from 1875 to 1901, if not, like the two preceding decades, conspicuously an age of creation, added at least three names to the roll of great judges. Lindley, who was born in 1828 and survived to 1921, was conspicuously the child of his time. He was the son of a Professor of Botany at University College, London, where he himself was educated. He studied Roman Law at Bonn and translated Thibaut's System des Pandektenrechts under the title Introduction to the Study of Jurisprudence. In 1860 he published his celebrated Treatise on the Law of Partnership, including its application to companies. In 1875 Lord Cairns, as if to symbolize the catholic jurisdiction of the new High Court of Justice, made him, though a Chancery practitioner, a judge of the Common Pleas Division. Here, and later in the Court of Appeal and in the House of Lords, he was the most versatile of lawyers, equally at home at common law and in equity, and, like Blackburn before him, he could claim to be both judge and jurist. Pollock, his grateful pupil, dedicated his *Contract* to him as he had dedicated his *Torts* to Willes.

Charles Bowen was, par excellence, the prize scholar. He won the Arnold Historical Prize, the Hertford and the Ireland Scholarships, and became in 1857 a Fellow of Balliol. Thirty years later, now a Lord Justice of Appeal, he translated into English verse the Eclogues and the first six books of the Aeneid. He preferred, indeed, to air his scholarship outside the law and dismissed with disdain the suggestion that he should write a textbook. But a judge's memorial must be sought in his judgments, and these bear on every page the mark of the scholar. His mind was subtle, sceptical and caustic. He once said that 'he had read Maine's works with the profoundest admiration for the genius of the author but with just a faint suspicion somewhere in the background of his mind that the results might turn out to be all nonsense.' Nor, if need be, did he spare his colleagues. The judges were once discussing the draft of an address to the Queen. To the words 'Conscious as we are of our shortcomings' it was objected that they ill fitted the dignity of the Bench. 'Suppose,' said Bowen, 'that we substitute "Conscious as we are of one another's shortcomings".' The man thus revealed was too remote from the bustle of life to be at ease with juries. He could not put himself in their place and he over-rated their intelligence. But his judgments display a mastery of the law expressed in fastidious prose; and a Court of Appeal of which he, Lindley and Lord Justice Fry were the members challenges comparison with any before or since.

Lord Macnaghten was an Ulsterman, educated first at Trinity College, Dublin, and then at Trinity College, Cambridge. He was both scholar and athlete. He was the senior Classic of his year and twice rowed in the Boat Race. He won the Chancellor's medal and the Diamond Sculls. For many years he was a busy member of the Chancery Bar and a Conservative Member of Parliament; and in 1887 he succeeded Blackburn as a Lord of Appeal, a promotion then un-precedented. Like Lindley, he was as happy with the common law as with equity. Unlike Blackburn, 'he had the gifts of listening with patience and deciding without doubt'. Two qualities are conspicuous in his judgments; the power to strip from a doctrine the encrustations of time, leaving it for future use naked and unashamed, and an exquis-ite sense of literary form. He could edge with irony the keenest obser-vation and adorn with elegance the most robust of minds.

One characteristic was shared by all the judges from Parke to Macnaghten: none had a legal education. There was none to have. Until 1852, when the Common Law Procedure Act furnished at once the need and the opportunity for judges to think in terms of principle, there was no serious study of the law at the Universities, and the old professional training in the Inns of Court had long disappeared. 'Dining in Hall was the only survival, and it was almost literally true that a man ate his way to the Bar.' Save for Blackstone, whether in the authorized version or as revised by Serjeant Stephen in 1841, there were few books which an intelligent man with a mind above drudgery could attempt to read without dismay or disgust. A witness before the Oxford University Commission of 1852 described the 'usual routine of what is now called a legal education'. A young man, 'entered at one of the Inns of Court, is received as a pupil for a year by some eminent conveyancer to whom he gives a hundred guineas for the privilege of going daily to his chambers. . . . He finds that he has purchased the right of walking blindfold into a sort of legal jungle. Masses of papers are placed daily before him, every sheet of which contains numberless terms as new and strange to him as the words of a foreign language and the bare meaning of which he rarely arrives at before the clerk announces that the client has called to take the papers away. . . . This unpropitious year at length over, the youth is doomed to go through a second year of the like probation, at the same cost and almost as unprofitably, in the chambers of a special pleader or an equity draftsman; and by the end of that year he is so bedevilled and so wearied that he gives up the attempt as hopeless and becomes a clergyman (an event of extremely common occurrence with Oxford men).' Such disillusion, if not a similar fate, awaited most men who later became eminent as judge or jurist. Sir Fitzjames Stephen 'was for a time in the chambers of Mr Field (afterwards Lord Field), then the leading junior on the Midland Circuit; but it was on the distinct understanding that he was to receive no instruction from his tutor.' He then went into the chambers of a conveyancer. 'I worked very hard with him, but I was incapable of being taught and he of teaching.' Lord Bowen, looking back upon his initiation into the law, remembered only 'the whitewashed misery of the pupil's room and the hopeless dinginess of the occupations of its inhabitants.' 'So bitter is the thought of it,' he said, 'that death itself can hardly be more bitter.' Sir Frederick Pollock was redeemed from bondage only by his good fortune in becoming a pupil of Lindley and a marshal to Willes.

It is true that the publication of Smith's Leading Cases offered the determined adventurer a *tabula in naufragio* and that considerable if desultory learning could be gleaned from the reports prepared by such men as Alderson, Blackburn, Campbell and Maule. But like Scott's hero in the first chapter of *Waverley*, though less agreeably, the pupil could be conscious only of 'driving through a sea of books, like a vessel without pilot or rudder'. Nor must it be supposed that the absence of organized education was felt by the profession as a reproach. The problems of litigation were to be solved, not in sedate seclusion by those who scanned the battle from afar, but more strenuously by those who lived in the thick of it and who knew by close and grim experience what legal conflict really meant. As late as 1883 Dicey sensed the predominant professional opinion to be little altered. 'If the question whether English law can be taught at the Universities could be submitted in the form of a case to a body of eminent counsel, there is no doubt whatever as to what would be their answer. They would reply with unanimity and without hesitation that English law must be learned and cannot be taught and that the only places where it can be learned are the law courts or chambers.' Dicey, it must be added, was speaking of those then prominent at the Bar or already on the Bench; and he was careful to mark the new era inaugurated for their successors in the second half of the century.

The renaissance began simultaneously in the Inns of Court and at the Universities. In the Inns of Court a scheme of education was adopted in 1852 largely through the pressure exercised by the formidable if acid personality of Lord Westbury. Five Readers were appointed, of whom the most prominent was Sir Henry Maine. In 1853 the first and voluntary examination was held and seven candidates attended. In 1872 the examination was made essential for call to the Bar. Many men, later distinguished judges, served as lecturers and examiners; among them were Sir Fitzjames Stephen, Lord Davey and Lord Sumner. But, after Lord Westbury had given the original impetus and had served indefatigably as Chairman for twenty-one years, Lord Macnaghten's association with the Council of Legal Education was perhaps the closest and the most inspiring. He was an examiner in 1864 and Chairman from 1895 to 1913.

The history of nineteenth-century Oxford illustrates the awakening of the Universities. A hesitant step was taken in 1850 by the creation of a new and combined school of Jurisprudence and Modern History. In the next year Convocation established a serious examination for the degree of Bachelor of Civil Law. The 'disputations' which it replaced are described by G. V. Cox, Esquire Bedel, who had himself taken part in them. A question was proposed to each candidate: *Quid existimas de hac quaestione, An dominium acquiri possit sine possessione?* The necessary and traditional arguments, in appropriate Latin, were then handed to the 'disputants' and, to occupy the hour prescribed by the statutes, they were accommodated with a folio *Justinian* and the relevant references. At the end of the hour the presiding examiner, who had meanwhile passed the time according to his taste, dismissed the candidates with the single word *Sufficit*. In 1852 the report of the University Commission was received. All concerned, members and witnesses alike, deplored the existing lethargy, but they differed upon the remedy. Baron Parke urged the University to teach 'the elements of legal science before the young men engaged in the complex and difficult details of its practice'. Lord Westbury preferred all legal education, preliminary and advanced, to be the monopoly of the Inns of Court. The Commissioners decided to support Baron Parke so that undergraduates might be spared the 'temptations and distractions of London life.' Solicitude for the tender plants raised at Oxford was doubtless proper but behind it a nice and more intractable problem was posed. Could law be used both as an instrument of general education and as a technical training? It was, indeed, not necessary to assume, with Savigny, that law was incompatible with culture; but the University must decide whether it was to be offered as one of several roads to intellectual discipline or whether it was to be a first step on the professional ladder.

At length in 1871 a separate School of Jurisprudence was established. In the same year James Bryce delivered his Inaugural Lecture as Regius Professor of Civil Law. When, as in duty bound, he recommended the study of Roman Law, he did not preach to deaf ears, though he may be thought to have opened his case in extravagant terms. He felt it incumbent upon him, or at least desirable, to rebuke contemporary judges for their lack of 'literary culture and polished taste' and to warn them that, if they wished not merely to be learned but even to remain honest, they should embrace the science, philosophy and ethics of the Roman jurists. In the syllabus of the new School, therefore, it was neither surprising nor unhappy that its academic character should be emphasized. It included papers on the Institutes of Gaius and Justinian, on International Law and on General Jurisprudence as understood by Bentham and Austin. The study of English law was confined to Constitutional History, exemplified by Stubbs' Charters, and to the History of Real Property. Contemporary Law was ignored. It may be said with some confidence that the School served its time well by bridging the gulf, hitherto dark and deep, between a liberal education and the mysteries of a craft.

The new academic interest in law provoked, and was itself sustained by, a new style of textbook, devoted primarily to the exposition of principle and designed especially for students. The first-fruits of this learning were gathered in the field of contract. Leake in 1867 made an heroic attempt to approach the subject scientifically and to see it as a coherent whole. In the preface to his *Law of Contracts* he observed that there existed no 'English work undertaken with the exclusive object of treating Contract in its general and abstract form, apart from its specific practical applications'; and this gap he endeavoured to fill. But it was in the next decade that two books revolutionized the teaching of English law. In 1876 Sir Frederick Pollock published his *Principles of Contract*. He sought, in harmony with the Judicature Acts, to examine the inter-play of law and equity, and he set the results not only against Roman, Continental and American models, but also against the Indian Contract Act, from which it might be supposed, insular eccentricities had been eliminated. In his interpretation of the Roman Law he acknowledged and accepted the influence and opinions of Savigny. In 1879 Sir William Anson published his *Law of Contract*. He was, even more fervently than Pollock, the disciple of Savigny, and it was through the superior vision of the master that he hoped to irradiate the concepts of obligation and agreement and to correct the English astigmatism. With these two books the foundations of the new learning were laid; and the inauguration in 1884 of the *Law Quarterly Review* emphasized its importance in professional as in academic circles.

Too much, however, must not be expected too soon. Queen Victoria's judges had been brought up in an older school, and while they might sympathize with youthful enthusiasm, could scarcely be diverted by it. Only in the next century were the men destined for the Bench to be bred upon Anson and Pollock. One of the first and greatest of the new generation was Lord Justice Scrutton. His was a career at which Parke or Bowen would have stared and might, or might not, have envied. After obtaining a First Class in the Law Tripos at Cambridge, he became a Bachelor of Laws in the University of London and Barstow Scholar in the Inns of Court. While reading in chambers he was Professor of Constitutional Law and Legal History at University College, London. Four times he won the Yorke Prize for a Legal Essay and upon such diverse topics as Copyright, Commons and Common Fields and the Influence of Roman Law on the Laws of England. He crowned his literary achievements by the completion in 1886 of his book on Charter-parties, to become at once the standard work.

It was natural, and perhaps inevitable, that the English writers should have drawn their inspiration from Continental jurists. But the results were not wholly happy. The *a priori* postulates of German scholars were not easy to apply to the tough and empirical fragments of case law, and they sometimes deflected, and even distorted, the instinctive grasp of practical needs and limitations which, whatever the defects of its qualities, made English law eminently serviceable. This incompatibility marred the work of Anson. Impelled by his admiration of Savigny to explain English, no less than German, doctrine in language fit for the ears of philosophers, he emphasized consent, and even more pedantically consensus, as the one root of contract. As an initial assumption it might pass muster; as the major premise of a syllogism it was perilous. One cause, at least, of the perplexities that have long darkened the treatment of mistake was Anson's insistence that it must be an exercise upon the theme of *Real Consent*. Pollock, though he at first shared the illusion, soon remembered that he was, after all, an English lawyer; and in the third edition of his book, published in 1881, he preferred to offer as the basis of contract the 'reasonable expectation of the parties'. If such a phenomenon as a national character does in truth exist and if in any degree it colours or shapes the jurisprudence of a country, it is surely this presumption rather than the alien consensus that suits the temper of the common law.

Sir Frank MacKinnon

Lord Justice Scrutton

The life of Lord Justice Scrutton, one of the greatest judges of his genera-
tion, comparable with the giants of the Victorian Era, was written for the
Dictionary of National Biography *by a former pupil who himself*
became a Lord Justice of Appeal.

Sir Frank Douglas MacKinnon (1871–1946) was one of the littérateurs
of the twentieth-century judiciary. His mental indolence, which was can-
didly self-confessed, and the variety of his extra-legal interests, deprived
the law of some of its finest literature. But his best known writing, On
Circuit *(1940), was a collection of stories about the legal world of the*
Assize towns.

His early years on the Bench were spent in the Commercial Court
where much less chance of displaying literary talents is afforded the judge;
but many a businessman can feel grateful to MacKinnon for the lucid way
in which his judgments on abstruse branches of mercantile law were
expressed.

MacKinnon came to the Court of Appeal in 1937 after thirteen years
as a puisne judge. It was here that his penchant for pithy and caustic
statements—an attribute acquired from his erstwhile master-in-the-law?
—were revealed to a wider audience. In one judgment he referred to the
Law Lords as the 'voices of infallibility' and in another case he referred to
the lawyers' talisman, 'the reasonable man or the man on the Clapham
omnibus' as the 'officious bystander'.

SCRUTTON, SIR Thomas Edward (1856–1934), judge, was born
28th August 1856 in the East India Dock Road, Poplar, the elder son
of Thomas Urquhart Scrutton, a prosperous shipowner, later of
Buckhurst Hill, Essex, by his wife, Mary, daughter of the Rev. Edward
Hickman. His father's family had for several generations run a line of
vessels, originally under sail, between the United Kingdom and the
West Indies. The father was a stalwart adherent of Congregationalism,
in the days when that persuasion and the Liberation Society were

a political force. Scrutton was accordingly educated at Mill Hill School.

On leaving school the relentless industry that he displayed throughout life spurred Scrutton to a pursuit of academic honours that can rarely have been equalled. At London University he took the degrees of B.A., M.A. and LL.B. (1882), with honours. He also won a scholarship at Trinity College, Cambridge, obtained a First Class in the Moral Sciences Tripos and was awarded the senior Whewell scholarship for International Law in 1879, and was placed first in the first class of the Law Tripos of 1880. He won the Barstow Scholarship in the Inns of Court in 1882. Finally, he won at Cambridge the Yorke Prize for a Legal Essay in 1882, 1884, 1885 and 1886: to win it four times is a feat which no one else has hitherto achieved. With such a record he may have hoped for a fellowship at Trinity. A remark made by Sir J. J. Thompson shortly after Scrutton's death may explain why he did not get one. 'I remember Scrutton. A very clever man, and of immense industry, *but*—no originality.'

As an undergraduate Scrutton was lanky and rather uncouth. He was possibly the only Englishman of his time who never shaved in his life. Somewhere in the Cambridge Union, of which he was President in 1880, there is, or was, a photograph of him with a downy beard. One of the few diversions from his books that he allowed himself was riding the old high bicycle, and he represented Cambridge in a contest with Oxford men of a like reckless courage.

Scrutton was called to the Bar by the Middle Temple in 1882, and formally joined the South-Eastern circuit: but he never went on it again. He became a K.C. in 1901, and a bencher of his Inn in 1908. He never took much part in the social life, or in the business of the Inn, and did not hold office.

Scrutton read in chambers with Sir A. L. Smith and was at the same time discharging the duties of Professor of Constitutional Law and Legal History at University College, London. After leaving Smith he had chambers for a time in Essex Court, and when his practice began to grow, as soon it did, moved to a large set of chambers at 3 Temple Gardens. The growth of his practice in commercial matters was hastened by the publication in 1886 of his book, *The Contract of Affreightment as expressed in Charter-parties and Bills of Lading.* This having been repeatedly, and carefully, revised by him and by others has remained the leading textbook on the subject: the fourteenth edition appeared in 1939. The subject for the Yorke prize which he won in 1882 was the laws of copyright. He turned his prize essay into a textbook, *The Laws of Copyright* (1883), and this was the source of another side of his practice. That was always mainly in commercial law, but his copyright business was considerable and lucrative.

During eighteen years in that court he displayed ever increasing judicial powers, and when for the last seven years he presided over one of its divisions, he had had few, if any, superiors in that position. When at the Bar he was, if anything, hampered by an immense knowledge of case law. Towards the end of his career he came to see the wood rather than the trees, and developed a mastery of legal principles. Indeed he achieved no little of that originality which Thompson failed to discover in his younger days. In 1936 an American professor published an article about him, in which he uses the phrases 'a matchless commercial lawyer', 'among the noblest of the judicial bench', 'a greater commercial judge than Mansfield', 'the greatest English-speaking judge of a century'.

With age, Scrutton became much more mellow. There was in 1932 an unhappy incident when he was very rude to H. A. McCardie (whom he probably despised intellectually) upon an appeal from him. McCardie was even more injudicious, and injudicial, in his protest in court by way of rejoinder. But the younger barristers, who only knew Scrutton as presiding in the Court of Appeal, would regard him as a dignified, imposing and kindly person.

Scrutton's intellectual interests besides the law were chiefly poetry, travel (before he was forty he had visited Palestine, Greece, Spain and Italy), music and church architecture. His only incursion into politics was in 1886, when, following the family tradition, he stood (but without success) as liberal candidate for the Limehouse division. When an undergraduate he became engaged to Mary, daughter of Samuel Crickmer Burton, solicitor, of Great Yarmouth, and they were married in 1884. They lived, a very devoted couple, at Westcombe Park, a suburb near Blackheath, and only moved to a flat in Piccadilly when Scrutton was on the bench. They had four sons, of whom the youngest was killed in the war of 1914–18, and a daughter. He and his wife were devoted to music and the opera. Keen attendants at orchestral concerts in London, they were never prevented by claims of work from attending throughout the season at Covent Garden, and in his travels in Germany his lodestar was the music at Bayreuth and Munich.

He was a member of the Reform Club and, when a judge, of the Athenaeum: but he was rarely seen in either club; if he had any spare time he spent it at home.

Early in life Scrutton took to bicycling and was a keen watcher of Rugby football, cricket and athletic sports and an enthusiastic, if not very skilful, golfer. He presented the Scrutton cup for an annual competition between the Inns of Court. It was in the course of a golfing holiday at Sheringham in the long vacation of 1934 that he was found to be suffering from a strangulated hernia. He was taken to hospital at Norwich and died there 18th August. He was buried in the Rosary cemetery at Norwich.

In 1892 a case of extreme technicality about general average came before Mr Justice J. C. Lawrence in the non-jury list. That unlearned judge (one of the political promotions of Lord Halsbury) was so palpably unfitted for such a task that it led to a movement for the establishment of a Commercial Court. That was achieved in 1895, and under Sir J. C. Mathew and his successors, who had a like qualification, the court for many years enjoyed its greatest prosperity. For some fifteen years Scrutton and his greatest rival, J. A. Hamilton (afterwards Lord Sumner) were the busiest practitioners in it.

In those years Scrutton got through an immense amount of work in the courts, or in the hideous room which he occupied in the hideous block called Temple Gardens, and in which it was characteristic of the man that a Spartan rigour reigned. He used to sit on a windsor chair, without a cushion, at a battered writing table, to the side of which was a table, loaded with papers, that had come out of one of his father's ships, with a rough piece of wood filling the hole that had enclosed the mast. When darkness set in the only source of light was a Victorian chandelier with fish-tail gas-burners. The other two rooms were filled with 'devils' and pupils: among them from time to time were the future Lord Atkin, Lord Wright, Lord Justice MacKinnon*, Mr Justice Fraser and Mr Justice Henn Collins. At 4.15 all the party met in one of the rooms for tea. The liquid was repulsive: and the only form of food was Bath Oliver biscuits. Scrutton, silently absorbed in thinking about his work, would stride about the room until, almost daily, the top of his head crashed into the knob of the chandelier that hung from the ceiling.

In February, 1909 Scrutton's rival, Hamilton, was promoted to the

* The author of this biography.

bench. Soon afterwards Scrutton was sent as special commissioner on the North-Eastern circuit, and discharged the duty to the general approval. In April 1910, on the recommendation of Lord Loreburn, he was appointed a judge of the King's Bench division, upon the resignation of Mr Justice Sutton.

Scrutton soon proved himself a very efficient judge, but not a popular one. He never had good manners (partly because he was a very shy man), and he indulged in petulant rudeness to counsel, and to solicitors' clerks on summonses. Eventually all the chief City solicitors, his former clients, gave a joint retainer to Alfred Chaytor, then a leading junior who took silk in 1914, to make a protest to the judge in court. Chaytor discharged his novel task with much tact, but with equal firmness. Scrutton listened without comment, but showed proof of his penitence in his subsequent conduct.

For six years Scrutton discharged with success the work of a judge of first instance in London (often in the Commercial Court) and upon circuit. He was very efficient in trying prisoners, although he had had no experience of such work at the Bar. In 1915, at the Old Bailey, he had to try a notorious murderer, George Joseph Smith, in the sensational 'Brides in the Bath' case, and the man in the street came to agree with the professional opinion that he was a great judge.

In October 1916, on the resignation of Lord Justice Phillimore, Scrutton was promoted to the Court of Appeal, and sworn of the Privy Council.

In addition to his books already mentioned, Scrutton produced in 1891 *The Elements of Mercantile Law* and in 1895 an annotated version of *The Merchant Shipping Act, 1894*. The other three Yorke prize essays, all of which were printed, are *The Influence of the Roman Law on the Law of England* (1885), *Land in Fetters* (1886), and *Commons and Common Fields* (1887). He also wrote a valuable article on 'The Work of the Commercial Courts' (*Cambridge Law Journal*, vol. i, no. 1, 1921).

Scrutton was a fine figure of a man. There can never have been a court of so many united inches as when he sat with Lord Sterndale and Lord Justice Bankes. As it had never been shaved, his beard became a feature rather than an appendage, and was so clipped as to give him the look of an Elizabethan. His portrait was never painted, but an excellent photograph is reproduced as the frontispiece to the fourteenth edition of his *Charter parties and Bills of Lading*. A cartoon of him by 'Ape Junior' appeared in *Vanity Fair*, 28th June, 1911: this depicts him in a characteristic pose.

5

FROM
THE BENCH

The only justice is to follow the sincere intuition of the soul,
angry or gentle. Anger is just, and pity is just, but judgment
is never just.

D. H. Lawrence

Mr Justice Maule

Address to a Convicted Bigamist

─────────

The heavy irony which Mr Justice Maule employed in sentencing a bigamist at Warwick Assizes in 1845 is said to have been the 'fons et origo' of the move to transfer matrimonial jurisdiction from the ecclesiastical to the secular courts. The Matrimonial Causes Act, 1857, which followed the recommendation of a Royal Commission seven years earlier, is the basis of our present-day divorce law.

Henry William Maule (1788–1858) was the son of a doctor; he had an intellectual prowess at the bar which was scarcely equalled among his contemporaries. He was a senior wrangler at Cambridge and was elected a fellow of Trinity College. He developed a commercial practice at the Bar, specializing in marine insurance. He was appointed to the Bench in 1839. Throughout his practising and judicial life he was an ardent Benthamite and always had an eye for law reform in his judicial pronouncements.

His ironical humour was at its best in the case of the errant bigamist. There are many bowdlerized versions of the judge's homily to the prisoner; and if the embellishments put upon the case enliven its literary quality Maule's judgment remains nevertheless a classic of its kind. Many of the more felicitously phrased versions conclude by stating that the prisoner was sentenced to one day's imprisonment thereby demonstrating the irony of the case. But in fact Hall was sentenced to four months in gaol. This was due to the fact that he had misled his 'second wife' into believing that he was free to marry her. Even then the sentence was extremely light by comparison with the punishment normally handed down by the judges of that period. The most reliable version of Maule's address, in The Times *for 3rd April, 1845, is printed here.*

THOMAS HALL, alias Thomas Rollins, a poor man not possessed of a farthing or a farthing's worth in the world, aged 35, was indicted for having on the 18th April, 1830 at the parish of Northleach in the County of Gloucester taken for his wife Mary Ann Nicholls and afterwards on the 15th February 1840 at the parish of Hampton-in-Arden in this County married and taken to wife Maria Hadley, his former wife being then alive, *contra formam*.

The offence was clearly proved but he stated that within a year or two of his marriage with Mary Ann she robbed him and sallied forth with the child and he has never since seen either, though he had at the time obtained a special warrant for her apprehension, armed with which he proceeded to the region of her seclusion or retirement, where he got sadly handled by ruffians and was made heartily glad to make the best of his way home to save his life, leaving his baggage in his precipitate departure from the profligate retreat. The substance of this, or at least much of this, he elicited from the witnesses for the prosecution. He had, however, represented to Maria that he had never entered into the holy state and she had given birth to two children by him.

He was of course under these circumstances convicted and Mr Justice Maule in passing sentence said that it did appear that he had been hardly used. It was hard for him to be so used and not be able to have another wife to live with him when the former had gone off to live in an improper state with another man. But the law was the same for him as it was for a rich man and was equally open for him through its aid to afford relief, but as a rich man would have done he also should have pursued the proper means pointed out by law whereby to obtain redress of his grievances. He should have brought an action against the man who was living in the way stated with his wife, and he should have obtained damages and then should have gone to the Ecclesiastical Court and obtained a divorce which would have done what seemed to have been done already, and then he should have gone to the House of Lords, and proving all his case and the preliminary proceedings have obtained full and complete divorce, after which he might, if he liked it, have married again. The prisoner might perhaps object to this that he had not the money to pay the expenses which would amount to about £500 or £600—perhaps he had not so many pence—but this did not exempt him from paying the penalty for committing a felony of which he had been convicted. His Lordship might perhaps have visited the crime more lightly if the prisoner had not misrepresented himself as a bachelor to Maria Hadley and so deceived her. If he had told her the circumstances and said 'Now I will marry you if you like to take the chance' etc. . . . but this he had not done and thus had induced her to live with him upon terms which she perhaps else would not have done.

It was a serious injury to her which he had no right to inflict because his wife and others had injured him. For this offence he must receive some punishment, and the sentence was that he be imprisoned and kept to hard labour for four months, which he hoped would operate as a warning how people trifled with matrimony.

Mr Justice Younger

'Three Weeks'

It has been said that the finest examples of the judiciary in England have been either Scots, Irish, Welsh, Jewish or Roman Catholic. Certainly when it comes to literary style the non-Sassenach has excelled in the judgments which permeate the law reports of England. Robert Younger, later Lord Blanesburgh, (1861–1946), was one in this class. He was an ardent lover of both literature and the arts and it was somewhat of a disappointment that more of his judgments were not infected with his strong non-legal interests. Within a year, however, of his appointment to the Chancery Bench he delivered the judgment in the case brought by the novelist Elinor Glyn to restrain a film company from allegedly pirating her book, Three Weeks. *Here at least his gifts were amply paraded.*

The case brought by the authoress does not figure prominently in the textbooks on copyright, since it only establishes the comparatively obvious point that a book which is grossly immoral or obscene cannot be the subject of copyright. But lawyers have long been aware of the case because of the curious manner in which it is reported. Odd words and phrases scattered throughout the text of the judgment appeared in darker and bolder type than the rest, as if the printer forgot himself in the excitement of reading the detailed highlights of sleazy literature, as recounted so elegantly by Mr Justice Younger.

THIS IS an action to stop the alleged infringement by means of a cinematograph film of the plaintiff's statutory copyright in a novel, to recover damages or an account of the defendants' profits in respect of the cinematograph representations and sales of the films already given and made, and to have the offending films in the possession of the defendants delivered up to the plaintiff.

The action was originally brought against two defendants, the Weston Feature Film Company and George Black. The defendant Black was settled with in the course of the proceedings, and the action was brought to trial only as against the Weston Feature Film Company. Although some distinction between the position of the two defendants appears in the pleadings, no point was made of this at the trial, and the defendant company, assuming full responsibility both for sales and representations of the film complained of, denied that the plaintiff was entitled as against them to any of the relief claimed by her in the action.

The plaintiff is the authoress of the novel in debate. It is entitled *Three Weeks*. First published in 1907, the book was from the point of view of notoriety fortunate enough to be condemned almost unanimously by the critics and to be banned by all the libraries. In consequence, I doubt not, of these attentions it has enjoyed a vogue denied to less daring rivals, and it has reached a sale in this country and America in numerous editions, expensive and cheap, of, I was told, far over a million copies.

The book is said to be an episode in a young Englishman's life without any real beginning or end. In a sense this is a correct enough description of the novel, but the episode referred to absorbs little more than half the book—160 pages out of a total of 319. The rest is taken up with a description of the young man's life and surroundings before the episode commenced and with a portrayal of the permanent influence upon his moral character and career which the authoress is pleased to attribute to the experience he went through during the episode in question.

The episode itself is a chance meeting at a Lucerne hotel between a beautiful lady of uncertain age and mysterious origin and the young Englishman sent by his parents on the grand tour to cure him of an unsuitable attachment at home. The meeting developed into a liaison which lasted for three weeks, after which the lady returned to the shadowy realm from which she had emerged and of which she was, as it happened, the queen. There, having given birth to a son of whom the young Englishman was the father, she was murdered by her husband, the dissolute king of the country. He in turn was assassinated by a faithful attendant of the queen's, leaving the child, the image of his handsome English father, to succeed to the throne.

In all its essentials the so-called episode is as hackneyed and commonplace a story as could well be conceived. If it is to be distinguished at all from innumerable anticipations in erotic literature, the distinction is to be found in the accessories of the tale. Mystery surrounds the lady. Of a loveliness unaffected by the passage of time, she is said to be polished, blasé, soignée. Even in a Swiss country hotel, but notably at Lucerne and Venice, she is pervaded by a luxury as sybaritic as it is incongruous: no wine can pass her lips which is not either of the deepest red or the richest gold; the roses she wears are matched in colour only by the red of her lips; the fruit with which she toys has to be out of season in order that it may be fabulously expensive. Although attended only by an elderly dignified male servant, the lady apparently carries about with her to Lucerne and Venice—if one may omit so-called mountain excursions to the Righi and the Burgenstock —baggage sufficient to fill an ordinary train; it is no extraordinary achievement for her dignified attendant in the space of a weekend to go from Lucerne to Venice, engage a palace on the Grand Canal, supplied with the essential convenience of a side door, and have it equipped with a retinue of Italian servants and, it would seem, an orchestra from Paris, in time to receive the lady on the following Monday travelling from Lucerne with all her baggage and apparently quite unaccompanied. These exaggerated incidents or others like them are of course quite absurd enough to be destitute of novelty in literature of the kind; but if the particular cachet of the plaintiff's novel is not to be found in this setting, then, so far as I can see, it has no cachet at all. At the best, the plaintiff has chosen a hackneyed theme for her episode, and her privilege as an authoress must be strictly confined to the method of treating it which she has adopted.

Now the defendants' film, which is styled 'Pimple's Three Weeks (without the Option)', is frankly farcical and is vulgar to an almost inconceivable degree. Designed to 'feature' the performance of a male artist who rejoices in the sobriquet of 'Pimple', whose speciality appears to be the impersonation of females of truly hideous mien, and who takes the part of the lady, the result is that 'Pimple' holds the centre of the stage throughout and dominates the film to the almost entire exclusion of the young man, as of everybody else. The young man's previous history and subsequent career, of which so much is made in the novel, have no place in the film, while on the other hand the lady's previous home experiences, during which incidentally she is depicted as a common vulgar scold, and all of which are entirely absent from the novel, monopolize the greater part of the film. The meeting in the novel between the lady and the young Englishman amid the surroundings of extravagant luxury to which allusion has already been made becomes in the film a meeting between 'Pimple' and the young man at one of Lockhart's coffee-houses amid every accompaniment of the broadest farce; and the incidents of the film to which even so remote a resemblance with any in the novel can be found are exceedingly few in number or importance. The great bulk of the film is taken up with happenings which have no counterpart in the novel; a great part of the novel is taken up with other incidents which have no counterpart in the film; and on the whole, after a careful consideration of both, and after the opportunity which was afforded me of seeing a representation of the film, I have arrived at the conclusion of fact that the film does not constitute any infringement of the plaintiff's copyright of the novel.

Of course no part of the letterpress is reproduced, and so far as there is any similarity of incident those of the film are so altered in effect and feeling and surrounding as to reproduce no element of any situation described in the novel for which the plaintiff can, as I think, claim any monopoly right at all.

This view of the case makes it unnecessary for me to do more than refer in passing to the important point raised by the defendants that their film is a mere burlesque of the plaintiff's novel, and that a genuine burlesque of a serious work constitutes no infringement of copyright although it may under certain conditions justify an action in the nature of slander of goods.

Making all allowance for the fact that prior to the Act of 1911 literary copyright did not include the acting right, it certainly is remarkable that no case can be found in the books in which a burlesque even of a play has been treated as an infringement of copyright, although burlesque, frequently more distinguished than the thing burlesqued, is as old as Aristophanes, to take Mr Hartree's example. It may well be that as far as English law is concerned one reason for this striking state of things is that the older cases insist upon the necessity of establishing that the alleged piracy is calculated to prejudice the sale or diminish the profits or supersede the objects of the original work, whereas it is well known that a burlesque is usually the best possible advertisement of the original and has often made famous a work which would otherwise have remained in obscurity. More probably, however, the reason is to be found involved in such observations as those of Lindley, L. J. in *Hanfstaengl v. Empire Palace*, or in such a decision as that of the Court of Appeal in *Francis, Day & Hunter v. Feldman & Co.*, or in the principle that no infringement of the plaintiff's rights takes place where a defendant has bestowed such mental labour upon what he has taken and has subjected it to such revision and alteration as to produce an original result. The same principle is illustrated in the law of designs by such cases as *Thom v. Syddall* and *Barran v. Lomas*; and if, in considering whether such a literary work as a novel has been infringed by such a thing as a cinematograph film, the true enquiry is, as I think it must be, whether, keeping in view the idea and general effect created by a perusal of the novel, such a degree of similarity is attained as would lead one to say that the film is a reproduction of incidents described in the novel or of a substantial part thereof, then in my opinion the answer in the present case must be in the negative. If, therefore, it were necessary for me to express an opinion upon this aspect of the case I should decide that on this ground also the plaintiff fails.

But there is involved in this case another and from the public point of view a much more important consideration which in my judgment entirely debars the plaintiff from obtaining any relief in this Court. The episode described in the plaintiff's novel, and which she alleges has been pirated by the defendants, is in my opinion grossly immoral in its essence, in its treatment, and in its tendency. Stripped of its trappings, which are mere accident, it is nothing more or less than a sensual adulterous intrigue. And it is not as if the plaintiff in her treatment of it were content to excuse or palliate the conduct described. She is not even satisfied with justifying that conduct. She has stooped to glorify the liaison in its inception, its progress, and its results; and she has not hesitated to garnish it with meretricious incident at every turn.

Now it is clear law that copyright cannot exist in a work of a tendency so grossly immoral as this, a work which, apart from its other objectionable features, advocates free love and justifies adultery where the marriage tie has become merely irksome. It may well be that the Court in this matter is now less strict than it was in the days of Lord Eldon, but the present is not a case in which in the public interest it ought, as it seems to me, to be at all anxious to relax its principles. We are constantly hearing of the injurious influence exercised upon the adventurous spirit of our youth by the penny dreadful which presents the burglar in the guise of a hero and so excites the imagination of the juvenile reader that, adopting in the spirit of true adventure the life of his idol, he presently finds himself in the dock branded by an unfeeling world as a common thief. So is a glittering record of adulterous sensuality masquerading as superior virtue, as it does in this book, calculated, with consequences as inevitable as they are sure to be disastrous, to mislead into the belief that she may without danger choose the easy life of sin many a poor romantic girl striving amidst manifold hardships and discouragements to keep her honour untarnished.

It is enough for me to say that to a book of such a cruelly destructive tendency no protection will be extended by a Court of Equity. It rests with others to determine whether such a work ought not to be altogether suppressed.

With one remaining aspect of this case I must deal. In her statement of claim the plaintiff in ordinary terms claims that the defendants' film reproduces substantial parts of her novel, and she alleges that the defendants have in their possession a number of the infringing films and that the defendants detain same from her: she asks for damages, or alternatively for an account of profits. In other words, the plaintiff's statement of claim is based upon the footing that the films are in law her own, and she claims their delivery up to her under s.7 of the Act. This renders it necessary for me to say a word about the film. It is, as I have already indicated, indescribably vulgar; but vulgarity is merely a question of taste, and with that I have here no concern. There are, however, in it isolated incidents and movements which in my judgment are more than vulgar; they are indecently offensive. The presence of these incidents in the film as I think disentitles it in its present form to protection in this Court, and would preclude the defendants as the owners of the film from maintaining any action for infringing it. It was, I do not doubt, permissible for the plaintiff, instead of framing her claim as she had done, indignantly to stigmatize the defendants' film as being not only an infringement of her copyright, but a libel upon her book, and I have no doubt that in an action so framed, provided of course that the libel had not been justified, it would have been possible for her had she proved her allegations to recover from the defendants damages for the injury to her property occasioned by this defamatory representation of it. But that is not the gist of the plaintiff's action, and no hint was given either in the pleadings or in the opening of her case that she had any such grievance against the defendants. Her whole case as pleaded and presented was that not only is she entitled to have the films delivered up to her as her own, but that she is entitled to the profit which the defendants have made by the appropriation of her property, or alternatively to damages which would be assessed upon the footing that every film sold is to be treated as the plaintiff's so that she recover the profit which she would have received had the sale of the film been made by herself: see *Pike v. Nicholas*. Such a presentation of her case has of course the advantage that it cannot be defeated by any plea of justification, but it has the disadvantage that the plaintiff accepts as her own work the defendants' production just as it stands, indecency and all, and it is quite clear in my opinion that, if the defendants' film truly bears the character which I hold it to bear, no inquiry as to damages nor any account of profits arising from it can or will in an action framed as this is be directed by the Court. On this ground also the plaintiff's claim in my judgment fails.

Under ordinary circumstances the action is one which would be dismissed with costs, but this is a case in which, as it appears to me, the Court owes it to its own self-respect to render no assistance whatever to either of the parties in respect of the subject of their litigation, and therefore I feel it my duty while dismissing the action to leave both parties to bear their own costs.

Lord Sumner

On Christianity and the Law

Lord Sumner, J. A. Hamilton (1859–1934), is recognized to have been as great a master of the English language as any judge who ever lived. His judgments, together with those of Lords Bowen and Macnaghten, are the only ones to have been included in the Oxford Book of English Prose.

A Mancunian by birth, Hamilton was a pupil at Manchester Grammar School and afterwards obtained first class in Mods. and Lit. Hum. at Oxford, where in 1882 he was President of the Union. He came to the Bar but was not immediately successful and filled in his spare time with journalism; he was particularly active in writing legal lives for the Dictionary of National Biography. *When he did begin to acquire a practice it was slow in developing although his qualities as a lawyer were evident. He had the distinction that Cosmo Gordon Lang asked to become his pupil. He turned Lang away on the grounds that he was not a busy enough junior to warrant taking a pupil. John Buchan did later become a pupil of his, but like Lang deserted the law for better things.*

Hamilton became a judge in 1909. He was promoted to the Court of Appeal in 1912 but almost instantly—in 1913—he was whisked off to the more rarefied atmosphere of the House of Lords. He had a profound influence on that Court in the years between the wars, many of his judgments becoming classics. His remark in Woolmington's case *that the burden of proof rests on the prosecution is a golden thread woven into the fabric of the English criminal law.*

Sumner, like so many who from poor origins have risen to the heights of professional and public life, became a diehard conservative. For example, he bitterly attacked the government for demoting General Dyer, the man responsible for the shooting on the masses at the Amritsar riots in 1919. He persistently used his position as a life peer (acquired through his appointment as a Law Lord) to speak on public debates in the Lords. This was probably the main reason why he failed to succeed Lord Finlay as Lord Chancellor.

In Bowman v. Secular Society, *Sumner demonstrated how literary gifts could be used to expound a complex aspect of the law. The case concerned the validity of a bequest to a society whose main object was to propagate anti-Christian doctrines. Sumner, delving deep into the history of the criminal offence of blasphemy, gave the quietus to the supposed doctrine that Christianity was a part of the law of England. Blasphemy, he said, was, in the absence of scurrility or indecency calculated to shake the fabric of society, not a criminal offence. In the course of this pronouncement he subjected the Ten Commandments to judicial interpretation.*

MY LORDS, the question is whether an anti-Christian society is incapable of claiming a legacy, duly bequeathed to it, merely because it is anti-Christian. The certificate proves that the incorporation is that of the statutory number of persons in accordance with the formalities of the Act, and that 'all the requisitions of this Act in respect of registration have been complied with' (Companies Act, 1862, s.18), and that the respondent society is a complete person in law. It does not prove that all the memorandum powers are lawfully exercisable.

What then are the society's character and powers? For them we must look at the memorandum, and then the question will be, Does the law permit their exercise?

Paragraph 3 (A) gives its principle. The first part is stated both as a positive proposition, namely, that human conduct should be based upon natural knowledge, and as a negative proposition, namely, that it should not be based on supernatural belief. The second part is expressed only positively, namely, that human welfare in this world is the proper end of all thought and action, but equally the negative of this proposition is implied. Since 'human welfare is the proper end of all thought and action', any object save the welfare of mankind in this world (for example, the glory of God) cannot be a proper end for any thought or action at all. The powers taken in the subsequent paragraphs are ancillary to the first and some are so expressed. It is true that object (K) is 'to publish books', and object (L) 'to assist by votes of money other societies or associated persons or individuals who are specially promoting any of the above objects', but are we to say that this company has among its memorandum powers the publication of Bibles and Prayer Books, the subvention of Bible Societies, and the doing of all lawful things conducive to the attainment of such objects, such as building a mission-hall for reading the Bibles and offering the prayers? If the memorandum is to be so construed it is decisive of the case, for I agree that this gift is not an imperfect gift nor impressed with any trust in the donee's hands, and a donee who sometimes acts legally and sometimes illegally cannot be deprived of his legacy for fear he might follow the evil and eschew the good. It is not a question of hoping for the best, as was argued; the law must presume that what is legal will be done, if anything legal can be done under the memorandum. Thus one just man may save the city. To my mind, if the memorandum be construed as it is by my noble and learned friend, who has immediately preceded me, any consideration of blasphemy or Christianity or their legal position is irrelevant, for the appeal fails without it, and before we come to it. I think we should look at the substance and that all the paragraphs should be construed as if they concluded with the words 'for the purposes and on the principle stated in paragraph (A).' Surely a society incorporated on such a principle cannot be supposed, as a matter of construction, to exercise ancillary powers on other principles or for independent purposes. Of course, it must be assumed that the powers taken are to be used, if possible, for lawful ends; for example, to subsidize a blaspheming lecturer would be an *ultra vires* act, and those who so disbursed the company's money would be personally liable to refund it, apart from aiding and abetting; but as I take the memorandum to be that of a society deliberately and entirely anti-Christian, in which opinion I believe the shareholders themselves would agree, I am constrained to deal with the question, What if all the company's objects are illegal *per se?* For I should be loth to dispose of this case on the narrow ground that, even if all its other objects are illegal, the company in law can always wind up and so dispose of its funds.

If the respondents are an anti-Christian society, is the maxim that Christianity is part of the law of England true, and if so, in what sense? If Christianity is of the substance of our law, and if a Court of law must, nevertheless, adjudge possession of its property to a company whose every action seeks to subvert Christianity and bring that law to naught, then by such judgment it stultifies the law. So it was argued, and if the premise is right, I think the conclusion follows.

It is not enough to say with Lord Coleridge, C. J., in *Ramsay's Case* that this maxim has long been abolished, or with my noble and learned friend the Master of the Rolls in the Court below that 'the older view', based on this maxim, 'must now be regarded as obsolete'. If that maxim expresses a positive rule of law, once established, though long ago, time cannot abolish it nor disfavour make it obsolete. The decisions which refer to such a maxim are numerous and old, and although none of them is a decision of this House, if they are in agreement and if such is their effect, I apprehend they would not now be overruled, however little Reason might incline your Lordships to concur in them. In what sense, then, was it ever a rule of law that Christianity is part of the law?

The legal material is fourfold: (1) statute law; (2) the criminal law of blasphemy; (3) general civil cases; (4) cases relating to charitable trusts. From statute law little is to be gleaned. During the sixteenth century many Acts were passed to repress objectionable doctrines, but plainly statutes were not needed if the common law possessed an armoury for the defence of Christianity as part and parcel of itself. Indeed, who but the King in Parliament could then say whether the Christianity, which for the time being formed part of the common law, was the Christianity of Rome or of Geneva or of Wittenberg? Certainly the Courts could not.

After the Revolution of 1688 there were passed the Toleration Act to give 'some ease to scrupulous consciences in exercise of religion', which, upon conditions, relieved certain dissenters (Papists and those who denied the Trinity excepted) from the operation of various existing statutes, and the Blasphemy Act, which recites that 'many persons have of late years openly avowed and published many blasphemous and impious opinions, contrary to the doctrines and principles of the Christian religion . . . and may prove destructive to the peace and welfare of this kingdom'. That the Blasphemy Act simply added new penalties for the common law offence of blasphemy, when committed under certain conditions, was held by Lord Hardwicke in *De Costa v. De Paz* and by the Court of King's Bench in *Richard Carlile's Case*; and Lord Eldon in *Attorney-General v. Pearson* said that the Toleration Act left the common law as it was and only exempted certain persons from the operation of certain statutes. Such, indeed, is the clear language of the statutes, nor can the fact that persons are singled out for special punishments who deny the Godhead of the Three Persons of the Trinity, the truth of the Christian religion, and the Divine authority of the Holy Scriptures, or who maintain that there be more gods than one, be accepted as showing that the common law offence of blasphemy consists in such denials and assertions and in nothing else. Later Acts have relieved various religious confessions from the

burthen [sic] of the Blasphemy Act and other statutes, but, except in
so far as they deal with charitable trusts for the purposes of such confessions, on which I do not now dwell, they seem to carry the present
matter no further.

The common law as to blasphemous libels was first laid down after
the Restoration, and here the statement that Christianity is part of the
law is first found as one of the grounds of judgment. Earlier opinions
of the same kind are curiously general in character. In *Bohun v.
Broughton*, on a *quare impedit*, it is said '*a tielx leis que ils de Saint
Eglise ont en ancien Scripture, covient a nous a doner credence; car ceo
common ley sur quel touts man(iere)s leis sont fondes.*' Again in the
Doctor and Student (dialogue 1, chs. 5, 6 and 7) three successive
chapters state the grounds of the law of England—the first, the law of
reason; the second, the law of God; and the third, the usage and
custom of the realm. When Lilburne was on his trial in 1649 he complained that he was not allowed counsel and appealed to the judges 'to
do as they would be done by'. 'You say well', replied Lord Keble. 'The
law of God is the law of England'. But all the same, Lilburne had to do
the best he could for himself. A passage from Lord Coke may also be
quoted. Brooke, J., had once observed casually (Y.B. 12 Hen. 8, fo, 4)
that a pagan could not have or maintain any action, and Lord Coke in
Calvin's Case, founding himself on this and on St Paul's Second
Epistle to the Corinthians (ch. 6, v. 15), stated that infidels are *perpetui
inimici*, and 'a perpetual enemy cannot maintain any action or get anything within the realm'. Of this Willes, C. J., in *Omichund v. Barker*
observes: 'Even the devils themselves, whose subjects he (Lord Coke)
says the heathens are, cannot have worse principles; and beside the
irreligion of it, it is a most impolitic notion and would at once destroy
all that trade and commerce from which this nations reaps such great
benefits.' Evidently in this interval the spirit of the law had passed from
the Middle Ages to modern times. So far it seems to me that the law
of the Church, the Holy Scriptures, and the law of God are merely
prayed in aid of the general system or to give respectability to propositions for which no authority in point could be found.

At the beginning of the seventeenth century a considerable change
of procedure took place in reference to religion. Legate was burnt at
Smithfield in 1612 upon a writ *de haeretico comburendo*, and another
heretic, named Wightman, at Lichfield about the same time, but they
were the last persons to go to the stake in this country *pro salute animae*.

No doubt this process was moribund. Before the Restoration the Court of Star Chamber and the Court of High Commission had been suppressed, and at length, by the statute, 29 Car. 2, c. 9, the writ *de haeretico comburendo* itself was abolished with all process and proceedings thereupon and all punishment of death in pursuance of any ecclesiastical censures. It is to be noted that the Act, in saving the jurisdiction of the Ecclesiastical Courts over 'atheism, blasphemy, heresy or schism,' distinguishes blasphemy from the profession of false doctrines, whether atheistical or heretical. The time of Charles II was one of notorious laxity both in faith and morals, and for a time it seemed as if the old safeguards were in abeyance or had been swept away. Immorality and irreligion were cognizable in the Ecclesiastical Courts, but spiritual censures had lost their sting and those civil Courts were extinct, which had specially dealt with such matters viewed as offences against civil order.

The Court of King's Bench stepped in to fill the gap. In 1663 Sir Charles Sedley was indicted for indecency and blasphemy. The indecency was so gross that little stress was laid on the blasphemy, which was probably both tipsy and incoherent. The Court told the prisoner that they would have him know that, although there was no longer any Star Chamber, they acted as *custos morum* for all the King's subjects, and it was high time to punish such profane actions, contrary alike to modesty and to Christianity.

Then follows *Taylor's Case* in 1675, when the indictment was for words only, though ribald and profane enough. This is the earliest trial for blasphemy. *Adwood's Case* in 1617 is not an instance. It is like *Traske's Case*, where the matter in hand was the making of conventicles as tending to sedition. The indictment in *Taylor's Case* is given in Tremaine's *Placita*, p. 226, and shows that the charge was not confined to the fact that Taylor's language was contrary to true religion, but it was considered dangerous to civil order, for it concludes: '*Ad grave scandalum professionis verae Christianae religionis in destructionem Christianae gubernationis et societatis . . . ac contra pacem dicti domini regis.*'

Now *Taylor's Case* is the foundation-stone of this branch of the law, and for a century or so there is no sign of carrying the law beyond it. The case repays scrutiny. The objection that the offence was an ecclesiastical one lay on the very face of the words charged, and in directing the jury Hale, C.J., found it necessary to show why it was also a civil offence. He said that such kind of wicked, blasphemous words, though of ecclesiastical cognizance, were not only an offence to God and religion, but a crime against the laws, State, and Government, and 'therefore punishable in this Court. For to say, religion is a cheat, is to dissolve all those obligations whereby the civil societies are preserved.' It is true that he added that Christianity was parcel of the laws of England, 'and therefore to reproach the Christian religion is to speak in subversion of the law', but this does not really enlarge the previous statement. Speaking in subversion of the law, without more, in the sense of saying that particular laws are bad and should be mended, has never been a criminal offence, and agitating against them has often led on to fortune. *Woolston's Case*, in 1728, supplies the completion of the doctrine. Upon a motion in arrest of judgment the Court followed *Taylor's Case* as settled law. The argument was that Woolston's crime, if any, was of ecclesiastical cognizance (he was a clergyman who joked about the miracles), and that 'mere difference of opinion is tolerated by law'. Lord Raymond's answer was, 'I would have it taken notice of that we do not meddle with any differences in opinion, and that we interpose only where the very root of Christianity itself is struck at. . . . To say, an attempt to subvert the established religion is not punishable by those laws upon which it is established, is an absurdity.' True it is that the last words somewhat invert Lord Hale's reasoning; for they seem to treat an attempt to subvert the established form of Christianity (not any other) as an offence, because it attacks the creature of the law, not because that form is the basis of the law itself and the bond of civilized society. At any rate the case leaves untouched mere differences of opinion, not tending to subvert the laws and organization of the realm.

Curl's Case, heard about the same time, was a case for publishing an obscene libel, but is of some incidental importance. The Courts were chary of enlarging their jurisdiction in this regard, and in Queen Anne's time judgment had been arrested in such a case for supposed want of precedent, and the offence was treated as one for ecclesiastical cognizance only. On a motion for arrest of the judgment on Curl it was argued that the libel, being only *contra bonos mores*, was for the spiritual Courts. The motion was refused, the Chief Justice saying, 'If it reflects on religion, virtue or morality, if it tends to disturb the civil order of society, I think it is a temporal offence'. He said, too, 'religion is part of the common law', but Probyn, J., clears this up, adding, 'It is punishable at common law as an offence against the peace in tending to weaken the bonds of civil society'.

At the end of the eighteenth and beginning of the nineteenth centuries various publishers of Paine's *Age of Reason* were prosecuted. The words indicted were chosen for their scoffing character, and indeed are often really blasphemous, but the idea throughout is that the book was the badge of revolution and tended to jeopardize the State. Thus in the trial of Williams, Ashhurst, J., passing sentence on him in the Court of King's Bench, stated the ground of this offence thus: 'All offences of this kind are not only offences to God, but crimes against the law of the land, and are punishable as such, inasmuch as they tend to destroy those obligations whereby civil society is bound together; and it is upon this ground that the Christian religion constitutes part of the law of England.'

If later cases seem to dwell more on religion and less on considerations of State, I think, when examined, they prove to be of small authority. In *Waddington's Case* there seems to have been little argument, and no decisions were cited. *Rex v. Davison* decides in effect that contempt of God in Court may be also contempt of Court. In 1838 Alderson, B., told a York jury *(Reg. v. Gathercole)* that 'a person may, without being liable to prosecution for it, attack Judaism, or Mahommedanism, or even any sect of the Christian religion (save the established religion of the country); and the only reason why the latter is in a different situation from the others is, because it is the form established by law, and is therefore a part of the constitution of the country. In like manner, and for the same reason, any general attack on Christianity is the subject of criminal prosecution, because Christianity is the established religion of the country.' The defendant, in fact, had not made any general attack on Christianity, but, being a Protestant clergyman, had foully aspersed a Roman Catholic nunnery. Whether this strange dictum was material or not, and whether it is right or not (and Baron Alderson's is a great name), it only shows that the gist of the offence of blasphemy is a supposed tendency in fact to shake the fabric of society generally. Its tendency to provoke an immediate breach of the peace is not the essential, but only an occasional feature. After all, to insult a Jew's religion is not less likely to provoke a fight than to insult an Episcopalian's; and, on the other hand, the publication of a dull volume of blasphemies may well provoke nothing worse than throwing it into the fire.

Hetherington's Case was a motion in arrest of judgment. Even here, alongside of the propositions that the Old Testament contains the law of God, and that 'it is certain that the Christian religion is part of the law of the land' (per Patterson, J.), we find Lord Denman, C.J., saying: 'As to the argument, that the relaxation of oaths is a reason for departing from the law laid down in the old cases, we could not accede to it without saying that there is no mode by which religion holds society together, but the administration of oaths; but that is not so, for religion . . . contains the most powerful sanction for good conduct.' *Reg. v. Moxon* is of small authority. Later prosecutions add nothing until Lord Coleridge's direction to the jury in *Reg. v. Ramsay and Foote.* For thirty years this direction has been followed, nor was it argued by the appellants that the publication of anti-Christian opinions, without ribaldry or profanity, would now support a conviction for blasphemy. It is no part of your Lordship's task on the present occasion to decide whether Lord Coleridge's ruling was or was not the last word on the crime of blasphemy, but the history of the cases and the conclusions reached at present go to show that what the law censures or resists is not the mere expression of anti-Christian opinion, whatever be the doctrines assailed or the arguments employed.

It is common ground that there is no instance recorded of a conviction for a blasphemous libel, from which the fact, or, at any rate, the supposition of the fact, of contumely and ribaldry has been absent, but this was suggested to be of no real significance for these reasons. Such prosecutions, it was said, often seem to be persecutions, and are therefore unpopular, and so only the gross cases have been proceeded against. This explains the immunity of the numerous agnostic or atheistic writings so much relied on by Secularists. All it really shows is that no one cares to prosecute such things till they become indecent, not that, decently put, they are not against the law. Personally I doubt all this. Orthodox zeal has never been lacking in this country. The Society for Carrying into Effect His Majesty's Proclamations against Vice and Immorality, which prosecuted Williams in 1797, has had many counterparts both before and since, and as anti-Christian writings are all the more insidious and effective for being couched in decorous terms, I think the fact that their authors are not prosecuted, while ribald blasphemers are, really shows that lawyers in general hold such writings to be lawful because decent, not that they are tolerable for their decency though unlawful in themselves. In fact, most men have thought that such writings are better punished with indifference than with imprisonment.

I may now turn to decisions in civil cases other than cases of charitable trusts. They are at least inconclusive. In *Murray v. Benbow* Byron's *Cain* was in question. Lord Eldon read it, and, as it happened, was able to compare it with *Paradise Lost*. 'You have alluded', he says, 'to Milton's immortal work. It did happen in the course of last Long Vacation, amongst the *sollicitae jucunda oblivia vitae*, I read that work from beginning to end. . . . Taking it altogether, it is clear that the object and effect were not to bring into disrepute, but to promote the reverence of our religion.' So judging *Cain* he doubted, and, as an injunction was matter of discretion and not of right, he refused an injunction till the plaintiff's right had been established at law. According to Smiles's *John Murray* (i., 428) the necessary action was brought, a jury upheld the copyright, and on a subsequent application the injunction was granted. About the same time, however, in 1822, in *Lawrence v. Smith* an injunction had been obtained *ex parte* to restrain the issue of a pirated edition of the plaintiff's *Lectures on Physiology*. As the lectures seemed to him to question the immortality of the soul, Lord Eldon dissolved it as a matter of discretion and in the absence of any judgment deciding the right at law, and observed that 'the law does not give protection to those who contradict the Scriptures', a dictum which, in its full width, imperils copyright in most books on geology. In the present case the respondents do not appeal for protection to the Court's discretion, but vindicate a right of property, as clearly established as if there were a verdict. Again in *Pare v. Clegg* Lord Romilly, M.R., gave judgment against the defendant, remarking that the society which he represented, though based on irrational principles, was not formed 'for the purpose of propagating irreligious and immoral doctrines', and so was liable. This is not authority for saying generally that a society formed for the purpose of propagating irreligious doctrines could not be made to pay its debts. At most they must be such irreligious doctrines as the law forbids, and that leaves open the whole question what it is that the law forbids. Whether or not it is an authority directly in favour of the respondents I am not prepared to say. *Cowan v. Milbourn* has long stood unchallenged. The judges meant to decide no new law, but to follow and apply the passages cited from Starkie on Libel. I cannot follow the observation of Lord Coleridge, C.J., in *Ramsay's Case* that the judgments, or at any rate that of Baron

Bramwell, turn on the effect of the statute of William III. The rooms had been engaged for two purposes. One was for a tea party and ball in memory of Tom Paine, and the other was the delivery of lectures in question. As to the first, the recorder left the case to the jury, who gave a farthing damages for the frustration of this dismal, but no doubt harmless, festivity. As to the other, some fear of a breach of the peace may have existed, for intervention by the chief constable is mentioned in the Law Reports, but not in the *Law Journal, Law Times*, or *Weekly Reporter*. The plea alleged a purpose 'to use the said rooms for certain irreligious, blasphemous, and illegal lectures', but they had not been delivered, and no indictable words could have been assigned. The recorder refused to leave the question of purpose to the jury with regard to the lectures. The argument in moving for the rule was that the case should have gone to the jury, for the placards *per se* did not prove an intention to insult or mislead, and temperate discussion of such subjects is lawful. Clearly the recorder had ruled that under such titles no lecture could be delivered that would not be unlawful. It is upon such a presentation of the case and, I suppose, on such a ruling at the trial that Chief Baron Kelly said, 'Such a lecture cannot be delivered . . . without blasphemy and impiety', and from this his colleagues do not dissent. I do not think that the Court were finding in the placards and the chief constable a *quia timet* justification for the defendant's breach of contract. Their ground was that the hiring was and could only be for an illegal object, and therefore the contract could not be enforced. The distinction is well settled between things which are illegal and punishable and things which, though not punishable, are illegal so as not to support a contract for good consideration. Prostitution is one of the common examples. Baron Bramwell evidently thought that Secularism was another. But this reasoning postulates that, whatever lectures were actually delivered, they could not but be unlawful. Lectures, lawful because decently expressed, could, however, have been delivered under those titles, and therefore the hiring was not conclusively shown to have been for an unlawful purpose and void. The case should have gone to the jury. The alternative view of the case must be that the whole Court held that any general denial or dispute of Christian faith is unlawful, which had not been held at law before. From this it would follow that a person, whose business it was to publish and sell anti-Christian books, need neither pay his printer's bill nor the poor rates for his shop, a proposition which is refuted by stating it, and from which at least two members of the Court in *Cowan v. Milbourn* would have recoiled. I think the decision was wrong.

As to *De Costa and De Paz*, Lord Hardwicke is reported as saying that there is a great difference between laying penalties on persons for the exercise of their religion and establishing them by acts of Court. So here I think there is a great difference between laying civil disabilities on a man for the profession of his irreligion or on a company for the exercise of its memorandum powers, however contrary to Christianity, and establishing them by the act of the Court. The appellants' claim is that the Court should deny the respondent company's right to receive this money on the ground that it cannot make any lawful use of it, not that it should establish the money in the company's hand as a charitable trust for un-Christian objects. It is true that Lord Hardwicke goes on to say that 'the intent of this bequest must be taken to be in contradiction to the Christian religion, which is a part of the law of the land . . . for the constitution and policy of this realm is founded thereon', and there are a good many other cases of the same kind, especially *Briggs v. Hartley* in which similar language is used; but charitable trusts form a particular and peculiar branch of the law, and I do not think that the reasoning, and still less the remarks, contained in those cases bear usefully on general principles. However right it may be to refuse the aid of the law in establishing a trust for Secularist purposes, I cannot see why a Secularist is not to receive a gift of money because he is a Secularist and says so. I will not further pursue the cases cited on charitable trusts, nor could I presume to add to what has fallen from my noble and learned friend, Lord Parker of Waddington.*

My Lords, with all respect for the great names of the lawyers who have used it, the phrase 'Christianity is part of the law of England' is really not law; it is rhetoric, as truly so as was Erskine's peroration when prosecuting Williams: 'No man can be expected to be faithful to the authority of man, who revolts against the Government of God.' One asks what part of our law may Christianity be, and what part of Christianity may it be that is part of our law? Best, C.J., once said in *Bird v. Holbrook* (a case of injury by setting a spring-gun): 'There is no act which Christianity forbids, that the law will not reach; if it were otherwise, Christianity would not be, as it has always been held to be,

---

* The father of the present Lord Chief Justice.

part of the law of England'; but this was rhetoric too. Spring-guns, indeed, were got rid of, not by Christianity, but by Act of Parliament. 'Thou shalt not steal' is part of our law. 'Thou shalt not commit adultery' is part of our law, but another part. 'Thou shalt love thy neighbour as thyself' is not part of our law at all. Christianity has tolerated chattel slavery; not so the present law of England. Ours is, and always has been, a Christian State. The English family is built on Christian ideas, and if the national religion is not Christian there is none. English law may well be called a Christian law, but we apply many of its rules and most of its principles, with equal justice and equally good government, in heathen communities, and its sanctions, even in Courts of conscience, are material and not spiritual.

Frequently as the proposition in question appears in one form or another, it is always as something taken for granted and handed down from the past rather than as a deliberate and reasoned proposition. It constantly has been used in charging juries as to unmistakably scurrilous words, where there was neither opportunity nor occasion for defining the limits of legitimate religious and irreligious opinion. I question if the foundations of the criminal law of blasphemous libel were ever fully investigated in any Court before *Ramsay's Case*. Even then Lord Coleridge passed over numerous decisions. To be sure his omissions were faithfully dealt with soon afterwards by Stephen, J., one of his own *puisnes*, in a popular periodical, and this paper your Lordships allowed Mr Talbot to read as part of his argument, to which, nevertheless, it added nothing either in learning or in cogency. Such observations, too, have often been employed by judges of first instance in cases relating to charitable trusts, where there was equally little need for any analysis of the proposition or for discussion, either historical or juridical, of its implications. It is fairly clear, too, that men of the utmost eminence have thought, and said advisedly, that mere denials of sundry essentials of the Christian faith are indictable as such. Hawkins, in his *Pleas of the Crown*, bk. i., ch. 26, p. 358, says that 'all blasphemies against God; as denying His being . . .' as well as 'all profane scoffing at the Holy Scripture' are punishable offences, and adds as the reason for punishing the latter that offences of this nature 'tend to subvert all religion and morality, which are the foundation of government'. Blackstone, bk. iv., p. 59, describes a class of 'offences more immediately against God and religion' consisting in 'blasphemy against the Almighty, by denying his being or providence' or 'contumelious reproaches of our Saviour Christ', and refers to this head 'all profane scoffing at the holy scripture or exposing it to contempt and ridicule.' Probably few great judges have been willing to go further in questions of religious liberty than Lord Mansfield in his eloquent address to this House in *Evans v. Chamberlain of London*. Yet there he says: 'The eternal principles of natural religion are part of the common law; so that any person reviling, subverting, or ridiculing them may be prosecuted at common law.' Again, the very careful Commissioners on the Criminal Law, of whom Serjeant Starkie was one and Sir William Wightman another, observe in their Sixth Report, p. 85: 'Although the law distinctly forbids all denial of the being and providence of God, or the truth of the Christian religion ... it is only where irreligion assumes the form of blasphemy, in its true and primitive meaning, and has constituted an insult both to God and man, that the interference of the criminal law has taken place.' Nevertheless, it seems to need no citation of authorities (the opinions of the majority of the Judges in your Lordships' House in *Shore v. Wilson* having been fully discussed) to show that a temperate and respectful denial, even of the existence of God, is not an offence against our law, however great an offence it may be against the Almighty Himself, and, except for *Cowan v. Milbourn*, it has never been decided outside of the region of charitable trusts that such a denial affects civil rights. I cannot bring myself to think that it does so. What, after all, is really the gist of the offence of blasphemy, or of its nature as a cause of civil disability? Ribaldry has been treated as the gist, which must be a temporal matter; as between creature and Creator, how can the bad taste or the provocative character of such a denial come into question? The denial itself, not the mode of it, must be what merits the Divine anger: but that is an offence against God. Our Courts of Law, in the exercise of their own jurisdiction, do not, and never did that I can find, punish irreligious words as offences against God. As to them they held that *deorum injuriae dis curae*. They dealt with such words for their manner, their violence, or ribaldry, or, more fully stated, for their tendency to endanger the peace then and there, to deprave public morality generally, to shake the fabric of society, and to be a cause of civil strife. The words, as well as the acts, which tend to endanger society differ from time to time in proportion as society is stable or insecure in fact, or is believed by its reasonable members to be open to assault. In the present day meetings or processions are held lawful which a hundred and fifty years ago would have been deemed seditious, and this is not because the law is weaker or has changed, but because, the times having changed, society is stronger than before. In the present day reasonable men do not apprehend the dissolution or the downfall of society because religion is publicly assailed by methods not scandalous. Whether it is possible that in the future irreligious attacks, designed to undermine fundamental institutions of our society, may come to be criminal in themselves, as constituting a public danger, is a matter that does not arise. The fact that opinion grounded on experience has moved one way does not in law preclude the possibility of its moving on fresh experience in the other; nor does it bind succeeding generations, when conditions have again changed. After all, the question whether a given opinion is a danger to society is a question of the times and is a question of fact. I desire to say nothing that would limit the right of society to protect itself by process of law from the dangers of the moment, whatever that right may be, but only to say that, experience having proved dangers once thought real to be now negligible, and dangers once very possibly imminent to have now passed away, there is nothing in the general rules as to blasphemy and irreligion, as known to the law, which prevents us from varying their application to the particular circumstances of our time in accordance with that experience. If these considerations are right, and the attitude of the law both civil and criminal towards all religions depends fundamentally on the safety of the State and not on the doctrines or metaphysics of those who profess them, it is not necessary to consider whether or why any given body was relieved by the law at one time or frowned on at another, or to analyse creeds and tenets, Christian and other, in which I can profess no competence. Accordingly, I am of opinion that acts merely done in furtherance of paragraph 3(A) and other paragraphs of the respondents' memorandum are not now contrary to the law, and that the appeal should be dismissed.

Mr Justice Eve

On Spiritual Copyright

Sir Harry Trelawney Eve (1856–1940) was for thirty years a judge of the Chancery Division. His elevation to the Bench in 1907 came at a time when a political career promised great things; he had won the Ashburton division of Devon for the Liberals in 1904 and retained the seat with an increased majority in 1906.

Physically a large and kindly man, Eve was always full of fun and good humour. But his way of expressing his sense of fun, by pungent sayings and skits in prose and verse, was not always taken kindly by his superiors or contemporaries. For a judge with such talent in the law it was a mystery why he was never promoted to the Court of Appeal, where he sat frequently as a supernumerary judge, but no doubt his indiscretions on the bench told against him.

In the following judgment Eve displayed his literary gifts to the full; the case aptly lent itself to such treatment. Eve held that a spiritualistic medium who had produced a script entitled The Chronicle of Cleophas *by automatic writing was the owner of copyright in it. The owner was therefore entitled to restrain a person who was present at the séances from publishing the article, annotated by himself, in book form.*

Mrs Cummins was a journalist and writer engaged in psychic research, acting as a spiritualist medium at séances. For some years she had practised automatic writing. The method of writing was as follows: Mrs Cummins covered her eyes with her left hand, took a pencil in her right hand and rested it on a wad of foolscap paper. After a while she passed into a dream state and her hand began to write very rapidly, sometimes over 2,000 words in an hour and a half without any pause.

Mr Bond was an architect and much interested in recent discoveries at the Abbey of Glastonbury and in automatic writing. He was invited by a mutual friend of his and Mrs Cummins, a Miss Gibbes, to join the séances when the automatic writing of an article The Chronicle of Cleophas, *began. After each sitting Mr Bond took away the original script with Mrs Cummins's consent and transcribed it, punctuated it and arranged it*

*in paragraphs, returning a copy to Mrs Cummins. From time to time
during the séances Mr Bond placed his fingers upon the back of Mrs
Cummins's hand when she was writing but it made no difference to the
mode of writing except that it became rather slower.*

*Mrs Cummins's claim to the copyright in the articles created as much
public interest as did the case of the Black Box tried before Mr Justice
Arthian Davies in the courts a quarter of a century later. Eve enjoyed
every minute of the action, which only lasted two days in the summer of
1926, and this is reflected by the lightness of touch in his cynical judgment.*

THE ISSUE in this action is reduced to the simple question who, if
anyone, is the owner of the copyright in this work. Prima facie, it is
the author, and so far as this world is concerned there can be no doubt
who is the author here, for it has been abundantly proved that the
plaintiff is the writer of every word to be found in this bundle of
original script. But the plaintiff and her witness and the defendant are
all of opinion—and I do not doubt that the opinion is an honest one—
that the true originator of all that is to be found in these documents is
some being no longer inhabiting this world, and who has been out of
it for a length of time sufficient to justify the hope that he has no reasons
for wishing to return to it.

According to the case put forward by those entertaining the opinion
I have referred to, the individual in question is particularly desirous of
assisting in further discoveries relating to the ancient Abbey of
Glastonbury, and he chooses the Brompton Road as the locality in
which, and the plaintiff as the medium through whom, his views as to
further works to be undertaken on the site of the Abbey shall be communicated to the persons engaged in the work of excavation. He is
sufficiently considerate not to do so in language so antiquated as not
to be understood by the excavators and others engaged in the interesting operations, but in order not to appear of too modern an epoch he
selects a medium capable of translating his messages into language
appropriate to a period sixteen or seventeen centuries after his death.
I am not impugning the honesty of people who believe, and of the
parties to this action who say that they believe, that this long departed
being is the true source from which the contents of these documents
emanate; but I think I have stated enough with regard to the antiquity
of the source and the language in which the communications are written
to indicate that they could not have reached us in this form without the

active co-operation of some agent competent to translate them from the language in which they were communicated to her into something more intelligible to persons of the present day. The plaintiff claims to be this agent and to possess, and the defendant admits that she does possess, some qualification enabling her, when in a more or less unconscious condition, to reproduce in language understandable by those who have the time and inclination to read it, information supplied to her from the source referred to in language with which the plaintiff has no acquaintance when fully awake.

From this it would almost seem as though the individual who has been dead and buried for some 1,900 odd years and the plaintiff ought to be regarded as the joint authors and owners of the copyright, but inasmuch as I do not feel myself competent to make any declaration in his favour, and recognizing as I do that I have no jurisdiction extending to the sphere in which he moves, I think I ought to confine myself when inquiring who is the author to individuals who were alive when the work first came into existence and to conditions which the legislature in 1911 [the year in which the Copyright Act was passed] may reasonably be presumed to have contemplated. So doing it would seem to be clear that the authorship rests with this lady, to whose gift of extremely rapid writing coupled with a peculiar ability to reproduce in archaic English matter communicated to her in some unknown tongue we owe the production of these documents. But the defendant disputes the plaintiff's right to be considered the sole author, alleging that he was an element and a necessary element in the production, and claiming, if the authorship is to be confined to persons resident in this world, that he is entitled to the rights incident to authorship jointly with the plaintiff.

In the course of the trial, after reading the correspondence, and hearing the evidence of Miss Gibbes, I expressed an unfavourable opinion of the defendant's conduct in certain respects. For one thing he had at a very early stage of his acquaintance with that lady commenced to borrow money from her, and when at a later date he was called upon to repay the sums so borrowed he set up a wholly insupportable story that the moneys had been paid to him as a gift; and for another, when he was submitting a complicated agreement for the approval of the two ladies and inducing them to believe that he desired them to take legal advice thereon, he was at the same time urging a mutual friend to obtain their approval and execution of the same without taking any such advice. Since I expressed that unfavourable opinion I have seen and heard the defendant in the box, and although his conduct in the matters I have referred to cannot but be regarded as involving grave errors of judgment, I do not think he was actuated by the sordid motives which his conduct was certainly calculated to suggest. He is an individual upon whose memory little reliance can be placed—he is of an imaginative temperament and regards the alleged supernatural incidents connected with this work with a reverence that is almost fanatical, and he has, I think, in more than one incident shown that he is occasionally subject to hallucinations. His claim to be considered a joint author is suggestive of an hallucination, for it is based upon the assertion that by his presence at the séances where the writing took place he in some way transmitted from his brain to the unconscious brain of the medium the classical and historical references which are to be found in these documents. He frankly admits that he does not appreciate how it was done, or to what extent he did it; but he has evidently brought himself to believe that he did contribute materially to the composition of the work and that his contribution was made by means of some silent transfer from his brain to that of the unconscious medium of phrases and allusions with which he was familiar but of which she knew nothing. But inasmuch as the medium is credited with a power to translate language of which she knew nothing into archaic English, of which she was almost equally ignorant, and at a phenomenal pace, it does not appear necessary to fall back on the defendant's presence in order to explain the classical and historical references which he maintains must have emanated from his brain. They may well have originated in the brain of the medium herself. In these circumstances I am quite unable to hold that the defendant has made out any case entitling him to be treated as a joint author. I think he is labouring under a complete delusion in thinking that he in any way contributed to the production of these documents.

Alternatively, failing to establish any claim on his own behalf, he submits that there is no copyright in the work at all, that it has come from a far-off locality which I cannot specify, and that the plaintiff is the mere conduit pipe by which it has been conveyed to this world. I do not think that is a fair appreciation of the plaintiff's activities. They obviously involved a great deal more than mere repetition; but, apart altogether from these considerations, the conclusion which the defendant invites me to come to in this submission involves the expression of an opinion I am not prepared to make, that the authorship and copyright rest with some one already domiciled on the other side of the inevitable river. That is a matter I must leave for solution by others more competent to decide it than I am. I can only look upon the matter as a terrestrial one, of the earth earthy, and I propose to deal with it on that footing. In my opinion the plaintiff has made out her case, and the copyright rests with her.

Lord Atkin

On Press Responsibility

Writing an in memoriam of Lord Atkin of Aberdovey (1867–1944), Lord Wright said that Atkin's work as a judge, spread over thirty years, was animated by a liberal philosophy of law. Law was to him not the function of deciding individual cases in isolation but a part of the complex nature of the living State.

Atkin's literary merits stand high in the annals of English law. He was not given to the smart epigrammatic phrases that characterize the efforts of lesser mortals. His style was, in Lord Wright's words, 'chaste, composed, easy and accurate'. But he could on occasions illuminate a thought with a sentence as felicitously phrased as any to be found in the vast bulk of law reports of this country. In one case, speaking of the nature of public policy, Atkin said that the doctrine should be invoked only in clear cases in which the harm to the public was substantially incontestable; he added, with these pregnant words, 'and does not depend upon the idiosyncratic inferences of a few judicial minds'. In another well-known case he referred to the forms of legal action which the legal historian, Maitland, had called the 'ghosts which haunted us from their graves'. Atkin supplied the gloss upon this epigram by saying, 'When these ghosts stand in the path of justice clanking their mediaeval chains the proper course for the judge is to pass through them undeterred'.

In the appeal from Trinidad and Tobago Lord Atkin handed down the locus classicus *on the subject of contempt of court, that misnomer of a doctrine which has put our modern press in a self-imposed strait-jacket. If only editors were to read and re-read Atkin's words the administration of justice would be the healthier for the informed criticism that the newspapers could and should make. Any cursory glance at the columnists and leader-writers of the nineteenth century would indicate how much more forthright they were when dealing with the workings of 'our lady, the Common Law'. Atkin's clarion call to the commentators of the twentieth century to comment without malice or imputation of ill-motive on the judiciary and their performance of public acts is plain for all to heed.*

THIS IS an appeal, by special leave, from an order of the Supreme Court of Trinidad and Tobago ordering the appellant to pay a fine of £25, or in default to be imprisoned for one month, for contempt of Court, and further ordering him to pay the costs of the proceedings as between solicitor and client.

In June, 1934, one, Joseph St Clair, was charged at the Sessions, Port of Spain, before Gilchrist, J., and a jury on an indictment containing two counts, one charging the accused with attempt to murder a superior officer, the second with shooting with intent to do grievous bodily harm. It appears that the accused fired his rifle at the officer but failed to hit him. He was found guilty on the second count, with a recommendation to mercy, and was sentenced on 12th June to eight years' hard labour. He did not appeal.

At the same sessions, one, John Sheriff, was charged before Robinson, J., and a jury on an indictment containing three counts, (1) wounding with intent to murder a particular woman, (2) wounding with intent to murder generally, (3) wounding with intent to do grievous bodily harm. It appears that he attacked with a razor, and seriously mutilated, a woman who was not the person he had intended to attack. He was convicted on the third count, and was sentenced on 14th June to seven years' hard labour. After sentence he said: 'I give notice of appeal', and on 20th June filed formal notice of appeal against his conviction. His appeal eventually succeeded, apparently on the ground of misdirection, and the conviction was quashed. Meanwhile, on 29th June, the present appellant, who is the editor-manager and part proprietor of a daily newspaper called the *Port of Spain Gazette*, published the article which has been found to constitute a contempt of Court. He did not write it, but revised it editorially before publication, and undoubtedly is fully responsible for its publication. It is necessary for the purposes of this case to consider the whole article. It was as follows:

THE HUMAN ELEMENT

Many years ago, it used to be a rather interesting feature of one of the English publications to draw pointed attention, in parallel columns to the strangely anomalous differences between the sentences imposed by various magistrates and judges in cases which seemed, from the reports, to present a fair similarity of facts. In some quarters, the criticism—often unexpressed in actual words—was resented as taking no account of circumstances which a judge was fully entitled to give effect to, though they might not strike the ordinary reader of the press reports. But on the whole, it was felt that, in the majority of instances, useful public service was rendered by this showing up of the inequalities of legal punishments. In Trinidad it must often have occurred to readers of the proceedings in our criminal courts, both inferior and. superior, how greatly the personal or human element seems to come into play in awarding punishment for offences. No question is here involved as to the justification for the convictions; it is assumed, and we believe it to be no unjustified assumption, that in the great majority of cases accused persons are seldom convicted except upon thoroughly satisfactory evidence; and a small number of appeals which succeed, when based upon the plea of the innocence of the prisoner of the offence charged, may be regarded as sufficient proof of that. It is the inequality of the sentences as fitting the circumstances of the offences that seems to often demand some comment. And if we here venture to draw attention to this, it is not by any means with the idea of confirming popular opinion as to the inherent severity or leniency of individual judges or magistrates, but simply with a view to inviting consideration of a matter that must, and in fact does, cause adverse comment amongst the masses as to the evenness of the administration of justice in Trinidad. In two recent cases has it been thought by the public that the sentences imposed by two different judges have been open to such criticism. In the one case, a man stood indicted for the seriously grave offence of shooting at his superior officer with intent to murder him. There seems no doubt that had it not been for the prisoner's failure to shoot straight—a thing at which he himself marvelled openly—he must have killed the officer. No doubt, as was brought out in evidence (and perhaps to an even greater degree than was proved), the man was suffering under the effects of constant provocation; but in addition to all else, there was this to aggravate the crime, that the offender was a trained member of a military body, presumably well disciplined, and that to have used a lethal weapon, to which his position gave him easy access, and with it to have attempted the murder of his officer is a thing regarded in most quarters as peculiarly heinous. The sentence imposed on conviction was eight years, which, on the assumption of good conduct, means release at the end of six years. The other case was one in which a man stood charged with a peculiarly brutal act of wounding with a razor his victim, a woman who was shortly to have become a mother, being so terribly injured that for a long time it seemed quite probable she would die. On conviction, the sentence imposed by another judge on this prisoner was seven years, which, on the assumption of good conduct means release at the expiration of five years and a quarter. Had either of these two cases stood alone, it is quite likely that the sentences would have passed uncommented upon; for neither of them is, in itself, what might be described as a lenient one. But coming together as they did at the same sessions and within a day or two of each other, they have created in the public mind an impression that the former was as unduly severe as the latter was lenient. Both, it is true, were for attempted murder. In both cases a deadly weapon was used. And while some may think that, as we stated above, the military relationship between the prisoner and his intended victim in the first case rendered the matter graver from an official standpoint, yet, on the other hand, in the shooting case, no one, providentially, was injured, and much provocation was proved, whereas in the razor slashing case (assuming the facts proved by the Crown to be true), there does not appear to have been any provocation, while, on the contrary, the attack was made on a woman unknown to or by the accused, whom he mistook for someone else. Surely there might have been expected rather more effect to have been given to the recommendation from the jury to mercy in the first case; and surely, in the other, it would have been more in accord with public opinion as to the need for stern suppression of such attacks had the learned judge been able to see his way to impose a considerably more severe term of imprisonment; the more so in view of the fact that there was absolutely no intimation from the jury that they thought any leniency might properly be shown. We fully realize that the infliction of the sentence is entirely in the discretion of the judge, who has a wide latitude, from a few days' to life-long imprisonment for the crime of attempted murder. But equally it is usually expected that the fullest consideration will be given to the recommendation of a jury for mercy. Assuming, therefore, that eight years' hard labour in lieu of the twenty years which many persons fully expected would be passed, fairly represents an effectual concession to the jury's views, the opinion had been fully expressed that the seven years passed on the razor slasher was far too little for the crime he had committed. And we do not think we are wrong in saying that, as a rule, some weight is given by judges to the question of whether a prisoner succeeded or failed in committing the crime he stands charged with. As we have pointed out, though in both of these cases, the Crown alleged and the jury found, an attempt to murder, in the one case that attempt failed completely—through no fault of the prisoner, it is true: in the other the attempt, while providentially failing resulted in terrible mutilation of the woman who was the victim. It is painful at all times to have to urge the insufficiency of a punishment inflicted; and we wish it to be distinctly appreciated that we dissociate ourselves from those who regard one judge as habitually severe or another as habitually lenient. Yet we do think that if some way could be devised for the great equalization of punishment with the crime committed, a great deal would have been achieved towards the removal of one frequent cause for criticism of the sentences passed in our various criminal courts.

On 3rd July the Attorney-General gave notice of motion to the Registrar of the Supreme Court that he would move for an order nisi calling upon the appellant to show cause why a writ of attachment should not issue against him for his contempt in publishing the article in question, and on the same date an order nisi was made by the Court in the terms of the notice of motion. The notice and the order nisi were at first limited to contempt in publishing an article calculated to interfere with the due course of justice, the complaint being that it was improper having regard to Sheriff's pending appeal. Later, it was amended so as to include a complaint that the article contained 'statements and comments which tend to bring the authority and administration of the law into disrepute and disregard'. In this amended form the matter came before the full Court consisting of the Chief Justice and Gilchrist and Robinson, JJ. It was heard on various days in July, and on 5th September the Chief Justice gave the judgment of the Court. He acquitted the appellant of contempt in respect of the pending appeal of Sheriff; and no more need be said on that point. But he found that the article was written with the direct object of bringing the administration of the criminal law by the judges into disfavour with the public, and desiring to impose a penalty which, if relatively light, would yet emphasize that, while the judges would place no obstruction in the way of fair criticism of their performance of their functions, untruths and malice would not be tolerated, he fined the respondent £25, in default, one month's imprisonment, and ordered him to pay the costs of the proceedings to be taxed between solicitor and client. The formal judgment, slightly departing from the wording of the oral judgment, recited that the appellant had committed a contempt of Court, the article having been written 'with the direct object of bringing the administration of the criminal law in this Colony by the judges into disrepute and disregard', so following the amended order nisi.

Their Lordships can find no evidence in the article, or in any facts placed before the Court, to justify either that the article was written with the direct object mentioned, or that it could have that effect: and they will advise His Majesty that this appeal be allowed. It will be sufficient to apply the law as laid down in *Reg. v. Gray* by Lord Russell of Killowen, C.J.*: 'Any act done or writing published calculated to bring a Court or a judge of the Court into contempt, or to lower his authority, is a contempt of Court. That is one class of contempt.

* In 1900.

Further, any act done or writing published calculated to obstruct or interfere with the due course of justice or the lawful process of the Courts is contempt of Court. The former class belongs to the category which Lord Hardwicke, L.C., characterized as "scandalizing a Court or a judge" *(In Re Read and Huggonson*)*. That description of that class of contempt is to be taken subject to one, and an important, qualification. Judges and Courts are alike open to criticism, and if reasonable argument or expostulation is offered against any judicial act as contrary to law or the public good, no Court could or would treat that as contempt of Court.'

And that, in applying the law, the Board will not lose sight of local conditions, is made clear in the judgment in *McLeod v. St Aubyn†*, where Lord Morris, after saying that committals for contempt of Court by scandalizing the Court itself had become obsolete in this country, an observation sadly disproved the next year in the case last cited, proceeds: 'Courts are satisfied to leave public opinion attacks or comments derogatory or scandalous to them. But it must be considered that in small colonies, consisting principally of coloured populations, the enforcement in proper cases of committal for contempt of Court for attacks on the Court may be absolutely necessary to preserve in such a community the dignity of and respect for the Court.'

But whether the authority and position of an individual judge, or the due administration of justice, is concerned, no wrong is committed by any member of the public who exercises the ordinary right of criticizing, in good faith, in private or public, the public act done in the seat of justice. The path of criticism is a public way: the wrong-headed are permitted to err therein; provided that members of the public abstain from imputing improper motives to those taking part in the administration of justice, and are genuinely exercising a right of criticism, and not acting in malice or attempting to impair the administration of justice, they are immune. Justice is not a cloistered virtue: she must be allowed to suffer the scrutiny and respectful, even though outspoken, comments of ordinary men.

In the present case the writer had taken for his theme the perennial topic of inequality of sentences, under the text, 'The Human Element', using as the occasion for his article the two sentences referred to. He expressly disclaimed the suggestion that one of the particular judges was habitually severe, the other habitually lenient. It is unnecessary

* In 1742.   † In 1899.

to discuss whether his criticism of the sentences was well founded. It is very seldom that the observer has the means of ascertaining all the circumstances which weigh with an experienced judge in awarding sentence. Sentences are unequal because the conditions in which offences are committed are unequal. The writer is, however, perfectly justified in pointing out, what is obvious, that sentences do vary in apparently similar circumstances with the habit of mind of the particular judge. It is quite inevitable. Some very conscientious judges have thought it their duty to visit particular crimes with exemplary sentences; others equally conscientious have thought it their duty to view the same crimes with leniency. If to say that the human element enters into the awarding of punishment be contempt of Court it is to be feared that few in or out of the profession would escape. If the writer had, as journalist, said that St Clair's sentence was, in his opinion, too severe: and on another occasion that Sheriff's sentence was too lenient, no complaint could possibly be made: and the offence does not become apparent when the two are contrasted. The writer in seeking his remedy, as has been remarked by the Supreme Court, has ignored the Court of Criminal Appeal: but he might reply that till such a Court has power, on the initiative of the prosecution, to increase too lenient sentences, its effect in standardizing sentences is not completely adequate. It appears to their Lordships that the writer receives less than justice from the Supreme Court in having untruths imputed to him as a ground for finding the article to be in contempt of Court. He has correctly stated both offenders to have been charged with intent to murder: and though he has subsequently inaccurately stated that the conviction of both affirmed that intent, yet seeing that both were convicted of the same intent—namely, to do grievous bodily harm, the reasoning as to unevenness of sentence appears to have been unaffected. And it seems of little moment that the writer thought that this sentence might be for life instead of in fact being for fifteen years. If criticisms of decisions could only safely be made by persons who accurately knew the relevant law, who would be protected? There is no suggestion that the law was intentionally mis-stated.

Their Lordships have discussed this case at some length because, in one aspect, it concerns the liberty of the Press, which is no more than the liberty of any member of the public, to criticize temperately and fairly, but freely, any episode in the administration of justice. They have come to the conclusion that there is no evidence upon which the

Court could find that the appellant has exceeded this right, or that he acted with untruth or malice, or with the direct object of bringing the administration of justice into disrepute. They are satisfied that the Supreme Court took the course they did with a desire to uphold the dignity and authority of the law as administered in Trinidad; there nevertheless seems to their Lordships to have been a misconception of the doctrine of contempt of Court as applied to public criticism. A jurisdiction of a very necessary and useful kind was applied in a case to which it was not properly applicable, and this, in the view of their Lordships, has resulted in a substantial miscarriage of justice. Acting therefore, on the principles enumerated in the first part of this judgment as applicable to appeals from convictions for contempt of Court, their Lordships will humbly advise his Majesty that this appeal be allowed, and that the order of the Supreme Court, dated 5th September, 1934, be set aside. The respondent must pay the costs here and in the Court below.

Lord Atkin

On Detention without Trial

Lord Atkin's dissent in the case of Liversidge v. Anderson *will rank among his greatest, simply because the subject matter involves the liberty of the individual. He knew that his sole dissent in that case would be unpopular and although he had been asked to omit some of his harsher comments about some members of the judiciary being more executive-minded than the executive he refused to compromise. He felt very strongly about the most fundamental principle in our law and no one would deflect him from what he regarded as the right course to adopt.*

During both World Wars the executive took power under Defence Regulations to detain without trial any person of 'hostile origin or associations' or anyone whose conduct was prejudicial to the safety of the country. Regulation 18B was used extensively to imprison a large number of aliens in Britain as well as British subjects like Sir Oswald Mosley. In Liversidge v. Anderson *a detainee sought to challenge the Home Secretary's right to order a detention without stating his reasons for believing that the person was liable to be detained under the Defence Regulations.*

MY LORDS, I have prepared an opinion which is applicable both to this case and to that of *Greene v. Secretary of State for Home Affairs**.

These cases raise the issue as to the nature and limits of the authority of the Secretary of State to make orders that persons be detained under regulation 18B of the Defence (General) Regulations, 1939. The matter is one of great importance both because the power to make orders is necessary for the defence of the realm, and because the liberty of the subject is seriously infringed, for the order does not purport to be made for the commission of an offence against the criminal law. It is made by an executive minister and not by any kind of judicial officer, it is not made after any inquiry as to facts to which the subject is party, it cannot be reversed on any appeal, and there is no limit to

---

* A case dealing with a similar point concerning a person detained under an order of the Home Secretary under Regulation 18B of the Defence (General) Regulations 1939.

the period for which the detention may last. The material words of the
regulation are as follows:

'If the Secretary of State has reasonable cause to believe any person to be
of hostile origin or associations and that by reason thereof it is necessary to
exercise control over him, he may make an order against that person directing
that he be detained.'

They are only simple words and as it appears to me obviously give
only a conditional authority to the minister to detain any person without trial, the condition being that he has reasonable cause for the belief
which leads to the detention order. The meaning, however, which for
the first time was adopted by the Court of Appeal in the Greene case
and appears to have found favour with some of your Lordships is that
there is no condition, for the words 'if the Secretary of State has
reasonable cause' merely means 'if the Secretary of State thinks that he
has reasonable cause'. The result is that the only implied condition is
that the Secretary of State acts in good faith. If he does that—and who
could dispute it or disputing it prove the opposite?—the minister has
been given complete discretion whether he should detain a subject or
not. It is an absolute power which, so far as I know, has never been
given before to the executive, and I shall not apologize for taking
some time to demonstrate that no such power is in fact given to the
minister by the words in question.

It is a curious fact that in both cases in the first emergence of the
issues raised no trace of this contention appeared. In the Liversidge
case the only question raised is in an action for false imprisonment
brought by the appellant. Following on a defence setting up detention
under an order of the Secretary of State the appellant asked for particulars of the reasonable cause. The only question raised on the
summons before the judge in chambers was on the onus of proof, and,
as both courts held that the onus was on the appellant to show that
there was no reasonable cause, the order for particulars was refused.
It is apparent that if at that time the courts had accepted the present
construction no question of onus would have arisen, for no issue as to
the actual existence of reasonable cause could arise. In the Greene case
the application was by summons for a writ of *habeas corpus*. The
Divisional Court took the same view of the onus as was adopted in the
Liversidge case, and held that in view of the Secretary of State's
affidavit in answer to the appellant's evidence the court was not satis-

fied that there had been no reasonable cause. These matters became irrelevant on the construction adopted by the Court of Appeal on appeal in Greene's case. The view there taken was that the words 'reasonable cause' cannot 'properly be construed as imposing an objective condition precedent of fact on which a person detained would be entitled to challenge the grounds for the Secretary of State's honest belief: in short, that the condition is subjective not objective'. This view of the case at once disposed of any objection to the different grounds adopted by the Divisional Court, and is of such overwhelming importance compared with the issues raised in both cases up to that point that I proceed at once to deal with it, reserving till later what has to be said on the original onus.

It is surely incapable of dispute that the words, 'if A has X' constitute a condition the essence of which is the existence of X and the having of it by A. If it is a condition to a right (including a power) granted to A, whenever the right comes into dispute the tribunal whatever it may be that is charged with determining the dispute must ascertain whether the condition is fulfilled. In some cases the issue is one of fact, in others of both fact and law, but in all cases the words indicate an existing something, the having of which can be ascertained. And the words do not mean and cannot mean 'if A thinks that he has'. 'If A has a broken ankle' does not mean and cannot mean 'if A thinks that he has a broken ankle'. 'If A has a right of way' does not mean and cannot mean 'if A thinks that he has a right of way'. 'Reasonable cause' for an action or a belief is just as much a positive fact capable of determination by a third party as is a broken ankle or a legal right. If its meaning is the subject of dispute as to legal rights, then ordinarily the reasonableness of the cause, and even the existence of any cause is in our law to be determined by the judge and not by the tribunal of fact if the functions deciding law and fact are divided. Thus having established, as I hope, that the plain and natural meaning of the words 'has reasonable cause' imports the existence of a fact or state of facts and not the mere belief by the person challenged that the fact or state of facts existed, I proceed to show that this meaning of the words has been accepted in innumerable legal decisions for many generations, that 'reasonable cause' for a belief when the subject of legal dispute has been always treated as an objective fact to be proved by one or other party and to be determined by the appropriate tribunal. I will go further and show that until June or July of this year in connection with this regulation 18B, there never has been any other construction even submitted to the courts in whatever context the words are found.

The power of arrest is confided by the common law both to constables and to private individuals. The constable has power within his district to arrest a person on reasonable suspicion of his having committed a felony. The private individual has power on two conditions: (1) that a felony has actually been committed; (2) that there is reasonable and probable cause of suspecting the person arrested. In these cases the grounds for suspicion must be brought before the court, the onus is on the person who arrested to prove the reasonable grounds, and the issue whether the cause is reasonable or not is to be determined by the judge. These propositions will be found in any elementary textbook. I will refer to authority that the defendant in an action for false imprisonment based on unlawful arrest is entitled to succeed if he pleads and proves that the imprisonment was legally justifiable:* that he must show the cause of suspicion so that the court may judge of the reasonableness†; that a man directing a constable to act on a suggestion of felony is bound to show probable cause of suspicion‡; that the plea must show reasonable and probable ground of suspicion, i.e., facts which raise a reasonable suspicion, not all the evidence (per Lord Campbell, C.J.), and it is for the court to say whether the facts pleaded show reasonable cause (per Wightman, J.)§; that it is a good plea that the man was arrested on a reasonable suspicion of felony, but not enough that the suspicion was *bona fide*¶; that the civilian defendant must make out a reasonable ground of suspicion and that a felony had actually been committed (per Lord Tenterden, C.J.)‖; and a more recent affirmation of the same principles in *Wallace v. W. H. Smith & Son Ltd***. In all these cases it is obvious that the courts were dealing with an objective fact to be proved before them by the defendant, and that their pronouncements would be nonsense if the inquiry had only been whether the defendant believed that he had reasonable ground.

So much for the constable's power of arrest at common law. He and other persons have also been armed with powers of arrest by statute and in all cases the condition of reasonable cause for suspicion

* *Allen v. Wright (1838).*
† *Mure v. Kaye (1811).*
  Stammers v. Yearsley (1833).
  Haynes v. Mewis (1826).
‡ *M'Cloughan v. Clayton (1816).*

§ *Broughton v. Jackson (1852).*
¶ *Sayer v. Lichfold (1854).*
‖ *Beckwith v. Philby (1827).*
** *1914.*

has been enacted. I select a list of thirteen statutes from the valuable work on Police Law by Dr Moriarty, the late chief constable of Birmingham, 6th ed., pp. 16, *seq.*

*   *   *

It is well settled that the onus of proving reasonable cause for belief is on the accused, and that the section means that the accused had reasonable cause to believe and did believe. It is so much an 'objective' fact that in this case reasonable belief is left to the jury. The subjective test would startle any judge versed in trying crimes. Similarly, by the Age of Marriage Act, 1929, s.6, which avoids marriage where either party is under sixteen it is a defence in proceedings under the Criminal Law Amendment Act for the accused to prove that he had reasonable cause to believe that the girl was his wife. A very familiar use of the words is in actions for malicious prosecution where the plaintiff has to establish the absence of reasonable or probable cause in the prosecutor for instituting the prosecution. The relevant facts known to the prosecutor are, if necessary, determined by the jury. The judge determines whether they constitute reasonable cause. The inquiry is 'objective', and the cause of action, if established with the essential element of malice, exists against any person, rich or poor, powerful or weak, including any member of the executive, whether Secretary of State or not. A further use of the words is to be found in the Directors Liability Act, 1890, s. 3, sub.s I(a) by which it is provided that a director of a company is liable for untrue statements unless he proves that he had reasonable ground to believe that they were true.

So far I have sought to establish that the words in question are not ambiguous, that they have only one plain and natural meaning, that with that meaning the words have been used at common law and in numerous statutes, and that whenever they are used the courts have given them the meaning I suggest, have considered that they give rise to a justiciable issue, and that as to the 'subjective' meaning now contended for by the Secretary of State it has never at any time occurred to the minds of counsel or judges that the words are even capable of meaning anything so fantastic.

I will now proceed to show that in the Defence Regulations themselves the persons responsible for the framing of them—may I call them for this purpose the legislators?—have shown themselves to be fully aware of the true meaning of the words, have clearly appreciated the difference between having reasonable cause to believe and believing without any condition as to reasonable cause, and have obviously used the words 'reasonable cause' in order to indicate that mere honest belief is not enough. The object is plainly that of the common law and previous statutes to secure some measure of protection for the public by providing a condition which, if necessary, can be examined by the courts. In the first place, when the decision is left to the minister or other executive authority without qualification the words omit the reference to reasonable cause. 'If it appears to the Secretary of State' that any 'person is concerned', etc. (order as to publication, reg. 2C); 'A Secretary of State . . . if it appears to him necessary may . . . (order as to giving information, reg. 6, para.(3)); 'If . . . it appears to a Secretary of State to be necessary . . . (order as to protected places, reg. 12, para (1)); so in regs. 14B, 16A, 18A, 21, 40B, 43B. The wording is sometimes varied with the same result. 'If the Secretary of State is satisfied' (publication in newspaper, reg. 2D) (articles likely to assist enemy, reg. 4C); 'satisfied that it is necessary or expedient' (prohibition of balloons, reg. 7, para (2)); 'satisfied . . . that . . . it is necessary' (restricting movements of persons: reg. 18A); 'satisfied . . . that it is subject to foreign influence' (organization subject to foreign influence, 18AA). Similar words occur in regs. 35, para (1), 39B, 39C.

In all these cases it is plain that unlimited discretion is given to the Secretary of State, assuming as everyone does that he acts in good faith. Now let us examine the regulations which import the words 'reasonable cause', some in reference to the commission of an offence, some to a defence to a charge, and some to the powers given to executive officers to do acts for the protection of the state.

[Lord Atkin then lists in numerical order 23 instances where the words 'reasonable cause' are inserted into the regulations.]

* * *

I have pointed out that the words in question have a plain and natural meaning, that that meaning has been invariably given to them in statements of the common law and in statutes, that there has been one invariable construction of them in the courts, and that the Defence Regulations themselves clearly recognize that meaning, using different words where it is intended that the executive officer should have unqualified discretion. I have not so far called attention to the working of reg. 18B itself which, as I venture to think, establishes within nine lines the distinction which the appellants rely on. '(1A) If the Secretary of State has reasonable cause to believe any person to have been or to be a member of [a certain organization] and that it is necessary to exercise control over him, he may make' a detention order. The organizations in question are defined as 'any organization as respects which the Secretary of State is satisfied that either: (a) the organization is subject to foreign influence or control, or (b) the persons in control of the organization have or have had associations with persons concerned in the government of, or sympathies with the system of government of, any Power with which His Majesty is at war'. The organizations, therefore, are impugned if the Secretary of State is satisfied as to their nature, but the person is not to be detained unless the Secretary of State has reasonable cause to believe that he is a member. The contrast is all the more marked when the words of 18B (1) 'If the Secretary of State has reasonable cause to believe any person to be of hostile . . . associations' are compared with the words of 18B (1A) which I have just quoted and which in substance say as to (b) if the Secretary of State is satisfied that the persons in control of the organization have hostile associations. Why the two different expressions should be used if they have the same 'subjective' meaning no one was able to explain. I suggest that the obvious intention was to give a safeguard to the individual against arbitrary imprisonment. Finally, if all these considerations failed, if there were a certain ambiguity in the words 'has reasonable cause to believe', the question would be conclusively settled by the fact that the original form of the regulation issued in September 1939 gave the Secretary of State the complete discretion now contended for: 'The Secretary of State if satisfied, etc.' But it was withdrawn and published in November, 1939, in its present form. It is not competent to us to investigate what political reasons necessitated this change, but it is at least probable that it was made because objection had been taken to the arbitrary power and it was seen that Parliament might intervene. What is certain is that the legislators intentionally introduced the well-known safeguard by the changed form of words.

If, then, the natural construction of the words indicates an objective condition to the power of the minister to detain, whose existence must, therefore, in case of dispute be cognizable by a court of law, what room is there for any other construction? I will deal with the suggested inconvenience to the minister or possible prejudice to the interests of the State later on. I venture to quote the words of the present Lord Chancellor in *Barnard v. Gorman**, a case turning on the meaning of the word 'offender' in a section of the Customs Consolidation Act, 1876. 'Our duty in the matter is plain. We must not give the statutory words a wider meaning merely because on a narrower construction the words might leave a loophole for frauds against the revenue. If on the proper construction of the section that is the result it is not for judges to attempt to cure it. That is the business of Parliament.' In that case the words were that 'the offender may be either detained or proceeded against by summons' and the question was whether the word 'offender' necessarily connoted that the person detained had in fact committed an offence, or included a person who was reasonably suspected of having committed an offence. Inasmuch as the very words referred to proceeding by summons which necessarily involved an investigation into the guilt or not of the person in question, it was considered by all members of this House quite clear that the word was capable of both meanings and could not have been used in the same sentence in the narrower meaning for detention and the broader for summons.

The respondents sought to find support in the decision in *Rex v. Halliday*†, in which this House affirmed a decision of the Court of Appeal and of a Divisional Court of which I happened to be a member. In that case the regulation undisputably gave to a Secretary of State unrestricted power to detain a suspected person, though only on the recommendation of an advisory committee presided over by a judge. The argument for the appellant was that the regulation was *ultra vires* because, though the words of the Defence of the Realm Act under which that regulation was made were plainly wide enough to enable a regulation to be made giving unrestricted powers, yet they ought to be read with a limitation in favour of liberty. Every judge who dealt with the case, including the noble Lords, refused to limit the natural meaning of the words, pointing out that a state of war would itself tend to confine the construction to the plain meaning of the words and would discourage any attempt to make the words lean in favour of liberty. What that case has to do with the present I cannot see. No one doubts that the Emergency Powers (Defence) Act, 1939, empowers His Majesty in Council to vest any minister with unlimited power over

---

* 1941—Viscount Simon.   † 1917.

the person and property of the subject. The only question is whether in this regulation His Majesty has done so.

In the present case there is, in the first place, no ambiguity at all, and, in the second place, even if it were open to a judge to consider the question of expediency, what are the suggested grounds which compel him to adopt the hitherto unheard of 'subjective' construction? It is said that it could never have been intended to substitute the decision of judges for the decision of the minister, or, as has been said, to give an appeal from the minister to the courts. But no one proposes either a substitution or an appeal. A judge's decision is not substituted for the constable's on the question of unlawful arrest, nor does he sit on appeal from the constable. He has to bear in mind that the constable's authority is limited and that he can only arrest on reasonable suspicion, and the judge has the duty to say whether the conditions of the power are fulfilled. If there are reasonable grounds, the judge has no further duty of deciding whether he would have formed the same belief any more than, if there is reasonable evidence to go to a jury, the judge is concerned with whether he would have come to the same verdict. For instance, the minister may have reasonable grounds on the information before him for believing that a person is of 'hostile origin'. If so, any ruling by the courts either in an action for false imprisonment or by way of habeas corpus is impossible though it should subsequently be proved beyond doubt that the minister's information was wrong and that the person was of purely British origin. The only remedy for such a mistake is to bring objections before the advisory committee whose advice is not binding, and to make representations to the minister himself.

But it is said that the grounds of belief will or may be confidential matters of public importance and that it is impossible to suppose that the Secretary of State was intended to disclose either his grounds or his information to the court. My Lords, the objection is answered by the very terms of the regulation itself. By paras. 3, 4 and 5 the detained person has the right to make objections to an advisory committee and it is the duty of the chairman 'to inform the objector of the grounds on which the order has been made against him and to furnish him with such particulars as are in the opinion of the chairman sufficient to enable him to present his case.' These grounds and particulars must, of course, be furnished to the chairman by the Secretary of State, for otherwise the chairman has no means of knowledge. What are these grounds and these particulars but the very facts constituting the 'reasonable cause' which on the true construction might have to be investigated by the court? I find myself unable to comprehend how it can be compulsory, as it is, to furnish the objector before the committee with the grounds and particulars, and yet impossible in the public interest to furnish the objector with them in court. The supposed difficulty is grossly exaggerated, even if it is not a fantasy. The present case of *Greene* illustrates this. On May 22, 1940, he was detained under an order which recited that the Home Secretary had reasonable cause to believe him to be a person of hostile associations and that by reason thereof it was necessary to exercise control over him. On 15th July, 1940, he was served with a document headed 'Home Office, Advisory Committee, 6 Burlington Gardens, W.1. Reasons for order under Defence Regulation 18B in the case of Benjamin Greene. The order under Defence Regulation 18B was made against you for the following reasons. The Secretary of State has reasonable cause to believe that you have been recently concerned in acts prejudicial to the public safety and the defence of the realm and in the preparation and instigation of such acts and that it is necessary to exercise control over you. Particulars.' Then follow six paragraphs of particulars referring to his being concerned in the management and control of two named organizations and of the nature of speeches and writings of his, and stating that he was privy to the activities of a named person in the publication of pro-German propaganda in a named periodical, that he was subsequently to the outbreak of war communicating with persons in Germany concerned in the government of Germany, that he was desirous of establishing a national socialist regime in Great Britain with the assistance, if received, of German armed forces, that he freely associated with persons of German nationality who he had reason to believe were agents of the German government, and that there was reasonable cause to believe that he desired and intended to continue the actions aforesaid. It is true that the 'reason' given was not that stated in the order, but it is explained that this was a mistake, and the 'particulars' are vouched in an affidavit of the Home Secretary as particulars of the original reason of 'hostile associations'. It is obvious that no important reasons of State prevented the Home Secretary from disclosing the causes of his belief. It is, however, said that the sources of his information may be confidential. I think this in some cases is likely to be so, but I cannot think that this creates any difficulty. The Home Secretary has the right to withold evidence that he can assure the court is confidential and cannot in the public interest be disclosed. He has in this case and in others sworn affidavits to the effect that the information he acted on was the result of reports and information from persons in responsible positions experienced in investigating matters of this kind and that he accepted their information. Before the era of 'subjective' cause, and, indeed, afterwards, the Divisional Court and the Court of Appeal have accepted these affidavits as satisfactory proof of the existence of reasonable cause. This was not a view favoured by the Attorney-General in the present case, for it weakens his case as to public mischief. But, in fact, if the affidavits are supported by statements by or on behalf of the Secretary of State vouching the necessity of withholding the names of the witnesses in the public interest, I personally agree with the former decisions and cannot see why, if the courts believe the Home Secretary and accept the substance of the information as constituting reasonable cause, they should not be satisfied that reasonable cause has been shown. The source of the information is merely a question going to the credibility of the person informed, and, no doubt, to the issue of reasonableness. But in police matters it is often withheld, and if, for instance, a constable defending an action for false imprisonment or wrongful arrest were to give in evidence that an informant whom he believed and had proved to be trustworthy had told him that the plaintiff was present at the scene of the felony in incriminating circumstances and the constable was corroborated by his inspector and sergeant but he declined to give the name of the informant, I think it clear that the court might accept the evidence as proving reasonable cause for suspicion. I agree with the Divisional Court in the case of Greene, in accepting what appears at that time to have been the contention of the Home Secretary that the Home Secretary's affidavit establishes the particulars as constituting reasonable cause. I think that the members of the Court of Appeal, though infected with the 'subjective' virus, took the same view. In addition to this, it must be remembered that by s.6 of the Emergency Powers (Defence) Act, 1939, there is complete power in the court to order proceedings to be heard in camera, and to prohibit the disclosure of any information concerning them. I cannot believe that proceedings for false imprisonment or for a writ of habeas corpus present more difficulties of this kind than does the trial of a spy. Lastly, on this question of expediency I would recall that for months after the regulation came into force this suggested difficulty never presented itself to the minds of the Home Secretary and his advisers, but, on the contrary, in *Rex v. Secretary of State for Home Affairs. Ex parte Lees**, the Home Secretary, when represented by the present Solicitor-General and the same junior counsel as in this case, frankly accepted the burden of proving reasonable cause.

It was further said that the provision of safeguards in the regulation itself, the resort to the advisory committee, the providing of 'grounds' and 'particulars', and the right to make representations to the Secretary of State indicate that the original power to detain was unconditional. But how unconvincing this appears. These safeguards are nothing compared with those given to a man arrested by a constable who must at once be brought before a judicial tribunal who investigates the case in public. Yet the constable or anyone else empowered to arrest on reasonable cause is liable to an action if he has exceeded his authority.

What appears to me to be the only argument as to expediency put forward by the respondents which has any weight was that derived from the second point of the powers given—'reasonable cause to believe ... that by reason thereof it is necessary to exercise control over him.' Adroitly the Attorney-General dealt with this first. Can it be supposed, he said, that it was intended that the accumulated experience, instinct and knowledge of the minister in coming to a decision on this matter could be replaced by a judgment of a court of law? But first things first. Before this decision is made there has to be a valid belief that the subject was of hostile origin, associations, etc. When once this is established, it is very unlikely that a court would not in most cases accept as reasonable the Home Secretary's decision to detain. But even on this part of the machinery for detention there is ample scope for an independent inquiry. Let us take the case of 'hostile origin'. If a man or a woman of hostile origin made the case that he or she had been a loyal subject for thirty or forty years, was a supporter of this country's war effort, and had never taken any part in any hostile activity, would it not be open to the courts to consider whether by reason of the hostile origin it was necessary to control him or her? Could the Home Secretary support a mere order to detain all persons of hostile origin regardless of age, sex or antecedents? Or could he support an order against a subject who had been a member of an organization which the Home Secretary was satisfied was now within

* 1941.

1A (a) or (b) but had ceased to be for years and had genuinely disclaimed any sympathy with its present objects. It must be remembered
that at the time of the issue of the regulation organizations of both
left and right were under suspicion, and there may well have been good
reasons for granting protection to persons who had merely at some time
or other been members of them without more.

I view with apprehension the attitude of judges who on a mere
question of construction when face to face with claims involving the
liberty of the subject show themselves more executive-minded than
the executive. Their function is to give words their natural meaning,
not, perhaps, in war time leaning towards liberty, but following the
dictum of Pollock, C.B., in *Bowditch v. Balchin**, cited with approval
by my noble and learned friend Lord Wright in *Barnard v. Gorman*†:
'In a case in which the liberty of the subject is concerned, we cannot go
beyond the natural construction of the statute'. In this country, amid
the clash of arms, the laws are not silent. They may be changed, but
they speak the same language in war as in peace. It has always been
one of the pillars of freedom, one of the principles of liberty for which
on recent authority we are fighting, that the judges are no respecters
of persons and stand between the subject and any attempted encroach-
ments on his liberty by the executive, alert to see that any coercive
action is justified in law. In this case I have listened to arguments
which might have been addressed acceptably to the Court of King's
Bench in the time of Charles I.

I protest, even if I do it alone, against a strained construction put on
words with the effect of giving an uncontrolled power of imprisonment to the minister. To recapitulate: The words have only one meaning. They are used with that meaning in statements of the common
law and in statutes. They have never been used in the sense now
imputed to them. They are used in the Defence Regulations in the
natural meaning, and, when it is intended to express the meaning now
imputed to them, different and apt words are used in the regulations
generally and in this regulation in particular. Even if it were relevant,
which it is not, there is no absurdity or no such degree of public
mischief as would lead to a non-natural construction.

I know of only one authority which might justify the suggested
method of construction: 'When I use a word,' Humpty Dumpty said
in rather a scornful tone, 'it means just what I choose it to mean,

* 1850.   † 1941.

neither more nor less.' 'The question is,' said Alice, 'whether you can make words mean so many different things.' 'The question is,' said Humpty Dumpty, 'which is to be master—that's all.' (*Through the Looking Glass*, c.vi.) After all this long discussion the question is whether the words 'If a man has' can mean 'If a man thinks he has'. I am of opinion that they cannot, and that the case should be decided accordingly.

If it be true, for the foregoing reasons, I am profoundly convinced it is, that the Home Secretary has not been given an unconditional authority to detain, the true decision in the two cases before us ought not to be difficult to make. In the Liversidge case the appellant has delivered a statement of claim averring that he was wrongly imprisoned by the respondent, the Secretary of State. The respondent traverses the wrongful imprisonment and contents himself with the admission that he ordered the appellant to be detained under the regulation. The appellant asked for particulars of his reasonable cause to believe (a) as to hostile associations, (b) as to necessity to control him. In my opinion, the apellant is not bound to rely on the traverse, though as a matter of pleading that, in my opinion, amounts to a positive allegation of authority to detain for which particulars may be asked. The appellant's right to particulars, however, is based on a much broader ground, a principle which again is one of the pillars of liberty in that in English law every imprisonment is *prima facie* unlawful and that it is for a person directing imprisonment to justify his act. The only exception is in respect of imprisonment ordered by a judge, who from the nature of his office cannot be sued, and the validity of whose judicial decisions cannot in such proceedings as the present be questioned. My noble friend, Lord Macmillan, suggests that under a more exacting system of pleading the appellant would have to aver the absence of reasonable grounds on the part of the Secretary of State. The English system of pleading was exacting enough a hundred years ago, but then and ever since, by reason of the presumption I have stated, the averment in an action against a constable for false imprisonment was in the form adopted in the present case, and the defendant had to plead his justification with particulars. There is no distinction of persons. The defendant has to justify with particulars, and in my opinion the appellant in this case was clearly right in asking for particulars. If the respondents were able to satisfy the court that they could not give particulars in the public interest, the court would either not order particulars or, if the objection came after the order, would not enforce it. There was no evidence of this kind at the hearing of this summons, and, in my opinion, the appeal ought to be allowed and an order made in the terms of the summons.

Lord Justice Harman

Two Judgments

Most, but not all, of the outstanding judgments in English law, both from a jurisprudential and literary viewpoint, have been reflective. The more important the case the more care the judge will devote to the giving of his reasons; in that process greater attention to the manner and style of expression can be lavished on the judicial product.

But there have been judges—few in number—who have excelled in their use of the English language even when delivering their judgments ex tempore. It has been said that Sir George Jessel in the late nineteenth century never reserved a judgment. Although that is a slight exaggeration Jessel was able to master the most complex case and rarely felt the need to cogitate upon his judgment. Although Jessel's judgments did not often rank as works of literature, they were models of clarity and precision and seldom fell foul of the appellate courts.

In modern times the exponent of the pithy and elegant ex tempore judgment has been Lord Justice Harman. His meticulous decision in the Shaw will case is reproduced on page 352. In contrast the two following judgments bear eloquent testimony to a felicity and conciseness of expression, straight off the cuff, which few possess and even fewer can ever acquire.

In the case of Campbell Discount Co. Ltd v. Bridge *the growing uneasiness of judges and lawyers about the practices of hire-purchase companies was touched on before the court, although the company involved had not in any way behaved improperly or unconscionably. A hirer of a car under a hire-purchase agreement with a finance company put down as a first payment, £105, and paid the first instalment on the total hire-purchase price of £482 10s. od. He then wrote to the finance company explaining that he could not afford to carry on the instalments and returned the car to them. A clause in the agreement provided that a hirer could terminate the agreement by giving notice, in which case a further clause in the agreement provided that the hirer should pay to the owners 'by way of compensation for depreciation of the vehicle' an amount which would raise the rentals to be paid to two-thirds of the hire-purchase price. The company claimed £206 3s. 4d. The County Court judge gave short shrift to the company's claim and simply noted as the reason for his judgment, 'Held penalty'. But the Court of Appeal disagreed and said that a sum which the parties agreed should be paid as compensation if the hirer terminated the contract as provided for in the agreement could not be considered as a penalty, and as such unenforceable in law. And the court could find no way of avoiding the right of the owner to claim the sum of money. What was particularly hard on the hirer was that if he had silently refused to pay and waited for the owner to come and claim his car, instead of frankly admitting his inability to continue paying, the compensation provision could not have operated, since then the claim would in law have been regarded as an exaction of a penalty.*

The second case, Solihull Corp. v. Gas Council, *involved one of the quillets of the law, rating and valuation. Apart from the Rent Restriction Acts hardly any branch of legislation has provoked so many judges to complain of the vagaries of the parliamentary draughtsman. In this case the West Midlands Gas Board purchased some land in the territory of the Solihull local authority for the erection of a gas research station. The board provided the money to buy the land and the buildings and paid the salaries of the employees. These expenses were reimbursed by the Gas Council; and there were other indications that the premises might have belonged to the Gas Council and not the Board. Of these two financially interconnected nationalized corporations, however, the premises of the West Midlands Gas Board but—for some undisclosed and inexplicable reason—not those of the Gas Council were exempted from rating. The Board made annual payments in lieu of rates, which was much less onerous. The Solihull Corporation on behalf of its ratepayers wished to extract the higher rating, which occupation of the premises by the Gas Council would have given them the right to expect. But the Court of Appeal, reversing the decision of the Lands Tribunal, clearly thought that occupation rested with the Board.*

Campbell Discount Co. Ltd v. Bridge

I AM of the same opinion and though I should like to emulate the laconic terms of the judgment of the county court judge who delivered judgment in two words, I feel constrained to add a word or two because of the uneasy feeling I have that the position of the law as it stands is not satisfactory. If the judgment of the majority in the *Cooden Engineering case* be right, then the position may be different according to whether there is somewhere behind the termination of the contract a breach by somebody. It has been pointed out quite rightly to us that it is unsatisfactory if the man who honestly admits to the finance company that he cannot go on may have to pay a penalty, but that if he waits for the finance company to exercise their rights and in the meanwhile breaks the contract, he may be able to escape paying it on the ground that penalty for breach of contract is not enforceable in law. I have felt myself oppressed by that consideration.

The solution may be that the minority view in *Cooden Engineering* was in fact the right one. I do not think anyhow that the discrepancy can be healed by some rather loose conception of what are called equitable principles. Equitable principles are, I think, perhaps rather too often bandied about in common-law courts as though the Chancellor still had only the length of his own foot to measure when coming to a conclusion. Since the time of Lord Eldon anyhow the system of equity for good or evil has been a very precise one and equitable jurisdiction is exercised only on well-known principles. There are some who would have it otherwise, and I think Lord Denning is one of them. He, it will be remembered, invented an equity called the equity of the deserted wife. That distressful female's condition has really not been improved at all now that this so-called equity has been analysed.

Similarly, I rather deprecate the attempt to urge the court on what are called equitable principles to dissolve contracts which are thought to be harsh, or which have turned out to be disadvantageous to one of the parties. It is pointed out in one of the cases cited to us yesterday (and Lord Nottingham's observation in *Maynard v. Moseley* is still true) that: 'the Chancery mends no man's bargain', and I do not therefore see my way to call in aid equity to mend what may be an unfortunate situation and one which, if it calls for remedy, calls for aid by the legislature rather than by the justiciary.

Solihull Corporation v. Gas Council

The not uncomplicated case with which we have been wrestling for the last three days is really a by-product of that particular piece of nationalization found in the Gas Act, 1948, which produced two full-grown corporations springing like Athena from the head of Zeus, fully armed with powers, one being, so to speak, the adviser of the other. The regional gas boards were the instruments designed to carry on the business of supplying gas to the public, and the Gas Council a body set up to advise the Minister of Fuel and Power and to co-ordinate the efforts of the various boards. These several corporations were, of course, never at arm's length. The Gas Council derived its finance by levying on the money earned by the gas boards; on the other hand, the Gas Council for certain purposes would reimburse one or other of the boards for expenditure that it incurred. Everything came out of the public's pocket in the end, being either borrowed from the Treasury and coming from the general tax-payer, or ex-tracted from the consumer of gas by way of payment for that com-modity. So you start with a position where the two corporations here involved are never at arm's length, nor do they ever deal with one an-other as if they were.

The dispute here is which of them is in rateable occupation of the hereditament in question; but as, owing to what is, I suppose, the accident of legislation, the board is immune from rates and the Gas Council is not, both of them stand on the same side of the fence, and urge that the board be treated as the rateable occupier although in a more rational world they would be on different sides, one arguing against the other. The outside party who wants the council to be treated as occupier is the rating authority, who can then levy a rate (and a considerable rate) on this hereditament, which is a gas research station.

Now it is one of the statutory duties of the Gas Council to establish research stations for the purpose of research into the useful application of gas, which had previously been carried on by a body set up by the various gas undertakings. The statute provides that one of the duties of the council is to conduct such research as seems good to them; and, as my Lord has pointed out, under section 3 of the Act the council may either do the research itself or make arrangements with, among other people, area boards to do it on its behalf. In this case one thing that is clear is that the council has made an arrangement, albeit a very vague and obscure one, with the board to conduct this particular piece of research into what are called 'complete gasification processes' on its behalf, in return for which (so far as can be gathered from the various rather wordy and unsatisfactory documents before us) the

Gas Council is to reimburse the board, albeit in the end out of the board's own money, for the expenses incurred or to be incurred. Under those arrangements the board has bought some land on which it has erected this gas research station, and has, I suppose, agreed to have inscribed upon it the name of the Gas Council, as if the object of the research station is to conduct research by the Gas Council itself. From this fact and certain notepaper headings and the like the Lands Tribunal has reached the conclusion that the council and not the board is in occupation of this hereditament.

In my judgment that is entirely contrary to the facts as revealed to us. I have found myself at a loss to appreciate how the Lands Tribunal could reach its conclusion; but I think perhaps my Lord hit upon the explanation when he said that they came to that conclusion because they started with a wrong premise. The premise which they should have started from was that this was a building to which the board not only had a title, but of which it was in fact in possession. Title, of course, in matters of rating is from one point of view quite unimportant; you can be occupying if you have no title at all; but where there is a competitor, matters of title often become extremely important. The subject is, I think, very well dealt with in Ryde on Rating, 10th ed., pp. 84, 85, and I do not think I need go into that. So far as I can see, the only theory now put forward in order to show that the council is occupier does not rest on any point of licence or tenancy— the contentions which were put forward below—but that in some way the very fact of the board's occupation is the occupation of the council.

That appears to me to be entirely contrary to all the facts found in the case. The station is owned and controlled by the board. The people who work there are the servants of the board. The controller of research is the board's servant, and no one else's. There are no indications of possession on the part of the council except its name on the façade. As to the board being the *alter ego* of the council, there is no evidence to support that either. The board is a separate corporation with which the council has made this arrangement to carry out this research on its behalf; but why the fact that it is being done on the council's behalf puts the council in occupation of the research station I am entirely unable to follow.

With all respect, therefore, to the Tribunal and the able argument of Mr Lyell, in my view this is a tolerably plain case; there was no ground on which the Tribunal could draw the inference which it drew on the facts put before it. If that be a true description of the position, then like my Lord, I think that an appellate court is not debarred from putting its own opinion in the place of that of the Tribunal. I agree that the appeal should be allowed.

Mr Justice Stable

On Obscenity

In 1954 the Director of Public Prosecutions launched a series of prosecutions against reputable publishers. They were charged with obscene libel for publishing books which were regarded by those in authority as less than reputable. Five publishers were taken to court during that period: Werner Laurie for Julie (convicted); Secker & Warburg for The Philanderer (acquitted); Hutchinson for September in Quinze (convicted); Heinemann for The Image and the Search (two juries failed to agree and a formal acquittal followed); and Arthur Barker for The Man in Control (acquitted). In the same year a desire to suppress other works which offended the senses of some more puritanical members of the public spread to the magistracy. Copies of Boccaccio's Decameron were condemned by the Swindon justices; their decision however was reversed on appeal. And in March 1955 the Doncaster police sought unsuccessfully to obtain a destruction order against copies of the Kinsey report.

In this state of threatened prosecution for books which by no standards of a civilized community could be called pornographic, reputable publishing houses organized themselves into an effective political pressure group and set about agitating their cause in Parliament. If books characterizing the hearty Falstaffian guffaws of a Rabelais or even the dirty sniggers of a Dean Swift were to be suppressed, publishers felt that much good and lasting literature would be lost to the reading public. The Society of Authors drafted new legislation which wended its tortuous way through Parliament—initial rejection, reference to a select committee, finally a Bill, which lapsed at the end of a Parliamentary session and whose ultimate success was somewhat tarnished by the removal of certain safeguarding clauses unacceptable to the Government.

The Obscene Publications Act, 1959, represented the triumph of compromise. The law was to have greater powers to deal with real pornography while literature was to be spared the armoury of the prosecutor by protective clauses redefining obscenity and allowing literary experts, for the first time, to testify to the work's eminence in the world of literature.

If publishers sat back secure in the knowledge that all was well with their world, two events reawakened them to the extant dangers. The publication by Weidenfeld and Nicolson of Nabokov's Lolita *during the final stages of the legislation was thought to arouse in the authorities the need to clamp down upon books which portrayed sexual perversions and aberrations. But if* Lolita *escaped the prosecutor's net (supposedly by a majority vote of 2 to 1, the Home Secretary and the Director of Public Prosecutions ganging up against an Attorney-General who was looking for a fight) Penguin Books with their projected publication of the unexpurgated version of D. H. Lawrence's* Lady Chatterley's Lover *did not eschew the drama and ultimately beneficial publicity attendant upon an Old Bailey trial.*

Lady Chatterley's Lover, *when first published in 1928, was heralded with strident criticism—'most evil outpourings—sewers of French pornography—literal cesspool—book snapped up by degenerate booksellers and British decadents'. In 1960 an English jury acquitted the publishers under the new Act. Kenneth Tynan's commentary on England's most celebrated litarery trial (printed on page 140) measures the interest which was focused on that stuffy Victorian courtroom and which engaged the attentions of some who were utterly in tune with their surroundings. If we are to make any qualification of Tynan's view it is that from the early stages of the trial with that jury—with its sprinkling of highly intelligent jurors—a verdict of guilty was never probable. The question throughout was whether the jurors would be able to arrive at an agreed verdict. A re-trial, with the advantages which that would tend to confer on a prosecution ill-handled in the first instance, might have been less favourable to the publishers.*

If the trial of Lady Chatterley—it seemed as if the lady herself were sitting in the empty dock in Court No. 1—was a milestone, so was the trial of Secker and Warburg in 1954. The enlightened and simple eloquence of Mr Justice Stable's summing up was the natural forerunner to the new legislation. Without it the forces of conservation might have stood in the path of the reformers. As it was, one member of the judiciary had pointed the need for change.

MEMBERS OF the jury, the charge against the accused is one of publishing what is called an obscene libel, and everybody agrees here that they all stand or fall together. The verdict that you will give is a matter of the utmost consequence, not only to the accused but also to the community in general. It is of great importance in relation to the future of the novel in the civilized world and the future generations who can only derive their knowledge of how we lived, thought and acted from the contemporary literature of the particular age in which they are interested. Your verdict will have a great bearing upon where the line is drawn between liberty and that freedom to read and think as the spirit moves us, on the one hand, and, on the other, a licence that is an affront to the society of which each of us is a member. The discharge of this important duty rests fairly and squarely on your shoulders. It is not what I think about this book; it is the conclusion that you come to, and you represent that vast diversity of minds and ages which is the reading public of the English-speaking world. You and you alone must decide this case and if, in the course of this sum-ming-up, I express my opinion about the matter, you are entitled to ignore it. The burden of proof in this, as in all criminal cases, rests on the prosecution from start to finish. You, in arriving at your verdict, must arrive at a unanimous verdict. If you can all agree, so much the better, but if there is any one of you, or more, who honestly cannot share the view of the others, then it is your duty so to say.

The test of obscenity to be applied today is extracted from a decision of 1868; it is this: '. . . whether the tendency of the matter charged as obscenity is to deprave and corrupt those whose minds are open to such immoral influences, and into whose hands a publication of this sort may fall.' Because this test was laid down in 1868, that does not mean that you have to consider whether this book is an obscene book by the standards of nearly a century ago. Your task is to decide whether you think that the tendency of the book is to deprave those whose minds today are open to such immoral influences and into whose hands the book may fall in this year, or last year when it was published in this country. Considering the curious change of approach from one age to another, it is not uninteresting to observe that in the course of the argument of the case in 1868 the rhetorical question was asked: 'What can be more obscene than many pictures publicly exhibited, as the Venus in the Dulwich Gallery?' There are some who think with reverence that man is fashioned in the image of God, and you know that babies are not born in this world, be they of either sex, dressed up in a frock-coat or an equivalent feminine garment.

We are not sitting here as judges of taste. We are not here to say whether we like a book of this kind. We are not here to say whether we think it would be a good thing if books like this were never written. You are here trying a criminal charge and in a criminal court you cannot find a verdict of 'Guilty' against the accused, unless, on the evidence that you have heard, you and each one of you are fully satisfied that the charge against the accused person has been proved.

Remember the charge is a charge that the tendency of the book is to corrupt and deprave. The charge is not that the tendency of the book is either to shock or to disgust. That is not a criminal offence. Then you say 'Well, corrupt or deprave whom?' and again the test: those whose minds are open to such immoral influences and into whose hands a publication of this sort may fall. What, exactly, does that mean? Are we to take our literary standards as being the level of something that is suitable for a fourteen-year-old schoolgirl? Or do we go even further back than that, and are we to be reduced to the sort of books that one reads as a child in the nursery? The answer to that is: Of course not. A mass of literature, great literature, from many angles is wholly unsuitable for reading by the adolescent, but that does not mean that the publisher is guilty of a criminal offence for making those works available to the general public.

You have heard a good deal about the putting if ideas into young heads. But is it really books that put ideas into young heads, or is it nature? When a child, be it a boy or a girl, passing from a state of blissful ignorance, reaches that most perilous part of life's journey which we call 'adolescence', and finds itself traversing an unknown country without a map, without a compass, and sometimes, I am afraid, from a bad home, without a guide, it is this natural change from childhood to maturity that puts ideas into its young head. It is the business of parents and teachers and the environment of society, so far as is possible, to see that those ideas are wisely and naturally directed to the ultimate fulfilment of a balanced individual life.

This is a book which obviously and admittedly is absorbed with sex, the relationship between the male and the female of the human species. I, personally, approach that great mystery with profound interest and at the same time a very deep sense of reverence. It is not our fault that but for the love of men and women and the act of sex, the human race would have ceased to exist thousands of years ago. It is not our fault that the moment in, shall we say, an over-civilized world—if 'civilized' is an appropriate word—sex ceases to be one of the great motive forces in human life, the human race will cease to exist. It is the essential condition of the survival and development of the human race, for whatever ultimate purpose it has been brought into this world. Speaking, as I am sure I do, to a representative group of people, nine men and three women, each one of you, I am sure, is of good will and anxious that in the solution of this great mystery today we should achieve some conception which will lead to great personal happiness between individuals of the opposite sex in millions of homes throughout this island, which, after all, is the only possible foundation upon which one could build a vigorous, a strong and a useful nation.

Rome and Greece, it is not uninteresting to reflect, elevated human love to a cult, if not a religion, but when we reach the Middle Ages we find an entirely different approach. The priesthood was compelled to be sexless, and a particular qualitative holiness was attached to the monks and nuns who dedicated themselves to cloisters and sheltered lives. You may think that it is lucky that they were not all quite as holy as that because otherwise, if they had been, we should none of us have been here today.

When you approach this matter which—let us face it—throughout the ages has been one of absorbing interest to men and women, you get these two schools of thought which are poles apart, and in between those two extremes you have a wide variety of opinion. At one extreme you get the conception, I venture to think, of the mediaeval church, that sex is sin; that the whole thing is dirty; that it was a mistake from beginning to end (and, if it was, it was the great Creator of life who made the mistake and not you or I); that the less that is said about this wholly distasteful topic the better; let it be covered up and let us pretend that it does not exist. In referring to the arrival of a particular day, reference is made to 'the happy event on Monday' instead of saying 'a baby was born on Monday'—it means exactly the same thing—and in speech and behaviour the utmost degree of reticence is observed. I suppose the high tide was obtained in the Victorian era, possibly as a reaction against the coarseness of the Georges and the rather libertine attitude of the Regency, when I understand that in some houses legs of tables were actually draped and rather stricter females never referred as such to gentlemen's legs but called them their 'understandings'.

At the other extreme you get the line of thought which says that nothing but mischief results from this policy of secrecy and covering up, that the whole thing is just as much a part of God's universe as anything else and the proper approach to the matter is one of frankness, plain speaking and the avoidance of any sort of pretence. Somewhere between those two poles the average, decent, well-meaning man or woman takes his or her stand.

The book that you have to consider is, as you know, in the form of a novel, and I venture to suggest for your consideration the question: what are the functions of the novel? I am not talking about historical novels when people write a story of some past age. I am talking about the contemporary novelist. By the 'contemporary novelist' I mean the novelist who writes about his contemporaries, who holds up a mirror to the society of his own day, and the value of the novel is not merely to entertain the contemporaries of the novel; it stands as a record or a picture of the society when it was written. Those of us who enjoy the great Victorian novelists get such understanding as we have of that great age from chroniclers such as Thackeray, Dickens, Trollope and many others. And where should we be today if the literature of Greece, Rome and the other civilizations portrayed, not how many people really thought and behaved, but how they did not think and how they did not speak and how they did not behave? The only real guidance we get about how people thought and behaved over the ages is in their contemporary literature.

It is equally important that we should have an understanding of how life is lived and how the human mind is working in those parts of the world which, although not separated from us in point of time, are separated from us in point of space. At a time like today, when ideas and creeds and processes of thought seem, to some extent, to be in the melting pot, this is more than ever necessary, for people are bewildered and puzzled to know in what direction humanity is headed. If we are to understand how life, for example, is lived in the United States, France, Germany, or elsewhere, the contemporary novels of those nations may afford us some guide, and to those of us who have not the time or the opportunity or the money or the inclination to travel, it may even be the only guide. This is an American novel written by an American, published originally in New York and purporting to depict the lives of people living today in New York, to portray their speech and their attitude in general towards this particular aspect of life. If we are going to read novels about how things go on in New York, it would not be of much assistance, would it, if, contrary to the fact, we were led to suppose that in New York no unmarried woman of teenage had disabused her mind of the idea that babies are brought by storks or are sometimes found in cabbage plots or under gooseberry bushes?

You may think that this is a very crude work; but that it is not, perhaps, altogether an exaggerated picture of the approach that is being made in America towards this great problem of sex. You may think that if this does reflect the approach on the other side of the Atlantic towards this great question, it is just as well that we should know it and that we must not close our eyes or our minds to the truth because it might conceivably corrupt or deprave any somewhat puerile young mind.

You may agree that it is a good book, or a bad book, or a moderate book. It is at least a book. It is the creation of a human mind and it depicts the people created in their particular environment. If you look at the front page, you will see the text. It is taken from a Victorian poet, Browning: 'What of soul was left, I wonder, when the kissing had to stop?' and I suppose men and women of all ages have wondered that.

The theme of this book is the story of the rather attractive young man who is absolutely obsessed with his desire for women. It is not presented as an admirable thing, or a thing to be copied. It is not presented as a thing that brought him happiness or any sort of permanent satisfaction, and throughout the book you hear the note of impending disaster. He is like the drunkard who cannot keep away from drink although he knows where it will land him in the end.

The author traces the moral thought of this man back to his childhood where the unhappy relations between his mother and his father left a sort of permanent bruise on his personality. He describes the pitfalls of slyness and filth into which the unhappy adolescent stumbles, without knowledge or experience, without the map and the compass and without the guiding hand of a wise parent or the example of a well-ordered, decent home. You will have to consider whether the author was pursuing an honest purpose and an honest thread of thought, or whether that was all just a bit of camouflage to render the crudity, the sex of the book, sufficiently wrapped up to pass the critical standard of the Director of Public Prosecutions. So far as his amatory adventures are concerned, the book does, with candour or if you prefer it, crudity, deal with the realities of human love and intercourse. There is no getting away from that, and the Crown says: 'Well, that is sheer filth.' Is the act of sexual passion sheer filth? It may be an error of taste to write about it. It may be a matter in which some, perhaps old-fashioned, people would prefer that reticence continued to be observed as it was yesterday. But is it sheer filth? That is a matter which you have to consider and ultimately to decide.

I do not suppose there is a decent man or woman in this court who does not wholeheartedly believe that pornography, the filthy bawdy muck that is just filth for filth's sake, ought to be stamped out and suppressed. Such books are not literature. They have got no message; they have got no inspiration; they have got no thought. They have got nothing. They are just filth and ought to be stamped out. But in our desire for a healthy society, if we drive the criminal law too far, further than it ought to go, is there not a risk that there will be a revolt, a demand for a change in the law, and that the pendulum may swing too far the other way and allow to creep in things that at the moment we can exclude and keep out?

That is all I have to say to you. Remember what I said when I began. You are dealing with a criminal charge. This is not a question or a case of what you think is a desirable book to read. It is a criminal charge of publishing a work with a tendency to corrupt and deprave those to whom it may fall. Before you can return a verdict of 'Guilty' on that charge you have to be satisfied, and each one of you has to be satisfied, that that charge has been proved. If it is anything short of that the accused are entitled to a verdict at your hands of 'Not Guilty'.

Verdict: Not Guilty.

Lord Justice Harman

On the Will of Bernard Shaw

It was almost inevitable that such a controversial figure in contemporary Britain as George Bernard Shaw should continue to provide argument and dispute even from his grave. Shaw's will—a long and complicated document, fatally composed by the twin hands of legal draftsman and lay critic—was held invalid in the Chancery Division, to the extent that the alphabet trusts he sought to set up were held not to be charitable and also void for uncertainty.

The legal tangle over his will was ultimately resolved when the case came before the Court of Appeal in December 1957 by way of a challenge to the decision of Mr Justice Harman (as he then was). On that occasion the Court was told that the Public Trustee was to receive up to £8,300 upon trust to carry out 'substantially' the alphabet trusts contained in the will. The trustee at that time offered a prize of £500 for the design of a new British alphabet of at least forty letters. The prize was shared by four out of 467 entrants; the Public Trustee declared that with the assistance of Mr P. A. D. MacCarthy, senior lecturer in the department of phonetics in the University of Leeds, these four contestants would co-operate to transliterate Androcles and the Lion *into a final British alphabet.*

It is ironical that Shaw himself anticipated the waywardness of the law in Clause 40 of his will where he made provision for his estate should 'such trusts fail through judicial decision'. But if he proved to be right he would have commended the manner in which the learned judge upheld his jibe at the law. Mr Justice Harman, himself an Irishman, did justice in more senses than one to Shaw's literary merits. The judgment was not only a successful parody of Shaw's caustic and cynical style but a model of clarity on a branch of the law which had been notoriously obscure until the recent Charities Act, 1960.

ALL HIS long life Bernard Shaw was an indefatigable reformer. He was already well known when the present century dawned, as novelist, critic, pamphleteer, playwright, and during the ensuing half-century

he continued to act as a kind of itching powder to the British public
to the English-speaking peoples, and, indeed to an even wider audience
castigating their follies, their foibles and their fallacies, and bombarding
them with a combination of paradox and wit that earned him in the
course of years the status of an oracle: the Shavian oracle; and the
rare distinction of adding a word to the language. Many of his projects
he lived to see gain acceptance and carried into effect and become normal. It was natural that he should be interested in English orthography
and pronunciation. These are obvious targets for the reformer. It is as
difficult for the native to defend the one as it is for the foreigner to
compass the other. The evidence shows that Shaw had for many years
been interested in the subject. Perhaps his best known excursion in
this field is *Pygmalion*, in which the protagonist is a professor of
phonetics: this was produced as a play in 1914 and has held the stage
ever since and invaded the world of the film. It is, indeed, a curious
reflection that this same work, tagged with versicles which I suppose
Shaw would have detested, and tricked out with music which he would
have eschewed (see the preface to *The Admirable Bashville*), is now
charming huge audiences on the other side of the Atlantic and has
given birth to the present proceedings. I am told that the receipts from
this source have enabled the executor to get on terms with the existing
death duties payable on the estate, thus bringing the interpretation of
the will into the realm of practical politics.

The testator, whatever his other qualifications, was the master of a
pellucid style, and the reader embarks on his will confident of finding
no difficulty in understanding the objects which the testator had in
mind. This document, moreover, was evidently originally the work
of a skilled equity draftsman. As such I doubt not it was easily to be
understood if not of the vulgar at any rate by the initiate. Unfortunately the will bears ample internal evidence of being in part the
testator's own work. The two styles, as ever, make an unfortunate
mixture. It is always a marriage of incompatibles: the delicate testamentary machinery devised by the conveyancer can but suffer when
subjected to the *cacoethes scribendi* of the author, even though the
latter's language, if it stood alone, might be a literary masterpiece.

This will is a long and complicated document made on 12th June,
1950, when the testator was already ninety-four years old, though it is
fair to say that it is rather youthful exuberance than the circumspection
of old age that mars its symmetry. By clause 2 the plaintiff is appointed

sole executor and trustee. Clause 5 is in these terms: 'I bequeath my copyrights performing rights filming rights television rights and all cognate rights now in existence or hereafter to be created with the manuscripts typescripts and other documents in which I have such rights to my trustees upon trust to apply the proceeds resulting from the exploitation of such rights or the sale or other lucrative use of such documents as income of my estate.'

Clause 7 begins as follows: 'I declare that my trustee shall manage and deal with my author's rights with all the powers in that behalf of an absolute owner (subject as hereinafter provided) for so long as may prove necessary or expedient during a period ending at the expiration of twenty years from the day of the death of the last survivor of all the lineal descendants of His late Majesty King George the Fifth who shall be living at the time of my death (hereinafter called the "special period").' A proviso is added forbidding the trustee to sell or assign the literary rights or to alienate them for more than a limited period. There follow clauses giving specific bequests and various directions including clause 16 in these words: 'I empower my trustees to procure all necessary assistance and expert advice legal artistic literary or other for the discharge of his relevant functions and to pay its cost out of my estate.'

Next come legacies and annuities to servants, relations and others, the trustee being empowered to provide the annuities out of the income of 'my residuary trust funds hereinafter defined', . . . The trustee is also given a discretion to increase annuities in certain events.

Clause 35 and its sequents I must read in full. Clause 35 is in these terms: 'I devise and bequeath all my real and personal estate not otherwise specifically disposed of by this my will or any codicil hereto and all property over which I have general power of appointment unto my trustee upon trust that my trustee shall (subject to the power of postponing the sale and conversion thereof hereinafter contained) sell my real estate and sell call in or otherwise convert into money as much as may be needed of my personal estate (other than any copyrights which as provided by clause 7 of this my will are not to be sold) to increase the ready moneys of which I may be possessed at my death to an amount sufficient to pay my funeral and testamentary expenses and debts estate duty legacy duty and all the duties payable on my death in respect of my estate or the bequests hereby made free of duty (other than testamentary expenses) and the legacies bequeathed by this my will or any codicil hereto or to make such other payments or investments or charge of investments as in his opinion shall be advisable in the interest of my estate and shall invest the residue of such moneys in manner hereinafter authorized and shall stand possessed of the said residuary trust moneys and the investments for the time being representing the same and all other investments for the time being forming part of my residuary estate (herein called my residuary trust funds) and the annual income thereof upon the trusts hereby declared of and concerning the same: (1) To institute and finance a series of inquiries to ascertain or estimate as far as possible the following statistics (a) the number of extant persons who speak the English language and write it by the established and official alphabet of twenty-six letters (hereinafter called Dr Johnson's alphabet); (b) how much time could be saved per individual scribe by the substitution for the said alphabet of an alphabet containing at least forty letters (hereinafter called the Proposed British alphabet) enabling the said language to be written without indicating single sounds by groups of letters or by diacritical marks, instead of by one symbol for each sound; (c) how many of these persons are engaged in writing or printing English at any and every moment in the world; (d) on these factors to estimate the time and labour wasted by our lack of at least fourteen unequivocal single symbols; (e) to add where possible to the estimates of time lost or saved by the difference between Dr Johnson's alphabet and the Proposed British alphabet estimates of the loss of income in British and American currency. The inquiry must be confined strictly to the statistical and mathematical problems to be solved without regard to the views of professional and amateur phoneticians, etymologists, spelling reformers, patentees of universal languages, inventors of shorthand codes for verbatim reporting or rival alphabets, teachers of the established orthography, disputants about pronunciation, or of the irreconcilables whose wranglings have overlooked and confused the single issue of labour saving and made change impossible during the last hundred years. The inquiry must not imply any approval or disapproval of the Proposed British alphabet by the inquirers or by my trustee. (2) To employ a phonetic expert to transliterate my play entitled *Androcles and the Lion* into the Proposed British alphabet assuming the pronunciation to resemble that recorded of His Majesty our late King George V and sometimes described as Northern English. (3) To employ an artist calligrapher to fair-copy the transliteration for reproduction by lithography photography or any other method that may serve in the absence of printers' types. (4) To advertise and publish the transliteration with the original Dr Johnson's lettering opposite the transliteration page by page and a glossary of the two alphabets at the end and to present copies to public libraries in the British Isles, the British Commonwealth, the American States North and South, and to national libraries everywhere in that order.'

Clause 36 is: 'I desire my trustee to bear in mind that the Proposed British Alphabet does not pretend to be exhaustive as it contains only sixteen vowels whereas by infinitesimal movements of the tongue countless different vowels can be produced all of them in use among speakers of English who utter the same vowel no oftener than they make the same fingerprints. Nevertheless they can understand one another's speech and writing sufficiently to converse and correspond.'

Clause 37 says: 'It is possible that the Ministry of Education may institute the inquiry and adopt the Proposed British alphabet to be taught in the schools it controls in which event subsection 1 of clause 35 foregoing and its relevant sequels will be contra-indicated as superfluous and clause 40 come into operation accordingly but the adoption must be exact and no account taken of the numerous alternative spelling reforms now advocated or hereafter proposed.'

[Clauses 38 and 39 set out the disposal of the income from the residuary trust funds during a period of twenty-one years after Shaw's death.] Clause 40 is: 'Subject to the trusts hereinbefore declared of my residuary trust funds and the income thereof or if and so far as such trusts shall fail through judicial decision or any other cause beyond my trustee's control my trustee shall stand possessed of my residuary trust funds and the income thereof but subject to a charge on the capital as well as the income thereof for payment of such of the annuities hereby bequeathed as shall be subsisting upon trust as to one third thereof for the trustees of the British Museum in acknowledgment of the incalculable value to me of my daily resort to the reading room of that institution at the beginning of my career as to one third of the same upon trust for the National Gallery of Ireland and as to the remaining one third of the same upon trust for the Royal Academy of Dramatic Art at 61 Gower Street in the County of London and should any of these three institutions be permanently closed at the date when the trust to accumulate the said balance of income of my residuary trust funds shall cease the others or other shall succeed to its share and if more than one equally.'

Finally, clause 47 reads thus: 'Having been born a British subject in Ireland in 1856, subsequently registered as a citizen of Eire, and finally privileged to remain a British subject by the Home Secretary's letter dated 27th June, 1949, I declare that my domicile of choice is English and desire that my will be construed and take effect according to English law.'

Apart from a minor question about certain annuities which I have already decided, the difficulties begin with clause 35 which is, in form, a normal residuary clause directing conversion of the estate, other than copyrights, and the payment of funeral and testamentary expenses and debts out of the proceeds and the ready money. These resources have proved inadequate, and it has been necessary to defray the death duties largely out of royalties accruing since the death, which, it will be remembered, are directed by clause 5 to be treated as income. The definition of 'my residuary trust funds' appears at first sight to exclude the copyrights and the proceeds of their exploitation, but no one suggested that the testator died intestate in this respect, and I am content to assume that these, directed as they are to be applied 'as income of my estate', form part of the residuary income. The trustee is by clause 7 directed to manage and deal with them as absolute owner for so long as may be necessary during the defined 'special period'.

The directions in clause 35 connected with what the testator calls the 'Proposed British alphabet' prescribe no limit of time, but clause 38 shows that not more than the income of the first twenty-one years after the death is to be devoted to these purposes. So much of this income as is not devoted to these purposes or the subsidiary purposes mentioned in clause 38 (which are, in my view, mere machinery incidental to the purposes stated in clause 35) is to be accumulated, and is to continue to be used during the special period unless the trusts 'shall fail through judicial decision or any other cause beyond my trustee's control' or unless the enterprise shall have been wound up on its successful achievement.

It appears that the residuary estate is likely to consist of nothing but copyrights and royalties arising out of them. These are to devolve at the end of the twenty-one-year period on the ultimate residuary legatees, the British Museum, the Royal Academy of Dramatic Art and the Irish National Gallery in equal shares. The first two of these now claim that what I may call the alphabet trusts are entirely void, and that the claimants are entitled therefore to come into their inheritance at once and to stop the accumulation of income. The grounds of this claim are two: first, that the trusts, being for an object and not for a person, are void trusts; secondly, that they are void for uncertainty.

The Attorney-General appears as *parens patriae* to uphold the trusts as being charitable trusts, and counsel for the Attorney-General at my request also supported the proposition of the executor that, even if not charitable, these trusts, not being tainted with the vice of perpetuity (as it is called), are a valid exercise by a man of his power of disposing of his own money as he thinks fit. The claimants retort that these trusts are not charitable trusts, and it seems to me that I should address myself first to that question. It is notorious that the word 'charitable', when used by a lawyer, covers many objects which a layman would not consider to be included under that word, but excludes benevolent or philanthropic activities which the layman would consider charitable. In construing a will the lawyer's sense must prevail in the absence of some special context. The four heads of charity are set out by Lord Macnaghten in *Commissioners for Special Purposes of the Income Tax v. Pemsel*. His words, as has often been pointed out, are not original, being drawn from the argument of Sir Samuel Romilly in his reply in *Morice v. Bishop of Durham*. They are almost too familiar to need repetition. Shortly stated the four heads are (i) religion, (ii) poverty, (iii) education, and (iv) 'other purposes beneficial to the community'. Sir Samuel Romilly describes the last head as being 'the most difficult', and the phrase he uses is 'the advancement of objects of general public utility.' Here, again, it is trite law that not every object coming within one or other of these categories is charitable—a college for pickpockets is no charity—but that every object which is to rank as charitable must either fit into one or more of the first three categories, or, if not, may still be held charitable because of general public utility.

The first object of the alphabet trusts is to find out by inquiry how much time could be saved by persons who speak the English language and write it by the use of the proposed British alphabet, and so to show the extent of the time and labour wasted by the use of our present alphabet and, if possible, further to state this waste of time in terms of loss of money. The second is to transliterate one of the testator's plays, *Androcles and the Lion*, into the proposed British alphabet assuming a given pronunciation of English, and to advertise and publish the transliteration in a page-by-page version in the proposed alphabet on one side and the existing alphabet on the other, and, by the dissemination of copies and, in addition, by advertisement and propaganda, to persuade the government or the public or the English-speaking world to adopt it. This was described by the Attorney-General as a useful piece of research beneficial to the public, because it would facilitate the education of the young and the teaching of the language and show a way to save time and therefore money. It was suggested that the objects could thus be brought within the third category and that a parallel could be found in the decision of Danckwerts, J., in *Crystal Palace Trustees v. Minister of Town and Country Planning*, where trusts 'for the promotion of industry commerce and art' were held charitable. So they were, but only in the context provided by the instrument (an Act of Parliament) in which they appeared. In my opinion, if the object be merely the increase of knowledge, that is not in itself a charitable object unless it be combined with teaching or education: see the speech of Rigby, L.J., in *In re Macduff*. The facts of that case bear no resemblance to the present, but Rigby, L.J., says: 'There is one other case to which I will refer—*Whicker v. Hume*—and in doing so I will refer also to the unreported case of *President of the United States of America v. Drummond*, which is mentioned in *Whicker v. Hume*. I say nothing about the wide extent of the gift in *Whicker v. Hume*, because there is no doubt now that the extensive nature of the gift as regards the range of the objects is no objection to it; but the gift was for advancement of education and learning, and the objection was taken by counsel who were impeaching the validity of the gift that education is no doubt a charitable purpose within the Statute of Elizabeth, but learning is not—that is to say, that the promotion of abstract learning would not be a charitable purpose. That was dealt with by Lord Chelmsford and Lord Cranworth, and both of them point out that, reading the word "Learning" as you find it in that will in connection with education, it must be taken as equivalent to teaching, and, therefore, as a certain branch of education; and I rather gather from their judgments, and from the pains which they take to draw out and to elucidate the meaning of the word "learning" in that will, that if they could not have put that interpretation upon it they would have doubted, at any rate, as to whether the advancement of learning as an abstract matter would be a charity at all. The Lord Chancellor, Lord Chelmsford, goes with great pains into the matter and deals with the word "learning"; and he says that the word in that will was used in the sense of teaching and instruction, "and, in that sense, it appears to me", he says, "that the case which was cited by the respondents, and which is printed in the respondent's case, of the *President of the United States v. Drummond*, may be applicable, where Lord Langdale decided, that a gift to the United States of America, to found, at Washington, under the name of the Smithsonian Institution, an establishment for the increase 'of knowledge among men', was a valid charity". The Lords evidently doubted whether a gift for the increase of knowledge would be a good charitable gift, unless it was understood to mean a gift for teaching and education. Yet the increase of knowledge would unquestionably in these days be taken to be a purpose of general utility, and the doubt of the noble Lords appears to me to be strongly in favour of the view taken by Lord Langdale that "purposes of general utility" will not make a good charitable gift.'

The research and propaganda enjoined by the testator seem to me merely to tend to the increase of public knowledge in a certain respect, namely, the saving of time and money by the use of the proposed alphabet. There is no element of teaching or education combined with this, nor does the propaganda element in the trusts tend to more than to persuade the public that the adoption of the new script would be 'a good thing', and that, in my view, is not education. Therefore I reject this element.

There remains the fourth category. As I have already said, this does not embrace all objects of public utility, as appears clearly in the case of *In re Strakosch* and perhaps even better in *Williams' Trustees v. Inland Revenue Commissioners*. The headnote reads: 'Every object of public general utility is not necessarily a charity, for in order to be charitable a trust must be within the spirit and intendment of the statute 43 Elizabeth, chapter 4. Accordingly, no trust can be charitable unless it is beneficial to the community in a way in which the law regards as charitable. A trust was established with the objects of promoting Welsh interests in London by social intercourse; discussing all questions affecting Welsh interests; fostering the study of the Welsh language by lectures on Welsh history, literature, music and art; maintaining a library of literature in the Welsh language or relating to Wales. The trustees were empowered (*inter alia*) to maintain an institute and meeting place for the benefit of Welsh people in London with a view to creating a centre to promote "the moral, social, spiritual and educational welfare of Welsh people". Held, that the trust was not

exempt from income tax under section 37, subsection (1) of the
Income Tax Act, 1918, since the ground on which a charitable character was sought to be attributed to it was not that it was beneficial in
a way which the law regards as charitable.' In his speech Lord Simonds
says: 'My Lords, the claim of the appellants that the property is vested
in them for charitable purposes is based on these contentions (a) that
"the dominant purpose of the trust is the fostering of Welsh culture
which is a purpose beneficial to the community composed of the people
of the United Kingdom", (b) that the purpose aforesaid is beneficial
to the community composed of the people of the Principality of Wales
and the county of Monmouth which is an integral part of the United
Kingdom and in itself constitutes a political body settled in a particular
territorial area and (c) "because the maintenance of the institute (the
expressed method of effectuating the purpose aforesaid) is itself a
purpose beneficial to a section of the British community which is
determined by reference to impersonal qualifications (namely persons
with Welsh connections who are resident in or near or visiting
London); and is not a selection of private individuals chosen on
account of personal qualifications." I have taken this statement of the
appellants' contentions from the formal reasons in their written case,
because in them so clearly appears the fallacious argument upon which
in this and other cases, which it has been my fortune to hear, an attempt
has been made to establish the charitable character of a trust. My Lords,
there are, I think, two propositions which must ever be borne in mind
in any case in which the question is whether a trust is charitable. The
first is that it is still the general law that a trust is not charitable and
entitled to the privileges which charity confers, unless it is within the
spirit and intendment of the preamble to the statute of Elizabeth (43
Elizabeth, chapter 4), which is expressly preserved by section 13 (3) of
the Mortmain and Charitable Uses Act, 1888. The second is that the
classification of charity in its legal sense into four principal divisions
by Lord Macnaghten in *Income Tax Special Purposes Commissioners
v. Pemsel* must always be read subject to the qualification appearing in
the judgment of Lindley, L.J., in *In re Macduff*...' Lord Simonds then
cites from that case as I have done. Then he goes on: 'But it is just
because the purpose of the trust deed in this case is said to be beneficial
to the community or a section of the community and for no other
reason that its charitable character is asserted. It is not alleged that the
trust is (a) for the benefit of the community and (b) beneficial in a way

which the law regards as charitable. Therefore, as it seems to me, in its mere statement the claim is imperfect and must fail.'

It is hard to ascertain what are the limits of purposes held to be beneficial to the community 'in a way which the law regards as charitable'. Lord Simonds, in the case last cited, grapples with this difficulty, and he admits that it is very difficult to reconcile all the cases. His Lordship opines that 'Each case must be judged on its own facts and the dividing line is not easily drawn . . .' It seems to me, however, that in the present case I am stopped on the threshold by the word 'beneficial'. Who is to say whether this project is beneficial? That, on the face of it, is a most controversial question, and I do not think that the fact that the testator and a number of other people are of opinion that the step would be a benefit proves the case, for undoubtedly there are a great many more people, at present at any rate, who think the exact contrary. That is why the testator directs the steps which he recommends to be taken. They are intended to overcome the opposition and sloth of the great majority who prefer to stick to what they know and to use that to which they are accustomed. I do not see how mere advertisement and propaganda can be postulated as being beneficial. Mr Isaac Pitman is the author of a singularly able piece of pleading on the subject in his affidavit, but, even if I were persuaded by him of the merits of the scheme, I cannot think that my opinion on that subject is relevant or can be the deciding factor.

I feel unable to pronounce that the research to be done is a task of general utility. In order to be persuaded of that, I should have to hold it to be generally accepted that benefit would be conferred on the public by the end proposed. But that is the very conviction which the propaganda based on the research is designed to instil. The testator is convinced, and sets out to convince the world, but the fact that he considers the proposed reform to be beneficial does not make it so any more than the fact that he describes the trust as charitable constrains the court to hold that it is.

A case on a parallel subject, spelling reform, came before Rowlatt, J., on an income tax point. That is *Trustees of the late Sir G. B. Hunter (1922) 'C' Trust v. Inland Revenue Commissioners*. The headnote reads: 'The appellants claimed that the income of a trust of which they were trustees was exempt from income tax under section 37(1) (b), Income Tax Act, 1918, on the ground that the trust was established for charitable purposes only, and that the trust income was applied to such purposes only. The trust deed provided that the net income and, after a period of years, the capital of the trust should be paid or applied to the benefit of the Simplified Spelling Society or in certain circumstances, as to which the trustees had wide discretionary powers, to the benefit of or to promote the formation of any other society or association having similar objects. The objects of the society were to recommend and to further the general use of simpler spellings of English words than those now in use. It engaged in propaganda to influence public opinion in favour of its objects and to gain for them the approval of education authorities. The appellants claimed that the purposes for which the society was established were charitable either as being educational or as being beneficial to the community. Held, that the trust was not established for charitable purposes.' In the case stated I find that it was contended for the society that its proposal had two practical advantages: (i) By the adoption of the system, spelling would be more quickly learned by a child, and the time so saved could be utilized in training the child's mind in other directions. The system would thus benefit education indirectly; (ii) The system was of general advantage, because by making the sound of words correspond with their written representation, it would lead to better speech, and by facilitating the learning of English by non-English speaking people, whether British subjects or foreigners, would help the adoption of English as an instrument of international communication. The trustees contended (1) That the society was established for educational purposes only; (2) That alternatively the society was established for purposes beneficial to the community only. The Crown claimed (1) That the trust was not established for educational purposes only or for purposes beneficial to the community but for the advancement of an idea or theory. With that view the Special Commissioners agreed, and there was an appeal which came before Rowlatt, J., who said: 'I think that the Commissioners were clearly right here. It must be distinctly understood that what the court has to decide in cases of this kind is not whether it appears that the society is pursuing a beneficial object or not, in the opinion of the court; I think that the court has nothing to do with that at all. But what the court has to decide is whether the object of the society is one that is charitable within the meaning of the rule governing courts of equity and the Income Tax Acts. The object of this society or any other society which would benefit under this trust is simply to make spelling more simple.

Everyone would agree up to a point that it is probably advantageous. Probably as you go on you will get differences of opinion; but, right or wrong, the question is whether that is a charitable object. You have people trying to promote the simplification of spelling, or the simplification of grammar, or the uniformity of pronouncing, or the simplification of dress, or the simplification or reform of any of the conveniences of life. But in my judgment they are nowhere near either of the express categories mentioned by Lord Macnaghten in the well-known judgment, *Income Tax Special Purposes Commissioners v. Pemsel* or within the classes of cases which come within the general classes in the Act. I think that this case is hardly arguable.' Such words of such a judge must have great weight with me.

It seems to me that the objects of the alphabet trusts are analogous to trusts for political purposes, which advocate a change in the law. Such objects have never been considered charitable. In his celebrated speech in *Bowman v. Secular Society* Lord Parker has this passage: 'Now if your Lordships will refer for a moment to the society's memorandum of association you will find that none of its objects, except, possibly, the first are charitable. The abolition of religious tests, the disestablishment of the Church, the secularization of education, the alteration of the law touching religion or marriage, or the observation of the Sabbath, are purely political objects. Equity has always refused to recognize such objects as charitable. It is true that a gift to an association formed for their attainment may, if the association be unincorporated, be upheld as an absolute gift to its members, or, if the association be incorporated, as an absolute gift to the corporate body; but a trust for the attainment of political objects has always been held invalid, not because it is illegal, for everyone is at liberty to advocate or promote by any lawful means a change in the law, but because the court has no means of judging whether a proposed change in the law will or will not be for the public benefit, and therefore cannot say that a gift to secure the change is a charitable gift.'

I therefore do not reach the further inquiry whether the benefit is one within the spirit or intendment (as it is called) of the Statute of Elizabeth, but, if I had to decide the point, I should hold that it was not.

It was argued for the ultimate legatees that, apart from any other consideration, the vice of uncertainty is fatal. Now, it has been often said that the vagueness with which a charitable bequest is stated will never be the cause of its failure. A modern instance is *In re Gott*. I will read from the headnote: 'A charitable trust cannot fail for uncertainty whether the charitable intention be general or only specific. There is no practical reason why certainty of the exact ambit of a charitable purpose should be required, as the court can settle a scheme for its administration.' Uthwatt, J., said: 'The argument is that where there is shown an intention to devote property to a particular charitable purpose only, but it is impossible to ascertain that purpose with certainty, the trust intended is not known, and there is, therefore, no trust to be enforced. The well-known statement that "a charitable trust does not fail for uncertainty" is said to be a slogan which does not apply save where there is an intent in favour of charity generally. No doubt, when a purpose is stated, no charitable trust is created unless the purpose is certainly charitable, but, given that certainty, uncertainty as to the particular charitable purpose intended is, in my opinion, immaterial. No authority was cited to me which supports the proposition that certainty in the definition of an intended specific charitable purpose is necessary and the proposition appears to be wrong in principle and never to have been accepted in practice. If a gift to charity generally does not fail for uncertainty—and that is a proposition which is not open to dispute—it appears to me to be a natural consequence, though it may not be a necessary consequence, that a specific charitable purpose may be vaguely set out. There is no practical reason why certainty of the exact ambit of a particular charitable purpose should be required, for the court has, as regards all charitable trusts, jurisdiction to settle a scheme for their administration—I am not referring to *cy-près* schemes—and it is settled practice that these schemes may deal, not only with methods of administration, but also with and define, the substance of the trust. The court, as Lord Eldon pointed out, in *Morice v. Bishop of Durham*, has taken strong liberties on the subject of charities.'

Once decided that the object is charitable and the law will provide the means of carrying it into effect by a scheme, and it seems to me that the fact that the testator has not selected any particular form of alphabet for his experiment would not be fatal if the experiment itself constituted a charitable object.

The question of certainty becomes far more difficult if there be no charitable intent. The objection here is that the Public Trustee would not know how to set about his task because he would not know the *corpus* on which to direct his appointed statistical and phonetic experts to work. No particular alphabet has been indicated by the testator, though there are indications of the kind of alphabet required. It is to have not less than forty letters of which at least fourteen are to be symbols for vowel sounds. The evidence before me showed that a great deal of work has been and is being done on these lines, and that among those skilled in the knowledge of phonetics a fit person could be selected who would be competent to advise the Public Trustee either to adopt one of the already existing scripts, or, if necessary, to procure the invention of a new one. I should not have considered the testator's omission or failure to choose an alphabet fatal. Once that is decided, I see no uncertainty. The statistical calculations could on the evidence be done, and the remaining directions are quite categorical.

Can, then, this project be upheld apart from charity? I feel bound to say at once that, as the authorities stand, I do not think I am at liberty to hold that it can. In *Houston v. Burns* Lord Haldane begins his speech in these terms: 'My Lords, by the law of Scotland, as by that of England, a testator can defeat the claim of those entitled by law in the absence of a valid will to succeed to the beneficial interest in his estate only if he has made a complete disposition of that beneficial interest. He cannot leave it to another person to make such a disposition for him unless he has passed the beneficial interest to that person to dispose of as his own. He may, indeed, provide that a special class of persons, or of institutions invested by law with the capacity of persons to hold property, are to take in such shares as a third person may determine, but that is only because he has disposed of the beneficial interest in favour of that class as his beneficiaries. There is, however, an apparent exception to the principle. The testator may indicate his intention that his estate is to go for charitable purposes. If these purposes are of the kinds which the law recognizes in somewhat different ways in the two countries as charitable, the court will disregard a merely subordinate deficiency in particular expression of intention to dispose of the entire beneficial interest to a class, and will even themselves, by making a scheme of some kind, give effect to the general intention that the estate should be disposed of for charitable purposes.'

Lord Parker in *Bowman v. Secular Society* categorically states: 'A trust to be valid must be for the benefit of individuals . . . or must be in that class of gifts for the benefit of the public which the courts in this country recognize as charitable . . .' In other words, one cannot have a trust, other than a charitable trust, for the benefit, not of individuals, but of objects. The reason has been often stated, that the court cannot control the trust. The principle has been recently restated by Roxburgh, J., in *In re Astor Settlement Trusts* where the authorities are elaborately reviewed. An object cannot complain to the court, which therefore cannot control the trust, and, therefore, will not allow it to continue. I must confess that I feel some reluctance to come to this conclusion. I agree at once that if the persons to take in remainder are unascertainable, the court is deprived of any means of controlling such a trust, but if, as here, the persons taking the ultimate residue are ascertained, I do not feel the force of this objection. They are entitled to the estate except in so far as it has been devoted to the indicated purposes, and in so far as it is not devoted to those purposes, the money being spent is the money of the residuary legatees of the ultimate remaindermen, and they can come to the court and sue the executor for a devastavit, or the trustee for a breach of trust, and thus, though not themselves interested in the purposes, enable the court indirectly to control them. This line of reasoning is not, I think, open to me. See, for instance, the statement by Lord Green, M.R., in *In re Diplock*. 'Those principles,' he says, dealing with uncertainty, 'I apprehend are really nothing more than the application of a fundamental principle of the law relating to trusts. In order that a trust may be properly constituted, there must be a beneficiary. The beneficiary must be ascertained or must be ascertainable. In the case of what I may call impersonal trusts, such as a gift to charitable purposes, or to benevolent purposes, there is no class of beneficiary which can be defined in the same sense as a class of beneficiaries such as a class of relatives. In the latter case, although no particular person in the class may be able to say that at any given moment he is entitled to anything out of the trust, the class as a whole can enforce the trust. Now in the case of charitable trusts in which no defined class is specified, nevertheless owing to the particular principles which have come to be applied to charitable gifts, the courts have not treated the trust as failing for that reason. There is a very good ground for that, namely that the Crown, as *parens patriae* taking all charities under its protection, is in a position to enforce the trust; and therefore, although there may be no specified charitable beneficiary who can come to the court and insist on having the trust performed, nevertheless the Attorney-General can appear and is entitled to insist on the trust being carried out, if necessary, by a scheme *cy près*. But that exception to the general rule, that there must be beneficiaries ascertained or ascertainable—if I may call it an exception—does not extend beyond what falls within the legal class of charity. It does not extend to other public-spirited purposes.' The same view is taken in the judgment of Jenkins, L.J., in *Commissioners of Inland Revenue v. Broadway Cottages Trust.*

I should have wished to regard this bequest as a gift to the ultimate residuary legatees subject to a condition by which they cannot complain of income during the first twenty-one years after the testator's death being devoted to the alphabet project. This apparently might be the way in which the matter would be viewed in the United States, for I find in Morris and Leach's work on the Rule against Perpetuities (1956), at p. 308, the following passage quoted from the American Law Institute's Restatement of Trusts: 'Where the owner of property transfers it upon an intended trust for a specific non-charitable purpose, and there is no definite or definitely ascertainable beneficiary designated, no trust is created; but the transferee has power to apply the property to the designated purpose, unless he is authorized so to apply the property beyond the period of the rule against perpetuities, or the purpose is capricious.' As the authors point out, this is to treat a trust of this sort as a power, for clearly there is no one who can directly enforce the trust, and if the trustees choose to pay the whole moneys to the residuary legatees, no one can complain. All that can be done is to control the trustees indirectly in the exercise of their power. In my judgment, I am not at liberty to validate this trust by treating it as a power. (See per Jenkins, L.J., in *Sunnyfields case* above: 'We do not think that a valid power is to be spelt out of an invalid trust.') This also was the view of the learned author of *Gray on Perpetuities* (4th ed.), the leading work on the subject (see Appendix H), and I feel bound to accept it.

The result is that the alphabet trusts are, in my judgment, invalid, and must fail. It seems that their begotter suspected as much, hence his jibe about failure by judicial decision. I answer that it is not the fault of the law, but of the testator, who failed almost for the first time in his life to grasp the legal problem or to make up his mind what he wanted.

Declarations accordingly.

6

CRIME AND PUNISHMENT

The mood and temper of the public in regard to the treatment of crime and criminals is one of the most unfailing tests of the civilization of any country. A calm dispassionate recognition of the rights of the accused and even of the convicted criminal against the state; a constant heart-searching of all charged with the deed of punishment; tireless efforts towards the discovery of regenerative processes; unfailing faith that there is a treasure, if you can find it, in the heart of every man. These are the symbols which in the treatment of crime and criminals make and measure the stored-up strength of a nation and are sign and proof of the living virtue in it.

Sir Winston Churchill as Home Secretary, 1912

Edward Gibbon

Crimes and Punishments in Roman Law

───────────

THE EXECUTION of the Alban dictator, who was dismembered by
eight horses, is represented by Livy as the first and the last instance
of Roman cruelty in the punishment of the most atrocious crimes. But
this act of justice or revenge was inflicted on a foreign enemy in the
heat of victory, and at the command of a single man. The Twelve
Tables afford a more decisive proof of the national spirit, since they
were framed by the wisest of the senate and accepted by the free voices
of the people; yet these laws, like the statutes of Draco, are written in
characters of blood. They approve the inhuman and unequal principle
of retaliation; and the forfeit of an eye for an eye, a tooth for a tooth,
a limb for a limb, is rigorously exacted, unless the offender can redeem
his pardon by a fine of three hundred pounds of copper.

The decemvirs distributed with much liberality the slighter chastise-
ments of flagellation and servitude; and nine crimes of a very different
complexion are adjudged worthy of death. 1. Any act of treason against
the state, or of correspondence with the public enemy. The mode of
execution was painful and ignominious; the head of the degenerate
Roman was shrouded in a veil, his hands were tied behind his back,
and, after he had been scourged by the lictor, he was suspended in the
midst of the forum on a cross, or inauspicious tree. 2. Nocturnal
meetings in the city, whatever might be the pretence—of pleasure, or
religion, or the public good. 3. The murder of a citizen; for which the
common feelings of mankind demand the blood of the murderer.
Poison is still more odious than the sword or dagger; and we are surprised to discover, in two flagitious events, how early such subtle
wickedness had infected the simplicity of the republic and the chaste
virtues of the Roman matrons. The parricide, who violated the duties
of nature and gratitude, was cast into the river or the sea, enclosed in
a sack; and a cock, a viper, a dog, and a monkey, were successively
added as the most suitable companions. Italy produces no monkeys;
but the want could never be felt till the middle of the sixth century

first revealed the guilt of a parricide. 4. The malice of an incendiary. After the previous ceremony of whipping, he himself was delivered to the flames; and in this example alone our reason is tempted to applaud the justice of retaliation. 5. Judicial perjury. The corrupt or malicious witness was thrown headlong from the Tarpeian rock to expiate his falsehood, which was rendered still more fatal by the severity of the penal laws and the deficiency of written evidence. 6. The corruption of a judge, who accepted bribes to pronounce an iniquitous sentence. 7. Libels and satires, whose rude strains sometimes disturbed the peace of an illiterate city. The author was beaten with clubs, a worthy chastisement; but it is not certain that he was left to expire under the blows of the executioner. 8. The nocturnal mischief of damaging or destroying a neighbour's corn. The criminal was suspended as a grateful victim to Ceres. But the sylvan deities were less implacable, and the extirpation of a more valuable tree was compensated by the moderate fine of twenty-five pounds of copper. 9. Magical incantations; which had power, in the opinion of the Latian shepherds, to exhaust the strength of an enemy, to extinguish his life, and to remove from their seats his deep-rooted plantations. The cruelty of the Twelve Tables against insolvent debtors still remains to be told; and I shall dare to prefer the literal sense of antiquity to the specious refinements of modern criticism. After the judicial proof or confession of the debt, thirty days of grace were allowed before a Roman was delivered into the power of his fellow-citizens. In this private prison twelve ounces of rice were his daily food; he might be bound with a chain of fifteen pounds weight; and his misery was thrice exposed in the market-place, to solicit the compassion of his friends and countrymen. At the expiration of sixty days the debt was discharged by the loss of liberty or life; the insolvent debtor was either put to death or sold in foreign slavery beyond the Tiber; but, if several creditors were alike obstinate and unrelenting, they might legally dismember his body, and satiate their revenge by this horrid partition. The advocates for this savage law have insisted that it must strongly operate in deterring idleness and fraud from contracting debts which they were unable to discharge; but experience would dissipate this salutary terror, by proving that no creditor could be found to exact this unprofitable penalty of life or limb. As the manners of Rome were insensibly polished, the criminal code of the decemvirs was abolished by the humanity of accusers, witnesses, and judges; and impunity became the consequence of immoderate rigour. The Porcian and Valerian laws prohibited the magistrates from inflicting on a free citizen any capital, or even corporal punishment; and the obsolete statutes of blood were artfully, and perhaps truly, ascribed to the spirit, not of patrician, but of regal, tyranny.

In the absence of penal laws and the insufficiency of civil actions, the peace and justice of the city were imperfectly maintained by the private jurisdiction of the citizens. The malefactors who replenish our gaols are the outcasts of society, and the crimes for which they suffer may be commonly ascribed to ignorance, poverty, and brutal appetite. For the perpetration of similar enormities, a vile plebeian might claim and abuse the sacred character of a member of the republic; but on the proof or suspicion of guilt the slave or the stranger was nailed to a cross, and this strict and summary justice might be exercised without restraint over the greatest part of the populace of Rome. Each family contained a domestic tribunal, which was not confined, like that of the praetor, to the cognizance of external actions; virtuous principles and habits were inculcated by the discipline of education, and the Roman father was accountable to the state for the manners of his children, since he disposed without appeal of their life, their liberty, and their inheritance. In some pressing emergencies, the citizen was authorized to avenge his private or public wrongs. The consent of the Jewish, the Athenian, and the Roman laws, approved the slaughter of the nocturnal thief; though in open daylight a robber could not be slain without some previous evidence of danger and complaint. Whoever surprised an adulterer in his nuptial bed might freely exercise his revenge; the most bloody or wanton outrage was excused by the provocation; nor was it before the reign of Augustus that the husband was reduced to weigh the rank of the offender, or that the parent was condemned to sacrifice his daughter with her guilty seducer. After the expulsion of the kings, the ambitious Roman who should dare to assume their title or imitate their tyranny was devoted to the infernal gods; each of his fellow citizens was armed with the sword of justice; and the act of Brutus, however repugnant to gratitude or prudence, had been already sanctified by the judgment of his country. The barbarous practice of wearing arms in the midst of peace, and the bloody maxims of honour, were unknown to the Romans; and during the two purest ages, from the establishment of equal freedom to the end of the Punic wars, the city was never disturbed by sedition, and rarely polluted with atrocious crimes. The failure of penal laws was more sensibly felt when every vice was inflamed by faction at home and dominion abroad. In the time of Cicero each private citizen enjoyed the privilege of anarchy— each minister of the republic was exalted to the temptations of regal power, and their virtues are entitled to the warmest praise as the spontaneous fruits of nature of philosophy. After a triennial indulgence of lust, rapine, and cruelty, Verres, the tyrant of Sicily, could only be sued for the pecuniary restitution of three hundred thousand pounds sterling; and such was the temper of the laws, the judges, and perhaps the accuser himself, that, on refunding a thirteenth part of his plunder, Verres could retire to an easy and luxurious exile.

The first imperfect attempt to restore the proportion of crimes and punishments were made by the dictator Sylla, who, in the midst of his sanguinary triumph, aspired to restrain the licence rather than to oppress the liberty of the Romans. He gloried in the arbitrary proscription of four thousand seven hundred citizens. But, in the character of a legislator, he respected the prejudices of the times; and instead of pronouncing a sentence of death against the robber or assassin, the general who betrayed an army or the magistrate who ruined a province, Sylla was content to aggravate the pecuniary damages by the penalty of exile, or, in more constitutional language, by the interdiction of fire and water. The Cornelian, and afterwards the Pompeian and Julian laws, introduced a new system of criminal jurisprudence; and the emperors, from Augustus to Justinian, disguised their increasing rigour under the names of the original authors. But the invention and frequent use of extraordinary pains proceeded from the desire to extend and conceal the progress of despotism. In the condemnation of illustrious Romans, the senate was always prepared to confound, at the will of their masters, the judicial and legislative powers. It was the duty of the governors to maintain the peace of their province by the arbitrary and rigid administration of justice; the freedom of the city evaporated in the extent of empire, and the Spanish malefactor who claimed the privilege of a Roman was elevated by the command of Galba on a fairer and more lofty cross. Occasional rescripts issued from the throne to decide the questions which, by their novelty or importance, appeared to surpass the authority and discernment of a proconsul. Transportation and beheading were reserved for honourable persons; meaner criminals were either hanged, or burnt, or buried in the mines, or exposed to the wild beasts of the amphitheatre. Armed robbers were pursued and extirpated as the enemies of society; the driving away of horses or cattle was made a capital offence; but simple theft was uniformly considered as a mere civil and private injury. The degree of guilt and the modes of punishment were too often determined by the discretion of the rulers, and the subject was left in ignorance of the legal danger which he might incur by every action of his life.

A sin, a vice, a crime, are the objects of theology, ethics, and jurisprudence. Whenever their judgments agree, they corroborate each other; but as often as they differ, a prudent legislator appreciates the guilt and punishment according to the measure of social injury. On this principle the most daring attack on the life and property of a private citizen is judged less atrocious than the crime of treason or rebellion, which invades the majesty of the republic; the obsequious civilians unanimously pronounced that the republic is contained in the person of its chief, and the edge of the Julian law was sharpened by the incessant diligence of the emperors. The licentious commerce of the sexes may be tolerated as an impulse of nature, or forbidden as a source of disorder and corruption; but the fame, the fortunes, the family of the husband, are seriously injured by the adultery of the wife. The wisdom of Augustus, after curbing the freedom of revenge, applied to this domestic offence the animadversion of the laws; and the guilty parties, after the payment of heavy forfeitures and fines, were condemned to long or perpetual exile in two separate islands. religion pronounces an equal censure against the infidelity of the husband, but, as it is not accompanied by the same civil effects, the wife was never permitted to vindicate her wrongs; and the distinction of simple or double adultery, so familiar and so important in the canon law, is unknown to the jurisprudence of the Code and Pandects. I touch with reluctance, and despatch with impatience, a more odious vice, of which modesty rejects the name, and nature abominates the idea. The primitive Romans were infected by the example of the Etruscans and Greeks; in the mad abuse of prosperity and power every pleasure that is innocent was deemed insipid; and the Scatinian law, which had been extorted by an act of violence, was insensibly abolished by the lapse of time and the multitude of criminals. By this law the rape, perhaps the seduction, of an ingenuous youth was compensated as a personal injury by the poor damages of ten thousand sesterces, or fourscore pounds; the ravisher might be slain by the resistance or revenge of chastity; and I wish to believe that at Rome, as in Athens, the voluntary and effeminate deserter of his sex was degraded from the honours and the rights of a citizen. But the practice of vice was not discouraged by the severity of opinion; the indelible stain of manhood was confounded with the more venial transgressions of fornication and adultery; nor was the licentious lover exposed to the same dishonour which he impressed on the male or female partner of his guilt. From Catullus to Juvenal, the poets accuse and celebrate the degeneracy of the times; and the reformation of manners was feebly attempted by the reason and authority of the civilians, till the most virtuous of the Caesars proscribed the sin against nature as a crime against society.

A new spirit of legislation, respectable even in its error, arose in the empire with the religion of Constantine. The laws of Moses were received as the divine origin of justice, and the Christian princes adapted their penal statutes to the degrees of moral and religious turpitude. Adultery was first declared to be a capital offence; the frailty of the sexes was assimilated to poison or assassination, to sorcery or parricide; the same penalties were inflicted on the passive and active guilt of paederasty; and all criminals, of free or servile condition, were either drowned, or beheaded, or cast alive into the avenging flames. The adulterers were spared by the common sympathy of mankind; but the lovers of their own sex were pursued by general and pious indignation; the impure manners of Greece still prevailed in the cities of Asia, and every vice was fomented by the celibacy of the monks and clergy. Justinian relaxed the punishment at least of female infidelity; the guilty spouse was only condemned to solitude and penance, and at the end of two years she might be recalled to the arms of a forgiving husband. But the same emperor declared himself the implacable enemy of unmanly lust, and the cruelty of his persecution can scarcely be excused by the purity of his motives. In defiance of every principle of justice, he stretched to past as well as future offences the operations of his edicts, with the previous allowance of a short respite for confession and pardon. A painful death was inflicted by the amputation of the sinful instrument, or the insertion of sharp reeds into the pores and tubes of most exquisite sensibility; and Justinian defended the propriety of the execution, since the criminals would have lost their hands had they been convicted of sacrilege. In this state of disgrace and agony two bishops, Isaiah of Rhodes and Alexander of Diospolis, were dragged through the streets of Constantinople, while their brethren were admonished by the voice of a crier to observe this awful lesson, and not to pollute the sanctity of their character. Perhaps these prelates were innocent. A sentence of death and infamy was often founded on the slight and suspicious evidence of a child or a servant; the guilt of the green faction, of the rich, and of the enemies of Theodora, was presumed by the judges, and paederasty became the crime of those to whom no crime could be imputed. A French philosopher has dared to remark that whatever is secret must be doubtful, and that our natural horror of vice may be abused as an engine of tyranny. But the favourable persuasion of the same writer, that a legislator may confide in the taste and reason of mankind, is impeached by the unwelcome discovery of the antiquity and extent of the disease.

The free citizens of Athens and Rome enjoyed in all criminal cases the invaluable privilege of being tried by their country. 1. The administration of justice is the most ancient office of a prince; it was exercised by the Roman kings, and abused by Tarquin, who alone, without law or council, pronounced his arbitrary judgments. The first consuls succeeded to this regal prerogative; but the sacred right of appeal soon abolished the jurisdiction of the magistrates, and all public causes were decided by the supreme tribunal of the people. But a wild democracy, superior to the forms, too often disdains the essential principles, of justice; the pride of despotism was envenomed by plebeian envy; and the heroes of Athens might sometimes applaud the happiness of the Persian, whose fate depended on the caprice of a single tyrant. Some salutary restraints, imposed by the people on their own passions, were at once the cause and effect of the gravity and temperance of the Romans. The right of accusation was confined to the magistrates. A vote of the thirty-five tribes could inflict a fine; but the cognizance of all capital crimes was reserved by a fundamental law to the assembly of the centuries, in which the weight of influence and property was sure to preponderate. Repeated proclamations and adjournments were interposed, to allow time for prejudice and resentment to subside; the whole proceeding might be annulled by a seasonable omen or the opposition of a tribune, and such popular trials were commonly less formidable to innocence than they were favourable to guilt. But this union of the judicial and legislative powers left it doubtful whether the accused party was pardoned or acquitted; and, in the defence of an illustrious client, the orators of Rome and Athens addressed their arguments to the policy and benevolence, as well as to the justice of their sovereign. 2. The task of convening the citizens for the trial of each offender became more difficult, as the citizens and offenders continually multiplied, and the ready expedient was adopted of delegating the jurisdiction of the people to the ordinary magistrates or to extraordinary inquisitors. In the first ages these questions were rare and occasional. In the beginning of the seventh century of Rome they were made perpetual; four praetors were annually empowered to sit in judgment on the state offences of treason, extortion, peculation, and bribery. And Sylla added new praetors and new questions for those crimes which more directly injure the safety of individuals. By these inquisitors the trial was prepared and directed; but they could only pronounce the sentence of the majority of judges, who, with some truth and more prejudice, have been compared to the English juries. To discharge this important though burdensome office, an annual list of ancient and respectable citizens was formed by the praetor. After many constitutional struggles, they were chosen in equal numbers from the senate, the equestrian order, and the people; four hundred and fifty were appointed for single questions, and the various rolls or decuries of judges must have contained the names of some thousand Romans, who represented the judicial authority of the state. In each particular cause a sufficient number was drawn from the urn; their integrity was guarded by an oath; the mode of ballot secured their independence; the suspicion of partiality was removed by the mutual challenges of the accuser and defendant; and the judges of Milo, by the retrenchment of fifteen on each side, were reduced to fifty-one voices or tablets, of acquittal, of condemnation, or of favourable doubt. 3. In his civil jurisdiction the praetor of the city was truly a judge, and almost a legislator; but as soon as he had prescribed the action of law, he often referred to a delegate the determination of the fact. With the increase of legal proceedings, the tribunal of the centumvirs, in which he presided, acquired more weight and reputation. But whether he acted alone or with the advice of his council, the most absolute powers might be trusted to a magistrate who was annually chosen by the votes of the people. The rules and precautions of freedom have required some explanation; the order of despotism is simple and inanimate. Before the age of Justinian, or perhaps the Diocletian, the decuries of Roman judges had sunk to an empty title; the humble advice of the assessors might be accepted or despised; and in each tribunal the civil and criminal jurisdiction was administered by a single magistrate, who was raised and disgraced by the will of the emperor.

A Roman accused of any capital crime might prevent the sentence of the law by voluntary exile or death. Till his guilt had been legally proved, his innocence was presumed and his person was free; till the votes of the last 'century' had been counted and declared, he might peaceably secede to any of the allied cities of Italy, or Greece, or Asia. His fame and fortunes were preserved, at least to his children, by this civil death; and he might still be happy in every rational and sensual enjoyment, if a mind accustomed to the ambitious tumult of Rome could support the uniformity and silence of Rhodes or Athens. A bolder effort was required to escape from the tyranny of the Caesars; but this effort was rendered familiar by the maxims of the Stoics, the example of the bravest Romans, and the legal encouragements of suicide. The bodies of condemned criminals were exposed to public ignominy, and their children, a more serious evil, were reduced to poverty by the confiscation of their fortunes. But, if the victims of Tiberius and Nero anticipated the decree of the prince or senate, their courage and despatch were recompensed by the applause of the public, the decent honours of burial and the validity of their testaments. The exquisite avarice and cruelty of Domitian appears to have deprived the unfortunate of this last consolation, and it was still denied even by the clemency of the Antonines. A voluntary death, which, in the case of a capital offence, intervened between the accusation and the sentence, was admitted as a confession of guilt, and the spoils of the deceased were seized by the inhuman claims of the treasury. Yet the civilians have always respected the natural right of a citizen to dispose of his life; and the posthumous disgrace invented by Tarquin to check the despair of his subjects was never revived or imitated by succeeding tyrants. The powers of this world have indeed lost their dominion over him who is resolved on death, and his arm can only be restrained by the religious apprehension of a future state. Suicides are enumerated by Virgil among the unfortunate, rather than the guilty, and the poetical fables of the infernal shades could not seriously influence the faith or practice of mankind. But the precepts of the Gospel or the church have at length imposed a pious servitude on the minds of Christians, and condemn them to expect, without a murmur, the last stroke of disease or the executioner.

The penal statutes form a very small proportion of the sixty-two books of the Code and Pandects, and in all judicial proceeding the life or death of a citizen is determined with less caution and delay than the most ordinary question of covenant or inheritance. This singular distinction, though something may be allowed for the urgent necessity of defending the peace of society, is derived from the nature of criminal and civil jurisprudence. Our duties to the state are simple and uniform; the law by which he is condemned is inscribed not only on brass or marble, but on the conscience of the offender, and his guilt is commonly proved by the testimony of a single fact. But our relations to each other are various and infinite; our obligations are created, annulled, and modified by injuries, benefits, and promises; and the interpretation of voluntary contracts and testaments, which are often dictated by fraud or ignorance, affords a long and laborious exercise to the sagacity of the judge. The business of life is multiplied by the extent of commerce and dominion, and the residence of the parties in the distant provinces of an empire is productive of doubt, delay, and inevitable appeals from the local to the supreme magistrate. Justinian, the Greek emperor of Constantinople and the East, was the legal successor of the Latian shepherd who had planted a colony on the banks of the Tiber. In a period of thirteen hundred years the laws had reluctantly followed the changes of government and manners; and the laudable desire of conciliating ancient names with recent institutions destroyed the harmony, and swelled the magnitude, of the obscure and irregular system. The laws which excuse on any occasions the ignorance of their subjects, confess their own imperfections; the civil jurisprudence, as it was abridged by Justinian, still continued a mysterious science and a profitable trade, and the innate perplexity of the study was involved in tenfold darkness by the private industry of the practitioners. The expense of the pursuit sometimes exceeded the value of the prize, and the fairest rights were abandoned by the poverty or prudence of the claimants. Such costly justice might tend to abate the spirit of litigation, but the unequal pressure serves only to increase the influence of the rich, and to aggravate the misery of the poor. By these dilatory and expensive proceedings the wealthy pleader obtains a more certain advantage than he could hope from the accidental corruption of his judge. The experience of an abuse from which our own age and country are not perfectly exempt may sometimes provoke a generous indignation, and extort the hasty wish of exchanging our elaborate jurisprudence for the simple and summary decrees of a

Turkish cadhi. Our calmer reflection will suggest that such forms and delays are necessary to guard the person and property of the citizen; that the discretion of the judge is the first engine of tyranny; and that the laws of a free people should foresee and determine every question that may probably arise in the exercise of power and the transactions of industry. But the government of Justinian united the evils of liberty and servitude, and the Romans were oppressed at the same time by the multiplicity of their laws and the arbitrary will of their master.

Charles Dickens

A Letter to the *Daily News* 28th February, 1846*

GENTLEMEN, IN the very remarkable Report made to the State Assembly of New York, in 1841, by a select committee of that body, who arrived at the conclusion, 'that the punishment of death, by law, ought to be forthwith and for ever abolished' in that part of America, there is the following suggestion:

'. . . Whether there sleep within the breast of man, certain dark and mysterious sympathies with the thought of that death, and that futurity which await his nature, tending to invest any act expressly forbidden by that penalty, with an unconscious and inexplicable fascination, that attracts his thoughts to it, in spite of their very shuddering dread; and bids his imagination brood over its idea, 'till out of those dark depths in his own nature, comes gradually forth a monstrous birth of Temptation. . . .'

Strongly impressed by this passage when I first read the report; and believing that it shadowed out a metaphysical truth, which, however wild and appalling in its aspect, was a truth still; I was led to consider the cases of several murderers, both in deed, and in intent, with a reference to it; and certainly it gathered very strong and special confirmation in the course of that inquiry. But, as the bearing, here, is on capital punishment in its influences on the commission of crime; and as my present object is to make it the subject of one or two considerations in its other influences on society in general; I, for the present, defer any immediate pursuit of the idea, and merely quote it now, as introducing this lesser and yet great objection to the punishment of death:

That there is, about it, a horrible fascination, which, in the minds—not of evil-disposed persons, but of good and virtuous and well-conducted people, supersedes the horror legitimately attaching to crime itself, and causes every word and action of a criminal under sentence of death to be the subject of a morbid interest and curiosity.

* Thanks for unearthing this letter, published here for the first time, are due to Mr Phillip Collins, one of the editors of the Pilgrim edition of the *Letters of Charles Dickens* to be published shortly.

Which is odious and painful, even to many of those who eagerly gratify it by every means they can compass; but which is, generally speaking, irresistible. The attraction of repulsion being as much a law of our moral nature, as gravitation is in the structure of the visible world, operates in no case (I believe) so powerfully, as in this case of the punishment of death; though it may occasionally diminish in its force, through strong reaction.

When the murderers HOCKER and TAWELL had awakened a vast amount of this depraved excitement, and it had attained to an unusually indecent and frenzied height, one of your contemporaries, deploring the necessity of ministering to such an appetite, laid the blame upon the caterers of such dainties for the Press, while some other news-papers, disputing which of them should bear the greater share of it, divided it variously. Can there be any doubt, on cool reflection, that the whole blame rested on, and was immediately and naturally refer-able to, the punishment of death?

Round what other punishment does the like interest gather? We read of the trials of persons who have rendered themselves liable to transportation for life, and we read of their sentences, and, in some few notorious instances, of their departure from this country, and arrival beyond sea; but *they* are never followed into their cells, and tracked from day to day, and night to night; *they* are never repro-duced in their false letters, flippant conversations, theological dis-quisitions with visitors, lay and clerical: or served up in their whole biography and adventures—so many live romances with a bloody ending. Their portraits are not rife in the print-shops, nor are their autographs stuck up in shop-windows, nor are their snuff-boxes handed affably to gentlemen in court, nor do they inquire of other spectators with eye-glasses why they look at them so steadfastly, nor are their breakfasts, dinners, and luncheons, elaborately described, nor are their waxen images in Baker-street (*unless they were in immediate danger, at one time, of the gallows*), nor are high prices offered for their clothes at Newgate, nor do turnpike trusts grow rich upon the tolls that people going to see their houses, or the scenes of their offences, pay. They are tried, found guilty, punished; and there an end.

But a criminal under sentence of death, or in great peril of death upon the scaffold, becomes, immediately, the town talk; the great subject; the hero of the time. The demeanour in his latter moments, of SIR THOMAS MORE—one of the wisest and most virtuous of men—

was never the theme of more engrossing interest, than that of HOCKER, TAWELL, GREENACRE, or COURVOISIER. The smallest circumstance in the behaviour of these, or any similar wretches, is noted down and published as a precious fact. And read, too—extensively and generally read—even by hundreds and thousands of people who object to the publication of such details, and are disgusted by them. The horrible fascination surrounding the punishment, and everything connected with it, is too strong for resistance; and when an attempt is made in this or that gaol (as it has been sometimes made of late), to keep such circumstances from transpiring, by excluding every class of strangers, it is only a formal admission of the existence of this fascination, and of the impossibility of otherwise withstanding it.

Is it contended that the fascination may surround the crime, and not the punishment? Let us consider whether other crimes, which have now no sort of fascination for the general public, had or had not precisely the gross kind of interest which now attaches to Murder alone, when they were visited with the same penalty. Was Forgery interesting, when Forgers were hanged? and is it less interesting now when they are transported for life? Compare the case of Dr Dodd, or Fauntleroy, or the Reverend Peter Fenn, or Montgomery, or Hunton, or any other generally known, with that of the Exchequer-Bill forgery in later times, which: with every attendant circumstance but death, or danger of death, to give it a false attraction, soon dwindled down into a mere item in a Sessions' Calendar. Coining, when the coiner was dragged (as I have seen one) on a hurdle to the place of execution; or Burglary, or Highway Robbery—did these crimes ever wear an aspect of adventure and mystery, and did the perpetrators of them ever become the town talk, when their offences were visited with death? Now, they are mean, degraded, miserable criminals; and nothing more.

That the publication of these Newgate court-circulars to which I have alluded, is injurious to society, there can be no doubt. Apart from their inevitable association with revolting details, revived again and again, of bloodshed and murder (most objectionable as familiarizing people's minds with the contemplation of such horrors), it is manifest that anything which tends to awaken a false interest in great villains, and to invest their greatest villainies and lightest actions with a terrible attraction, must be vicious and bad, and cannot be wholesome reading. But it is neither just nor reasonable to charge their publication on the newspapers, or the gleaners for the newspapers. They are published because they are read and sought for. They are read and sought for: not because society has causelessly entered into a monstrous and unnatural league on this theme (which is would be absurd to suppose), but because it is in the secret nature of those of whom society is made up, to have a dark and dreadful interest in the punishment at issue.

Whether public executions produce any good impression on their habitual witnesses, or whether they are calculated to produce any good impression on the class of persons most likely to be attracted to them, is a question, by this time, pretty well decided. I was present, myself, at the execution of Courvoisier. I was, purposely, on the spot, from midnight of the night before; and was a near witness of the whole process of the building of the scaffold, the gathering of the crowd, the gradual swelling of the concourse with the coming-on of day, the hanging of the man, the cutting of the body down, and the removal of it into the prison. From the moment of my arrival, when there were but a few score boys in the street, and those all young thieves, and all clustered together behind the barrier nearest to the drop—down to the time when I saw the body with its dangling head, being carried on a wooden bier into the gaol—I did not see one token in all the immense crowd; at the windows, in the streets, on the house-tops, anywhere; of any one emotion suitable to the occasion. No sorrow, no salutary terror, no abhorrence, no seriousness; nothing but ribaldry, debauchery, levity, drunkenness, and flaunting vice in fifty other shapes. I should have deemed it impossible that I could have ever felt any large assemblage of my fellow-creatures to be so odious. I hoped, for an instant, that there was some sense of Death and Eternity in the cry of 'Hats off!' when the miserable wretch appeared; but I found, next moment, that they only raised it as they would at a Play—to see the Stage the better, in the final scene.

Of the effect upon a perfectly different class, I can speak with no less confidence. There were, with me, some gentlemen of education and distinction in imaginative pursuits, who had, as I had, a particular detestation of that murderer; not only for the cruel deed he had done, but for his slow and subtle treachery, and for his wicked defence. And yet, if any one among us could have saved the man (we said so, afterwards, with one accord), he would have done it. It was so loathsome, pitiful, and vile a sight, that the law appeared to be as bad as he, or worse; being very much the stronger, and shedding around it a far more dismal contagion.

The last of the influences of this punishment on society, which I shall notice in the present letter, is, that through the prevalent and fast-increasing feeling of repugnance to it, great offenders escape with a very inadequate visitation. Only a few weeks have elapsed since the streets of London presented the obscene spectacle of a woman being brought out to be killed before such a crowd as I have described, and, while her young body was yet hanging in the brutal gaze, of portions of the concourse hurrying away, to be in time to see a man hanged elsewhere, by the same executioner. A barbarous murderer is tried soon afterwards, and acquitted on a fiction of his being insane—as any one, cognizant of these two recent executions, might have easily foreseen.

I will not enter upon the question whether juries be justified or not justified in evading their oaths, rather than add to the list of such deeply degrading and demoralizing exhibitions, and sanction the infliction of a punishment which they conscientiously believe, and have so many reasons for believing, to be wrong. It is enough for me that juries do so; and I presume to think that the able writer of a powerful article on Johnstone's trial in *The Daily News*, does not sufficiently consider that this is no new course in juries, but the natural result and working of a law to which the general feeling is opposed. MR ABERCROMBIE, five-and-thirty years ago, stated it in the House of Commons to have become a common practice of juries, in cases of Forgery, to find verdicts 'contrary to the clearest and most indisputable evidence of facts'; and cited the case of a woman who was proved to have stolen a ten-pound note, which the jury, with the approbation of the judge, found to be worth only thirty-nine shillings. SIR SAMUEL ROMILLY, in the same debate, mentioned other cases of the same nature; and they were of frequent and constant occurrence at that time.

Besides—that juries have, within our own time, in another class of cases, arrived at the general practice of returning a verdict tacitly agreed upon beforehand, and of making it applicable to very different sets of facts, we know by the notable instance of Suicide. Within a few years, juries frequently found that a man dying by his own hand, was guilty of self-murder. But this verdict subjecting the body to a barbarous mode of burial, from which the better feeling of society revolted (as it is now revolting from the punishment of death), it was abrogated by common consent, and precisely the same evasion established, as is now, unfortunately, so often resorted to in cases of murder. That it is an evasion, and not a proceeding on a soundly-proved and established principle, that he who destroys his own life must necessarily be mad—the very exceptions from this usual course in themselves demonstrate.

So it is in cases of Murder. Juries, like society, are not stricken foolish or motiveless. They have, for the most part, an objection to the punishment of death: and they will, for the most part, assert such verdicts. As jurymen, in the Forgery cases, would probably reconcile their verdict to their consciences, by calling to mind that the intrinsic value of a bank note was almost nothing, so jurymen in cases of Murder probably argue that grave doctors have said all men are more or less mad, and therefore they believe the prisoner mad. This is a great wrong to society; but it arises out of the punishment of death.

And the question will always suggest itself in jurors' minds—however earnestly the learned judge presiding, may discharge his duty—'which is the greater wrong to society? To give this man the benefit of the possibility of his being mad, or to have another public execution, with all its depraving and hardening influences?' Imagining myself a juror, in a case of life or death: and supposing that the evidence had forced me from every other ground of opposition to this punishment in the particular case, as a possibility of irremediable mistake, or otherwise: I would go over it again on this ground; and if I could, by any reasonable special pleading with myself, find him mad rather than hang him—I think I would.

CHARLES DICKENS

Judge David L. Bazelon

The Dilemma of Punishment*

Judge Bazelon, who is a member of the United States Court of Appeals in Washington D.C., is a strange phenomenon in the Anglo-Saxon world— a criminologist on the Bench. Since he joined the Federal Bench in 1949 he has delivered more than twenty-five judgments touching on the defence of insanity in criminal cases. The most celebrated of these was his judgment in Durham v. United States *in 1954, which created a wider test of criminal responsibility.*

The Durham case, to which Judge Bazelon alludes in his address, concerned a 23-year-old man who broke into a Georgetown (Washington D.C.) house and was caught pilfering clothes. Since the age of sixteen Durham had been charged with passing bad cheques, embezzlement, violation of parole, car theft and attempted suicide. Three times he had been committed to mental institutions. Psychiatrists had variously diagnosed him as 'psychotic with psychopathic personality' and, oddly, 'without mental disorder but with a psychopathic personality'.

Following the indictment for housebreaking Durham was adjudged of unsound mind and again sent to a mental institution. Sixteen months later the hospital's superintendent certified that 'prolonged psychiatric study had established that Durham suffers from psychological illness but is mentally competent to stand his trial. . . .' At his trial the only medical witness was the government psychiatrist who had originally found him incompetent to stand trial; his evidence was unequivocal that Durham was of unsound mind at the time of his crime. The trial judge applied the legally-hallowed but medically-maligned M'Naghten rules. Was the accused suffering from such a defect of reasoning, from disease of the mind, as not to know the nature and quality of the act he was committing, or if he did know it, that he did not know what he was doing was wrong? The psychiatrist could not categorically say whether Durham knew the difference between right and wrong. The trial judge therefore dismissed the plea of insanity.

The Court of Appeals substituted its broader and medically-acceptable

* The Louis D. Brandeis Memorial Lecture for 1960

test that the accused is not to be held criminally responsible if his unlawful act was the product of mental disease or mental defect. The court said that the test would be whether the accused acted because of a mental disorder and not whether he has displayed particular symptoms which medical science has long recognized do not necessarily, or even typically, accompany even the most serious mental disorder.

Thus in one decision psychiatry and law were brought into harmonious relationship when dealing with criminal behaviour instead of being kept, as they are in England, almost at loggerheads. An American psychiatrist, Dr Karl Menninger, called the Durham decision 'more revolutionary in its total effect than the Supreme Court decision regarding segregation'.

A NUMBER of my distinguished predecessors on this platform have assessed various aspects of the character and accomplishments of Louis D. Brandeis. An image has emerged of a brilliant intellectual technician possessing a degree of moral strength beyond the capacity of most of us. Many details of his life and work have been presented to round out this impressive image, and also to convey the range of his probing interests. Unhappily, the legal and social problems of criminal law administration were not within this range—with at least one notable exception in his prophetic dissent in the *Olmstead* case, an early wire-tapping decision. Crime and society's treatment of the criminal were not publicly a dominant source of concern for Justice Brandeis.

Not directly, that is. For there is nevertheless an abiding connection between the Brandeis heritage—both in outlook and in method—and the outburst of modern concern with the great problems of criminal justice. Let me spell out this important connection. Above all else, Brandeis believed in fructifying the law by making it responsive to scientific developments and general intellectual advance. He felt that survival of basic social respect for the law on the part of the populace required no less—that the 'living law' had to maintain its vital relation to general intellectual advance and changing social life. This, he noted, was specially difficult for the law because of its deep traditional aspect. But not thereby any the less necessary. Those of you who are lawyers will understand this remark as referring to what is undoubtedly the most profound issue in the philosophy of law—the inner mechanism of change. Brandeis' outlook thereon was clear, dramatically forward-looking and established him as a creative leader and, indeed, as a prophet to later generations of lawyers. In 1916 he quoted approvingly a psychologist who had said 'that a lawyer who has not studied economics and sociology is very apt to become a public enemy'. Justice Brandeis was talking to us today—and, moreover, telling us something we still need to know.

It is interesting that Brandeis should have borrowed the words of a psychologist to express this strong view because it applies in our day *a fortiori* (as we lawyers say) to the behavioural sciences, including psychology. The phrase 'public enemy' is perhaps too strong, since through special newspaper use after 1916 it has lost its traditional quality. But lawyers working in the field of the criminal law who resist or ignore the facts, the insights, the whole considerable offering of sociology, psychiatry, and allied disciplines, do a deep disservice to the public, for that public expects its experts to improve our ways of carrying on the business of society. Such a lawyer is no friend of the public, nor is he a good servant of the law. And he is not working within the Brandeis heritage. This can be asserted, I think, without reference to the current shortcomings or ultimate limits of these behavioural disciplines.

I said there is a true connection between this heritage and the current agitation in the criminal law not only with respect to outlook but also as to method. Naturally I refer to that deservedly famous event in the history of American law when Brandeis filed a 112-page brief in the case of *Muller v. Oregon*, which he argued before the United States Supreme Court in January 1908. This initiated the startling legal tradition of what came to be known as the 'Brandeis brief'; as his biographer has characterized the event—'he made the law grow a hundred years in a day'. A recent use of this still new, still vital form of legal argument was, as many of you know, appellant's brief in *Brown v. Board of Education*, the chief of the desegregation cases. The brief in *Muller v. Oregon*, which concerned the constitutionality of a state statute limiting the hours women might work in industry, amounted to a major sociological treatise. It referred in full, cogent detail to the more important scientific studies—factual, statistical, and theoretical—concerning the actual and very urgent problem of women *then working* in American industry. Nothing quite like that had ever been done before. The law was supposed to be concerned with something called The Law, and its technique of adjustment to changing experience was lost somewhere among the higher mysteries of the

Law-Fact dichotomy. Then Brandeis overwhelmed the highest court of the land with the full, relevant weight of modern social scientific facts. And he won his case.

I am not suggesting that the Brandeis brief has finally resolved—or that it was designed finally to resolve—the very difficult problems of both substance and procedure which centre around the continuous adjustment of existing rules of law and changing circumstances. Hardly that. It is not my purpose this evening to discuss the complex theory of when and how the law properly takes cognizance of new facts and altered awareness in society, and the differing roles of the legislature and the courts in this process. I simply note that the law *does* change, through both instruments of government, and that the Brandeis brief remains a still vital weapon in the methodological arsenal of such change. Of course everyone—especially judges, I assure you—would rest more comfortably if administration of the law were a mechanical process, and all law was initiated by a democratic legislature after full public hearings. But our system, and life itself, is much more complex than that. The courts unavoidably have their unique role to play.

In both the *Muller* and the desegregation cases, scientific material was used referring to the important psychological effects of overwork on women and segregated education on negro children. When the law welcomes science, psychological insight plays its specific and important role in depicting reality by its focus on the inner effect of circumstances on the individual and the resulting generation of healthy or distorted motive.

In the criminal law, where one might expect the assistance of the behavioural sciences and especially psychiatry to be most eagerly solicited—because most obviously relevant—the fact of the matter is that they are not. In my opinion, not nearly enough. I will not burden your patience by recounting again the century-old struggle against the exclusionary M'Naghten Rules. These Rules have dominated the administration of the insanity defence in England and most American jurisdictions. It should suffice to remind you of their continued vitality. The M'Naghten formula emphasizes the rational capacity of the mind, and excuses from criminal responsibility only the individual who at the time of the crime 'was labouring under such a defect of reason, from disease of the mind, as not to know' what he was doing or that it was wrong. However this test *might* have been interpreted—volumes have been written on the possible meanings of the words—it had in fact worked to exclude medical evidence. I am almost tempted to say that under M'Naghten practice the psychiatrist appears in the proceeding at all only to testify to the irrelevance of psychiatry—that is, to confirm the irrelevance that 'the law' has already decided upon. It assigns to the psychiatric expert in court a sacrificial role in a ritual of condemnation. The expert is asked a question which—most leaders of the profession inform us—cannot be answered within the terms of their discipline. And unless the Rules are breached—as they frequently are on the trial level—the psychiatrist is not encouraged or permitted to address himself to the clinical questions which are the only ones he is truly expert in answering.

That is the scientific expert testifying at the trial level. But on appeal, you may ask, have there been no 'Brandeis briefs' setting forth the relevant facts and insights of modern scientific psychiatry? Yes, for example, many psychiatric works were referred to in the appellant's brief in the *Durham* case, which, as many of you know, resulted in the adoption in the District of Columbia of a broadened insanity test—a rule designed to relax the rigours of M'Naghten and to welcome genuine psychiatric testimony presented in its own terms. The Durham test simply asks whether the accused was suffering from a mental disease or defect and inquires as to the relation between any such condition and the criminal act. But the District of Columbia is only one out of a multitude of jurisdictions. A judge in another jurisdiction had this to say in rejecting the Durham Rule:

'The District of Columbia Court was persuaded to this doctrine chiefly by treatises on subjects other than law to which the decision refers, by Weihofen, Zilboorg, Deutsch, Glueck, Guttmacher, Overholser, Reik, and others doubtless learned in the field of psychiatry. I am not willing to accept their teachings and to reject completely the philosophies of such eminent jurists as Blackstone . . .'

—And so on. This judge preferred to follow what he called 'guides furnished by accepted principles of the law.'

In the administration of the criminal law today, we desperately need all the help we can get from modern behavioural scientists—before trial, and after trial. The law by itself, without these workers, is cast in the hopeless role of a socially isolated, traditional bulwark against the welter of personal, social and economic forces which create today's problem of crime and the so-called criminal population. And in this losing struggle, the law—by which I mean police, judges, lawyers, and prison guards—would have at its disposal a limited set of concepts honoured largely by time alone. In brief, the law would have the *lex talionis*—the idea of retributive punishment based on absolute moral principles of purportedly universal application. *By itself,* the law would dispose of both the problem of crime and the criminal himself with the one idea of punishment. The 'programme' would be: Repress crime and all anti-social behaviour by punishment alone; rehabilitate the offender by punishment alone; achieve social understanding of wrongdoing and the wrong-doer by the sole mechanical response—'Punish them—they deserve it!'

If the foregoing remarks seem intemperate, that is of course because they do *not* describe our actual system of criminal law administration. For one thing, stern retributive justice has always been tempered by mercy and forgiveness—by the ubiquitous impulse to afford the transgressor a 'second chance'. This happens in practice even when it is not allowed by theory. We simply find it too difficult, too non-human to punish, punish, punish—even though we may hold most seriously the moral imperative to punish, and even though our feeling is that we are wrong when we do not. And for another thing, the behavioural scientists—along with their facts, ideas, and methodology—have as a matter of fact intervened increasingly at many stages of the administrative process. Social workers, clinicians, welfare agencies, even the police, as well as many others, attempt to deal constructively with the juvenile delinquent before he is sent to a reformatory to begin his professional training as the criminal of the future. The psychiatrist comes to court and sometimes his presence there *does* have something other than a ritualistic effect on the outcome of the proceeding. Again, he and his co-workers are more and more frequently consulted in the course of sentencing, probation, parole, and even— as the light of a new dawn—in the institutional rehabilitative process. Occasionally all of this activity ends up having its effect in a judicial decision, even one delivered from an appellate bench.

So clearly our criminal system is a very mixed affair—some would say a very *mixed-up* affair. But things are happening, there is agitation and movement, much heat and a certain amount of light. To put it simply, it is a system in transition. We are, painfully and slowly, coming to a clearer understanding of alternatives and necessities. We are also making some practical progress in working out institutional and administrative means. While much of the intellectual ferment has centred around the wording of the jury instruction when the defence of insanity has been raised, I think it is obvious that this can be compared to the peak of an iceberg that is visible above the waterline. The peak is important chiefly as an indication of the general whereabouts of the much more significant eight-ninths lurking beneath the surface. It is foolhardy to take the visible peak for the whole massive obstruction.

Well, what *is* this iceberg? If our system is in transition, then the question properly arises—Transition from what to what? From M'Naghten to Durham? Hardly. Certainly *from* M'Naghten—but not *just* from that ritualistic phrase, except perhaps symbolically. And Durham—even viewed as a concept, as an approach, which is the way I prefer to view it, rather than nineteen words of a jury instruction—is merely one way of welcoming the psychiatrist into the courtroom. It is a beginning, not an ending—and it relates to the insanity defence, which is only that visible one-ninth of the iceberg.

I believe that the deeper part of the iceberg consists of the retributive urge to punish irrespective of effect, and the accompanying intellectual justification of this primitive urge, the so-called theory of deterrence. A deep emotion and a complicated rationalization.

But before I elaborate these speculations of mine, I want to say that they are my own opinions, which I hold as an interested citizen. While I do not stand alone with these views, not by any means, I am afraid that I cannot even vouch for the faithfulness of my presentation of borrowed ideas. If they seem original, that is probably due as much to lack of scholarship as to anything else. They should be taken merely as one man's speculative opinions.

Wherever one turns in an effort at reform in the treatment of offenders, one comes up against this need to punish and its defence by the theory of deterrence. Of course there are many other arguments put forward at various times in justification of the present system, with its great emphasis on punishment for its own sake or punishment as the answer to all problems. For example, both Judge Learned Hand in this country and Lord Denning in England—the first sadly and the latter more firmly—have referred to the *public's* demand that the sinner shall suffer. Judge Hand stated that he did 'not share that feeling, which is a vestige . . . of very ancient primitive and irrational belief and emotions.' Lord Justice Denning spoke more strongly by saying:

'It is a mistake to consider the objects of punishment as being deterrent or reformative or preventive, and nothing else. . . . The truth is that some crimes are so outrageous that society insists on adequate punishment, because the wrongdoer deserves it, irrespective of whether it is a deterrent or not.'

I can assure you that similar views are frequently expressed from the bench in courts throughout our land—and often enough when the crime is no more 'outrageous' than juvenile car-theft. Sometimes the court in relieving itself of these sentiments will refer to society's demand for retribution—communicated to the court by some unknown intermediary, or perhaps so obvious as not to require communication. On other occasions a court will abandon that rhetorical flourish and speak directly, saying—'You are going to be punished good and proper because you deserve it, and because too many of you hoodlums have been getting away with it.'

So it is still the need to punish that confronts us—although at times not *my* need, but somebody else's. All this, as Judge Hand suggests, is highly irrational. I am sure that we must recognize this irrational need as a social fact, but I cannot see that we must abandon attempts at reform because of it. After all, that public out there that needs to punish also needs to forgive—and it especially needs to be given, for its own protection and well-being, the most rationally effective administration we can devise for it. It is not getting it now. The excessive emphasis on punishment, with the consequent neglect of genuine rehabilitation, is accompanied by a disastrously high level of recidivism. In the relatively progressive Federal Prison System, for example, the rate increased between 1949 and 1958 from 61 per cent to 67 per cent. In this same period, the number of serious offenders who have had two or more previous convictions has grown from 39 per cent to 46 per cent. Please realize what these figures mean: In two-thirds of the cases, punishment neither reforms nor deters the individual who has served one sentence. And with those who have served a second sentence, it fails again in nearly half of the cases.

Another point of view towards this problem is put forward by Harry Elmer Barnes. He says that two-thirds of the criminal population is always at large and that moreover the ones on the outside tend to be the smartest and the most dangerous of the lot. So that while he feels lack of funds and the fear of escape, rather than the urge to punish, are the greatest obstacles to needed reforms, he argues for more rehabilitation as follows:

'The public is unmindful of the fact that convicts, on the average, will serve less than three years in prisons and law-abiding citizens can only be protected from their depredations by successful rehabilitation during this brief term of incarceration.'

From more than one point of view, then, punishment rather than rehabilitation just does not work.

This being the case, why such persistent, irrational emphasis on punishment? I think one thing is the deep childish fear that with any reduction of punishment, multitudes would run amok. It seems to me this fear must be based on exaggerated notions of the role of punishment when we were children. The reasoning is: We are good adults because we were punished when we were bad children; any adult who is bad should get some more of what we got when we were children. '*They*' must be punished to reconfirm our adulthood and our goodness —to distinguish us from them. But most of us who have been good for many years—or at least haven't been caught—have not maintained our high estate because of witnessing frequent public hangings and whippings or stopping to observe a malefactor being drawn-and-quartered on the corner of a busy intersection. Quite the opposite. According to the famous Warden Lawes of Sing Sing Prison, this is especially true of the prosecutors and judges who so zealously take upon themselves the rhetorical burden of carrying out society's need to punish. He sent invitations to the appropriate officers of the law to attend each of the 114 executions carried out at Sing Sing while he was warden. Not one ever found time to attend.

Perhaps one should be encouraged by the fact that the modern urge to punish is no longer so immediately personal. I suppose we should all be pleased by the recent report from Saudi Arabia announcing an important reform in criminal law administration—that hereafter a thief's hand will be cut off by an 'expert surgeon' using anaesthetics rather than by an amateur with a hatchet. An accompanying reform is that adulteresses will no longer be stoned to death, as in biblical times. As Saudi Arabia enters the modern world, they will now be shot.

So there is something like progress in these matters. I would remind you that not half a century before the M'Naghten Rules were enunciated, more than 200 crimes were punishable by death in England. It is interesting to speculate as to whether England could possibly have become the civilized place it is today if the number of capital crimes had not been reduced. But Lord Denning still believes in punishment for its own sake—or still believes that society believes in it.

The belief in punishment-at-a-distance was strikingly illustrated by a report from South Africa last April. It seems that the flogging of offenders was being carried out in a magistrates' court located near the centre of Cape Town. Sentences up of to ten strokes are inflicted on malefactors beginning with eight-year-old boys. The matter became newsworthy when the public began to object to the practice. The objection, however, was not to the punishment itself, but to the uncomfortable circumstance that it was administered in the business district of the city. One citizen complained, 'We can clearly hear the swish and smack of the cane and the pleadings and screams of people being beaten'. It appears that this 'noise' was upsetting women office workers, one of whom expressed herself as follows: 'I sympathize with the police. It cannot be nice to have to deal out these beatings. But I wish we didn't have to listen to it.' Not only the women were disturbed. One man said that 'his conversations with important clients had been interrupted by the "howling of somebody being thrashed."' The problem was solved by police assurances that the beatings would thereafter be administered in a basement, where they would not disturb the public.

I think we are, generally speaking, very confused about the whole subject of punishment. And it is in truth a very complicated matter, with a large admixture of deep emotions concerning views of our own childhood and the child within us, half-spoken beliefs about the nature of our daily self-control, fear of other people, complex attitudes towards authority, and so on. All this helps to indicate for me the direction at least of an explanation of the dilemma of punishment. Because what has to be explained—and finally understood—is the really frightening scope of the irrationality of our notions and practices regarding punishment. It seems that we just do not know how to be practical about the matter. For example, most of us, I imagine, have achieved major control over our own aggressive and vindictive impulses. We would be revolted to watch a hanging or a beating, and even more to participate in one. When we are personally called upon to administer punishment or any form of serious deprivation, we take the task as a heavy duty and think very hard to make certain that we do no more and no less than we feel to be necessary and effective in the circumstances. This would be so in the disciplining of our own children or any subordinates. But when it comes to the administration of crime, we hand the whole matter over to a distant bureaucratic machine, and we want to hear no more about it. Our attitude is—Let the State take care of 'them'.

In other words, our personal resolution of the issue of vindictiveness seems to be achieved at the cost of our human capacity to identify with the offender. Isn't it strange that the criminal law tradition which not so long ago was based on the supposedly deterrent spectacle of public punishment has come full circle and now can be said to be based in effect on the distance and even the secrecy of actual punishment? I wonder how many in this audience have ever seen the inside of a prison? What you would see there can be justified only on the assumption that the prisoners are less than human, and that therefore the obviously de-humanizing process they are undergoing is appropriate for them. Because they have stolen property or committed acts of violence, they are outside the pale of human society, and that is the end of the matter. But of course, after having further brutalized them, after having failed to deal with the causes of their behaviour, and having failed to effect any serious rehabilitation, we then release them into society where they can experience their second or third or fourth opportunity to fail. As Karl Menninger has said, these people are failures first and 'criminals' later. To be a criminal is not strictly speaking merely to have committed a crime—it is a social branding plus penitentiary training, all of which serves only to confirm the initial personal failure which led to the first anti-social act. (As I speak of crime and the criminal tonight, I should emphasize that I am thinking of the delinquent car-thief, the mugger, the amateur burglar and armed robber, the sex offender, and the man who commits assault and other crimes of violence—my attention is not directed towards the special problems represented by the criminal élite consisting of competent professionals, the organization men of the syndicates, or the whole separate area of white-collar crime.)

It is as if society co-operates with certain human beings who are social failures to create this object called the criminal. Our present system of punishment is an essential part of *this* process, not of any process that can be called reforming or rehabilitative. Why does society go to all the trouble and expense of creating this special class of human beings? I think chiefly because we really do not comprehend what we are doing, because we do not want to deal with the facts of social failure to begin with, and because we are not prepared to follow out the logic of our attitude and 'dispose' of these failures outright. There results a sort of half-way house, neither disposal nor rehabilitation, but a new class of human beings to mirror society's confusion on the profound issue of failure in the educative process—and reliance on punishment to cure or cover over all such failure.

What I am suggesting is that the criminal serves as a 'scapegoat'. And this as much as anything is impeding obvious and sorely needed reform in the treatment of offenders. I use the word 'scapegoat' in the specific sense in which it has become a key term in the psycho-sociological analysis of prejudice. That is, a deeply held, unrealistic, projective image of a minority group indulged by members of a dominant group. The essential fact in this form of prejudiced perception is that the member of the dominant group refuses ordinary, human one-to-one identification with representatives of the minority group, sometimes for lack of opportunity, sometimes because of a deeper unwillingness. But, as the analysis of prejudice has revealed, there is a very meaningful if distorted identification nevertheless. Just as the Jew is avaricious and the Negro lazy and lascivious, so the criminal is violent and impetuous in trying to achieve his ends—he has been foolish (if caught), has lost control over himself, and has done what he wanted to do just when he wanted to do it. Don't you and I have these impulses? Doesn't the anti-Semite envy the Jew as he imagines him, and doesn't the Negrophobe believe that the Negro has more primitive pleasures in his life? First we bestow upon them our repressed desires, then we place them outside the pale, thus neatly disposing of them *and* our forbidden impulses.

But of course it doesn't work. Eventually one meets and gets to know a Jew, a Negro or a criminal, and then the trouble begins. The Jew may be poor, the Negro deprived and unhappy—and in any event, both are recognizably and disturbingly *human*, that is, 'like us'. Like-wise the criminal. We can see that he would like to master his impulses, and we see that we might have responded as he did to his provocations, to his miserable social and psychological background. We identify on a one-to-one human basis—if we retain the capacity to do so—and behold! the whole complexion of the problem has changed. *He is like us*—only somewhat weaker, and he has failed in a primary obligation of the mature citizen. He needs help if he is going to bring out the good in himself, and restrain the bad. But first, we must stop treating him like a pariah, as a person who is entitled to punishment and only punishment, because if we treat him that way he will become that way.

Another point to be understood about punishment is that it is not a universal solvent. Different people react differently to it. This is perfectly obvious with regard to children, and needs no elaboration. Our response to punishment is like anything else we learn; some learn better than others, and some learn the same lesson differently than others. In this broad sense, the criminal is the person who has been mis-educated with respect to punishment and the threat of punishment. His re-education must consist of something in addition to just more of the same, more punishment. To conceive otherwise would be like giving harder and harder lessons in algebra to a student who has already evidenced his inability to absorb the basic lessons. Only an incompetent teacher, a man of ill-will or one with very limited resources, would go about destroying a student in such a fashion. But that is just what we do with so many people who, if they had had the proper capacity to respond to punishment, would not have gotten into trouble in the first place. We do just the wrong thing by confirming all of their wrong feelings about punishment. And so we create a class of hopelessly recidivistic criminals.

I think that all I have been saying about punishment can be summed up under the headings—punishment without thinking, punishment as a mechanical and exclusive response, punishment unaccompanied by a rational view of its purpose and effect. As the late George Dession, one of the most careful, creative legal thinkers about these matters, has said—'punishment is never good in itself'. That proposition is perhaps the first step toward wisdom in thinking about the criminal law system. Professor Dession, in re-thinking the whole matter and attempting to devise a more rational and effective approach, preferred to use different words in describing the criminal law system so as to get away from the idea that it concerned only this special class of people called 'criminals' and from the sole response of punishment. He felt that this was self-defeating both in its effect on offenders and on the public, in that it broke the crucial conduit of identifications, and limited the role of imagination. He preferred to speak of a system of sanctions having application to proscribed behaviour, with the purpose of preserving public order. Punishments—called negative sanctions or deprivations

—naturally have their part in this system, but it is a functional part no greater than may be necessary to do what can be done to prevent anti-social behaviour, and to account for it when despite our efforts it does occur. 'Accounting' for it means, again, doing what practically can be done to ensure that the particular individual alters his course of behaviour thereafter. Moreover, sanctions were to be recognized as 'positive' as well as 'negative'—rewards as well as deprivations were to be used as proper techniques for inducing proper behaviour. Our moral education as youngsters was based on both techniques—and if an individual's moral upbringing was faulty, both techniques were deemed necessary in correcting it. This sounds so reasonable and so simple—but it is a never-never land compared to our present system!

This point about the utility of punishment perhaps requires some emphasis. I would not want to leave you with the impression that I am opposed to all measures of punishment, or deprivation. It seems super-fluous to state that I recognize their necessity, but perhaps I had better do so because thinking in this field tends to be characterized by an either-or, all-or-nothing attitude. It is just this attitude which I object to and from which I wish to dissociate myself. Let me illustrate its unfortunate effects. When the *Durham* case was decided in the Dis-trict of Columbia, a great hue and cry was raised that great numbers of vicious criminals would soon be roaming the streets of the city. Nothing could have been more off the mark, as subsequent events have shown. But at the time many people felt that *either* offenders are pun-ished by execution or a penitentiary term, *or* they in effect get off scot-free—that *all* of them must be punished and just punished, or *nothing* would be done to protect society against them. Our Court of Appeals was compelled to reverse a number of cases on the ground that the jury was not properly instructed regarding the consequences of an acquittal by reason of insanity. The Court now requires a positive instruction to the effect that the defendant acquitted by reason of insanity will be put in a mental institution until cured and judicially determined to be no longer a danger to himself or others. Such com-mitments, incidentally, may continue for a longer term than would have been served in a penitentiary for the offence charged. They are clearly a deprivation, a negative sanction—and in this sense a 'punish-ment'—but with the very important difference that it is not retributive, it is no more than may be necessary, and it is punishment subordinate to the purpose of rehabilitation.

On another point. Some people seem to feel that whenever trained workers including psychiatric therapists supplement the work of police and prison guards, or play any independent role at all, the offender will be molly-coddled and consequently society's bulwark against crime will crumble. This is nonsense, but the attitude persists. Dr Melitta Schmideberg of the Association for the Psychiatric Treatment of Offenders is one of the most devoted and distinguished workers in her field. I am not competent to underwrite the validity of her views, but she is a richly experienced therapist in this special and rather neglected area of treatment. She believes in a strongly directive therapy, and in the course thereof gives practical recognition to the fact that the threat of loss of liberty—of going to gaol or going back to gaol—plays an important part in her work with probationed offenders or repeaters. This threat is an ever-present backdrop to her efforts to help the patient get along with his probation officer, to stop breaking the law, to get a job and hold it, and so on. She feels that—'Fear of punishment and guilt keep normal people in check, but an overdose of anxiety can react in the opposite direction on criminals.' She states the problem as follows: 'If the therapist condemns the offender out and out, he cannot treat him; if he condones his offence, he cannot change him.' This is certainly not a molly-coddling approach. On the other hand, she objects eloquently to the psychological effect on offenders of a period in the usual penitentiary. She feels one of the most imperative uses of therapy is to help the ex-convict overcome the effects of prison! Now does it strike anyone here as sensible to deny early treatment of first offenders, send them to a penitentiary where their dangerous problems will be dangerously augmented, and then end up with an infinitely more difficult problem-personality to deal with later on?

Why do we do it? Why do we treat offenders this way? I trust that by this time you are aware that I do not really have a neat answer, and that any satisfactory answer will be found to lie very deep indeed—probably at the core of man's inhumanity to man, in each of us and in the history of all of us. As of today, the main problem is that the problem has been with us so long. Its insolubility has been sanctified by history. But as regards the similar and not unrelated problem of poverty, more and more people are now refusing to be stopped by this traditional historical *impasse*. Perhaps this revolutionary century of ours will also effect a little revolution on behalf of the fallible humans who cannot live up to even the more obvious rules of social order, without somewhat more help than most of us get or need. One doesn't have to be a wild radical to see this problem as one with which we are doing very poorly and one which calls for top-to-bottom re-thinking. As Morris Cohen reminds us, 'It was the conservative President Taft, later Chief Justice of the United States, who character-ized our criminal law as a disgrace to civilization.'

But when we transcend our emotional urge to punish, and begin to think seriously about crime and the criminal without such undue reliance on the one idea of punishment, we very shortly come right up against an intellectually much more formidable barrier. And that is the ubiquitous theory of deterrence. On the intellectual level, it turns out to be the greatest barrier to progress in the criminal law.

This theory proposes that actual malefactors be punished in order to deter potential malefactors. In its pure form, it is willing to assume *arguendo* that punishment may not reform and may even damage the particular individual being punished. But this unfortunate person must be sacrificed to the common good—he must be punished as an example to all, to keep all the rest of us from committing his crime. Of course the theory is not always stated in this pure form. Indeed, there is a common confusion which you may notice in arguments based on the premise of deterrence—a confusion between deterrence of the person being punished and deterrence of all others. Now clearly the convicted prisoner was not deterred by the prior punishment of others from committing the crime which placed him in prison. And to speak of deterring him from committing another offence later takes us back to the previous discussion of the effectiveness of punishment, and concerns rehabilitation not deterrence. So the theory, properly considered, involves only the justification of punishment because of its show-effect, its supposed effect on others. I need not labour the point that the individual so used is a scapegoat, a sacrificial victim. This is an admitted feature of the theory.

Logically, of course, the more we witness the pains of punishment, the more apt they would be actually to deter us from crime. (That is, if active fear deters.) Originally, this logic was a part of the deterrence theory. But in our day it is not. To illustrate this I would like to quote from the 1953 Report of the Royal Commission on Capital Punishment:

'In the first half of the nineteenth century executions still took place in public. This indeed was thought to be an essential part of the deterrent value of the death penalty. But public executions, "though the publicity was deterrent in intention . . . became in practice a degrading form of popular entertainment, which could serve only to deprave the minds of the spectators".'

Parliament ended the practice in 1868. The Report also suggests that the method of hanging was invented and found favour because of its 'advertisement value'. But at the hearings before the Commission, 'witness after witness' defended hanging because it was the most humane method of execution! The Report notes this 'surprising inversion' succinctly as follows:

'Thus a method of execution whose special merit was formerly thought to be that it was peculiarly degrading is now defended on the ground that it is uniquely humane.'

So clearly the deterrence theory is not quite so logical as it used to be. (And just as well!)

I understand that what empirical studies have been made of the deterrent value of capital and other forms of punishment can properly be characterized as 'Inconclusive'. If this is so, and as long as it is so, we are free to speculate about the problem—but I think we do have an accompanying obligation to avoid rigid formulations and dogmatic stands.

A common argument offered in support of deterrence is this: The ordinary citizen would not obey traffic signals if sanctions were not imposed on all drivers for breach of the rules. This argument, please notice, depends for its persuasiveness on a supposed identity between a traffic violation, on the one hand and murder, assault and grand theft, on the other, all these being 'breach of the rules'. Although I suppose they all do come under this category, the empirical differences are more impressive to me than the abstract similarity. But more important, because of the preconditioning of licensing, the persons to whom traffic rules are addressed are a select group to begin with: Those who are incompetent to conform to the rules, for whatever reasons are weeded out before the sanction system is applied. And that is an important point. Although traffic rules have very little moral force behind them, the system works tolerably well just because reliance is not placed solely on sanctions, but also on the judgment of competence.

I think we all understand that the maintenance of public order must be backed up by a system of sanctions ... deprivations ... *punishments*, if you please. Neither law nor morality can sustain itself, from generation to generation, without the threat of some form of punishment. But the difficult point to be comprehended here is that the system requires the *threat* of punishment, not punishment itself. An internal control system generated by our mores and received beliefs keeps most of us from stealing. For those who require external controls, it is the threat of going to gaol, not actual time spent there, that keeps them from stealing. Actual sanctions are needed—as far as the system is concerned—only to give substance to the threat, to keep it from being reduced to impotence. The problem really posed by the question of deterrence is, how much actual punishment—and what kind of actual punishment—is required in order to sustain the threat of punishment at an effective level? Or, stated inversely—now looking at the problem from the point of view of the individual rather than the system—how much non-punishment, how much besides punishment, can be allowed in treatment of the individual without inviting a breakdown of the system of sanctions?

I do not propose to solve this problem, even stated in such fashion, from this platform, this evening. But I do want to conclude with a few observations about this critical and perplexing question. First of all, I believe that in the absence of decisive empirical data, we should take a developmental approach. That is, we should view the issue historically and not assume that any particular *status quo* is ultimate and unalterable. I will confess that I am subjectively distrustful of many ponderous proponents of deterrence who answer the question, how much punishment is necessary, with the quick reply, exactly as much as we now have. And those who use the necessity of deterrence to justify the scandal of our prison system, also earn my suspicion.

Some people have argued in favour of the M'Naghten ritual on the grounds of a deterrent effect—that the mentally-ill offender should not be recognized as such and treated as such because to do so would encourage crime and perhaps even mental illness. This argument I consider beneath contempt. The M'Naghten Rules were adopted twenty-five years before the English saw fit to do away with public hangings. As Dr Eliot Slater has stated, '. . . the effect of the Rules has been to stabilize the law at the time of 1843 into being the law of the country for all time. This is an event without equal in the history of English common law.' Whether or not without equal, it is certainly rare, and certainly contrary to the modification by experience that we are told is the genius of the common law. Why I wonder, are these Rules considered still necessary to deter crime, when public hangings and capital punishment for petty offences are not? And if M'Naghten is so necessary for this purpose, why do the same people justify it by reminding us that trial courts frequently ignore it?

To sum up briefly: Punishment has a role to play in the education and re-education of the individual. The threat of some form of deprivation is of course essential in the functioning of any moral or legal system—and the threat must have substance. But these basic requirements of the criminal law have been used—I will say misused—to justify the present system which contains a preposterous predominance of senseless punitive elements. The theory of deterrence, as too frequently applied, results in degrading the individual for a purported social purpose—contrary to the democratic ethos and with no convincing evidence that the purpose is promoted. In doing so, in casting the individual offender in the role of a scapegoat, it begs the entire question of justice. And while no socio-legal system can reach a perfect incarnation of justice, none can survive in the hearts of the people which by-passes or does not engage the issue seriously.

If we were not so set on punishing the offender for the sake of punishment, if we did not justify this practice by reference to its deterrent effect, we could understand that rehabilitation lies at the spiritual heart of any vital moral system. The alternative can only be destructiveness. Even the violent corporal punishments of the past were designed to rehabilitate the wrongdoer's soul, which was held to be of much greater concern than his body. In our secular age, we have lost sight of this spiritual truth. But we still punish—without hope of reformation, without belief in saving the soul by damning the earthly body. And our entire moral system necessarily suffers thereby.

Would it really be the end of the world if all gaols were turned into hospitals, or 'Rehabilitation Centres'? The offender would then—just as the committed mental patient is today—be deprived of his dearest possession, his personal liberty. 'Punishment' enough, I should think —to satisfy our punitive urge and to induce a deterrent fear. The offender's purpose in such a Rehabilitation Centre would be to change his personality, his very style of responding to life. I would like to suggest, quite seriously, that the effort towards such a personal alteration is the greatest sanction of them all. To make this is indeed the true command of all religion and all morality. And it is the normal law-abiding person's most profound and continuous 'punishment'. The difference between the offender or the mental patient and the rest of us happily normal citizens, is that 'they' have a special problem and need special help in living up to society's expectations. A few of us have had 'special problems' in the course of our lives but were lucky enough to get the help we needed, or strong enough to get by on our own. We are entitled to congratulate ourselves on the superiority of our endowment or good fortune—but not, I think, to celebrate our triumphs by degrading our less fortunate neighbours. Is it in any way necessary for our own benefit to perpetuate the shame of our penitentiaries—where a youthful offender, having been processed through the homosexual auction block, will be taught the ways of crime and perversity by a hardened expert?

I am at the end of my remarks—for this evening, at least. I have not said enough, and perhaps I have also said too much. I know that I have oversimplified, because my purpose has been to emphasize a pervasive and half-hidden factor in a highly complex matter. The ubiquitous and irrational quality of the need to punish is an essential *key*, I believe, to an analysis of criminal law problems—but it is of course not a substitute for that analysis itself. Among the many serious issues I have *not* discussed this evening, prominent mention should be made of the current and future limits of that omnibus grouping called the behavioural sciences. How much of their promise is valid hope, how much wishful thinking? We can only find out by trying—by experimenting. Take the question of psychiatric 'treatment', for example. It seems clear that new, more sophisticated techniques will have to be developed with more pointed relevance to the problems of offenders. But where are the experimental clinics, where are the budgets to attract competent staff, where is the administrative approach that would welcome and facilitate this urgent work? Blocked, I have suggested, by the belief in punishment. Many critics of the reforming attitude in criminal law administration fear the unknown contours of a future dominated by the experimental ideas of rehabilitation. Reformers may share some of these fears, but they are motivated even more by fear of the consequences of continuing our present practices. For example, I am deeply disturbed by the whole question of the indeterminacy of the period of incarceration, which is a very serious problem today and will undoubtedly grow in importance as reforms favouring rehabilitation are instituted. The image of one class of experts administering the lives of another class of 'unfortunates' has some very disquieting aspects. I comfort myself with the thought that images of the future are frequently discomfiting, and that early surgery, for example, was probably greeted with the same disquiet. Imagine one man cutting up another! But it has worked out tolerably well.

Perhaps we can take comfort that new problems have a way of begetting new solutions and that, in this instance, solutions may be found which are consonant with our traditional concern for civil liberties. I, for one, have no intention of ushering in permanent incarceration for behaviour not seriously dangerous to society.

After all this speculation of mine, I would like to leave you at least with a restored sense of reality. Crime and criminals belong very much to their particular time and place. They grow out of very specific social settings. Moreover, any system of sanctions and any system of rehabilitation applies to and within a society, it does not substitute for one. And these systems cannot be much better than the society in which they exist. On the other hand, they should not be worse. I leave you with the question whether they in fact are.

Albert Camus

Reflections on the Guillotine

———

SHORTLY BEFORE World War I, a murderer whose crime was particularly shocking (he had killed a family of farmers, children and all) was condemned to death in Algiers. He was an agricultural worker who had slaughtered in a blood delirium, and had rendered his offence still more serious by robbing his victims. The case was widely publicized, and it was generally agreed that decapitation was altogether too mild a punishment for such a monster. I have been told that this was the opinion of my father, who was perfectly outraged by the murder of the children. One of the few things I know about him is that this was the first time in his life he wanted to attend an execution. He got up while it was still dark, for the place where the guillotine was set up was at the other end of the city, and once there, found himself among a great crowd of spectators. He never told what he saw that morning. My mother could only report that he rushed wildly into the house, refused to speak, threw himself on the bed, and suddenly began to vomit. He had just discovered the reality concealed beneath the great formulas that ordinarily serve to mask it. Instead of thinking of the murdered children, he could recall only the trembling body he had seen thrown on a board to have its head chopped off.

This ritual act must indeed be horrible if it can subvert the indignation of a simple, upright man; if the punishment which he regarded as deserved a hundred times over had no other effect than to turn his stomach. When the supreme act of justice merely nauseates the honest citizen it is supposed to protect, it seems difficult to maintain that this act is intended—as its proper functioning *should* intend it—to confer a greater degree of peace and order upon the city. Justice of this kind is obviously no less shocking than the crime itself, and the new 'official' murder, far from offering redress for the offence committed against society, adds instead a second defilement to the first. This is so apparent that no one dares speak openly of the ritual act itself. The officials and the journalists whose responsibility it is to speak of it, as if conscious of the simultaneously provocative and shameful aspects of such justice, have devised a kind of ceremonial language for dealing with it, a language reduced to the most stereotyped formulas. Over breakfast we may read, on some back page of our newspaper, that the condemned man 'paid his debt to society', that he 'expiated his crime', or that 'at five o'clock this morning justice was done'. Officials deal with this man as 'the accused', 'the patient', or merely refer to him as the C.A.M. (*Condamné à mort*). Capital punishment, one might say, is written about only in whispers. In a highly organized society such as ours we acknowledge a disease is serious by the fact that we do not dare speak of it openly. In middle-class families, it was long the rule to say that the oldest daughter had a 'weak chest', or that Papa suffered from a 'growth': to have tuberculosis or cancer was regarded as something of a disgrace. This is even more certainly true in the case of capital punishment: everyone does his best to speak of it only in euphemisms. The death penalty is to the body politic what cancer is to the individual body, with perhaps the single difference that no one has ever spoken of the necessity of cancer. Yet we do not usually hesitate to describe the death penalty as a *regrettable necessity*, justifying the fact that we are killing someone because it is 'necessary', and then not speaking of what we are doing because it is 'regrettable'.

My intention, on the contrary, is to speak of it crudely. Not out of a taste for scandal, and not, I think, because I am morbidly inclined. As a writer I have always abhorred a certain eagerness to please, and as a man I believe that the repulsive aspects of our condition, if they are inevitable, must be confronted in silence. But since silence, or the casuistry of speech, is now contributing to the support of an abuse that must be reformed, or of a misery that can be relieved, there is no other solution than to speak out, to expose the obscenity hiding beneath our cloak of words. France shares with Spain and England the splendid distinction of being among the last countries on this side of the Iron Curtain to retain the death penalty in its arsenal of repression. This primitive rite survives in our country only because an ignorant and unconcerned public opinion has no other way to express itself than by using the same ceremonial phrases with which it has been indoctrinated: when the imagination is not functioning, words lack the resonance of their meanings and a deaf public scarcely registers a man's condemnation to death. But expose the machinery, make people touch the wood and the iron, let them hear the thud of heads falling, and a suddenly aroused public imagination will repudiate both vocabulary and punishment alike.

When the Nazis staged public executions of hostages in Poland, they first gagged their prisoners with rags soaked in plaster so they could not cry out some final word of liberty or rebellion. It may seem an effrontery to compare the fate of these innocent victims with that of our condemned criminals, but apart from the fact that it is not only criminals who are guillotined in France, the method is the same: we gag our guilty with a stuffing of words, though we cannot justly affirm the legitimacy of their punishment unless we have first considered its reality. Instead of saying, as we always have, that the death penalty is first of all a necessity, and afterwards that it is not advisable to talk about it, we should first speak of what the death penalty really is, and only then decide if, *being what it is*, it is necessary.

Speaking for myself, I believe the death penalty is not only useless but profoundly harmful, and I must record this conviction here before proceeding to the subject itself. It would not be honest to allow it to appear as if I had arrived at this conclusion solely as a result of the weeks of inquiry and investigation I have just devoted to the question. But it would be equally dishonest to attribute my conviction to sentimentality alone. I stand as far as possible from that position of spineless pity in which our humanitarians take such pride in, in which values and responsibilities change places, all crimes become equal, and innocence ultimately forfeits all rights. I do not believe, contrary to many of my illustrious contemporaries, that man is by nature a social animal; the opposite, I think, is probably nearer the truth. I believe only that man cannot now live outside a society whose laws are necessary to his physical survival, which is a very different thing. I believe that responsibility must be established according to a reasonable and effective scale of values by society itself. But the law finds its final justification in the benefit it provides, or does not provide, the society of a given place and time. For years I have not been able to regard the death penalty as anything but a punishment intolerable to the imagination: a public sin of sloth which my reason utterly condemns. I was nevertheless prepared to believe that my imagination influenced my judgment. But during these weeks of research, I have found nothing which has modified my reasoning, nothing which has not, in all honesty, reinforced my original conviction. On the contrary. I have found new arguments to add to those I already possessed; today I share Arthur Koestler's conclusion without qualification: capital punishment is a disgrace to our society which its partisans cannot reasonably justify.

It is well known that the major argument of those who support capital punishment is its value as an *example*. We do not chop off heads merely to punish their former owners, but to intimidate, by a terrifying example, those who might be tempted to imitate their actions. Society does not take revenge—society merely protects itself. We brandish the newly severed head so that the next prospective murderer may therein read his future and renounce his intentions. All of which would indeed be an impressive argument if one were not obliged to remark: (1) That society itself does not believe in the value of this much advertised example. (2) That it has not been ascertained whether capital punishment ever made a single determined murderer renounce his intentions, while it is certain that its effect has been one of fascination upon thousands of criminals. (3) That the death penalty constitutes from other points of view, a loathsome example of which the consequences are unforeseeable.

First of all, then, society does not believe its own words. If it did, we would be shown the heads. Executions would be given the same promotional campaign ordinarily reserved for government loans or a new brand of *apéritif*. Yet it is well known on the contrary, that in France executions no longer take place in public—they are perpetrated in prison yards before an audience limited to specialists. It is less well known why this should be so, and since when it has been so. The last public execution took place in 1939—the guillotining of Weidmann, a murderer several times over whose exploits had brought him much notoriety. On the morning of his execution, a huge crowd rushed to Versailles; many photographers attended the ceremony and were permitted to take photographs from the time Weidmann was exposed to the crowd until the moment he was decapitated. A few hours later *Paris-Soir* published a full page of pictures of this appetizing event, and the good people of Paris were able to discover that the lightweight precision instrument used by their executioner was as different from the scaffold of their history books as a Jaguar is from an old de Dion-Bouton. The officials connected with the event and the government itself, contrary to every hope, regarded this excellent publicity in a very dim light, declaring that the press had only appealed to the most sadistic impulses of its readers. It was therefore decided that the public would no longer be permitted to witness executions, an arrangement which, shortly afterwards, made the work of the Occupation authorities considerably easier.

Logic, in this case, was not on the side of the lawmakers. Logically, in fact, they should have voted a medal to the editor of *Paris-Soir* and encouraged his staff to do still better next time. If punishment is to be exemplary, then the number of newspaper photographs must be multiplied, the instrument in question must be set up on a platform in the Place de la Concorde at two in the afternoon, the entire population of the city must be invited, and the ceremony must be televised for those unable to attend. Either do this, or stop talking about the value of an example. How can a furtive murder committed by night in a prison yard serve as an example? At best it can periodically admonish the citizenry that they will die if they commit murder; a fate which can also be assured them if they do not. For punishment to be truly exemplary, it must be terrifying. Tuaut de la Bouverie, representative of the people in 1791 and a partisan of public execution, spoke more logically when he declared to the National Assembly: 'There must be terrible spectacles in order to control the people.'

Today there is no spectacle at all—only a penalty known to everyone by hearsay and, at long intervals, the announcement of an execution couched in soothing formulas. How shall a future criminal, in the very act of committing his crime, keep in mind a threat which has been made increasingly abstract by every possible effort? And if it is really desirable that the incipient murderer preserve a vision of his ultimate fate that might counterbalance and ultimately reverse his criminal intent, then why do we not burn the reality of that fate into his sensibility by every means of language and image within our power?

Instead of vaguely evoking a debt that someone has paid to society this morning, would it not be more politic—if we are interested in setting an example—to profit by this excellent opportunity to remind each taxpayer in detail just what sort of punishment he can expect? Instead of saying, 'If you kill someone you will pay for it on the scaffold', would it not be more politic—if we are interested in setting an example—to say instead: 'If you kill someone, you will be thrown into prison for months or even years, torn between an impossible despair and a constantly renewed fear, until one morning we will sneak into your cell, having taken off our shoes in order to surprise you in your sleep, which has at last overcome you after the night's anguish. We will throw ourselves upon you, tie your wrists behind your back, and with a pair of scissors cut away your shirt collar and your hair, if it should be in the way. Because we are perfectionists we will lash your arms together with a strap so that your body will be arched to offer unhampered access to the back of your neck. Then we will carry you, one man holding you up under each arm, your feet dragging behind you, down the long corridors, until, under the night sky, one of the executioners will at last take hold of the back of your trousers and throw you down on a board, another will make sure your head is in the lunette, and a third one will drop, from a height of two metres twenty centimetres, a blade weighing sixty kilograms that will slice through your neck like a razor.'*

For the example to be even better, for the terror it breeds to become in each of us a force blind enough and powerful enough to balance, at the right moment, our irresistible desire to kill, we must go still further. Instead of bragging, with our characteristic pretentious ignorance, that we have invented a swift and humane† means of killing those condemned to death, we should publish in millions of copies, read out in every school and college, the eyewitness accounts and medical reports that describe the state of the body after execution. We should particularly recommend the printing and circulation of a recent communication made to the Academy of Medicine by Doctors Piedelièvre and Fournier. These courageous physicians, having examined, in the interests of science, the bodies of the condemned after execution, have considered it their duty to sum up their terrible observations thus: 'If we may be permitted to present our opinion on this subject, such spectacles are horribly painful. The blood rushes from the vessels according to the rhythm of the severed carotids, then coagulates. The muscles contract and their fibrillation is stupefying. The intestine undulates and the heart produces a series of irregular, incomplete, and convulsive movements. The mouth tightens, at certain moments, into a dreadful grimace. It is true that the eyes of a decapitated head are immobile, the pupils dilated; fortunately, they cannot see, and if they exhibit no signs of disturbance, none of the characteristic opalescence

---

* A description of the actual procedure in French prisons. Cf. the movie *We are All Murderers*.—Translator.

† According to the optimistic Dr Guillotine, the condemned man would feel nothing at all—at most a 'slight coolness at the back of his neck'.

of a cadaver, they at least have no capacity for movement: their transparency is that of life, but their fixity is mortal. All this may last minutes, even hours, in a healthy subject: death is not immediate. . . . Thus each vital element survives decapitation to some extent. There remains, for the physician, the impression of a hideous experiment, a murderous vivisection followed by a premature burial.'*

I doubt that many readers can read this dreadful report without blanching. We can, in fact, count on its power as an example, its capacity to intimidate. What is to prevent us from adding to it the reports of witnesses that further authenticate the observations of medical men? If the severed head of Charlotte Corday is supposed to have blushed under the executioner's hand, we shall hardly be surprised after examining the accounts of more recent observers. Here is how one assistant executioner, hardly likely to cultivate the sentimental or romantic aspects of his trade, describes what he has been obliged to see: 'There was one wild man, suffering from a real fit of delirium tremens, whom we had to throw under the knife. The head died right away. But the body literally sprang into the basket, where it lay struggling against the cords that bound it. Twenty minutes later, in the cemetery, it was still shuddering.'† The present chaplain of La Santé, the Reverend Father Devoyod, who does not appear to be opposed to the death penalty, tells, nevertheless, the following remarkable story in his book Les Délinquants‡ (which renews the famous episode of a man named Languille whose severed head answered to its name§): 'The morning of the execution, the condemned man was in a very bad humour, and refused to receive the succour of religion. Knowing the depths of his heart and his true regard for his wife, whose sentiments were genuinely Christian, we said to him, "For the love of this woman, commune with yourself a moment before you die." And the condemned man consented, communing at length before the crucifix, and afterwards scarcely seemed to notice our presence. When he was executed, we were not far from him; his head fell on to the trough in front of the guillotine, and the body was immediately put into the basket. But contrary to custom, the basket was closed before the head could be put in. The assistant carrying the head had to wait a moment until the basket was opened again. And during that brief

* *Justice sans bourreau*, No. 2, June, 1956.
† Published by Roger Grenier, in *Les Monstres*, Gallimard.
‡ Editions Matot-Braine, Reims.
§ In 1905, in Loiret.

space of time, we were able to see the two eyes of the condemned man fixed on us in a gaze of supplication, as if to ask our forgiveness. Instinctively we traced a sign of the cross in order to bless the head, and then the eyelids blinked, the look in the eyes became gentle again, and then the gaze, which had remained expressive, was gone. . . .' The reader will accept or reject the explanation proposed by the priest according to his faith. But at least those eyes that 'remained expressive' need no interpretation.

I could cite many other eyewitness accounts as hallucinatory as these. But as for myself, I hardly need or know how to go further. After all, I make no claim that the death penalty is exemplary: indeed, this torture affects me only as what it is—a crude surgery practiced in conditions that deprive it of any edifying character whatsoever. Society, on the other hand, and the State (which has seen other tortures) can easily bear such details; and since they favour preaching examples, they might as well make them universally known so that a perpetually terrorized populace can become Franciscan to a man. For who is it we think we are frightening by this example constantly screened from view; by the threat of a punishment described as painless, expedient, and on the whole less disagreeable than cancer; by a torture crowned with all the flowers of rhetoric? Certainly not those who pass for honest (and some are) because they are asleep at such an hour, to whom the *great example* has not been revealed, and who drink their morning coffee at the hour of the premature burial, informed of the operation of justice, if they happen to read the newspapers, by a mealy-mouthed bulletin that dissolves like sugar in their memory. Yet these same peaceful creatures furnish society with the largest percentage of its homicides. Many of these honest men are criminals without knowing it. According to one magistrate, the overwhelming majority of the murderers he had tried did not know, when they shaved themselves that morning, that they were going to kill someone that night. For the sake of example and security alike, we should brandish rather than disguise the agonized face of our victim before the eyes of every man as he shaves himself in the morning.

This is not done. The State conceals the circumstances and even the existence of its executions, keeps silent about such reports and such accounts. It does not concern itself with the exemplary value of punishment save by tradition, nor does it trouble to consider the present meaning of its act. The criminal is killed because he has been killed for centuries, and furthermore he is killed according to a procedure established at the end of the eighteenth century. The same arguments that have served as legal tender for centuries are perpetuated as a matter of routine, contradicted only by those measures which the evolution of public sensibility renders inevitable. The law is applied without consideration of its significance, and our condemned criminals die by rote in the name of a theory in which their executioners no longer believe. If they believed in it, it would be known, and above all it would be seen. But such publicity, beyond the fact that it arouses sadistic instincts of which the repercussions are incalculable and which end, one day or another, by satisfying themselves with yet another murder, also risks provoking the disgust and revolt of public opinion itself. It would become more difficult to execute by assembly line, as we do in France at this moment, if such executions were translated into the bold images of popular fantasy. The very man who enjoys his morning coffee while reading that justice has been done would certainly choke on it at the slightest of such details. And the texts I have quoted may go far towards supporting the position of certain professors of criminal law who, in their evident incapacity to justify the anachronism of capital punishment, console themselves by declaring with the sociologist Tarde that it is better to kill without causing suffering than it is to cause suffering without killing. Which is why we can only approve the position of Gambetta, who as an adversary of the death penalty nevertheless voted against a bill proposing the exclusion of the public from executions, asserting: 'If you do away with the horror of the spectacle, if you perform executions in the prison yards, you will also do away with the public reaction of revolt which has shown itself in recent years, and thereby establish the death penalty all the more firmly.'

We must either kill publicly, or admit we do not feel authorized to kill. If society justifies the death penalty as a necessary example, then it must justify itself by providing the publicity necessary to *make* an example. Society must display the executioner's hands on each occasion, and require the most squeamish citizens to look at them, as well as those who, directly or remotely, have supported the work of those hands from the first. Otherwise society confesses that it kills without consciousness of what it does or what it says; or that it kills yet knows, too, that far from intimidating belief, these disgusting ceremonies can only awaken a sense of criminality, and thoroughly undermine public morale. Who could be more explicit than a judge at the end of his career?—Counsellor Falco's courageous confession deserves careful attention: 'On only one occasion during my years on the bench I recommended a verdict in favour of execution of the accused and against the commutation of his punishment; I decided that despite my position I would attend the ceremony—with complete objectivity, of course. The man in question was not at all sympathetic, not even interesting: he had brutally murdered his little daughter and then thrown her body down a well. Nevertheless, after his execution, for weeks, and even for months, my nights were haunted by this memory. . . . I served in the war like everyone else, and I saw an innocent generation killed before my eyes; yet confronted with the memory of that dreadful spectacle, I still can say I never once experienced the same kind of bad conscience I felt as I watched the kind of administrative assassination known as capital punishment.'*

But after all, why should society believe in the value of such an example, since it does not affect the incidence of crime, and since its effects, if they exist at all, are invisible? For capital punishment cannot intimidate a man who does not know he is going to commit murder, who decides on it in an instant and prepares his action in the heat of passion or an *idée fixe*; cannot intimidate a man who starts off for an assignation carrying with him a weapon to frighten his faithless mistress or his rival and then, at the last minute, makes use of it, although without any such intention—or without thinking he had any such intention. In short, capital punishment cannot intimidate the man who throws himself upon crime as one throws oneself into misery. Which is to say that it is ineffective in the majority of cases. It is only fair to point out that in France, at least, capital punishment is rarely applied in cases of 'crimes of passion'. Yet even 'rarely' is enough to make one shudder.

But does the death penalty act as a deterrent, at least, upon that 'race' of criminals it claims to affect—those who live by crime? Nothing is less certain. Arthur Koestler reminds us that in the period when pickpockets were punished by hanging in England, other thieves exercised their talents in the crowds surrounding the scaffold where their fellow was being hanged. Statistics compiled during the past fifty years in England show that out of 250 men hanged, 170 had previously attended one or even two public executions. Even as late as 1886, out of 167 men condemned to death in the Bristol prison, 164 had attended

* The magazine *Réalités*, No. 105, October, 1954.

at least one execution. Figures corresponding to these cannot be ascertained in France because of the secrecy which surrounds executions here. But those we have remind us that in that crowd my father stood among to watch a public execution, there must have been a considerable number of future criminals who did not run home and vomit. The power of intimidation operates only on those timid souls who are not dedicated to crime, and gives way before precisely those incorrigibles whom it is concerned to correct.

Yet it cannot be denied that men fear death. The deprivation of life is certainly the supreme punishment, and arouses in each of us his decisive fear. The fear of death, rising from the obscurest depths, ravages the self; the instinct for life, when threatened, panics and flounders among the most dreadful agonies. The legislator may with some justice assume that his law affects one of the most mysterious and powerful motives of human nature. But the law is always simpler than nature. When, in its attempt to establish its sovereignty, the law ventures into the blind realms of being, it runs a terrible risk of being impotent to control the very complexity it attempts to set in order.

Indeed if the fear of death is one kind of evidence, the fact that this same fear, no matter how great it may be, has never sufficed to discourage human passions, is still another. Bacon was right: no passion is so weak that it cannot confront and master the fear of death. Vengeance, love, honour, grief, even fear of something else—all are victorious over the fear of death in one circumstance or another. And shall cupidity, hatred, or jealousy not accomplish all that love or patriotism or the human passion for liberty are able to achieve? For centuries the death penalty, often accompanied by various barbarous refinements, has tried to restrain the incidence of crime; yet crime persists. Why? Because the instincts which confront and war against each other within man are not, as the law would have them, constant forces in a state of equilibrium. They are variable forces that die and triumph one after another, whose successive imbalances nourish the life of the mind in the same way that electrical oscillations, occurring with sufficient frequency, establish a current. Consider the series of oscillations passing from desire to satiation, from decision to renunciation, which all of us experience in a single day and then multiply these variations to infinity and we may form an idea of the extent of our psychological proliferation. These imbalances, these disequilibriums are generally too fugitive to permit any one force to gain control of the entire self.

Yet it sometimes happens that a single element of the soul's resources can break free and occupy the entire field of consciousness; no instinct, even that of self-preservation, can then oppose the tyranny of this irresistible force. In order that the death penalty be really intimidating, human nature itself would have to be different from what it is, would have to be as stable and serene as the law itself. It would no longer be life, but still-life.

But life is not still-life, is not stable, not serene. Which is why, surprising as it may seem to those who have not observed or experienced in themselves the complexity of the human situation, the murderer for the most part considers himself innocent when he commits his crime. Before being judged, the criminal acquits *himself.* He feels he is—if not entirely within his rights—at least extenuated by circumstances. He does not reflect; he does not foresee; or if he does, it is only to foresee that he will be pardoned—altogether or in part. Why should he fear what he regards as highly unlikely? He will fear death after being judged, not before his crime. Therefore, in order to intimidate effectively, the law must permit the murderer *no escape*, must be implacable *in advance*, must admit no possibility of an extenuating circumstance. Who among us would dare to demand this?

And even if we did, there is still another paradox of human nature to consider. The instinct of self-preservation, if it is a fundamental one, is no more so than that other instinct less often discussed by academic psychologists: the death instinct which at certain times demands the destruction of the self or of others. It is probable that the desire to kill frequently coincides with the desire to die or to kill oneself.* The instinct of self-preservation thus finds itself confronted in variable proportions by the instinct of self-destruction. The latter is the only means by which we can altogether explain the numerous perversions which—from alcoholism to drug addiction—lead the self to a destruction of which it cannot long remain ignorant. Man desires to live, but it is vain to hope that this desire can control all his actions. He desires to be annihilated as well—he wills the irreparable, death for its own sake. It so happens that the criminal desires not only his crime, but the misery that accompanies it, especially if this misery is unbounded and inordinate. When this perverse desire grows until it gains control of the self, the prospect of being put to death is not only impotent to

---

* One can read week after week in our press about criminals who wavered between killing others and killing themselves.

restrain the criminal, but probably deepens even further the abyss into which he plunges: there are situations in which one kills in order to die.

Such singularities suffice to explain how a punishment that seems calculated to intimidate the normal mind has in reality nothing whatever to do with ordinary psychological processes. All statistics show, without exception—in the countries which have abolished it, as well as in others—that there is no connection between the death penalty and the incidence of crime.* This incidence, in fact, neither rises nor falls. The guillotine exists; crime exists; between them there is no other apparent connection than that of the law. All we are entitled to conclude from the figures provided by statisticians is this: for centuries crimes other than murder were punished by death, and this supreme punishment, deliberately repeated, caused none of these crimes to disappear. For several centuries these crimes have no longer been punished by death, yet they have not increased in number, and the incidence of some has even diminished. Similarly, murder has been punished by capital punishment for centuries, yet the race of Cain has not disappeared from the earth. In the thirty-three nations that have abolished the death penalty or no longer impose it, the number of murders has not increased. How can we therefore conclude that the death penalty is really intimidating?

Its partisans can deny neither these facts nor these figures. Their only and ultimate reply is significant; it explains the paradoxical attitude of a society which so carefully conceals the executions it claims as exemplary: 'It is true that nothing proves that the death penalty is exemplary; it is even certain that thousands of murderers have not been intimidated by it. But we cannot know who *has* been intimidated by such a penalty; consequently, nothing proves that it does not serve as an example.' Thus the greatest of all punishments, the penalty that involves the ultimate forfeiture of the condemned man and concedes the supreme privilege to society, rests on nothing more than an unverifiable possibility. Death, however, does not admit of degrees of likelihood; it fixes all things—blame and body alike—in its definitive rigidity. Yet it is administered in our country in the name of a possibility, a calculation of likelihood. And even if this possibility

* *Vide* the report of the English Select Committee of 1930 and of the Royal commission (1949–53) which has continued this study recently: 'All the figures that we have examined confirm our statement that the abolition of the death penalty has provoked no increase in the number of crimes committed.'

should be reasonable, would it not have to be certitude itself to authorize certain and absolute extinction? Yet the man we condemn to die is
cut in two not so much for the crime he has committed as for the sake
of all the crimes that might have happened, but which *have not* happened—which could occur, but somehow *will not* occur. Hence, the
greatest possible uncertainty appears to authorize the most implacable
certitude of all.

I am not the only one to be astonished by this dangerous contradiction. The State itself disapproves, and its bad conscience explains in
turn all the contradictions of the official attitude. This attitude sup-
presses the publicity of executions because it cannot affirm, faced with
the facts, that they have ever served to intimidate criminals. It cannot
escape the dilemma which Beccaria had already pointed to when he
wrote: 'If it is important to show the people frequent proof of power,
then executions must be frequent; but in that case crimes must be
frequent too, which will prove that the death penalty is far from
making the desired impression; thus this penalty is at the same time
useless and necessary.' What can the State do about a punishment
both useless and necessary, except conceal it without abolishing it?
And so it will be preserved in obscurity, continued with perplexity and
hesitation, in the blind hope that one man at least, one day at least, will
be intimidated by consideration of the punishment that lies ahead, and
will abandon his murderous intent, thereby justifying, though no one
will ever know it, a law which has no support in reason or experience.
To persist in its claim that the guillotine is exemplary, the State must
raise the incidence of real murders in order to avoid an unknown
murder of which it cannot be sure (will never be sure) that it would
ever have been committed at all. Is it not a strange law, that recognizes
the murder it commits, and remains forever ignorant of the crime it
prevents?

But what will remain of this power of example, if it is proved
that capital punishment has another power, this one quite real,
which degrades men to the worst excesses of shame, madness, and
murder?

The exemplary effects of these ceremonies can readily be traced in
public opinion—the manifestations of sadism they reveal, the terrible
notoriety they arouse in the case of certain criminals. Instead of an
operatic nobility of attitude at the foot of the scaffold, we find nothing

but disgust, contempt, or perverse pleasure. The effects are well known. Propriety too has had its share in effecting the removal of the scaffold from the square in front of the city hall to the city walls, and from the walls to the prison yard. We are less well informed about the sentiments of those whose business it is to attend this kind of spectacle. Let us listen to the words of the director of an English prison, who speaks of 'an acute sense of personal shame', of a prison chaplain who speaks of 'horror, shame, and humiliation';* and let us consider especially the feelings of the man who kills because it is his trade—I mean the executioner. What shall we think of these civil servants of ours, who refer to the guillotine as 'the bike', the condemned man as 'the client' or 'luggage', except, in the words of the priest Bela Just, who served as prison chaplain for more than thirty executions, that 'The idiom of the executors of justice yields nothing in point of cynicism or vulgarity to that of its violators.'† Here, furthermore, are the reflections of one of our assistant executioners on his official travels across the country: 'When it came time for our trips to the provinces, the real fun began: taxis, good restaurants, everything we wanted!'‡ The same man, boasting of the executioner's skill in releasing the knife, says: 'One can *indulge oneself in the luxury* of pulling the client's hair.' The depravity expressed here has other, more profound aspects. The clothing of the condemned man belongs, by custom, to the executioner. We learn that old father Deibler hung all the clothing he had collected in a shack and that he used *to go and look at his collection from time to time*. There are more serious examples. Here is our assistant executioner again: 'The new executioner has guillotine fever. Sometimes he stays at home for days at a time, sitting in a chair, ready to go, his hat on his head, his overcoat on, waiting for a summons from the public prosecutor.'§

And this is the man of whom Joseph de Maistre said that his very existence was accorded by a special decree of divine power and that without him, 'order gives way to chaos, thrones collapse, and society disappears.' This is the man by means of whom society gets rid of its culprit, and once the executioner signs the prison release, he is permitted to walk out, a free man. The honourable and solemn example, as conceived by our legislation, has had one certain effect, at least—it

* Report of the Select Committee, 1930.
† Bela Just, *La Potence et la croix*, Fasquelle.
‡ Roger Grenier, *op. cit.*
§ *Ibid.*

perverts or destroys the human quality and reason of all who participate in it directly. It will be objected that we are discussing only a few exceptional creatures who make a living out of such degradation. There might be fewer protests if it were known that there are hundreds of men who offer their services as executioner *without pay*. Men of my generation, who have survived the history of our times, will not be surprised to learn this. They know that behind the most familiar, the most peaceful face lies the instinct to torture and to kill. The punishment which claims to intimidate an unknown murderer unquestionably provides a number of known monsters with their vocation as killers. Since we are not above justifying our cruellest laws by considerations of probability, let us not hesitate to admit that out of these hundreds of men whose services are refused, one, at least, has satisfied in some other way the bloody impulses which the guillotine awakened within him.

If we are to maintain the death penalty, let us at least be spared the hypocrisy of justification by example. Let us call by its right name the penalty about which all publicity is suppressed, this intimidation which does not operate upon honest men to the degree that they are honest, which fascinates those who have ceased to be honest, and which degrades and disorders those who lend their hands to it. It is a punishment, certainly, a dreadful physical and moral torture, but one offering no certain example save that of demoralization. It forbids, but it prevents nothing—when it does not in fact arouse the will to murder itself. It is *as if it were not*, except for the man who suffers it—in his soul for months or years, and in his body during the desperate and violent moment when he is cut in two without being altogether deprived of life. Let us call it by a name which, lacking all patents of nobility, at least provides that of truth—let us recognize it for what it ultimately is: a revenge.

Punishment, penalizing rather than preventing, is a form of revenge; society's semi-arithmetical answer to violation of its primordial law. This answer is as old as man himself, and usually goes by the name *retaliation*. He who hurts me must be hurt; who blinds me in one eye must himself lose an eye; who takes a life must die. It is a feeling, and a particularly violent one, which is involved here, not a principle. Retaliation belongs to the order of nature, of instinct, not to the order of law. The law by definition cannot abide by the same rules as nature. If

murder is part of man's nature, the law is not made to imitate or reproduce such nature. We have all known the impulse to retaliate, often
to our shame, and we know its power: the power of the primaeval
forests. In this regard, we live—as Frenchmen who grow justifiably
indignant at seeing the oil king of Saudi Arabia preach international
democracy while entrusting his butcher with the task of cutting off a
thief's hand—in a kind of Middle Ages ourselves, without even the
consolations of faith. Yet if we still define our justice according to the
calculations of a crude arithmetic,* can we at least affirm that this
arithmetic is correct, and that even such elementary justice, limited as
it is to a form of legal revenge, is *safeguarded* by the death pentalty?
The answer must again be: No.

We scarcely need to point out how inapplicable the law of retaliation has become in our society: it is as excessive to punish the pyro-
maniac by setting his house on fire as it is insufficient to punish the
thief by deducting from his bank account a sum equivalent to the
amount he has stolen. Let us admit instead that it is just and even
necessary to compensate the murder of the victim by the death of the
murderer. But capital punishment is not merely death. It is as different,
in its essence, from the suppression of life as a concentration camp from
a prison. It is undeniably a murder which arithmetically cancels out
the murder already committed; but it also adds a regularization of
death, a public premeditation of which its future victims are informed,
an *organization* which in itself is a source of moral suffering more
terrible than death. There is thus no real compensation, no equivalence. Many systems of law regard a premeditated crime as more serious than a crime of pure violence. But what is capital punishment if
not the most premeditated of murders, to which no criminal act, no
matter how calaculted, can be compared? If there were to be a real
equivalence, the death penalty would have to be pronounced upon a
criminal who had forewarned his victim of the very moment he would
put him to a horrible death, and who, from that time on, had kept him

---

* Several years ago I urged the reprieve of six Tunisians who had been condemned to
death for the murder of three French policemen in a riot: the circumstances during which
the killing had occurred made responsibility difficult to determine. A note from the office
of the President of the Republic informed me that my petition was being considered by
the appropriate authorities. Unfortunately, by the time this note was in the mail I had
already read that the sentence had been carried out two weeks before. Three of the
condemned men had been put to death, the other three reprieved. The reasons for
reprieving the latter rather than those who were executed had not been decisive. I conclude
that because there were three victims there had to be three death penalties.

confined at his own discretion for a period of months. It is not in private life that one meets such monsters.

Here again, when our official jurists speak of death without suffering, they do not know what they are talking about, and furthermore they betray a remarkable lack of imagination. The devastating, degrading fear imposed on the condemned man for months or even years* is a punishment more terrible than death itself, and one that has not been imposed on his victim. A murdered man is generally rushed to his death, even at the height of his terror of the mortal violence being done to him, without knowing what is happening: the period of his horror is only that of his life itself, and his hope of escaping whatever madness has pounced upon him probably never deserts him. For the man condemned to death, on the other hand, the horror of his situation is served up to him at every moment for months on end. Torture by hope alternates only with the pangs of animal despair. His lawyer and his confessor, out of simple humanity, and his guards, to keep him docile, unanimously assure him that he will be reprieved. He believes them with all his heart, yet he cannot believe them at all. He hopes by day, despairs by night.† And as the weeks pass, his hope and despair increase proportionately, until they become equally insupportable. According to all accounts, the colour of his skin changes: fear acts like an acid. 'It's nothing to know you're going to die,' one such man in the Fresnes prison said, 'but not to know if you're going to live is the real torture.' At the moment of his execution Cartouche remarked, 'Bah! a nasty quarter of an hour and it's all over.' But it takes months, not minutes. The condemned man knows long in advance that he is going to be killed and that all that can save him is a reprieve which operates, so far as he is concerned, like the will of heaven itself. In any case he cannot intervene, plead for himself: he is no longer a man, but a thing waiting to be manipulated by the executioners. He is kept in a state of absolute necessity, the condition of inert matter, yet within him is the consciousness that is his principal enemy.

---

* Roemen, condemned to death at the time of the Liberation, remained in chains 700 days before being executed: a scandal. Those condemned by common law wait, as a general rule, three to six months until the morning of their death. Yet if one wishes to preserve their chances of reprieve, it is not advisable to shorten the delay. I can bear witness, moreover, that the examination leading to a recommendation of mercy is conducted in France with a gravity that does not exclude an evident willingness to reprieve to the full extent that law and public opinion will allow.

† Since there are no executions on Sunday, Saturday night is always a good night in death row.

When the officials whose trade is to kill such a man refer to him as 'luggage', they know what they are saying: to be unable to react to the hand that moves you, holds you, or lets you drop—is that not the condition of some package, some *thing*, or better still, some trapped animal? Yet an animal in a trap can starve itself to death; the man condemned to death cannot. He is provided with a special diet (at Fresnes, diet No. 4 with *extras* of milk, wine, sugar, preserves, and butter); he is encouraged to eat well—if necessary he is forced to eat. The animal must be in good condition for the kill. The thing—the animal—has a right only to those corrupted privileges known as caprices. 'You'd be surprised how sensitive they are!' declared one sergeant at Fresnes without a trace of irony. Sensitive? Unquestionably—how else recover the freedom and dignity of will that man cannot live without? Sensitive or not, from the moment the death sentence is pronounced, the condemned man becomes part of an imperturbable mechanism. He spends several weeks within the cogs and gears of a machine that controls his every gesture, ultimately delivering him to the hands that will lay him out on the last device of all. The luggage is no longer subjected to the operations of chance, the hazards that dominate the existence of a living being, but to mechanical laws that permit him to foresee in the minutest perspective the day of his decapitation.

His condition as an object comes to an end on this day. During the three-quarters of an hour that separates him from his extinction, the certainty of his futile death overcomes everything: the fettered, utterly submissive creature experiences a hell that makes a mockery of the one with which he is threatened. For all their hemlock, the Greeks were humane: they provided their criminals a relative liberty at least, the possibility of postponing or advancing the hour of their own death; and of choosing between suicide and execution. For reasons of security, we carry out our justice by ourselves. Yet there could not be real justice in such cases unless the murderer, having made known his decision months in advance, had entered his victim's house, tied him up securely, informed him he would be put to death in the next hour, and then used this hour to set up the apparatus by which his victim would be dispatched. What criminal has ever reduced his victim to a condition so desperate, so hopeless, and so powerless?

This doubtless explains the strange quality of submission that is so often observed in the condemned man at the moment of his execution.

After all, those who have nothing to lose by it might make a last desperate effort, preferring to die by a stray bullet or to be guillotined in a violent struggle that would numb every sense: it would be a kind of freedom in dying. And yet, with very few exceptions, the condemned man walks quite docilely to his death in dismal impassivity. Which must be what our journalists mean when they tell us the condemned man died courageously. What they *really* mean, of course, is that the condemned man made no trouble, no attempt to abandon his status as luggage, and that we are all grateful to him for his good behaviour. In so disgraceful a business the accused has shown a commendable sense of propriety in allowing the disgrace to be disposed of as soon as possible. But the compliments and character references are just another part of the general mystification that surrounds the death penalty. For the condemned man often behaves 'properly' only to the degree that he is afraid, and deserves the eulogies of our press only if his fear or his despair are sufficiently great to sterilize him altogether. Let me not be misunderstood: some men—political prisoners or not —die heroically, and we must speak of them with the admiration and respect they deserve. But the majority of those condemned to death know no other silence than that of fear, no other impassivity than that of horror, and it seems to me that the silence of fear and horror deserves still more respect than the other. When the priest Bela Just offered to write to the relatives of one young criminal only a few minutes before he was to be hung, and received these words in answer: 'I don't have the courage, not even for that,' one wonders how a priest, at such a confession of weakness, could keep from falling on his knees before what is most miserable and most sacred in man. As for those who do not talk, those who show us what they have gone through only by the puddle they leave in the place they are dragged from, who would dare say they died as cowards? And by what name shall we call those who have brought these men to their 'cowardice'? After all, each murderer, at the moment of his crime, runs the risk of the most terrible death, while those who execute him risk nothing, except perhaps a promotion.

No—what the condemned man experiences at this moment is beyond all morality. Neither virtue, nor courage, nor intelligence, not even innocence has a share in his condition at that moment. Society is reduced at one blow to that condition of primitive terror in which nothing can be judged and all equity, all dignity, have vanished. 'The sense of his own innocence does not immunize the executed man against the cruelty of his death. . . . I have seen terrible criminals die courageously, and innocent men walk to the knife trembling in every limb.'* When the same witness adds that, in his experience, such failures of nerve are more frequent among intellectuals, he does not mean that this category of men has less courage than any other, but that they have more imagination. Confronted with an inescapable death, a man, no matter what his convictions, is devastated throughout his entire system.† The sense of powerlessness and solitude of the fettered prisoner, confronted by the public coalition which has *willed* his death is in itself an unimaginable punishment. In this regard, too, it would be far better if the execution were held in public: the actor that is in every man could then come to the aid of the stricken animal, could help him keep up a front, even in his own eyes. But the darkness and the secrecy of the ceremony are without appeal: in such a disaster, courage, the soul's consistency, faith itself—all are merely matters of chance. As a general rule, the man is destroyed by waiting for his execution long before he is actually killed. Two deaths are imposed, and the first is worst than the second, though the culprit has killed but once. Compared to this torture, the law of retaliation seems like a civilized principle. For that law, at least, has never claimed that a man must be blinded in both eyes to pay for having blinded his brother in one.

This fundamental injustice, moreover, has its repercussions among the relatives of the man who is executed. The victim has his relatives too, whose sufferings are generally infinite, and who, for the most part, wish to be revenged. They *are* revenged, in the manner I have described, but the relatives of the executed man thereby experience a misery that punishes them beyond the bounds of all justice. A mother's or a father's expectation during the endless months, the prison parlour, the awkward conversations which fill the brief minutes they are allowed to spend with the condemned man, the images of the execution itself —all are tortures that have not been inflicted on the relatives of the victim. Whatever the feelings of the latter, they cannot require their revenge to exceed the crime to such an extent, and torment those who violently share their own grief. 'I have been reprieved, Father,' writes one man condemned to death, 'and I still don't really believe in my

* Bela Just, *op. cit.*
† A great surgeon, himself a Catholic, told me that he had learned never to tell his patients, even when they were believers, that they were suffering from an incurable cancer. The shock, he believed, was too dangerous, and even risked jeopardizing their faith.

good luck. The reprieve was signed 30th April, and they told me Wednesday, on my way back from the parlour. I sent them to tell Papa and Mama, who had not yet left the prison. You can imagine their happiness.'* We can imagine their happiness only to the degree that we can imagine their unceasing misery until the moment of the reprieve, and the utter despair of those who receive another kind of news, the kind that unjustly punishes their innocence and their misery.

As for the law of retaliation, it must be admitted that even in its primitive form it is legitimate only between two individuals of whom one is absolutely innocent and the other absolutely guilty. Certainly the victim is innocent. But can society, which is supposed to represent the victim, claim a comparable innocence? Is it not responsible, at least in part, for the crime which it represses with such severity? This theme has been frequently developed elsewhere, and I need not continue a line of argument which the most varied minds have elaborated since the eighteenth century. Its principal features can be summed up, in any case, by observing that every society has the criminals it deserves. As far as France is concerned, however, it is impossible not to draw attention to circumstances which might make our legislators more moderate. Answering a questionnaire on capital punishment in *Figaro* in 1952, a colonel declared that the establishment of perpetual forced labour as the supreme penalty amounted to the same thing as the establishment of schools of crime. This superior officer seems to be unaware—and I am happy for his sake—that we already have our schools of crime, which differ in one particular from our reformatories —the fact that one can leave them at any hour of the day or night: they are our bars and our slums, the glories of our republic. And on this point, at least, it is impossible to express oneself with moderation.

According to statistics, there are 64,000 overcrowded living accommodations (three to five persons to a room) in the city of Paris alone. Now of course the man who murders children is a particularly unspeakable creature, scarcely worth working up much pity over. It is probable, too (I say probable), that none of my readers, placed in the same promiscuous living conditions, would go so far as to murder children: there is no question of reducing the guilt of such monsters.

---

* Devoyod, *op cit.* It is impossible to read objectively the petitions for reprieve presented by fathers and mothers who evidently cannot comprehend the punishment that has suddenly fallen upon them.

But would such monsters, in decent living conditions, have an occasion to go so far? The least one can say is that they are not the only guilty parties: it is difficult to account for the fact that the right to punish these criminals is given to the very men who prefer to subsidize sugar beets rather than new construction.*

But alcohol makes this scandal all the more striking. It is well known that the French nation has been systematically intoxicated by its parliamentary majority for generally disgraceful reasons. Yet even with such knowledge in our grasp, the determined responsibility of alcohol for crimes of blood is still astounding. One lawyer (Guillon) has estimated that it is a factor in 60 per cent of all such cases. Dr Lagriffe sets the rate somewhere between 41.7 and 72 per cent. An investigation conducted in 1951 at the distribution centre of the Fresnes prison, among inmates guilty of breaches of common law, revealed that 29 per cent were chronic alcoholics and 24 per cent had alcoholic backgrounds. Finally, 95 per cent of all murderers of children have been alcoholics. These are all fine figures, but there is one we must consider which is still finer: that of the *apéritif* manufacturer who declared a profit of 410,000,000 francs in 1953. A comparison of these figures authorizes us to inform the stockholders of this company, and the assemblymen who voted for sugar beets rather than for buildings, that they have certainly killed more children than they suspect. As an adversary of capital punishment I am far from demanding the death penalty for these individuals. But to begin with, it seems to me an indispensable and urgent duty to conduct them under military escort to the next execution of the murderer of a child, and at the conclusion of the ceremony to present them with a table of statistics which will include the figures I have been discussing.

When the state sows alcohol, it cannot be surprised if it reaps crime.† And it is *not* surprised, after all—it merely restricts itself to chopping off the same heads for which it poured out so much alcohol. It imperturbably executes its justice and sets itself up as a creditor: its good conscience is not affected. Hence we have one representative of the interests of alcohol indignantly answering the *Figaro* questionnaire: 'I

---

* France ranks ahead of all other nations in consumption of alcohol, fifteenth in construction.

† At the end of the last century, the partisans of capital punishment made much of an increase in the incidence of crime after 1880, which seemed to parallel a diminution in the application of the death penalty. It was in 1880, however, that the law permitting retail liquor establishments to set up shop without previous authorization was promulgated. Such facts are not difficult to interpret!

know what the most outspoken abolitionist of capital punishment would do if he were suddenly to discover assassins on the point of killing his mother, his father, his children, or his best friend . . . *Alors!*' This '*alors!*' seems a little drunk already. Naturally the most outspoken abolitionist of capital punishment would fire, and with every justification, at the assassins, and without affecting in the slightest his reasons for outspokenly urging the abolition of capital punishment. But if his ideas led to consequences of any value, and if the same assassins smelled a little too much of alcohol, would he not subsequently turn his attentions to those who make it their business to intoxicate our future criminals? It is even a little surprising that the parents of victims of alcoholic crimes have never had the notion of requesting a few elucidations from the floor of the Assembly itself. But the contrary is the rule, and the State, armed with the confidence of all, with the full support of public opinion, continues to punish murderers, even and especially when they are alcoholics, somewhat the way a pimp punishes the hard-working creatures who provide his livelihood. But the pimp doesn't preach about his business. The State does. Its jurisprudence, if it admits that drunkenness occasionally constitutes an extenuating circumstance, is unaware of chronic alcoholism. Drunkenness, however, accompanies only crimes of violence, which are not punishable by death, whereas the chronic alcoholic is also capable of premeditated crimes, which gain him the death penalty. The State thus maintains the right to punish in the very case in which its own responsibility is profoundly involved.

Does this come down to saying that every alcoholic must be declared non-responsible by a State which will strike its breast in horror until the entire populace drinks nothing but fruit juice? Certainly not. No more than it comes down to saying that the facts of heredity eliminate responsibility and guilt. A criminal's real responsibility cannot be determined exactly. All calculation is powerless to take into account the total number of our ancestors, alcoholic or not. At the other end of time, such a number would be 10^{22} times greater than the number of inhabitants of the earth at present. The total of diseased or morbid tendencies which could be transmitted is thus incalculable. We enter the world burdened with the weight of an infinite necessity, and according to logic must agree on a situation of a general non-responsibility. Logically, neither punishment nor reward can be distributed accurately, and therefore all society becomes impossible. Yet the instinct of self-preservation, in societies and individuals alike, requires, on the contrary, the postulate of individual responsibility; a responsibility that must be accepted, without daydreaming of an absolute indulgence which would coincide with the death and disappearance of any society whatsoever. But the same line of reasoning that compels us to abandon a general non-responsibility must also lead us to conclude that there is never, on the other hand, a situation of total responsibility, and consequently no such thing as absolute punishment or absolute reward. No one can be rewarded absolutely, not even by the Nobel prize. But no one must be punished absolutely if he is found guilty, and with all the more reason if there is a chance he might be innocent. The death penalty, which neither serves as an example nor satisfies the conditions of retaliative justice, usurps in addition an exorbitant privilege by claiming the right to punish a necessarily relative guilt by an absolute and irreparable penalty.

If, in fact, the death penalty serves as a questionable example of our gimcrack justice, one must agree with its supporters that it is eliminative: capital punishment definitely eliminates the condemned man. This fact alone, actually, ought to exclude, especially for its partisans, the discussion of all the other dangerous arguments which, as we have seen, can be ceaselessly contested. It would be more honest to say that capital punishment is definitive because it must be, to point out that certain men are socially irrecoverable, constituting a permanent danger to each citizen and to the social order as a whole, so that, before anything else, they must be suppressed. No one, at least, will question the existence of certain beasts in our society, creatures of incorrigible energy and brutality that nothing seems capable of subduing. And although the death penalty certainly does not solve the problem they present, let us at least agree that it goes a long way toward eliminating it.

I will return to these men. But first, is capital punishment confined only to them? Can we be absolutely certain that not one man of all those executed is recoverable? Can we even swear that one or another may not be *innocent*? In both cases, must we not admit that capital punishment is eliminative only to the degree that it is irreparable? Yesterday, 15th March, 1957, Burton Abbott, condemned to death for the murder of a 14-year-old girl, was executed in California: it was certainly the kind of crime that I imagine would class him among the irrecoverables. Although Abbott had constantly protested his innocence, he was condemned. His execution was scheduled for 15th

March at 10.00 in the morning. At 9.10 a reprieve was granted to allow the defence to present an appeal.* At 11 o'clock the appeal was rejected. At 11.15 Abbott entered the gas chamber. At 11.18 he began to breathe the first fumes of gas. At 11.20 the secretary of the reprieve board telephoned the prison: the board had changed its decision. The governor had been called first, but he had gone sailing, and they had called the prison directly. Abbott was removed from the gas chamber: it was too late. If the weather had been bad the day before, the governor of California would not have gone sailing. He would have telephoned two minutes earlier: Abbott would be alive today and would perhaps see his innocence proved. Any other punishment, even the most severe, would have permitted this chance. Capital punishment, however, permitted him none.

It may be thought that this case is exceptional.† Our lives are exceptional too, and yet, in the fugitive existence we have been granted, this exception occurred not ten hours by plane from where I am writing. Abbott's misfortune is not so much an exception as it is one news item among many others, an error which is not at all isolated, if we examine our newspapers (for example, the Deshay case, to instance only the most recent). The jurist Olivecroix, applying a calculus of probabilities to the chance of judiciary error, concluded in 1860 that approximately one innocent man was condemned out of every 257 cases. The proportion seems low, but only in relation to moderate punishment. In relation to capital punishment, the proportion is infinitely high. When Hugo wrote that he preferred to call the guillotine Lesurques,‡ he did not mean that every man who was decapitated was a Lesurques, but that one Lesurques was enough to wipe out the value of capital punishment forever. It is understandable that Belgium definitely abjured pronouncing capital punishment after one such judiciary error, and that England brought up the question of its abolition after the Hayes case. We can readily sympathize with the conclusions of that Attorney-General who, consulted on the petition for reprieve of a criminal who

* It should be pointed out that it is the custom in American prisons to conduct the condemned man to a new cell on the eve of his execution, thus informing him of the ceremony that awaits him.

† Not so exceptional. When Caryl Chessman was executed on 2nd May, 1960, after twelve years in death row, a brief stay of execution granted by a Federal Judge in San Francisco failed to be communicated to San Quentin prison in time because the judge's secretary misdialled the prison's telephone number. By the time the message was relayed to the governor the pellets of potassium cyanide had done their job.—Editor.

‡ The name of an innocent man guillotined in the *Courrier de Lyon* case.

was most probably guilty but whose victim's body had not been recovered, wrote as follows: 'The survival of X assures the authorities the possibility of effectively examining at their leisure every new sign that may subsequently be discovered of the existence of his wife [the victim, whose body had not been recovered]. . . . On the other hand, his execution, eliminating this hypothetical possibility of examination, would give, I fear, to the slightest evidence of her still being alive a theoretical value, a pressure of regret which I consider it inopportune to create.' The man's feeling for both justice and truth are admirably expressed, and it would be advisable to cite as often as possible in our assize courts that 'pressure of regret' which sums up so steadfastly the danger with which every juryman is confronted. Once the innocent man is dead, nothing more can be done for him except to re-establish his good name, if someone is still interested in asking for such a service. His innocence is restored—actually he had never lost it in the first place. But the persecution of which he has been the victim, his dreadful sufferings, and his hideous death have been acquired forever. There is nothing left to do but consider the innocent men of the future, in order to spare them such torments. It has been done in Belgium; but in France, apparently, there are no bad consciences.

Why should our consciences be bad if they are based on our conception of justice: has not this conception made great progress, does it not follow in the footsteps of science itself? When the learned expert gives his opinion in the assize courts, it is as if a priest had spoken, and the jury, raised in the religion of science—the jury nods. Nevertheless several recent cases—particularly the Besnard affair—have given us a good idea of the comedy such expertise can provide. Guilt is not better established because it can be demonstrated in a test tube. Another test tube can prove the contrary, and the personal equation will thereby maintain all its old significance in such perilous mathematics as these. The proportion of scientists who are really experts is the same as that of judges who are really psychologists—scarcely more than that of juries that are really serious and objective. Today, as yesterday, the chance of error remains. Tomorrow another expert's report will proclaim the innocence of another Abbott. But Abbott will be dead, scientifically enough, and science, which claims to prove innocence as well as guilt, has not yet succeeded in restoring the life it has taken.

And among the guilty themselves, can we also be sure of having killed only 'irrecoverables'? Those who like myself have had to attend hearings in our assize courts know that a number of elements of sheer accident enter into a sentence, even a death sentence. The looks of the accused; his background (adultery is often regarded as an incriminating circumstance by some jurors: I have never been able to believe that all are completely faithful to their wives and husbands); his attitude (which is only regarded as being in his favour if it is as conventional as possible, which usually means as near play-acting as possible); even his elocution (one must neither stutter nor speak too well) and the incidents of the hearing sentimentally evaluated (the truth, unfortunately, is not always moving)—all these are so many accidents that influence the final decision of a jury. At the moment the verdict recommending the death penalty is pronounced, one can be sure that this most certain of punishments has only been arrived at by a great conjunction of uncertainties. When one realizes that the verdict of death depends on the jury's estimation of the extenuating circumstances, particularly since the reforms of 1832 gave our juries the power to admit *undetermined* extenuating circumstances, one can appreciate the margin left to the momentary humours of the jurors. It is no longer the law which establishes with any precision those cases in which the death penalty is recommended, but the jury which, after the event, estimates its suitability by guesswork, to say the least. As there are no two juries alike, the man who is executed might as well have been spared. Irrecoverable in the eyes of the honest citizens of Île-et-Vilaine, he might well be granted the shadow of an excuse by the good people of Var. Unfortunately, the same knife falls in both departments. And it is not concerned with such details.

The accidents of the times combine with those of geography to reinforce the general absurdity. The Communist French worker who was just guillotined in Algeria for having planted a bomb, discovered before it could explode, in the cloakroom of a factory was condemned as much by his act as by the times, for in the Algerian situation at present, Arab public opinion was to be shown that the guillotine was made for French necks too, and French public opinion, outraged by terrorist activities, was to be given satisfaction at the same time. Nevertheless, the minister in charge of the execution counted many Communist votes in his constituency, and if the circumstances had been slightly different the accused would have got off lightly and perhaps one day, as his party's deputy, might have found himself drinking at the same bar as the minister. Such thoughts are bitter and one might wish they remained fresh a little longer in the minds of our governors. These gentlemen should be aware that times and manners change; a day comes along when the criminal who was executed too quickly no longer seems quite so guilty. By then it is too late, and what can you do but repent or forget? Naturally, one forgets. But society is nonetheless affected: one unpunished crime, according to the Greeks, infects the whole city. Innocence condemned to death, or crime excessively punished, leaves a stain no less hideous in the long run. We know it, in France.

Such is the nature of human justice, it will be said, and despite its imperfections, after all, even human justice is better than the operation of despotism or chance. But this rueful preference is tolerable only in relation to moderate punishment. Confronted by death sentences, it is a scandal. A classic work on French law excuses the death penalty from being subject to degree in the following words: 'Human justice has not the slightest ambition to ensure proportion of this nature. Why? Because it knows itself to be imperfect.' Must we therefore conclude that this imperfection authorizes us to pronounce an absolute judgment, and that society, uncertain of realizing justice in its pure state, must rush headlong with every likelihood of error, upon the supreme injustice? If human justice knows itself to be imperfect, might not that knowledge be more suitably and modestly demonstrated by leaving a sufficient margin around our condemnations for the eventual reparation of error?* This very weakness in which human justice finds extenuating circumstances for itself in every case and on every occasion— is it not to be accorded to the criminal himself as well? Can the jury in all decency say, 'If we condemn you to death by mistake, you will surely forgive us in consideration of the weaknesses of the human nature we all share. But we nevertheless condemn you to death without the slightest consideration of these weaknesses or of this common nature'? All men have a community in error and in aberration. Yet must this community operate in behalf of the tribunal and be denied to the accused? No, for if justice has any meaning in this world, it is none other than the recognition of this very community: it cannot, in its very essence, be separated from compassion. Let it be understood that by compassion I mean only the consciousness of a common suffering,

---

* Satisfaction was expressed over the recent reprieve of Sillon, who killed his four-year-old daughter in order to keep her from her mother, who had asked for a divorce. During his detention it was discovered that Sillon was suffering from a brain tumour that could account for the insanity of his action.

not a frivolous indulgence that takes no account of the sufferings and rights of the victim. Compassion does not exclude punishment, but it withholds an ultimate condemnation. It is revolted by the definitive, irreparable measure that does injustice to man in general since it does not recognize his share in the misery of the common condition.

As a matter of fact, certain juries know this well enough, and often admit the extenuating circumstances of a crime which nothing can extenuate. This is because they regard the death penalty as too extreme and prefer to punish insufficiently rather than to excess. In such cases, the extreme severity of the punishment tends to sanction crime instead of penalizing it. There is scarcely one session of the assize courts of which one cannot read in our press that a verdict is incoherent, that in the face of the facts it appears either insufficient or excessive. The jurors are not unaware of this. They simply prefer, as we should do ourselves, when confronted with the enormity of capital punishment, to appear confused rather than compromise their sleep for nights to come. Knowing themselves imperfect, at least they draw the appropriate consequences. And true justice is on their side, precisely to the degree that logic is not.

There are, however, great criminals that every jury will condemn, no matter where and when they are tried. Their crimes are certain, and the proofs elicited by the prosecution correspond with the admissions of the defence. What is abnormal and even monstrous in their crimes unquestionably determines their category as pathological, though in the majority of such cases psychiatrists affirm the criminal's responsibility. Recently, in Paris, a young man of rather weak character, but known for the sweetness and affection of his nature and his extreme devotion to his family, described himself as being annoyed by his father's remarks on the lateness of the hours he had been keeping. The father was reading at the dining-room table. The young man took an axe and struck his father several mortal blows with it from behind. Then, in the same fashion, he struck down his mother, who was in the kitchen. He removed his bloody trousers and hid them in the closet, changed his clothes, and after paying a visit to the family of his fiancée without revealing the slightest discomposure, returned to his own house and informed the police his parents had been murdered. The police immediately discovered the bloody trousers, and easily obtained the parricide's unperturbed confession. The psychiatrists agreed on his responsibility for these 'murders by irritation'. The young man's strange indifference, of which he gave other indications in prison (rejoicing that his parents' funeral had been so well attended: 'Everyone liked them,' he said to his lawyers), can nevertheless scarcely be considered as normal. But his reason was apparently intact.

Many 'monsters' offer a countenance just as impenetrable. They are therefore eliminated upon consideration of the facts alone. Because of the nature or the degree of their crimes it is inconceivable that they would repent or even wish to change their ways. In their case, a recurrence is what must be avoided, and there is no other solution than to eliminate them. On this—and only this—aspect of the question is the discussion of the death penalty legitimate. In all other cases the arguments of its partisans cannot withstand the criticism of its opponents. At this point, in fact, at our present level of ignorance, a kind of wager is established: no expertise, no exercise of reason can give the deciding vote between those who think a last chance must always be granted to even the last of men and those who consider this chance as entirely illusory. But it is perhaps possible, at this very point, to override the *eternal* opposition between the partisans and opponents of the death penalty, by determining the advisability of such a penalty *at this time, and in Europe*. With considerably less competence, I shall attempt to parallel the efforts of Professor Jean Graven, a Swiss jurist who writes in his remarkable study of the problems of capital punishment: '. . . Regarding the problem that once again confronts our conscience and our reason, it is our opinion that the solution must be based not upon the conceptions, the problems and the arguments of the past, nor on the theoretical hopes and promises of the future, but on the ideas, the given circumstances, and the necessities of today.'* One could, in fact, argue forever about the advantages or devastations of the death penalty as it has been through the ages or as it might be contemplated in some eternity of ideas. But the death penalty plays its part here and now, and we must determine here and now where we stand in relation to a contemporary executioner. What does the death penalty mean for us, half-way through the twentieth century?

For the sake of simplification, let us say that our civilization has lost the only values that, to a certain degree, could justify the death penalty, and that it suffers, on the contrary, from every evil that necessitates its suppression. In other words, the abolition of the death

* *Revue de Criminologie et de Police technique*, Geneva, special number, 1952.

penalty should be demanded by the conscious members of our society on grounds of both logic and fidelity to the facts.

Of logic, first of all. To decide that a man must be definitively punished is to deny him any further opportunity whatsoever to make reparation for his acts. It is at this juncture, we repeat, that the arguments for and against capital punishment confront one another blindly, eventuating in a fruitless checkmate. Yet it is exactly here that none of us can afford to be positive, for we are all judges, all party to the dispute. Hence our uncertainty about our right to kill and our impotence to convince others on either side. Unless there is absolute innocence, there can be no supreme judge. Now we have all committed some transgression in our lives, even if this transgression has not put us within the power of the law and has remained an unknown crime: there are no just men, only hearts more or less poor in justice. The mere fact of living permits us to know this, and to add to the sum of our actions a little of the good that might partially compensate for the evil we have brought into the world. This right to live that coincides with the opportunity for reparation is the natural right of every man, even the worst. The most abandoned criminal and the worthiest judge here find themselves side by side, equally miserable and jointly responsible. Without this right, the moral life is strictly impossible. None among us, in particular, is entitled to despair of a single man, unless it be after his death, which transforms his life into destiny and admits of a final judgment. But to pronounce this final judgment before death, to decree the closing of accounts when the creditor is still alive, is the privilege of no man. On these grounds, at least, he who judges absolutely condemns himself absolutely.

Barnard Fallot of the Masuy gang, who worked for the Gestapo, confessed to the entire list of terrible crimes of which he was accused, and later went to his death with great courage, declaring himself beyond hope of reprieve: 'My hands are too red with blood,' he said to one of his fellow prisoners.* Public opinion and that of his judges certainly classified him among the irrecoverables and I would have been tempted to put him in that category myself, had I not read one astonishing piece of evidence: after having declared that he wanted to die bravely, Fallot told the same prisoner: 'Do you know what I regret most of all? Not having known sooner about the Bible they gave me here. If I had, I wouldn't be where I am now.' It is not a question

---

* Jean Bobognano, *Quartier des fauves, prison de Fresnes*, Édition du Fuseau.

of surrendering to the sentimentality of conventional imagery and conjuring up Victor Hugo's good convicts. The age of enlightenment, as it is called, wished to abolish the death penalty under the pretext that man was fundamentally good. We know, of course, that he is not (he is simply better or worse). After the last twenty years of our splendid history we know it very well. But it is because man is not fundamentally good that no one among us can set himself up as an absolute judge, for no one among us can pretend to absolute innocence. The verdict of capital punishment destroys the only indisputable human community there is, the community in the face of death, and such a judgment can only be legitimated by a truth or a principle that takes its place above all men, beyond the human condition.

Capital punishment, in fact, throughout history has always been a religious punishment. When imposed in the name of the king, representative of God on earth, or by priests, or in the name of a society considered as a sacred body, it is not the human community that is destroyed but the functioning of the guilty man as a member of the divine community which alone can give him his life. Such a man is certainly deprived of his earthly life, yet his opportunity for reparation is preserved. The real judgment is not pronounced in this world, but in the next. Religious values, especially the belief in an eternal life, are thus the only ones on which the death penalty can be based since according to their own logic they prevent that penalty from being final and irreparable: it is justified only insofar as it is not supreme.

The Catholic Church, for example, has always admitted the necessity of the death penalty. It has imposed the penalty itself, without avarice, at other periods. Today, its doctrines still justify capital punishment, and concede the State the right to apply it. No matter how subtle this doctrine may be, there is at its core a profound feeling which was directly expressed by a Swiss councillor from Fribourg during a discussion of capital punishment by the national council in 1937; according to M. Grand, even the worst criminal examines his own conscience when faced with the actuality of execution. 'He repents, and his preparation for death is made easier. The Church has saved one of its members, has accomplished its divine mission. This is why the Church has steadfastly countenanced capital punishment, not only as a means of legitimate protection, but *as a powerful means of salvation.* . . . [My italics.] Without becoming precisely a matter of doctrine, the death penalty, like war itself can be justified by its quasi-divine efficacity.'

By virtue of the same reasoning, no doubt, one can read on the executioner's sword in Fribourg the motto 'Lord Jesus, thou art the Judge'. The executioner is thereby invested with a divine function. He is the man who destroys the body in order to deliver the soul to its divine judgment, which no man on earth can foresee. It will perhaps be considered that such mottos imply rather outrageous confusions, and certainly those who confine themselves to the actual teachings of Jesus will see this handsome sword as yet another outrage to the body of Christ. In this light can be understood the terrible words of a Russian prisoner whom the executioners of the Tsar were about to hang in 1905, when he turned to the priest who was about to console him with the image of Christ and said: 'Stand back, lest you commit a sacrilege.' An unbeliever will not fail to remark that those who have placed in the very centre of their faith the overwhelming victim of a judicial error should appear more reticent, to say the least, when confronted by cases of legal murder. One might also remind the believer that the emperor Julian, before his conversion, refused to give official posts to Christians because they systematically refused to pronounce the death sentence or to aid in administering it. For five centuries Christians believed that the strict moral teaching of their master forbade them to kill. But the Catholic faith is derived not only from the teachings of Christ, it is nourished by the Old Testament, by Saint Paul, and by the Fathers as well. In particular the immortality of the soul and the universal resurrection of the body are articles of dogma. Hence, capital punishment, for the believer, can be regarded as a provisional punishment which does not in the least affect the definite sentence, but remains a disposition necessary to the terrestrial order, an administrative measure which, far from making an end of the guilty man, can promote, on the contrary, his redemption in heaven. I do not say that all believers follow this reasoning, and I can imagine without much difficulty that most Catholics stand closer to Christ than to Moses or Saint Paul, I say only that the belief in the immortality of the soul has permitted Catholicism to formulate the problem of capital punishment in very different terms, and to justify it.

But what does such a justification mean to the society we live in, a society which in its institutions and manners alike has become almost entirely secular? When an atheist—or sceptic—or agnostic judge imposes the death penalty on an unbelieving criminal, he is pronouncing a definitive punishment that cannot be revised. He sits upon God's throne,* but without possessing God's powers and, moreover, without believing in them. He condemns to death, in fact, because his ancestors believed in eternal punishment. Yet the society which he claims to represent pronounces, in reality, a purely eliminative measure, destroys the human community united against death, and sets itself up as an absolute value because it pretends to absolute power. Of course society traditionally assigns a priest to the condemned man, and the priest may legitimately hope that fear of punishment will help effect the condemned man's conversion. Yet who will accept this casuistry as the justification of a punishment so often inflicted and so often received in an entirely different spirit? It is one thing to believe and 'therefore know not fear,' and another to find one's faith through fear. Conversion by fire or the knife will always be suspect, and one can well understand why the Church renounced a triumph by terror over infidel hearts. In any case, a secularized society has nothing to gain from a conversion concerning which it professes complete disinterest: it enacts a consecrated punishment, and at the same time deprives that punishment of its justification and its utility alike. Delirious in its own behalf, society plucks the wicked from its bosom as if it were virtue personified. In the same way, an honourable man might kill his son who had strayed from the path of duty, saying, 'Really, I didn't know what else I could do!' Society thus usurps the right of selection, as if it were nature, and adds a terrible suffering to the eliminative process, as if it were a redeeming god.

To assert, in any case, that a man must be absolutely cut off from society because he is absolutely wicked is the same as saying that society is absolutely good, which no sensible person will believe today. It will not be believed—in fact, it is easier to believe the contrary. Our society has become as diseased and criminal as it is only because it has set itself up as its own final justification, and has had no concern but its own preservation and success in history. Certainly it is a secularized society, yet during the nineteenth century it began to fashion a kind of ersatz religion by proposing itself as an object of adoration. The doctrines of evolution, and the theories of selection that accompanied such doctrines, have proposed the future of society as its final

---

* The decision of the jury is preceded by the formula 'before God and my conscience. . . .'

end. The political utopias grafted on to these doctrines have proposed, at the end of time, a Golden Age that justifies in advance all intermediary enterprises. Society has grown accustomed to legalizing whatever can minister to its future, and consequently to usurping the supreme punishment in an absolute fashion: it has regarded as a crime and a sacrilege everything that contradicts its own intentions and temporal dogmas. In other words, the executioner, formerly a priest, has become a civil servant. The results surround us. Half-way through the century, our society, which has forfeited the logical right to pronounce the death penalty, must now abolish it for reasons of realism.

Confronted with crime, how does our civilization in fact define itself? The answer is easy: for thirty years crimes of State have vastly exceeded crimes of individuals. I shall not even mention wars—general or local—although blood is a kind of alcohol that eventually intoxicates like the strongest wine. I am referring here to the number of individuals killed directly by the State, a number that has grown to astronomic proportions and infinitely exceeds that of 'private' murders. There are fewer and fewer men condemned by common law, and more and more men executed for political reasons. The proof of this fact is that each of us, no matter how honourable he is, can now envisage the *possibility* of someday being put to death, whereas such an eventuality at the beginning of the century would have appeared farcical at best. Alphonse Karr's famous remark, 'Let my lords the assassins begin', no longer has any meaning: those who spill the most blood are also those who believe they have right, logic, and history on their side.

It is not so much against the individual killer that our society must protect itself then, as against the State. Perhaps this equation will be reversed in another thirty years. But for the present, a legitimate defence must be made against the State, before all else. Justice and the most realistic sense of our time require that the law protect the individual against a State given over to the follies of sectarianism and pride. 'Let the State begin by abolishing the death penalty' must be our rallying cry today.

Bloody laws, it has been said, make bloody deeds. But it is also possible for a society to suffer that state of ignominy in which public behaviour, no matter how disorderly, comes nowhere near being so bloody as the laws. Half of Europe knows this state. We have known it in France and we risk knowing it again. The executed of the Occupation produced the executed of the Liberation whose friends still dream of revenge. Elsewhere, governments charged with too many crimes are preparing to drown their guilt in still greater massacres. We kill for a nation or for a deified social class. We kill for a future society, likewise deified. He who believes in omniscience can conceive of omnipotence. Temporal idols that demand absolute faith tirelessly mete out absolute punishments. And religions without transcendence murder those they condemn *en masse* and without hope.

How can European society in the twentieth century survive if it does not defend the individual by every means within its power against the oppression of the State? To forbid putting a man to death is one means of publicly proclaiming that society and the State are not absolute values, one means of demonstrating that nothing authorizes them to legislate definitively, to bring to pass the irreparable. Without the death penalty, Gabriel Péri and Brasillach would perhaps be among us still; we could then judge them, according to our lights, and proudly speak out our judgment, instead of which they now judge us, and it is we who must remain silent. Without the death penalty the corpse of Rajk would not still be poisoning Hungary, a less guilty Germany would be received with better grace by the nations of Europe, the Russian Revolution would not still be writhing in its shame, and the blood of Algeria would weigh less heavily upon us here in France. Without the death penalty, Europe itself would not be infected by the corpses accumulated in its exhausted earth for the last twenty years. Upon our continent all values have been overturned by fear and hatred among individuals as among nations. The war of ideas is waged by rope and knife. It is no longer the natural human society that exercises its rights of repression, but a ruling ideology that demands its human sacrifices. 'The lesson the scaffold always provides,' Francart wrote, 'is that human life ceases to be sacred when it is considered useful to suppress it.' Apparently it has been considered increasingly useful, the lesson has found apt pupils, and the contagion is spreading everywhere. And with it, the disorders of nihilism. A spectacular counterblow is required: it must be proclaimed, in institutions and as a matter of principle, that the human person is above and beyond the State. Every measure which will diminish the pressure of social forces on the individual will also aid in the de-congestion of a Europe suffering from an afflux of blood, will permit us to think more clearly, and to make our way toward recovery. The disease of Europe is to believe in nothing and to claim to know everything. But Europe does not know everything, far from it, and to judge by the rebellion and the hope in which we find ourselves today, Europe does believe in something: Europe believes that the supreme misery of man, at its mysterious limit, borders on his supreme greatness. For the majority of Europeans faith is lost, and with it the justifications faith conferred upon the order of punishment. But the majority of Europeans are also sickened by that idolatry of the State which has claimed to replace their lost faith. From now on, with divided goals, certain and uncertain, determined never to submit and never to oppress, we must recognize both our hope and our ignorance, renounce all absolute law, all irreparable institutions. We know enough to be able to say that this or that great criminal deserves a sentence of perpetual forced labour. But we do not know enough to say that he can be deprived of his own future, which is to say, of our common opportunity for reparation. In tomorrow's united Europe, on whose behalf I write, the solemn abolition of the death penalty must be the first article of the European Code for which we all hope.

From the humanitarian idylls of the eighteenth century to its bloody scaffolds the road runs straight and is easily followed; we all know today's executioners are humanists. And therefore we cannot be too suspicious of humanitarian ideologies applied to a problem like that of capital punishment. I should like to repeat, by way of conclusion, that my opposition to the death penalty derives from no illusions as to the natural goodness of the human creature, and from no faith in a Golden Age to come. On the contrary, the abolition of capital punishment seems necessary to me for reasons of qualified pessimism, reasons I have attempted to explain in terms of logic and the most realistic considerations. Not that the heart has not made its contribution to what I have been saying: for anyone who has spent several weeks among these texts, these memories, and these men—all, intimately or remotely, connected with the scaffold—there can be no question of leaving their dreadful ranks unaffected by what one has seen and heard. Nevertheless, I do not believe there is no responsibility in this world for what I have found, or that one should submit to our modern propensity for absolving victim and killer in the same moral confusion. This purely sentimental confusion involves more cowardice than generosity, and ends up by justifying whatever is worst in this world: if everything is blessed, then slave camps are blessed, and organized murder, and the

cynicism of the great political bosses—and ultimately, blessing everything alike, one betrays one's own brothers. We can see this happening
all around us. But indeed, with the world in its present condition the
man of the twentieth century asks for laws and institutions of *convales-
cence* that will check without crushing, lead without hampering. Hurled
into the unregulated dynamism of history, man needs a new physics,
new laws of equilibrium. He needs, most of all, a reasonable society,
not the anarchy into which his own pride and the State's inordinate
powers have plunged him.

It is my conviction that the abolition of the death penalty will help
us advance toward that society. In taking this initiative, France could
propose its extension on either side of the Iron Curtain; in any case she
could set an example. Capital punishment would be replaced by a
sentence of perpetual forced labour for criminals judged incorrigible,
and by shorter terms for others. As for those who believe that such
punishment is still more cruel than capital punishment itself, I wonder
why, in that case, they do not reserve it for Landru and his like and
relegate capital punishment to secondary offenders. One might also
add that such forced labour leaves the condemned man the possibility
of choosing his death, whereas the guillotine is a point of no return.
On the other hand, I would answer those who believe that a sentence
of perpetual forced labour is too mild a punishment by remarking first
on their lack of imagination and then by pointing out that the privation
of liberty could seem to them a mild punishment only to the degree
that contemporary society has taught them to despise what liberty
they have.*

That Cain was not killed, but bore in the sight of all men a mark of
reprobation is, in any case, the lesson we should draw from the Old
Testament, not to mention the Gospels, rather than taking our inspiration from the cruel examples of the Mosaic law. There is no reason why
at least a limited version of such an experiment should not be attempted
in France (say for a ten-year period), if our government is still capable
of redeeming its vote for alcohol by the great measure in behalf of

* See also the report on the death penalty made by Representative Dupont to the
National Assembly on 31st May, 1791: 'He [*the assassin*] is consumed by a bitter, burning
temper; what he fears above all is repose, a state that leaves him to himself, and to escape it
he continually faces death and seeks to inflict it; solitude and his conscience are his real
tortures. Does this not tell us what kind of punishment we should impose, to what
agonies he is most sensitive? *Is it not in the very nature of the disease that we must seek the
remedy which can cure it.*' I italicize this last sentence, which makes this little-known
Representative a real precursor of our modern psychological theories.

civilization which total abolition would represent. And if public opinion and its representatives cannot renounce our slothful law which confines itself to eliminating what it cannot amend, at least, while waiting for a day of regeneration and of truth, let us not preserve as it is this 'solemn shambles' (in Tarde's expression) which continues to disgrace our society. The death penalty, as it is imposed, even as rarely as it is imposed, is a disgusting butchery, an outrage inflicted on the spirit and body of man. This truncation, this living severed head, these long gouts of blood, belong to a barbarous epoch that believed it could subdue the people by offering them degrading spectacles. Today, when this ignoble death is secretly administered, what meaning can such torture have? The truth is that in an atomic age we kill as we did in the age of steelyards: where is the man of normal sensibility whose stomach is not turned at the mere idea of such clumsy surgery? If the French state is incapable of overcoming its worst impulses to this degree, and of furnishing Europe with one of the remedies it needs most, let it at least reform its means of administering capital punishment. Science, which has taught us so much about killing, could at least teach us to kill decently. An anaesthetic which would permit the accused to pass from a state of sleep to death, which would remain within his reach for at least a day so that he could make free use of it, and which in cases of refusal or failure of nerve could then be administered to him, would assure the elimination of the criminal, if that is what we require, but would also provide a little decency where today there is nothing but a sordid and obscene exhibition.

I indicate these compromises only to the degree that one must sometimes despair of seeing wisdom and the principles of civilization impose themselves upon those responsible for our future. For certain men, more numerous than is supposed, knowing what the death penalty really is and being unable to prevent its application is physically insupportable. In their own way, they suffer this penalty too, and without any justification. If we at least lighten the weight of the hideous images that burden these men, society will lose nothing by our actions. But ultimately even such measures will be insufficient. Neither in the hearts of men nor in the manners of society will there be a lasting peace until we outlaw death.